Silicon Valley
Imperialism

Silicon Valley Imperialism

Techno Fantasies and
Frictions in Postsocialist Times

ERIN McELROY

Duke University Press   *Durham and London*   2024

Project Editor: Liz Smith
Typeset in Portrait and Trade Gothic by Westchester Publishing Services

Library of Congress Cataloging-in-Publication Data
Names: McElroy, Erin, [date] author.
Title: Silicon Valley imperialism : techno fantasies and frictions in
postsocialist times / Erin McElroy.
Description: Durham : Duke University Press, 2024. | Includes
bibliographical references and index.
Identifiers: LCCN 2023026644 (print)
LCCN 2023026645 (ebook)
ISBN 9781478030218 (paperback)
ISBN 9781478025962 (hardcover)
ISBN 9781478059219 (ebook)
Subjects: LCSH: Gentrification—Social aspects—Romania. | Technology—
Social aspects—Romania. | Racism—Romania. | Human geography—
Romania. | Gentrification—Social aspects—California—San Francisco. |
Technology—Social aspects—California—San Francisco. | Romania—
Social conditions—1989- | BISAC: SOCIAL SCIENCE / Human Geography |
SOCIAL SCIENCE / Technology Studies
Classification: LCC HT178.R6 M345 2024 (print) | LCC HT178.R6 (ebook) |
DDC 303.48/3309498—dc23/eng/20231117
LC record available at https://lccn.loc.gov/2023026644
LC ebook record available at https://lccn.loc.gov/2023026645

Cover art: Untitled. © Alex Horghidan. Courtesy the artist.

Contents

Acknowledgments

This book has emerged through over a decade's worth of connections and political commitments in both Romania and the United States, and ultimately it is dedicated to those organizing against Siliconization and racial dispossession in and across both. I can't understate how indebted I am to everyone who I have learned from and with on this journey.

I could have never asked for a more supportive adviser and mentor throughout this book's emergence into its finalized iteration than Neda Atanasoski, whose generosity, brilliance, and ongoing support is woven into each page. Not only has her scholarship on postsocialism, technology, liberalism, and race been an unending source of inspiration, but even now, as I prepare this text's final touches, she has continued to offer steadfast mentorship. From our first meeting as I began graduate school in the Feminist Studies Department at the University of California, Santa Cruz, to the present, I owe her mountains of gratitude for never having stopped believing in this work. At UCSC, I was also lucky to have worked with Karen Barad, Megan Moodie, and Lisa Rofel, each of whom helped shape this book and my thinking on postsocialism, the Cold War, feminist technoscience, and connectivity, and each of whom has offered important mentorship along the way. I am thankful too for helpful conversations there with Neel Ahuja, Miriam Greenberg, Christine Hong, Jennifer Kelly, Marisol LeBrón, Steven McKay, Nick Mitchell, Jenny Reardon, and Felicity Amaya Schaeffer. I additionally want to thank Alaina Lemon, who was pivotal early on in my theorizing of race and Eastern Europe, and Liviu Chelcea, who enthusiastically joined my committee and helped me think through complex dynamics of housing, privatization, and anticommunism. Ananya Roy's work on property, race, and banishment has been hugely influential for me too, and I am honored to have received mentorship from her for many years now as well.

Elizabeth Roberts has also been an informal mentor of sorts over the years of navigating academia, for which I am grateful. And if it weren't for Angana Chatterji and Richard Shapiro, I might have never pursued justice-oriented scholarship in the first place. Thanks too to those who sat by me in those formative years of thinking difference together and who still do, in particular Heidi Andrea Restrepo Rhodes and Pei Wu.

Time dedicated to researching and writing this book was made possible by fellowships from the Cota-Robles Dissertation Fellowship, the Fulbright Institute of International Education, and the Social Science Research Council's International Dissertation Fellowship. I was also fortunate to receive funding from the Antipode Foundation, the Creative Work Fund, the Foreign Language and Area Studies program, the Kala Institute, the University of California Humanities Research Institute, the UCSC Humanities Institute, and the Office of the Vice President of Research, the College of Liberal Arts, and the Department of American Studies at the University of Texas at Austin. I was grateful too to receive a residency with the UCHRI and a postdoctoral fellowship at the AI Now Institute at New York University, both of which allowed me to carve out manuscript time and workshop ideas. Thanks to the many postdocs, researchers, and workers whom I thought with and organized alongside at AI Now, including Shazeda Ahmed, Alejandro Calcaño Bertorelli, Roel Dobbe, Theodora Dryer, Genevieve Fried, Ben Green, Joan Greenbaum, Casey Collan, Amba Kak, Elizabeth Kaziunas, Varoon Mathur, Mariah Peebles, Inioluwa Deborah Raji, Joy Lisi Rankin, Noopur Raval, Rashida Richardson, Julia Bloch Thibaud, Nantina Vgontzas, Sarah Myers West, and Meredith Whittaker.

So much of this book is based on housing justice struggles in Bucharest, Cluj, and the San Francisco Bay Area. In Bucharest, I am appreciative of everyone at the Frontul Comun pentru Dreptul la Locuire, and in Cluj, of those at Căși Sociale ACUM! I can only hope that the stories that I share here are resonant with ongoing work. In the Bay Area, I hold immense gratitude for everyone who I have worked with over the years in the Anti-Eviction Mapping Project, Eviction Free San Francisco, and partner groups in creating protests, maps, art, and political analysis against gentrification. Some of us have been working together for over a decade now, which blows my mind! Thanks also to support from collaborative research spaces that I have been a part of, including the *Radical Housing Journal*, the Housing Justice in Unequal Cities Network at UCLA, and the Beyond Inhabitation Lab at the Polytechnic University of Turin. All of these spaces ground me in the power of international solidarities, as do ongoing conversations with so many comrades especially Rob Robinson.

There are also many justice-based artists whose inspiring work I invoke throughout this book, including Mihaela Drăgan, Fernando Martí, Mircea Nicolae (who sadly passed away before this was published), Veda Popovici, David Schwartz, Florin Tudor, and Mona Vătămanu. I am especially grateful to Alex Horghidan, whose brilliant illustration appears on this book's cover. I love it so much! Ultimately, I owe my deepest debts to those who shared such brilliant analysis about race, eviction, technology, capitalism, postsocialism, and empire with me during my research, many of whom appear in this book with pseudonyms.

The ideas that I traverse in this book have emerged out of a multitude of conversations and connected projects. My thinking with Veda Popovici on housing justice, coloniality, and decoloniality in Eastern Europe permeates this entire writing, as does everything that I've learned throughout our ongoing friendship. I can only hope this text does partial justice to the depths of our thinking together. Thanks as well to years of exchange on housing struggles in Eastern Europe with dear friends including Ioana Florea, Michele Lancione, Ana Vilenica, Enikő Vincze, and George Zamfir, and to ongoing conversations on fascist formations with Adina Marincea, Manuel Mireanu, and Mary Taylor. Bogdan Popa has been an invaluable thinking partner regarding communism, queerness, and ethnicity, and I am lucky to have been able to workshop parts of this book with him. Thanks to Alex Ghiț for providing tips about archival treasures, and to Andrada Fiscutean for discussions on postsocialist technoculture. Michele Lancione in particular has offered in-depth feedback on this entire manuscript, for which I am deeply indebted. Everything that I've learned from Ovidiu Țichindeleanu and Manuela Boatcă on postsocialism and decoloniality, as well as from Neda Atanasoski and Kalindi Vora on technology, race, labor, and postsocialism, also permeate the pages of this book.

In the Bay Area, ongoing collaborations with Manissa M. Marahawal have been crucial in my thinking about tech, gentrification, colonialism, and activism. We can't seem to stop writing together, which I love! Similarly, collaborating with Alex Werth in theorizing deracinated dispossession has been especially influential in this text, as has thinking with Daniela Aiello, Lisa Bates, and Terra Graziani against universal methods of analyzing evictions. I am lucky to have been able to write and research with so many brilliant AEMP members and anti-eviction organizers over the years. While there are far too many people to name here, perhaps our recently published *Counterpoints: A San Francisco Bay Area Atlas of Displacement and Resistance* (2021) does justice to many of those involved in this collective work in the Bay Area. Special thanks to Mary Shi for being my co-wrangler in the atlas, and to longtime AEMP members who I've worked with for years now who are still plugging away at collective work including Ariana Faye Allensworth, Azad Amir-Ghassemi, Bianca Ceralvo, Ciera Dudley, Terra Graziani, Gracie Harris, Nathan Kim, Alexandra Lacey, Sam Rabiyah, Dan Sakaguchi, and Manon Vergerio. I also want to thank those who taught me about the power and histories of tenant organizing there, in anti-eviction meetings, on the streets blocking tech buses, and in books, zines, murals, oral histories, and more.

I am lucky to have been able to workshop this book's chapters with many generous scholars. Chapter 1 in particular benefited from feedback from Kim TallBear and Angela Willey on an earlier but connected paper in *Imaginations: Journal of Cross Cultural Image Studies,* and from guidance from Matthew Hayes and Hila Zaban related to writing in *Urban Studies.* I am also grateful for feedback from participants at the International Workshop on Racial Capitalism conference at the University of Texas at Austin organized by Zachary Levenson. While Neda Atanasoski's expertise informs this entire book, our collaborative writing together on postsocialism has very much informed chapters 2 and 3. Chapter 3 also benefited from collaboration with Mary Taylor in workshopping possibilities of antifascist anthropology. My studies on underground computing cultures, meanwhile, are indebted to ongoing exciting collaborations with Luis Felipe R. Murillo, which alongside conversations with Sareeta Amrute and Héctor Beltrán inspired an earlier version of chapter 5 that appeared in *Catalyst: Feminism, Theory, and Technoscience.* Similarly, chapter 6 benefited from a workshop with Environmental Humanities @ UT thanks to Heather Houser and with the Center for Women's and Gender Studies at UT thanks to Christen Smith. The book's coda, meanwhile, has been grounded in conversations with everyone involved in the Landlord Tech Watch project and Anti-Eviction Lab. Special thanks too to Desiree Fields for inspiring conversations on property and technology over the course of many years now.

At UT, I was lucky to find helpful colleagues in the Department of American Studies including Alex Beasley, Iván Chaar López, Lina Chhun, Cary Cordova, Janet Davis, Lauren Gutterman, Rich Heyman, Steven Hoelscher, Stephanie Kaufman, Randolph Lewis, Stephen Marshall, Julia Michenberg, Karla Peña, and Shirley Thompson, all of whom have supported this work. It was also wonderful to work with so many creative and astute students at UT and to workshop ideas woven throughout this book in classes. Collaboration with Iván Chaar López in creating the Critical Digital Studies Group was especially rich, where Edgar Gómez-Cruz, Amelia Acker, and other remarkable faculty and graduate students have inspired my thinking on digitality. I am also grateful to everyone in the Feminist Geography Collective, especially Caroline Faria, Kaily Heitz, Laurel Mei-Singh, and Pavithra Vasudevan.

Thanks too for support from Simone Browne, Tanya Clement, Edmund Gordon, Alison Kafer. While I will miss everyone there, I am thankful for the warm and welcoming Department of Geography at the University of Washington, especially for Sarah Elwood and Megan Ybarra in being so supportive throughout the transition. Thanks too to so many generous new colleagues including Kessie Alexandre, Mia Bennett, Michael Brown, Lindsay Cael, Kam Wing Chan, Mark Ellis, Kim England, Nell Gross, Parwati Martin, Gunwha Oh, Jen Rose Smith, Gretchen Sneegas, Suzanne Withers, Bo Zhao, Danya Al-Saleh, Marika Cifor, Kavita Dattani, Michelle Habell-Pallán, Brett Halperin, Cleo Wölfle Hazard, Nassim Parvin, Aditya Ramesh, Chandan Reddy, Daniela Rosner, Amir Sheikh, Sasha Su-Welland, Amanda Lock Swarr, and Melanie Walsh.

At the end of the day, I can't express enough gratitude to Elizabeth Ault for the invaluable feedback and guidance throughout what has become many years of making this book a reality. From the first phone call we had when I barely knew what I was talking about to this final version, thank you for believing in this work and helping me think through crucial moments of articulation, framing, and contextualization. Thanks also to everyone who I've worked with at Duke University Press, and to Gracie Harris and Ideas on Fire for editing support and feedback. Amron Lehte designed this book's wonderful index, and I'm lucky to have learned more about indexing from her.

If it weren't for dear friends who have bolstered me tirelessly throughout these years of working on this project, none of it would have materialized. Many of you have been mentioned already, yet so many have not. Thanks to Aiden, Alex, Alexi, Ana, Ariel, Bogdan, Carla, Chris, Dani, Elisa, Emma, Heidi, Iox, Jackie, Kaily, Kate, Kevin, Laurel, Lauren, Lee, Liviu, Luis Felipe, Magie, Manissa, Manon, Manu, Marko, Mary, Rakhee, Russel, Shamsher, Terra, Veda, and Zoltán for crucial phone calls, chats, hikes, meals, drinks, visits, places to stay, and more. And of course I need to express my appreciation for Ziggy, the boss cat of Bucharest. So much gratitude is owed to the Brownsteins/Olmans, and especially to Murray for tales from the "old country" and for his encouragement to "get into politics." I'm also appreciative of Zach for the generous back support, and of the Roberts for ongoing enthusiasm. At the end of the day, I can't imagine what this project would have looked like if it weren't for Candace and now Lily too, who have supported me with unwavering patience, perspective, and chuckles as we've moved from place to place. And of course, I am beyond indebted to Meryl, John, and Jenna, who have been there all the while.

"Is this what it's really like in Silicon Valley?" my friend asks me, imagining that
the recent rebranding of the Romanian city of Cluj as "the Silicon Valley of
Eastern Europe" implies a sort of mimicry. Somehow, we've managed to find
our way inside what has become an emblem of Cluj's transformation—the
tall, jutting tower of NTT Data, which flashes a colossal sign, godlike onto the
city's tech horizon. Now that we're inside, feelings of curiosity and clandes-
tineness have overcome us as we study the interior of the building's fake wall
plants, human-shaped robots, and large, soft mushroom statues, all appealing
to the astrofuturist science fiction aesthetic of outer space travel and speculative futures—though perhaps more that of an Elon Musk imaginary than that
of the cosmonautical communist futurism popular during state socialism in
Romania, which lasted from 1947 to 1989. NTT Data, a Japanese-based information technology (IT) firm, set up shop in the aftermath of Romania's transition in what are now considered ongoing postsocialist times. While numerous
global (and primarily Western) tech corporations rushed in to capitalize on the
labor and infrastructural spoils of the 1989 transition, it was later, in 2013, that
NTT acquired the Cluj-based EBS software company. Soon after, NTT remod-
eled the building and employed new aesthetic grammars of *Siliconization*, or the
technopolitics and processes caught up in fantasies of becoming Silicon Valley.
In the case of NTT, this meant distributing software services replete with "real-
time solutions" and "global delivery capabilities" to forty countries, and having
a Romanian staff fluent in English. Soon enough, wEBSite Bistro was opened on
the building's fourth floor, accessible to guests who have since been able to order
food and drinks from electronic tablets on the balcony while surrounded by
cranes and the echoing sounds of so-called smart city development. And this

is where my friend and I are sitting, hovering above the threshold of Eastern Europe's supposed new Silicon Valley.

Over the last decade, Romania's tech industry has gained international attention, with the country boasting some of the continent's fastest internet and a growth of start-ups and firms, particularly in Cluj and Bucharest (but also in cities such as Timișoara, Iași, and Brașov). Real estate speculators chase technocapitalist development, particularly proximate to newly constructed and revitalized office buildings. Often, a prerequisite for this entrepreneurial techno-urban remaking is the cleansing of poor and working-class residents, particularly Roma families and people squatting in buildings that otherwise have been neglected by the city for decades. Skyrocketing rents, alongside brutal evictions, manifest racial expulsion to interstitial wastelands squeezed between the urban and rural made a catchment for those rendered disposable by planners, developers, speculators, and the state. Ananya Roy refers to such expulsion processes as forms of "racial banishment" through which subaltern communities are pushed to the far edges of urban life.[1] Earlier today, for instance, my friend and I ran into a couple she knew from down the street who will be displaced later this month. Living on a crumbling lot without running water or utilities, squeezed between the shiny City Casa residential complex and the glistening German iQuest campus, they knew that their time was limited as soon as the cranes came in. "All of the space around here is becoming too valuable," they shrugged on their break from recycling cardboard around the neighborhood.

Racial banishment amid the onslaught of technocapitalism is motored through methods of Siliconization alongside anticommunist processes of property restitution (*restituire*), or the reprivatization of homes that had been nationalized and made public during state socialism's early years. Today, these homes are being returned to the heirs of the presocialist bourgeois under the anticommunist auspices of transitional justice and Westernization. Due to centuries of anti-Roma racism—which included practices such as slavery, forced labor, eugenic technoscience, and mandated assimilation—few Roma owned property prior to socialism. Socialist property nationalization altered this landscape, providing public housing opportunities that many people have since lived in for generations now. Such provisions are being eviscerated today through the anticommunist mandates of reprivatization, which render state socialism a dark and deadened stain to be cleansed by embracing the logics of private property. This means rendering socialist projects such as housing nationalization retrograde. It also means championing evictions as a means of cleansing the socialist past and restituting capitalism, now recoded as smart city urbanization. In Veda Popovici's words, the neoliberal consensus of anti-communism following the Cold War "has been signified as a 'return to Europe,' a correction towards the so-called *natural* way of being part of the Western world."[2] Smart city ideals are thus espoused by local administrations eager to distance themselves from the backward past and catch up to the Western future. Against this backdrop, leftist projects such as housing and racial justice, never mind public or social housing, get interpreted as primitive and are thus ejected from urban futurity. As Enikő Vincze has found, roughly 30 percent of housing became nationalized (and thus social, or public) during socialism, but only 2 percent is now.[3]

In Cluj, smart city making has led to a rise in rents and evictions alongside new racial geographies of dispossession and segregation. Many evictees are Roma, and frequently people end up banished to the local waste site, Pata Rât, situated eighteen kilometers outside the city center. There, four different communities reside, the most recent having arrived in 2010 during a moment of newfound tech development led by the company Nokia. A militarized eviction followed suit, with over three hundred people forcibly expelled from their homes in the middle of a freezing December night. Over a decade later, displaced tenants continue to reside around the dump, crammed into tiny homes circumscribed by toxic waste. This injustice is put into stark relief as a new tech development project, Transilvania Smart City, is being erected next door. George Zamfir argues that while banishing Roma from Cluj's urban center in 2010 was a "prerequisite for Westernization," this new "smart" development will result in "10 thousand new luxury apartments whose residents will benefit from drone delivery and gondolas . . . located less than 500 meters from the homes of evicted Roma."[4] It is this disjuncture marked by technocapitalist fantasy and racial disavowal alike that the dispossessed are forced to rehearse.

The collapsing of racial and communist renunciation here strategically ignores that despite its many failures, state socialism had provided housing, employment, and education for many previously abandoned. This dismissal supports what Liviu Chelcea and Oana Druță critique as "zombie socialism," a neoliberal rhetorical technique that erases the nuances, temporalities, victories, and catastrophes that state socialism produced.[5] Zombie socialism holistically conflates socialism with totalitarianism, authoritarianism, and even fascism, negating its more emancipatory and antifascist histories. This is not to erase the racial and chauvinist violence that the Communist Party deployed, such as forced assimilation into the deracinated communist worker and instances of forced eviction. Nor is it to overlook the fact that throughout its tenure, the party became increasingly repressive, nationalistic, and surveillance driven, as

Katherine Verdery has well documented.[6] But it is significant to note that in the postsocialist present, emancipatory socialist inheritances such as public housing get cast as retrograde through a zombie socialist lens.

Zombie socialist epistemologies on one hand understand Siliconization as a path toward Westernization. On the other, they fetishize a presocialist urban past often described as Romania's "golden era." It was then that cities such as Bucharest were recognized as "the Little Paris of the East" and Timișoara "the Little Vienna of the East." Yet this was also a fascistic time led by groups such as the Iron Guard and the Legionnaires who were determined to exterminate Jews, Roma, communists, queers, and deviants. Thus, while proponents of anticommunist futurity find comfort in the golden era, so does a growing neofascist movement—one today embodied by the Alianța pentru Unirea Românilor (Alliance for the Union of Romanians/AUR). Although "the Little Silicon Valley of the East" is conjured not by AUR members but rather by liberals, that their vision restitutes the same golden era speaks to the strange bedfellows that anticommunism produces. I am particularly interested in the contours of this alignment and what they say about tech fantasies throughout this book.

While *Silicon Valley Imperialism* is concerned with the racial and spatial violence that anticommunist Siliconization conjures, it also refrains from only reading socialism as a matter of the state. As writing by Neda Atanasoski and Kalindi Vora, as well as by Mary Taylor and Noah Brehmer, importantly illustrate, there are many socialisms that have long existed beyond the enclosure of the state within Eastern Europe and beyond.[7] In this regard, postsocialism emerges not as a simple spatiotemporal marker of state socialism's end, but rather as a theoretical concept useful for marking the cessation of state socialism as a dominant discourse overdetermined by Cold War knowledge production. Conceptually, postsocialism thus facilitates an exploration of socialist legacies on multiple scales beyond the state, offering insight regarding past and present radical imaginaries of collective action.

Committed to mapping anticapitalist threads and fabrics through postsocialist analytics, this book also attends to the racial and spatial violence that processes of Siliconization and anticommunism conjointly inhere in state socialism's remains. While their interlocked power manifests racial dispossession, it also encloses revolutionary potentiality. For instance, in 2017 and 2018, Romania experienced a surge of anticommunist and anti-corruption protests largely designed by members of the country's burgeoning tech sector, as well as by architects fixated on presocialist urbanism. Known as the Light Revolution, demonstrations gained international acclaim for their use of digitality to disavow the undead ghosts of Romania's "corrupt" socialist past. Many expressed allegiance to the European Union (EU), the United States, and the North Atlantic Treaty Organization (NATO). Rather than acknowledging the violence of global capital, protests instead upheld an anticommunist imaginary in which socialist deviation and its corrupt ghosts could be pacified, corrected, and eradicated through Siliconization.

As I question throughout this book, What does it mean that liberal and fascist glorifications of presocialism align amid today's anticommunist conjunctures? Lilith Mahmud's understanding of liberalism as a cosmological reaffirmation of "the moral superiority of the Occident" is helpful here.[8] Liberalism, she finds, peaked during the Enlightenment but continues to inform feelings of belonging and political subjectivity for many Western (and in this case Western aspirational) subjects. Drawing on this, I am particularly interested in how post–Cold War liberal cosmologies chart new conduits between the Enlightenment and Silicon Valley. I am also concerned with how liberal negations of illiberalism messily collapse fascism, authoritarianism, communism, and un-Americanism—basically anything that stands in the way of Western-becoming. In this sense, throughout this book I assess a post–Cold War paradigm that positions liberalism and illiberalism as an epistemological impasse within the political-ideological spectrum, one that obfuscates how the material violence of capital and empire spectrally haunts both the so-called East and West today.

This spatiotemporal conjuncture highlights the multiple imperial legacies haunting postsocialist times. The space now known as Romania has long been occupied by multiple imperial projects, from the Roman to the Ottoman, from the Russian to the Austro-Hungarian. And while Romanian and Hungarian nationalists' respective struggles over Moldova and Transylvania today can spark questions regarding whether Romania itself bears empire-like qualities, the United States also has found its way into the fold. Although the simultaneity of empires and their phantoms is nothing new, the Cold War worked wonders in reducing the capacity to understand imperial multiplicity. Yet "imperial formations," as Ann Laura Stoler and Carole McGranahan put it, are not monolithic steady states, but rather "states of becoming, macropolities in states of solution and constant formation."[9] Processes of becoming and unbecoming, of blurring and realigning, show that despite claims of one empire dying, ending, or being abdicated by another, imperial formations continue their work of haunting. Imperial formations, in this sense, serve as a critical analytic for theorizing "not the inevitable rise and fall of empires, but the active and contingent process of their making and unmaking."[10] By foregrounding the role of Western and US technoculture, technocapital, and their imaginaries throughout this book, I remain attentive to the reality that many other empires and relationships to the state are at play.

With this in mind, in this book I forge the analytic of *Silicon Valley imperialism*, or a global condition in which Silicon Valley's existence is necessitated by its unending growth and in which it penetrates and devours people's intimate lives, local epistemologies, and personal data while also consuming global and even outer space imaginaries in novel ways. While Silicon Valley is emboldened by and often co-constitutive of US empire, it is not synonymous with it. Nor has it replaced US empire or co-opted the entrenched space of Western Europe in presocialist golden era fantasies. Rather, Silicon Valley imperialism coexists on a mutating playbook of schisms and captures, of post-Enlightenment liberal and illiberal imaginaries, and of desires and horrors—all informing various states of becoming and unbecoming.

Writing of neoliberalization amid post-Mao China, Lisa Rofel locates the formation of "desiring subjects" in postsocialist cultural publics.[11] For her, desire encapsulates an aspirational politic that informs public understandings of postsocialist materialities, one that seeks coherence despite the instability and unpredictability of transition. Similar desires can be located in postsocialist Romania, ones that mobilize zombie socialist grammars to justify and make sense of the predation of socialist-era infrastructure, all the while capturing space for the global capital investment geographies of creative capital, tech start-ups, and outsourcing. Cranes and cacophonous sounds of construction fill the air throughout Cluj's Mărăști neighborhood, where NTT Data and dozens of new outsourcing firms are based. Once home to socialist-era textile factories and other working-class manufacturing plants, many of its tech workers earn up to five times more than their neighbors today.[12] That said, there are plenty of others who are paid far less to engage in more menial tasks "behind the curtain" of automation. Nevertheless, the dream of entrepreneurialism is strong. As Oana Mateescu writes, "With the professionalization of the hipster into the upster (which, in Cluj, signals involvement in the start-up ecosystem), labor becomes a form of social and urban belonging framed in the terms of a technomoral governance that can refashion the entire city into a laboratory."[13] Yet these fantasies are only accessible to some. Very few upsters are Roma, and many aspire to move to higher corporate echelons to eventually land gigs at Google or Oracle. Yet for the most part, technocapitalist logics reduce these workers to surrogate cogs in a machine that accumulates wealth in California's San Francisco Bay Area region—a space that first "became" Silicon Valley during the Cold War.

While Silicon Valley imperialism has unevenly transformed both Bay Area and Cluj postindustrial presents, neither actually *is* Silicon Valley. That said, Silicon Valley imperialism is hard at work in both, sowing the seeds for what I describe as its twin concept of *racial technocapitalism*. By this, I refer to the technocapitalist imperatives undergirding racialized processes of data, land, infrastructure, and housing theft. Racial capitalism, in Lisa Lowe's words, "suggests that capitalism expands not through rendering all labor, resources, and markets across the world identical, but by precisely seizing upon colonial divisions, identifying particular regions for production and others for neglect, certain populations for exploitation, and others, disposal."[14] Racial technocapitalism conceptually homes in on how Silicon Valley imperialism disparately materializes racial and spatial dispossession while fabricating anticommunist techno fantasies. Sometimes, racial technocapitalism mobilizes *technofascist* formations, or the techniques through which anticommunist, white nationalist, populist, neoliberal, and even liberal ideologies mechanize fascist conditions of possibility. Racial technocapitalism and technofascism alike offer Silicon Valley imperialism new imaginative and material transits. Yet at the same time, both predate and are not reliant on Silicon Valley's existence. For instance, prior to the formation of Silicon Valley, interwar counting machines made by IBM were used by the Romanian state to map racialized populations as disposable (as I explore in chapter 4).

There are also socialist-era computing histories that predate processes of Silicon Valley imperialism that need to be taken into account in understanding Romania's technological past and present. Indeed, despite today's Siliconizing sea change, this is not the first era in which Romania has experienced a tech boom. To conflate technological development in Romania with Western incursion epistemologically gentrifies the socialist period, which also was a time of rapid industrialization, urbanization, and cyber development. It was then that the country produced the most third-generation computers (1960s and 1970s machines with integrated circuits and miniaturized transistors) in the Eastern bloc, while also fostering deviant practices of cloning Western fourth-generation microprocessor home personal computers (PCs) underground. Other clandestine practices such as internet cabling, software piracy, and media bootlegging have thrived in socialism's aftermath, much of which embrace an ethos of *șmecherie*—a Romanian word with Roma roots inferring cunningness, or a sort of street-smart cleverness.[15]

Siliconization has meant the co-optation of both state computing and hardware production, along with the predation of technodeviant practices and infrastructures, not to mention the cheap surrogate labor that outsourcing provides. After 1989, the land that state socialist factories (computer and otherwise) sat on was largely bought by real estate speculators, divided into joint stock trades, and sold. Firms such as Hewlett-Packard, Microsoft, Oracle, and IBM (again) swept in, absorbing socialist-era tech workers and embracing the grammar of zombie socialism in order to justify intervention. This co-optation has only augmented in recent years, getting at what Silvia Lindtner describes as "displacements of technological promise," or nonlinear, recursive moves that recuperate spatial and technological pasts into the frameworks of neoliberal futurity, casting those who don't fit into its vision into the waiting room of history.[16]

Technological promises infiltrate postsocialist urbanity throughout Cluj, yet sometimes they get corrupted by other technological futures past that refuse Silicon predation. As Tung-Hui Hu, Brian Larkin, and Shannon Mattern have each illustrated, while present-day infrastructures often co-opt those of prior eras, remnants of the past also refuse complete assimilation.[17] Sometimes in Cluj then the past seeps out despite the shiny veneer of Siliconization. For instance, although NTT absorbed EBS, much of the area's "chic modernist" development sits on former industrial and residential exoskeletons. The German iQuest campus, along with iQuest Real Estate and Taco Development, all balance upon the ruins of the Flacăra textile factory. The factory's former canteen now houses tech firms with abstruse names such as Doc.Essensis and CCSCC. One block down the road, the old Napochim plastics factory, known as "The Red Flag" when it first opened in 1947, is being transformed into an apartment block to house tech workers. The former Arbator Butchery, meanwhile, is becoming the "Oxygen Mall." Still lounging on NTT's balcony, my friend and I laugh, "See, it's not the greenwashing of postsocialism—it's the oxygen-washing!" Oxygen-washing, as a form of Siliconization, paves the way for what Neferti Tadiar describes as "uber-urbanization," a process that signposts "the imaginative and techno-infrastructural value-propelled project behind the global fantasy of city everywhere, whose defining tropes also act as programmatic codes for the enterprise."[18]

My friend and I are in the midst of a collaborative mapping project led by the housing justice collective, Căși Sociale ACUM! (Social Housing NOW!), which she cofounded in 2016 in Cluj. We are currently working on a Căși project made in collaboration with the Anti-Eviction Mapping Project (AEMP), which I cofounded in 2013 in Siliconizing San Francisco. While Căși organizes tenants and evictees in Cluj to create social housing alternatives and stop evictions, the AEMP emerged to map landscapes of dispossession and create tools for housing justice. I had been studying housing injustice in Romania for some years prior to cofounding the AEMP, which in part inspired me to ground the project in visions of international solidarity, anti-imperialism, and spatial justice. Now, back in Romania, I find myself circling through the merits and pitfalls of applying AEMP digital cartographic methods since honed in the Bay Area to map Siliconizing Cluj. Committed to not transposing universalizing mediations of space, race, and tech gentrification onto Romanian topographies, I am nevertheless invested in tracing the Silicon connections between the two locales in order to help sow the seeds for anti-imperial future-making. These commitments to housing justice and anti-imperial solidarities across Bay Area and Romanian urban space animate this book, as do questions about what other worlds become possible when refusing to read Silicon Valley as the zero point of spatiotemporal and technological analysis. *Silicon Valley Imperialism* thus traverses an array of socialist and postsocialist tech projects and anticapitalist visions that corrupt Silicon promises.

Geographically, this book's chapters transit the Romanian cities of Bucharest, Cluj, and Râmnicu Vâlcea, and the Moldovan city of Chișinău, while also engaging spaces now comprising California's so-called Silicon Valley region. Employing ethnographic and interdisciplinary reading practices, I analyze three phenomena unique to Romania's relationship with Silicon Valley imperial circuits: (1) geographic entanglements of Silicon Valley and Romanian technological, racial, and urban lifeworlds; (2) presocialist, socialist, and Cold War technohistories as they inform, haunt, and inspire those of the postsocialist/post–Cold War spectral present; and (3) the spatiotemporal entwining of divergent techno-imaginaries and materialities in postsocialist times. As I show, imaginaries and materialities, when studied together, underpin how meanings, dreams, and desires inform and are informed by lived realities. Here I invoke Karen Barad's feminist concept of "agential realism," in which politics, ethics, and observations are inherently composed of material and discursive intra-actions.[19] Producers of knowledge and their imaginative worlds thus directly inform the construction of what becomes material.

While situating my inquiry into the spacetime of Silicon Valley imperialism, I also chart visions and practices of unbecoming. In Angela Willey's words, "Knowledge and power are not only always enmeshed with one another but also always implicated in possibilities for new becomings" and practices of "becoming otherwise."[20] There is analytic agency, then, sewn into aspirations of both *becoming* and *unbecoming* Silicon Valley. This work of unbecoming reveals that while Siliconization is real and ongoing, so are other techno-urban practices unrecognizable through Google Glass or its search engine results.

Their endurance imparts frictions that slow down and at times undo Silicon materialities and imaginaries. Anna Tsing's work on frictions of global connection is helpful here in revealing how globalization processes produce not simply culture clashes or one-way influences, but rather messy, awkward zones of encounter.[21] She also shows that because speculative enterprises often require imaginative work prior to materialization—not only by companies, but also by places (for instance, Cluj's elite dreams up becoming "the Silicon Valley of Eastern Europe")—anticapitalist conjuring work can be just as powerful in processes of unbecoming. Throughout this book, I unearth practices of unbecoming by engaging in the work of activists, organizers, artists, performers, technologists, and theorists who look to past, present, and future refusals of Siliconization. It is through their work that Silicon Valley imperialism becomes unhinged and unraveled—sometimes overtly, sometimes in back-end code. In tracing these practices as well as the violent structures that their work refutes, this book's chapters dip in and out of technopolitical moments and intimate spaces alike in order to theorize interconnected spatiotemporalities always in flux.

Racial Technocapitalism

One might assume that racial technocapitalism is an import into Romania given the power of Silicon Valley imperialism and US empire; history, however, is far more complex. Yes, Silicon Valley transports US understandings of race and racialization, with the whole of Eastern Europe often being racialized as backward and requiring Western technological salvation. However, if following Cedric Robinson's observation that capitalism has always been co-constituted by racism, beginning within Europe's borderlands, things become more muddled.[22] As feudal landlording practices transitioned into capitalism (by enclosing the commons, creating new markets, and suppressing anticapitalist uprisings),[23] so did racializing practices, which exploited the labor and dispossessed the land of Roma people, Jews, Slavs, Tartars, the Irish, and others. With this in mind, Robinson's intervention positions capitalism as inherently racist from the start. In the Romanian provinces of Moldova and Wallachia, Roma slaves were forced to work the lands of boyars (landlords) and churches for five centuries and were never offered reparations after mid-nineteenth-century abolition. In Transylvania, landownership too depended on racialized serfdom. As Anca Parvulescu and Manuela Boatcă observe, "Although historians have foregrounded the labor of the enslaved in the transatlantic trade and different forms of indentured labor that were enmeshed with it globally,

FIGURE I.1. Sign advertising NTT Data's new café, wEBSite Bistro, in the streets headed to their offices in downtown Cluj. Photo taken by author, 2018.

enslaved rural populations rarely appear in labor histories of modern East Europe."[24] Or, as Ioanida Costache articulates, "Any discussion of racism and colonialism in Europe remains incomplete without a critical integration of the situation of the Roma," who have been subjected to racialized exploitation "from the extraction of their labor as an enslaved people to their genocide."[25] This is why, per Piro Rexhepi, today's Roma displacement cannot simply be chalked up to neoliberalism, but rather needs to take into account "histories of racial capitalism underwritten by colonial mappings of population, place, and time."[26]

State socialism, as a project, was established in part to obliterate the capitalist regime that preceded it, one that had been informed by imperiality, racialization, fascism, and aspirations to become European. This, however,

FIGURE I.2. Robot at
NTT Data. Photo taken
by author, 2018.

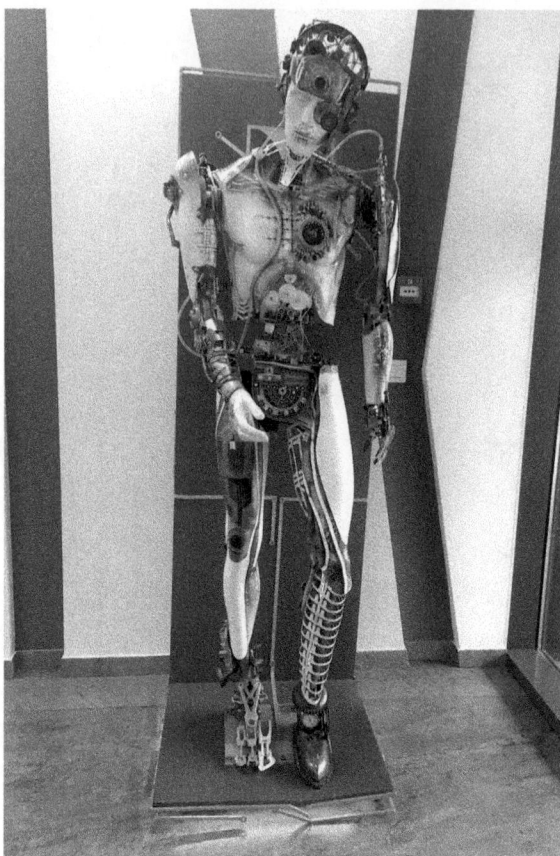

is not to suggest that the socialist project obliterated racism.[27] Per Rexhepi,
"The protracted racialization of Roma populations across different (post)Ot-
toman spaces betrays the supposed racelessness of socialism."[28] While many
socialists referred to racism as *șovinism*, or chauvinism, many Roma recall experiences of *ură de rasă*, or race hate, during the era. As Manuel Mireanu has
traced, anti-Roma racism was augmented in the 1980s in Romania, with Roma
people often rendered social problems, school dropouts, nomads, and squatters.[29] Despite this, many Roma who experienced race hate during socialism's
latter years are quick to acknowledge how much worse it became in the 1990s,
a period marked by austerity, unemployment, and also racist pogroms. Enikő
Vincze and George Zamfir write that today, as has been the case historically,
"Racialized nationalism does not consider Roma as people with an ethnic background similar to other ethnics, but as lesser humans belonging to an inferior
race."[30] Given this, we can see that while racism is not a recent import into

Romania, there are new racial transits that do need to be studied, be they of so-called presocialist "returns" or of those that accompany Silicon Valley imperial grammars.

While Robinson, along with other scholars of Black Marxism, positions capitalism as an inherently racial project, other Marxists have additionally foregrounded its historic reliance on innovation and technology. Yet those interested in capitalism's technological reliance have not always attended to the significance of race and coloniality. Some of this came to a head during the 1974–1982 Brenner debate, which saw Robert Brenner argue against Immanuel Wallerstein regarding primitive accumulation—Karl Marx's concept of how precapitalist modes of production, including those of feudalism and slavery, preconditioned capitalist economics. While Wallerstein's world-systems theory found primitive accumulation reliant on the West's ability to exploit peripheral and semiperipheral lands including Eastern Europe,[31] Brenner, whose theorizations were largely based on examples from the English countryside, believed that capitalism emerged through the alienation of the means of production.[32] This, he claimed, inspired new techniques of market competition and technological revolution within Europe, or "innovation via accumulation."[33] Yet in *Capital*, while Marx does back some of Brenner's ideas, he also supports Wallerstein's. As the famous passage goes: "The discovery of gold and silver in America, the extirpation, enslavement and entombment in mines of the aboriginal population, the beginning of the conquest and looting of the East Indies, the turning of Africa into a warren for the commercial hunting of black-skins, signalized the rosy dawn of the era of capitalist production."[34] While his remark connects slavery, imperialism, and capitalism to new technologies of exploitation beyond Eastern Europe, in *Capital* he also looked to Romanian provinces to exemplify the appropriation of peasant labor by wealthy boyars such as Vlad Țepeș, known today as Count Dracula.[35] Marx was however hazier regarding the role of racialization within Eastern Europe, not to mention the role that slavery and colonization continued to play within capitalist contexts elsewhere.

David Harvey's concept of "accumulation by dispossession" has served as a partial antidote here, particularly in assessing the dispossessive violence that capitalist innovation inheres.[36] He looks to how processes of primitive accumulation are requisite on new territories of acquisition and therefore dispossession, often made accessible through financial crises. Yet as Paula Chakravartty and Denise Ferreira da Silva argue, missing from his analysis are how such new territories protract historic racial and imperial practices, epistemologies, and geographies.[37] They also suggest returning to Cedric Robinson, C. L. R. James, and Frantz Fanon to better understand "how historical materialism alone cannot account for the ways in which capitalism has lived off—always backed by the colonial and national state's means of death—of colonial/racial expropriation."[38] Or, as Brenna Bhandar puts it, colonial encounters have long relied on the logics of private property in order to create capitalist markets, in turn producing racial regimes of ownership that haunt the present. Such confrontations have manifested "a conceptual apparatus in which justifications for private property ownership remain bound to a concept of the human that is thoroughly racial in its makeup."[39] As she notes, while racial capitalism was indeed a core tenet of feudal Europe prior to the colonization of the Americas, it became globalized in the era of modern colonialism, which relied on new technologies of economic, racial, and spatial measurement, codification, and abstraction. Such techniques were used to render colonized peoples "outside of history, lacking the requisite cultural practices, habits of thought, and economic organization to be considered as sovereign, rational economic subjects."[40] Prior imperial violence is thus not simply stuck in the past but is rather an ongoing condition of possibility that very much informs capitalist logics and their racial technologies.

Returning to Romania then, historic formations of empire, racial capitalism, and technocapitalism require a similar approach—one that takes into account the simultaneity of multiply existing imperial formations over time. This is in part what informs Parvulescu and Boatcă's formulation of an "inter-imperial approach" to the region, one that provides a corrective to linear narratives of industrialization as requisite for capitalism. Rather, they argue that imperial histories in East Europe "left indelible marks on both the socioeconomic organization and the self-conceptualization of its subjects, which placed them in a different relationship to the West European core than the American colonies."[41] Drawing on world-systems analysis, they note how while racial capitalist difference in the colonies marked *"colonial difference* from the core,"* ethnic and class-based hierarchies within East Europe illustrated the *"imperial difference* between European empires and their former subjects."[42] This, in Boatcă's words, has long positioned East European spaces to serve as "laboratories of modernity at the level of global capitalism."[43] The semiperipheral East, portrayed as white Christian Europe's incomplete and darker self,[44] gets mapped then as "culturally alien by definition."[45] While state socialism concretized this alien otherness to the West, it also wrought the region free (or freer) from Western imperial control through industrialization. In this sense, histories of technological development, empire, and ethnic/racial difference in Eastern Europe do not easily map onto Western capitalist trajectories and need to be explored through unique historic contexts.

US empire helped engineer and then capitalize on the collapse of communism (though of course this had to do with a range of factors notwithstanding increased authoritarian rule, nationalism, and a shift away from the antifascist ideals that originally contoured the socialist project). Silicon Valley imperialism in particular orchestrated the co-optation of socialist-era infrastructure, knowledge, and technofuturity. This then adds a new layer of empire into the mix, one that embraced technoliberal grammars. Here, by *technoliberalism*, I invoke what Atanasoski and Vora describe as a "political alibi of present-day racial capitalism that posits humanity as an aspirational figuration in relation to technological transformation, obscuring the uneven racial and gendered relations of labor, power, and social relations that underlie the contemporary conditions of capitalist production."[46] Technoliberalism then unevenly powers the appropriation of space, race, labor, and futurity to embolden racial technocapitalism. Not only does it transit Western understandings of race and technology into the East, but it also galvanizes the coloniality undergirding California's so-called Silicon Valley. In this way, racial technocapitalism in Romania is a stratified constellation marked by variegated imperial histories, each of which transits different relational understandings of race, ethnicity, and class.

Silicon Valley Imperialism

Most of the tech companies scattered about Cluj, but also Bucharest and other Romanian cities, are not from Silicon Valley per se (although plenty are); many are in fact based in the United Kingdom, Germany, France, Japan, and beyond. That said, they cumulatively serve as an alibi for Silicon Valley imperial visions, while also being hooked into Silicon Valley venture capital circuits, software, servers, data centers, and code. Today, not only does California's Silicon Valley contain more billionaires, venture capitalists, and patents per square foot than anywhere else on earth, but also, the region hosts fifty of the top one hundred most expensive zip codes in the United States and most of the firms that power much of networked life globally. As scholars such as Margaret O'Mara and Linda Weiss have each observed, Silicon Valley economics have everything to do with the United States' Cold War pursuit of technological supremacy and defense.[47] This has continued in Cold War aftermaths, with Google's former CEO, Eric Schmitt, leading a Pentagon advisory board while Meta's Mark Zuckerberg embraces Cold War 2.0 logics which suggest that breaking up Facebook's monopolies would empower Chinese tech. Though these companies remain reliant on military contracts, they work to avoid government regulation, oversight, and taxes. They would rather, per Facebook's original motto, "Move fast and break things." Yet as Ruha Benjamin saliently questions, "What about the people and places broken in the process?"[48]

Not only does Silicon Valley maintain material and military infrastructural dominance, but it also manufactures and disseminates aspirational and entrepreneurial desires. As Richard Walker writes, "The mythology of the plucky tech entrepreneur has diffused around the world, becoming a key element in the capitalist dream world of today."[49] Many of these entrepreneurs find themselves in places like Cluj, looking to capitalize on cheap outsourcing, technological prowess, English language capacity, and more. Upon the ruins of socialist technofuturism, Silicon Valley–based start-ups and "digital nomad" remote workers offer workshops, TED talks, and more on how to become better at capitalism, how to successfully amass big data, and how to mobilize artificial intelligence, machine learning, and algorithmic automation.

However, as Lilly Irani cautions in her work on "entrepreneurial citizenship" in India, by looking for Silicon Valley everywhere, older forms of power relations that have perhaps more explanatory and political strength (for instance, British colonialism) remain hidden in plain sight.[50] By only seeing Siliconization as responsible for technological development in Cluj, an array of histories remain buried. As Andrew Schrock summarizes, "Silicon Valley was always a promise, never a place."[51] This promise is not dissimilar to that which Sara Ahmed critiques as "the promise of happiness," which imparts a moral and affective fantasy.[52] Conversant with Lauren Berlant's "cruel optimism" and its unfulfillable promises of upward mobility,[53] Silicon Valley conjures fantasies of liberal assimilation despite the material and imaginative violence it yields. While this may look different in the array of "Silicon Valleys" popping up around the globe—from Silicon Plateau in Bangalore to Silicon Wadi in Israel—promises, disavowals, and spatial erasure do ensue.

Just as Cluj is not and never will *be* Silicon Valley, neither will the many lands of the San Francisco Bay Area. As Kim Tran writes, "I have never heard a poor person of color from the South Bay ever call where I'm from 'Silicon Valley.'"[54] Yet even the South Bay, San Jose, and San Francisco—cities collectively recognized as Silicon Valley—bear imperial toponymies, referencing lands violently stolen from Ohlone and Miwok peoples by Spanish missionaries, Anglo gold rushers, and then US empire. This process, in Jodi Byrd's words, "cohered and transformed external lands into internal domestic spaces that now seamlessly exist."[55] Massacre by massacre, the US government sought to expand the country to the western edge of continental space by killing California Indians rather than honoring treaties.[56] It was the hydraulic mining frenzy that fol-

lowed the gold rush, that, in Malcolm Harris's words, manifested a new crea-
ture: "the California engineer, master of water, stone, and labor."[57] As he traces,
it was nineteenth-century frontier scientists who set the stage for technologies
of racial capitalist production vis-à-vis the "California model," an exportable
formula that legitimized white supremacy and resource grabbing.[58] Per Harris, "California engineers became the heralds of proletarianization around the
world, the shock troops of global enclosure, drawing the lines that so many
were forced to follow."[59] This set the stage for geographies of racial technocapitalism in the Valley today.

Thus, despite popular understandings that position US imperialism fomenting through its external island conquests beginning in the late nineteenth
century, as well through its Cold War nuclear-armed global superpower status
gained by protecting the "free world" from communism, in fact US empire is
rooted in the ongoing and incomplete project of settler colonialism (incomplete in that Native peoples and lands are still here). Not that this model did
not seep into Cold War science; on the contrary, it laid the groundwork for
the very formation of Stanford University and the tech companies that the
institution later helped grow. US empire continues to expand today by trans-
ferring "Indianness" onto an array of extractable materialities—including data
accumulated "at home" in the Silicon Valley region and abroad (for instance,
in Eastern Europe).

Building on the foundations of US empire, then, Silicon Valley imperialism
reiterates Native erasure through ongoing practices of gentrification. In Nick
Estes's words, "Gentrification doesn't only happen in cities, and it doesn't only
mimic colonial processes—it is colonialism. Settler colonialism, whether in
border towns, rural areas, or urban geographies, is fundamental to the history
of US expansion that has required the removal, dispossession, and elimination of Indigenous peoples."[60] Although "gentrification" discursively traffics in
popular understandings of housing financialization, the whitening of neighborhoods, and practices of forced expulsion globally, its vernacular utilization
can, and often does, deracinate the present from centuries of racial dispossession and violence. This is in part why Roy prefers the analytic of racial banishment, which signals "the public means of evictions as well as forms of racialized
violence, such as slavery, Jim Crow, incarceration, colonialism, and apartheid,
that cannot be encapsulated within sanitized notions of gentrification and displacement."[61] In Romania, racial banishment is useful for apprehending how
presocialist fascist spatiality maps onto the Siliconized present.

In the San Francisco Bay Area, racial banishment marks centuries of colonial violence, not to mention segregation, exploitation, and dispossession

imposed upon Natives, immigrants, and people of color during the development of a number of capitalist projects that followed the gold rush. Railroad development, canaries and fruit production, microelectronics manufacturing, and more preyed upon hazardous immigrant labor, all of which laid the foundation for Silicon Valley economics.[62] Though the term "Silicon Valley" did not appear until 1971 in reference to semiconductor success by known eugenicist William Shockley,[63] such events had everything to do with Stanford University, which had established a research park in 1951 that became home to many of the Valley's earliest companies. Yet Stanford University would not have come into being in the first place if it weren't for capital from founder Leland Stanford's prior frontier ventures in gold and railroads. In this sense, the bedrock of Cold War Silicon Valley has always been stained by the ravages of empire.

In addition to trafficking racial technocapitalist tactics of innovation, exploitation, and accumulation, Silicon Valley imperialism rehearses anticommunist ideologies. It was in 1950 that Norbert Wiener, the "father of cybernetics," argued that the solution to authoritarianism and fascism required remodeling the world through distributed communications systems managed by computers.[64] This framework was used to position the region's technologies, as well as neoliberal economics, as salvific in the battle against illiberalism (often equated with communism)—be it at home or abroad.[65] It was communist visions led by groups such as the Black Panther Party that soon became feared as the illiberal sparks capable of dismantling US empire locally—in turn incentivizing state-backed repression.[66] Silicon Valley technologies and ideologies were in turn developed to maintain US imperial power both at home and abroad in the liberal war against racialized communism/illiberalism. Per Atanasoski and Vora, the United States "morally underwrote its imperial projects as a struggle for achieving states of freedom abroad over illiberal states of unfreedom, racializing illiberal systems of belief as a supplement to the racialization of bodies under Western European imperialism."[67] The Cold War paradigm and its development of weapons, computers, and semiconductors thus racialized the illiberal communist other—not to supplant existing racial difference, but rather to add a new genre of raciality into the mix that Silicon Valley technologies could help discipline.

As the Cold War was coming to a close, Ronald Reagan synthesized this logic by proclaiming that "the Goliath of totalitarianism will be brought down by the David of the microchip," or the "oxygen of the modern age."[68] Thus not only did Reagan offer a discursive prototype to today's "oxygen washing" in Cluj, but he also allegorized Silicon Valley imperialism through biblical tropes. Of course, these myths have long been used to justify colonial technologies of control upon "savages" imagined as technologically unsophisticated and thus without legitimate claims to land. Sylvia Wynter writes that with the Spanish colonization of the Americas, jurists and theologians transitioned from solely categorizing those requiring domination as "Enemies of Christ/Christ Refusers" to those of a different race.[69] In other words, through imperialism, race became an "extrahuman" trait that required remapping the "space of Otherness . . . defined in terms of degrees of rational perfection/imperfection."[70] A master code was thus established of racialized rationality/irrationality, and it has been used since to justify imperial rights to sovereignty upon stolen land, not to mention the institutionalization of the plantation system. While this master code haunts the present, it has also, Wynter notes, grown to rationalize the superiority of the First World over "underdeveloped" places and to render the "Invisible Hand" of the free market as inevitable. This master code reifies the authority of what she describes as the contemporary "biocentric ethno-class genre of the human, of which our present techno-industrial, capitalist mode of production is an indispensable and irreplaceable, but only a proximate function."[71] And so, per Reagan, the microchip became an object through which to reproduce the master code of Western capitalist authority.

It was the microchip, then, that Silicon Valley ideologues imagined manifesting Francis Fukuyama's overdetermined and unfulfilled proclamation of the post-1989/1991 "end of history," in which the entire world would be blanketed by liberal democracy.[72] This end-of-history imaginary, coupled with shifts toward consumer markets and ongoing US imperial formations, has razed new and uneven space for Siliconization. Perhaps it should be of no surprise that in 2008, tech evangelist Chris Anderson penned an op-ed suggesting that with the rise of big data, we have also reached the "end of theory," where it no longer matters why things happen as long as they can be modeled, predicted, and scaled.[73] Elided from this temporal apogee are the racial asymmetries undergirding geographies of datafication and digitality, so that digital universalism remains, in Anita Say Chan's words, a myth at best.[74] Or, perhaps, this end of theory/history is a new instantiation of the same master code critiqued by Wynter, which seeks to dampen class conflict and revolutionary uprisings by trafficking imaginaries of assimilation into the tech bourgeoisie and its fictive projections of liberal universality.

In 2014, a lengthy article in *Time* featured a story detailing Zuckerberg's project Internet.org, designed to supply even the most "remote" spaces of the planet with internet. The cover image of the article depicted a tall, white Zuckerberg surrounded by shorter, brown children from the rural town of Chandauli, India. As Kentaro Toyama chastised, "Internet.org is a form of colonialism that whitewashes Facebook's techno-imperialism under a cloak of doing good."[75] Such a salvific mission, one to effectively "save the world" with one's own product, gets echoed in Silicon Valley spaces far and wide. Sam Altman, CEO of OpenAI and past president of YCombinator, has built an economy within Silicon Valley to be "a guild of hyper-capitalist entrepreneurs who will help one another fix the broken world."[76] Meanwhile, Elon Musk, the world's wealthiest person (as of 2023), who maintains power through leadership positions in SpaceX, Tesla, Twitter/X, the Boring Company, and more, claims his ventures such as colonizing Mars and preserving "free speech" will save the world, or at least some wealthy humans on it.[77]

In such contexts of Silicon Valley imperialism, data, materials, imaginaries, outer space, and even sociality are for the taking, often under the pretense of saving humanity within the endless end of history. At the same time, Silicon Valley imperialism functions to accumulate capital on stolen lands where Native worlds and histories have suffered numerous assassination attempts. In this sense, the grabbing of land and the grabbing of data go hand in hand in order to destroy worlds for some and protract them of others. As Katherine McKittrick contextualizes, "Land grabbing is a self-replicating system that provides the avaricious conditions for the data grab. . . . The task of the data grab is to remake our sense of place, heartlessly."[78] Ohlone lands have been actively made and remade through Spanish and US empire before being remade again through Silicon Valley imperialism. And in Cluj, where Western tech firms launch outsourcing exploitations upon the ruins of socialist modernity, place is also actively being reshaped. Yet despite Siliconized subsumption, other futures past and present remain, many of which crystallize through anti-imperial politics and postsocialist analytics.

Postsocialism

By tracking Silicon Valley imperialism and racial technocapitalism together, in this book I theorize a particular postsocialist moment. By postsocialism, I refer to a post-1989 condition that has endured in both Eastern Europe and the West and that unevenly recodes configurations of race and empire today. At the same time, I find it a useful analytic for theorizing anticapitalist practices that exceed the spatiotemporal borders of state socialism and the Cold War. In other words, I find postsocialism germane to everyday life, infrastructure, and politics in the former Eastern bloc and beyond.[79] My take here is particularly inspired by the feminist collaboration between Atanasoski and Vora, who suggest that postsocialism resists "the revolutionary teleology of what was before," materializing space to explore socialisms' ongoing legacies today.[80] To this end, they offer the framework of pluralizing postsocialisms, highlighting "current practices, imaginaries and actions that insist on political change at a variety of scales, including local, state, and transnational ones." By unmooring postsocialism from its oft-assumed spatiotemporality, anticapitalist practices that exceed the boundaries of state socialism surface.

While mid-twentieth-century decolonial movements have been understood as globally significant, just as noteworthy have been twentieth-century moves to disavow socialist practices within and beyond Eastern Europe. As Redi Koobak, Madina Tlostanova, and Suruchi Thapar-Björkert write, "Never fully realised in any of the spaces that claimed to be socialist, the state socialist utopia is still crucial as a dream, as an alternative to the capitalist liberal or neoliberal model."[81] While socialism—as utopic and anticipatory project—has been discredited as a dream from the past, in fact, it has never fully arrived. Postsocialism thus highlights the ongoing practice of imagining and actualizing anticapitalist alternatives, lifeworlds, and futures to come. This aligns with Lisa Lowe's suggestion that the past conditional temporality, or "what could have been," offers a way past Western universalist epistemological enclosures of revolutionary change.[82] By revisiting "times of historical contingency and possibility to consider alternatives that may have been unthought in those times,"[83] anticolonial and non-Western Marxist futures past resurface.

At the same time, postsocialism also marks the temporal uncanniness imbued in the process of living on amid the aftermaths of state socialism. David Scott writes of melancholy and hopelessness associated with "the temporal disjunctures involved in living on in the wake of past political time, amid the ruins, specifically, of postsocialist and postcolonial futures past."[84] As he illustrates, the emancipatory dreams guiding revolution can crumble in its aftershocks, particularly when nationalist and neoliberal futures take over. Thus, while postsocialism is a useful analytic for mapping the material, imaginative, and epistemological legacies of the socialist project, it is also conceptually helpful in apprehending the brutality of global capital. It meanwhile remains theoretically germane in examining Soviet socialism in itself as an imperial project, one that broke from some of the Marxist and anti-imperialist ideals that originally inspired it. In its plurality then, postsocialism shows that the legacies of Marx and Lenin have multiple lives beyond and in excess of European spatiality.[85] But also, as liberation theorists such as Enrique Dussel have observed, there are Indigenous socialisms and communalisms in the Americas that predate and coagulate with Marxism.[86] David Graeber and David Wengrow have more recently suggested that perhaps it was these Native communalisms that inspired French Enlightenment critiques of private property before Marx, ultimately igniting revolution.[87] All of this underscores the need for postsocialist theory to take into account socialisms' multiplicities.

Despite postsocialism's plurality, Cold War area studies formations have long quarantined it as a conceptual apparatus only related to the aftermaths of state socialist spatiotemporality. This has animated a breadth of scholarship on the merits of postsocialist theory and its connections to postcolonial theory, as well as whether or not to abandon the term entirely given that it has now been over three decades since the collapse of the Iron Curtain. While the "post" in postcolonialism has been accepted as signaling not colonialism's end but rather historic and entangled endurances of empire, race, and struggle globally, scholars such as Martin Müller have suggested that postsocialism is not worthy of such affordances and that it be retired in favor of new formations such as the "Global East."[88] While this move elides theoretical interventions about postcolonialism's relevancy in the North and West,[89] it also obviates the imperiality of the United States and the Soviet Union throughout the Cold War.[90] Further, just as capital remains global, so are practices of capitalist refusal in ways that postsocialist analytics are productive in apprehending. Postsocialist theory is also still useful in assessing the hauntings of disaster capitalism in the so-called post–Cold War "East" (which has not abated despite wishful thinking).

Müller's rejoinder is hardly the first regarding the theoretical merits (or lack thereof) of postsocialism. Postsocialism emerged as a term in academic writing in the 1990s and which, unlike postcolonialism (which entered academic discourses years after decolonization movements began and which was at its inception a theoretical concept), initially stood as a spatiotemporal descriptor applied mostly to post-1989/1991 Central and Eastern European nations and at times, when modified, to China, Vietnam, and Cuba.[91] Yet postsocialism was also important in portraying, as Verdery argues, "reorganization on a cosmic scale," and the redefining and reordering of "people's entire meaningful worlds" via processes of privatization, lustration, democratization, transition, neoliberalism, and other modes of liberal-democratic governance[92]—in other words, the remaking of persons from socialist to capitalist subjects. To this end, postsocialist theory was used to study the pandemonium brought about by injections of post-1989 neoliberalism, which sought to transform what Koobak, Tlostanova, and Thapar-Björkert describe as "the eternal present of the consumer paradise" associated with history's end and the expansion of NATO and global trade.[93] It also documented leftist organizing against such paradises.[94] While the left has continued to organize for anticapitalist futures, postsocialist theory has begun to accept the inevitability of the capitalist global order. It has seen, in Tlostanova's words, socialist state modernity accepted as a nonviable project, uncritical of the ongoing work of training its practitioners "on how to become fully modern (in the only remaining neoliberal way) and therefore, fully human."[95]

This not-yet-human stance, one of ex-socialist subjects lagging behind the humanity of their Western counterparts, was recently reified by a CBS reporter referring to Ukrainians as "semi-civilized" upon Russia's 2022 invasion.[96] While complicated by very stark stratifications of ethnic and racial difference within the former Eastern bloc—this semicivilized positionality does nevertheless bring into light the ongoing saliency of postsocialist theory, particularly regarding temporality, globality, and race. Whereas postcolonial theory has importantly studied the backwardness with which subaltern subjects are interpellated, postsocialist theory is particularly well situated to analyze the temporal disjuncture that the collapse of state socialism imposed. After all, the socialist project was both one in which time was supposed to speed up to materialize a communist utopic future, but also one, especially in the 1980s, that many associated with temporal stagnation.[97] Theorizing state socialism's demise, Boris Groys writes that the postsocialist subject travels "not from the past to the future, but from the future to the past; from the end of history . . . back to historical time. Post-Communist life is life lived backward, a movement against the flow of time."[98] This forges what Anita Starosta describes as postsocialist "common time," or "a process of never-finished synchronization among multiple temporalities—and by the same token, the process of forging the only possible authentic 'we.'"[99] The never-finished nature of this time, or what David Scott calls "leftovers from a former future stranded in the present,"[100] reflects that despite the best attempts of Westernization and Silicon Valley imperialism alike, spatiotemporal otherness persists.

When it comes to analyzing the ruins, dreams, and disasters contouring formerly socialist cities, this spatiotemporal otherness often remains a shallow marker of topography and periodization rather than a time-space theoretic. The Cold War again is to blame here, as it was then that the field of urban studies was revitalized to better theorize the newly accessible "world of cities"[101]—many of which were transforming through rampant injections of post–Cold War neoliberalism. Through this, a dominant analytic emerged, one that understood postsocialist urbanities as "correcting" themselves, catching up to their Western counterparts. As Martin Ouřednícek argues, pervasive anticommunism and Western admiration has "created ideal conditions for an uncritical implantation of Western theoretical concepts, for the westernization of the spoken language in general, and in academic vocabulary in particular."[102] Three decades after the collapse of the Cold War, postsocialist urbanists today are more apt to acknowledge the limitations of Western conceptual frames by engaging postcolonial theory. But here postcoloniality does the heavy theoretical lifting, while postsocialist cities are remaindered as what Örjan Sjöberg calls "case studies onto themselves,"[103] confined into what Michael Gentile depicts as "the peripheries of urban knowledge."[104] Ana Vilenica, in a brilliant critique of Western theory dominating conversations on urban commoning, also blames "neocolonial 'transitional' narratives" for creating an Eastern distrust of collective projects, which get interpellated as Western humanitarian interventions rather than homegrown anticapitalist struggles.[105] In this sense, producing urban studies of commoning and anti-eviction work in Eastern Europe requires contending not only with Western Cold War epistemic dominance, but also the internalized anticommunism that the Cold War has wrought.

In an attempt to address some of the politics undergirding paradoxes such as this, Sharad Chari and Katherine Verdery have contemplated the possibilities of welding postcolonial and postsocialist studies together. "Just as postcoloniality had become a critical perspective on the colonial present," they write, "postsocialism could become a similarly critical standpoint on the continuing social and spatial effects of Cold War power and knowledge."[106] To this end, and in recognition of the Cold War as an epistemological limit to how the world could be known in the second half of the twentieth century, they argue for a new post–Cold War framing: "It is time to liberate the Cold War from the ghetto of Soviet area studies and post-colonial thought from the ghetto of Third World and colonial studies. The liberatory path proposed here the jettisoning of these two posts in favor of a single overarching one: the post–Cold War."[107] Their intervention points to the ongoing necessity of thinking empire, socialist modernity, and global capitalism together. Yet perhaps part of the problem remains in that much of the Western left today still only imagines the alternative to capitalism being state socialism. By pluralizing postsocialisms, new paths for investing in anticapitalist frameworks beyond the state percolate. In this way, by connecting postsocialisms and postcolonialisms in their pluralities—not simply for postsocialism to theorize the West nor just for postcolonialism to chart the East—we can better apprehend the spatiotemporalities of neoliberalism, liberalism, and illiberalism alongside ongoing anticapitalist collectivity and anti-imperial revolution.[108]

Il/liberalism

Given the revival of the Cold War as a geopolitical framework amid Putin's invasion of Ukraine and before that the blaming of Russian and Eastern European hackers for Trump's electoral victory, postsocialism also offers an important corrective to the dehistoricized and decontextualized framing of democracy and authoritarianism as the only (and opposing) political forms. Today's so-called Cold War 2.0 transpires in a moment when although state socialism has receded into the past, the US/Russian antipodal battling for imperial control of "satellite" states appears alive and well. This gets inscribed as a contest between liberalism and illiberalism, between democracy and authoritarianism, between lightness and darkness, and weirdly enough, between communism and capitalism (even though Russia and Eastern Europe are capitalist today). At the same time, mythology and media networks reify Cold War paranoia, informing what Sorin Cucu describes as a double allegorical formation: "Historical events such as the end of the Cold War are not what they appear to be, yet even this new Cold War is not what it purports to be. Double deception!"[109] As a "postmodern pastiche" of the Cold War, its 2.0 form resuscitates prior fears of information leakage and espionage through what Alaina Lemon describes as "technologies for intuition."[110] This highlights the need to better engage with fiction, speculation, and technology in charting Cold War 2.0 verisimilitudes, where the Cold War's mythological powers materialize undead fantasies of bipolarity.

While powerful in its framing of democracy and authoritarianism as opposites, this bipolarity fails to accommodate a critique of capitalism. In the words of Alexei Yurchak, "The opposition of 'democracy' and 'authoritarianism,' . . . instead of providing analytical clarity, in fact, contributes to decoupling 'democracy' from 'capitalism' and thus concealing and depoliticizing the real conditions."[111] Yet capitalism and liberal democracy have been historically entangled, as has been evidenced through zombie socialist property restitution schemas as well as through the predation of socialist infrastructure by Silicon Valley firms. Thus, given the resurgence of the "Cold War," postsocialism remains salient in assessing contested political terrains and their undead fictions. At the same time, as Wendy Brown warns, many of today's "fascist returns," such as Make America Great Again (MAGA) Trumpism in the United States, hinge not just on updating interwar fascist pasts, but also on the fruits of neoliberalism coming to bear—many of which are also intimately tethered to liberal anticommunist frameworks.[112] This aligns with interventions made by scholars such as Robinson and James who decades ago now pointed out the need to theorize fascism, capitalism, and Western imperialism as connected.[113] Similarly, Evgeny Morozov dissuades against a growing belief on both the left and right that we are somehow in the midst of a feudal return, one marking the end of capitalism and a return to rule by tech elite lords.[114] This is because technofeudal analytics negates the ongoing might of technocapitalism, which, while perhaps not as sensational as technofeudalism, remains the name of the game. Thus, studying liberal, capitalist, and imperial epistemologies remains just as important as ever in assessing today's "illiberal returns."

In December 2020, amid the COVID-19 pandemic, Romanians voted to grant parliamentary power to the fascist-leaning AUR party. AUR, which means "gold" in Romanian, has openly sympathized with the Iron Guard Legionnaire movement, which, while tethered to Orthodox Christian mysticism, powered fascist populism in presocialist times to rid the country of its Jews, Roma, deviants, and communists. One of AUR's leaders, Sorin Lavric, had been fanning racist flames during this time, blaming Roma people for being the main harbingers of the COVID-19 virus.[115] Such a sentiment had already been spreading widely in mainstream culture, with articles and social media posts fashioning Roma as nomadic vectors for transmission.[116] One op-ed written by a disgruntled Romanian flight attendant bemoaned having to bring diasporic Roma back to Romania from their homes abroad. "I was so happy when I took you to other countries," she addressed to her Roma passengers. "I was thinking, 'My God, one less,' and now you come back with skirts full of stolen money, with the same raffia nets, a bit arrogant and disgusting! You come to kill our elders, our parents, and the worst thing is that we also bring you and welcome you home!"[117] Such biological racist ideology has since been spreading like wildfire, updating older histories of anti-Roma racism beyond fringe far right groups. As Costache summarizes, "Put simply, if civilization is synonymous with science, medicine, modernity, and technology, then it is foiled by those living in poverty, and squalor like many Roma, who lack access to all things that index 'civilization,' like running water."[118] To return to the pure, presocialist past and to restore possibilities of Westernization through Siliconization, figures like the fascist Antonescu are invoked to complete the eugenicist project.

Today's ethno-nationalist move to restitute fascism's "golden era" is nationalistically anchored in what Anders Hellström, Ov Cristian Norocel, and Martin Bak Jørgensen describe as "the nostalgic longing for an ethnically homogenous past that never quite existed."[119] In theorizing nationalism in postsocialist contexts, Anikó Imre suggests its legitimacy "is grounded in mythical origin stories that can be resourced to posit collective beginnings, which then put the nation on a path towards a future destiny, a narrative journey shaped by power holders in the present."[120] For instance, during the summer of 2022, Hungarian prime minister Viktor Orbán delivered an eerie speech in the small Romanian town of Băile Tușnad (which maintains an ethnic Hungarian majority) against the mixing of races, or what he called "species."[121] In his words, "We [Hungarians] are not a mixed species . . . and we do not want to become a mixed species." Following his oration, Orbán traveled to the United States to speak on a Trumpian panel in Dallas, Texas, leading critics to theorize that his Romanian speech was just as much intended for US white supremacists as Hungarian fascists. Yet in Eastern Europe, his rhetoric also speaks to post-1989 promises of joining, or perhaps returning to, the European body. There, nationalists seek to purge racial "others within," while preventing Romania from being "colonized" with refugees.[122] Not coincidentally, this language invokes the presocialist period when Jews were described as having colonized Romania. To this end, AUR references "Jewish colonization" while also aspiring for a "revolution" to remove the "rotten system" allegedly controlled by George Soros.[123]

The spatiotemporal connections between the East and West, presocialist and postsocialist temporality, and liberalism and illiberalism invoke the conditions that communism first emerged to combat. It was as state socialism was solidifying across the Eastern bloc that Hannah Arendt and Karl Polanyi each charted connections between liberal democracy and fascism, suggesting that fascism (particularly Nazism) emerged from crises in liberal empires.[124] Arendt offered Nazism as a genealogy rooted in the late nineteenth-century German colonial expansion and genocide in Namibia. Meanwhile, Polanyi (who defended his dissertation in Cluj in 1909) saw the 1930s rise of fascism as an effect of state-enforced laissez-faire and self-regulating market economies. These markets, left unhindered, could not help but produce imperial domination, he observed. Nikhil Pal Singh argues that although these two thinkers offer much to study that connects liberalism, imperialism, racism, and fascism, they both fail to fully understand the raciality of US liberalism as well as its implications in Cold War socialist space.[125] Further, Arendt's critiques of Stalinist totalitarianism and German Nazism have too easily merged in popular interpretations, inspiring some of the conflations of fascism and socialism saturating liberal mythologies today. Cold War understandings of Soviet illiberal technologies have been mapped onto post-9/11 imaginaries of technoterrorism, for instance. As Atanasoski and Vora suggest, "As fascism was excised from the realm of the West to that of the East, then, certain modes of automation, especially those that reduced the human to the machine, came to be associated with ongoing states of unfreedom justifying US 'humanizing' imperial violence in the decolonizing world where the Cold War was fought."[126]

Robinson's theorization of fascism serves as antidote here, particularly his observation that for many non-Western peoples, "fascism—that is militarism, imperialism, racial authoritarianism, choreographed mob violence, millenarian crypto-Christian mysticism, and a nostalgic nationalism" has been "no more an historical aberration than colonialism, slave trade, and slavery."[127]

Even in Italy, fascism emerged as part of Mussolini's strategy to gain control of colonized peoples in Palestine, Libya, and East Africa, particularly in Ethiopia, and to suppress communist possibility.[128] In other words, capitalism and imperialism predate and inform fascist possibility. Similarly, in reflecting on the interwar imbrication of capitalism and fascism, James offers, "More and more groups of German capitalists began to see their way out in Hitler."[129] Anticolonial and Black radical thinkers continued to make these correlations throughout the Cold War. Yet in its aftermaths, liberals have mobilized what Lilith Mahmud describes as "fascism's spectral powers by invoking it as an imminent threat to political life."[130]

While liberalism has generally opposed what fascism stands for, Mahmud warns that "its own values of moderation, rationality, and freedom have at times displaced to the margins of legitimate political discourse not only fascist positions but also antifascist ones."[131] As has been made evident amid Light Revolution protests that discredit anticapitalist, antifascist organizing, but also within the broader project of Siliconization—which while framed as a liberal project, materials racial banishment and chastises antifascist work—fascism maintains power by stupefying "a normative liberal subjectivity into disarming antifascist resistance, thus abetting fascism's rise."[132] It is because of this that Mahmud calls for an anthropology of spectral fascism as well as an antifascist anthropology in order to locate how and why white supremacy sits at the core of both fascism and liberalism. Adrienne Pine builds on this in suggesting that an antifascist anthropology, as opposed to an anthropology of fascism, means explicitly taking a political stand in one's work. This requires disavowing liberalism while interrogating its conceptions of illiberalism. It also means reimagining ethnography beyond "individualistic neoliberal logics of funding and employment" and instead reframing it as "part of a collective, emancipatory project of anti-imperialist, anticapitalist struggle."[133] As Mahmud puts it, "An antifascist, illiberal anthropology, must be willing to name fascism even when it haunts democratic sites, when it latches onto liberal thought, when it sounds civilized and reasonable, when it incarnates in police uniforms rather than black shirts" (or green shirts in the case of Romania's Legionnaires who the AUR party venerates).[134] Embracing an antifascist anthropology then means not only studying AUR formations and supporting antifascist organizing, but also interrogating liberal constellations that, in reifying the Cold War inimical, fodder racial capitalist, neoliberal, and fascist specters.

Throughout this book, I participate in an antifascist ethnographic and reading practice invested in how antifascist postsocialist frameworks can apprehend the post–Cold War bifurcation of liberalism and illiberalism. Postsocialist analytics, alongside antifascist reading and ethnographic practices, are well positioned to assess this impasse, but also the time and space of political action. Indeed, amid the cosmic ruptures of today's Cold War 2.0, marked by white supremacist leaders and Russia's invasion of Ukraine, as well as liberal constellations opposing the two, postsocialism is far from a place of retirement. With this in mind, *Silicon Valley Imperialism* aims to reshape the spatial extent of postsocialism, positioning it as an emerging theoretical concept useful in assessing contestations of race, space, empire, technology, liberalism, and illiberalism, as well as anticapitalist, antifascist, and anti-imperial collectives that have inherited socialist legacies.

Unbecoming

Part of the work of crafting a postsocialist ethnography means charting the ongoing work of refusing, refuting, and unbecoming subsumed by capital, and in this case, Siliconized. After all, despite its real powers, Silicon Valley imperialism is also a project that continually fails to absorb, explain, and transform all that it desires. While it champions figments of ingenuity and novelty, Siliconization depends on the predation of prior technofuturisms—some of which, when conjured anew, can lead to its own corruption. Perched on NTT's balcony, staring out at the new construction surrounding us, my friend, a couple of decades older than me, begins to remember the thrill she had as a child in the 1970s when the nearby Central Commercial Center—then a marker of socialist modernity—opened its doors to the public for the first time. As Stephen Collier offers, perhaps what was most remarkable during this era was not the state's ability "to create 'ideal cities of the future' but its utterly pathological inability to do anything else."[135] Indeed, techno-urban modernity was part and parcel of the social project.

Today, amid the ruins of this future past, the Central Commercial Center's top floor has been transformed into ClujHub—a coworking space with daily talks in which successful Westerners attempt local entrepreneurial inculcation, and in which Romanian technologists teach successful business practices. It also houses Uber, much to the chagrin of local taxi drivers, many of whom are working class and/or Roma and many of whom have protested against its transportation monopolization. Recounting her first visit to the Central Commercial Center with her mother in the 1970s, my friend pauses, and then begins to question if that not-so-distant memory mirrors that of NTT opening its cosmological fourth floor up to us today. Rather than trumpeting socialist prosperity though, the imagery surrounding us at NTT is one of global capital.

And yet, its success depends on the exoskeletons of socialist infrastructure, not to mention the computing prowess of many who grew up during socialism and its aftermaths. Might Silicon Valley imperialism's own proclamations of ingenuity then be a fiction of sorts—one corrupted by the ghosts of a techno-futurity that came before?

With this in mind, *Silicon Valley Imperialism* focuses on the entanglements, ruptures, frictions, and fictions caught up in Siliconization. By fictions, I signal the speculative fantasies and desires entrenched in both socialist and postsocialist technocultures. Becoming Silicon Valley, after all, is only one of many imagined anticipatory trajectories that, while partly true, also elides other visions and futures. It was only during the Cold War that Bay Area geographies "became" Silicon Valley, recoding settler technologies of enclosure onto stolen lands. Despite this, Ohlone land rematriation projects led by groups such as the feminist Sogorea Te' Land Trust are hard at work reclaiming stolen land within ever-expanding Siliconized borders.[136] At the same time, housing and racial justice organizing work continue its undoing in Romania. Groups such as Căși Sociale ACUM! in Cluj and its sister organization, the Frontul Comun pentru Dreptul la Locuire (FCDL/The Common Front for Housing Rights) in Bucharest, organize daily against technologies of dispossession—thereby also undoing Siliconization. Underground cyber projects also endure, many driven by *șmecherie* practices of deviancy. There are also art and theater collectives engaging in technological worldmaking projects illegible to Silicon imperial reading practices. By worldmaking, here I build on Adom Getachew's description of a venture that while critical of imperial inheritances, nevertheless aims to create new movements, worlds, and connections against empire.[137]

Engagement with these worlds allows me to illustrate how post–Cold War end-of-history narratives are only some of many postsocialist speculations. In other words, anti-imperial worldmaking projects effectively corrupt Siliconization by speculating on other futures past. Speculation, as Aimee Bahng illustrates, is not solely the domain of finance capital.[138] Speculation can also invoke Samir Amin's proposition to move beyond negative critique by anticipating "the world we wish to see."[139] This allows us to reactivate, as Gary Wilder suggests, "repeating traces of unrealized past possibilities, of alternative forms of life."[140] Sometimes then, acts of speculation involve extrapolating technological futures past to undo Silicon Valley imperial circuits of reproduction. Aligned with what Karen Barad describes as the work of "re-membering," speculation then regenerates "what never was but might yet have been."[141] This does not mean wallowing in the genre of socialist nostalgia, but rather engaging in pluralistic postsocialist possibilities past and present beyond the state and beyond empire.

Connections

The worldmaking projects against Silicon Valley imperialism mapped throughout this book take place in Eastern Europe and the United States. Rather than compare Siliconization across these spaces, I trace connections and entanglements. In observing that comparative approaches to traditional area studies might force false reductions, Sanjay Subrahmanyam once suggested that perhaps a connected approach might be more useful in understanding spatial tethering and transactions.[142] Lisa Lowe has similarly argued that comparative methods have become too institutionalized, used to produce modern knowledge by mapping deviations from Western rationality and ideals.[143] With this in mind, Gillian Hart writes, "Political stakes are especially important since much of what travels under the banner of 'comparison' tends to be deeply retrograde."[144] To this end, Ananya Roy has noted that for some time now, poor people's movements and the work of nonalignment has maintained "an imagination of trans-national thinking and global inter-connectivity." Their vision, she writes, "is not one of comparison . . . but can the critical theory catch up?"[145] Indeed, what would it mean to produce interconnected studies driven by poor people's movements in alignment with anti-imperial and antifascist organizing rather than simply comparative studies of urban spaces or Silicon Valley from up above?

Building on this, rather than employing a comparative framework in which two distinct spaces are compared side by side—in this case, Romania and Silicon Valley—here I employ *connected methods* to foreground relationalities that center housing, racial, and technological justice as entwined fields of inquiry. Aligned with what Donna Haraway describes as feminist practices of situated knowledge production[146] as well as what Kim TallBear offers as practices of "standing with" by conducting research in good relations,[147] this book interrogates imperial modes of knowledge production. It draws on ethnographic engagement and collaborative mapping projects, as well as interdisciplinary reading practices. In combining and connecting methods, I embrace what Mel Y. Chen describes as an "exceedingly, rudely feral transdisciplinarity,"[148] one rooted in connections across an array of sources and spacetimes. Inspired by Lowe's tactic of "reading across archives" to understand the "intimacies and contemporaneities that traverse distinct and separately studied 'areas,'"

I aim to unsettle "the discretely bounded objects, methods, and temporal frameworks canonized by a national history invested in isolated origins and in dependent progressive development."[149] Or, as McKittrick writes: "Connections. Reading across a range of texts and ideas and narratives—academic and nonacademic—encourages multifarious ways of thinking through the possibilities of liberation and provides clues about living through the unmet promises of modernity."[150] Lingering in spaces of connection then means refusing to objectify people as data or sites from which to apprehend difference. It also means refusing the boundaries and comparativities of Western modern knowledge production.

Connection also requires rootedness to the ground itself. Here I draw on Jodi Byrd, Alyosha Goldstein, Jodi Melamed, and Chandan Reddy's provocation that by maintaining a relationship to the land itself, by seeing it as "an ontological condition for a different concept of the political that refuses conquest," futures beyond "economies of dispossession" are possible.[151] I have strived to maintain such grounded relationalities in conducting research for this book, which does not feign a semblance of objective distance and which refrains from reducing the dispossessed to sites of authenticity, but rather takes place through my relationships, commitments, and collaborations on the ground—all of which revolve around an explicit vision of spatial/racial justice and anti-imperialism. In the Bay Area, much of this grounded thinking generates from my work with the AEMP. I cofounded the AEMP in 2013 to support direct action and mutual aid housing justice work. Since then, I have been plugged into the collective daily, working with a brilliant group of volunteer researchers, mappers, storytellers, and software developers, all committed to producing work that supports tenant organizing despite Silicon Valley. I have also mobilized countermapping techniques to support housing justice knowledge in Bucharest and Cluj, where I have lived and visited off and on for over a decade. Much of this book draws on time spent in community there between 2011 and 2019, with a heavier concentration between 2016 and 2019, during which I participated in housing justice research while attending art events, protests, and political theater performances. Much of this time was spent with the FCDL in Bucharest, as well as with Căși in Cluj. These two collectives prioritize work that directly empowers on-the-ground anti-eviction organizing.

Groups such as the FCDL are deeply embedded in local anarchist, feminist, and anti-racist social centers where countless hours are spent meeting, learning, cooking, collaborating, and dancing. Much of my time in Bucharest was spent within the space of the Macaz Bar Teatru Coop (Macaz Bar Theater Cooperative). There, I attended countless talks, organizing meetings, parties, and political theater performances, constantly learning from the organizing, artistic, and community-building work of colleagues, collaboratives, and comrades. Artist, organizer, and political theorist Veda Popovici served as an important teacher, friend, and comrade in many of these spaces, and this book is in large part indebted to ongoing conversations with her. I also spent time in Macaz's sister space, A-casă in Cluj, a feminist anarchist social center then situated on Someșului Street. There, if you sit in the garden where the collective grows fruits and vegetables, NTT's tower peeks out above the bustling technoscape of new tech construction.

While this book is based on these collective commitments, I have also ventured into tech conferences, meetings, and hubs in the spirit of what Laura Nader calls "studying up."[152] Ethnographic work in these spaces has helped me chart not only the material impacts of Siliconization, but also how different understandings of futurity, technology, and postsocialism collide. This has also allowed me to weave together complex perspectives, from tech workers staffing US call centers to former hackers from Râmnicu Vâlcea—the Romanian mountain town infamously nominated as "Hackerville" by the West. While studying technocultural conjunctures, frictions, and fantasies in these spaces, my analysis of Silicon Valley imperialism remains deeply grounded in and through my commitment to anti-imperial worldmaking.

Chapter Map

Silicon Valley Imperialism is divided into two parts: "Silicon Valley Spatiotemporality" and "Techno Frictions and Fantasies." The first focuses on geographies of Siliconization and racial dispossession both in Romania and in the San Francisco Bay Area. The latter more broadly explores the multiple temporalities of socialism, the Cold War, and their aftermaths, providing a view of the present Siliconizing trajectory and its dominant (fascist) futures before exploring alternatives. While any chapter can be read on its own and in any order, I nevertheless recommend reading them sequentially to follow the threads that this book sews.

Chapter 1, "Digital Nomads and Deracinated Dispossession," positions the figure of the digital nomad as an avatar for Silicon Valley imperialism. It investigates how the landing of digital nomads and Western tech in Cluj cannibalizes Roma housing and personhood, updating presocialist racial property logics. It also shows how the digital nomad, while complicit in postsocialist processes of gentrification, discursively recodes Orientalist fantasies of the "free and wandering Gypsy," a literary trope that emerged within the heart of nineteenth-century Western Europe to allegorize imperiality. The deracinated nomad's fetishization today indexes Silicon Valley's imperial status, while transiting presocialist private property relations into postsocialist times. To better illustrate imperial violence but also resistance to it, this chapter engages in a close reading of a storymapping project coproduced with Căși, as well as ethnographic work assessing the racial geographies of digital nomadism and smart city production.

Chapter 2, "Postsocialist Silicon Valley," transits to the San Francisco Bay Area, where I assess how the Cold War and its aftermaths recode colonial spatiality through a series of dispossessive booms and busts that encroach upon common spaces and anticapitalist politics. I look at the Valley's imperial formation, assessing how gold rush legacies and Cold War technocultures have morphed into consumerist playgrounds for the rich today. By mapping the cooptation of socialist ideals such as sharing, I track technoliberal moments in postsocialist contexts. At the same time, the chapter mobilizes postsocialist analytics to apprehend anticapitalist pasts, presents, and futures that refuse Silicon Valley imperial plans. Throughout, I engage with housing justice work in which I have been a part while also weaving in historical uprisings and illustrations from political artist Fernando Martí.

Chapter 3, "The Technofascist Specters of Liberalism," investigates how liberal property and protest formations on both sides of the former Iron Curtain enable technofascism to spread. Refusing the post–Cold War trope that positions "the dangerous East" as the harbinger of authoritarianism that liberalism will save the world from, I instead suggest that the East offers important lessons regarding how liberalism prefigures fascist possibility. In compiling a genealogy of Romanian populist protest movements that have slowly seen anticapitalist politics get co-opted by the anticommunist right, I chart the increasingly cramped space from which to foster dissent. Engaging a counterfactual exercise, this chapter also describes a protest that never came to be against the furniture company IKEA. While Romanian liberals have mobilized against the incursions of a Canadian gold mining company that has sought to plunder the country's minerals, they have failed to organize against the largest owner of Romanian forestlands in part due to the liberal fantasies of Western intimacy that IKEA affords.

Chapter 4, "The Most Dangerous Town on the Internet," looks at how Silicon Valley imperialism builds on Cold War imaginaries while disavowing its own technofascist past. It explores the role of IBM in powering Romania's presocialist genocidal project while also looking at the company's postsocialist incursion aimed at capitalizing on socialism's remains. At the same time, the chapter investigates how Western technological imaginaries collapse communism and fascism together, promising salvation through Siliconization. By drawing on ethnographic research and archival investigations, it explores Romanian computing histories. It also follows a theater play made by the Bucharest-based playwright David Schwartz that brings to the fore lived experiences of postsocialist technological transition.

Chapter 5, "Corruption, Șmecherie, and Clones," further explores socialist and postsocialist technoculture in Romania, focusing on retrospective and speculative accounts of what did, and what could have, transpired beyond the purview of the state, capitalist transition, and the Siliconized present. Against a backdrop of anticommunist politics, the chapter looks to deviant technological practices that existed, and that perhaps could have corrupted, Silicon Valley imperialism from materializing. While describing a collaborative art piece by Veda Popovici and Mircea Nicolae, *Istoria (Nu) Se Repetă* (History [Does Not] Repeat Itself), I pepper in ethnographies of scammers, computer cloners, and political artists who illustrate practices of *șmecherie*. These *șmecherie* narrations, technocultures, imaginations, and speculations, I suggest, corrupt Siliconization.

Chapter 6, "Spells for Outer Space," builds on ongoing speculative themes, weaving together socialist astrofuturism portrayed in Romanian and Moldovan film, art, and speculative fiction with ethnographic observations of capitalist ruination. I begin with a close reading of the film *Gagarin's Tree* by Mona Vătămanu and Florin Tudor, which features the Romanian scholar of decolonization Ovidiu Țichindeleanu considering socialist visions of developing an anticapitalist utopia in outer space. While illustrating materialities that emerged from these dreams, I also question why they crumbled after 1989. While communist utopianism was based on friendships with other Second and Third World peoples, and while it in large part developed in resistance to presocialist fascism, state socialism never managed to fully resolve anti-Roma racism. What might have happened if socialist astrofuturism could have better integrated what Roma feminist playwright Mihaela Drăgan describes as Roma futurism?[153] Might this, coupled with anticapitalist and antifascist organizing, helped avert the Siliconized genre of astrofuturity dominating cosmological imaginaries today?

The book's coda, "Unbecoming Silicon Valley," looks at frictions engendered in both the United States and Romania through practices of outsourcing landlordism. Today, US corporate landlords use digital "proptech" platforms to facilitate scalable property management and sell fantasies of frictionless automation. Yet in fact many deploy outsourced labor in locales such as Cluj. On one hand, by deploying Romanian workers behind the magical curtain of automation, novel circulations of race, labor, tenancy, and capital are animated. On the other, propertied frictions also bear potentiality for new transnational geographies of resistance, ones connected by housing and labor movements. Such resistance is part and parcel of the project of unbecoming Silicon Valley as it weakens the Silicon grip on technology, property, and futurity. As the stories woven together throughout this book evoke, anti-imperial worldmaking projects necessitate new transnational solidarities and connections, ones also grounded in the ongoing work of racial, spatial, and technological justice.

PART I

Silicon Valley Spatiotemporality

Digital Nomads and Deracinated Dispossession

It was in the middle of a freezing December night in 2010 that military police, bulldozers, and city hall officials forcibly evicted a community of seventy-six Roma families totaling close to 350 people from their homes on Coastei Street in Cluj's city center.[1] Of the many overlapping plans tied up in this act of racial dispossession, one involved the Finnish IT company Nokia. The firm had hoped to construct a downtown office building in what is now the epicenter of the city's Silicon Valley mimicry.[2] In short, it had been offered a two-year tax break to move one of its German branches to Cluj through a city-initiated program to incentivize tech growth, one that heralded the dawn of Romania's newfound "Silicon Valley of Eastern Europe" status. While many Cluj residents expressed enthusiasm for Nokia's migration to Romania—seeing it as a welcome manifestation of the country's newfound status as a European Union (EU) member, not to mention as an employment instigator in the aftermaths of the 2008 financial crisis[3]—those expelled from their city-center homes felt differently.

Upon eviction, the dispossessed were forcibly relocated eighteen kilometers outside the city center to tiny barracks adjacent to the city's municipal waste site, Pata Rât. There, they became neighbors with communities already banished to the dump living in three preexisting settlements: Cantonului, where 800 people have been living in makeshift homes following a wave of evictions following state socialism's 1989 demise; Dallas, where 300 people have been living since the 1960s despite housing protections afforded by the socialist state; and Rampa, where roughly 100 people live, wastelanded on the landfill itself.[4] By wastelanding, I draw on Traci Voyles's conception of "a racial and spatial signifier that renders landscapes pollutable."[5] Rehearsing a playbook already perfected in California,[6] Siliconization mobilizes wastelanding logics to expel those rendered unassimilable to its fantasies into the dumps of modernity. At the same time, it conjures an Enlightenment history of racial disposability in Eastern Europe endemic to dreams of Westernization. As Veda Popovici writes, fantasies of the "smart city, the civilised city, the city for the respectable tax-paying citizens . . . cater to a performative, aspirational desire of becoming Western."[7] Racial dispossession is a precondition imagined as necessary for manifesting such fantasies.

While Nokia did manage to establish a short-lived factory building in the outskirts of Cluj in Jucu—a former state farmland and industrial zone—it never completed its downtown office building. Yet the assembly plant, "Nokia Village," provided temporary employment for hundreds of Romanians hungry for work in the postrecession economy. There, workers processed keyboards, screens, motherboards, headphones, chargers, and more into packaged products to be shipped to retail stores. At the time, the press heralded Nokia Village as the "factory of the future," one that would create at least fifteen thousand jobs and make Romania "the seventh power of Europe."[8] While these aspirational promises set in motion ongoing Silicon fantasies, soon after, Nokia was offered a deal to relocate to China, where new tax breaks awaited. They quickly closed up shop and left the city before completing their downtown office building (though Nokia does maintain offices in Bucharest and Timișoara today). A five-thousand-square-meter parcel of the Coastei Street region where the Cluj office was going to be built was instead handed over to the Christian Orthodox Archbishop to build a Faculty of Theology, replete with student dormitories. The church's leader baldly suggested that the education perks of the project would "make up" for the eviction of Roma residents.[9] There were even conversations of developing an IKEA in the area.

Writing of dispossession inhered by frictions of global capital, or what she calls "spectacular accumulation," Anna Tsing suggests that as "old residents become aliens, as the familiar landscape is transfigured by trauma, danger, and the anxiety of the unknown . . . mystery can flourish, and unexpected discoveries can be made." However, "When the spectacle passes on, what is left is rubble and mud, the residues of success and failure. People with other stakes and stories will have to pick up the pieces."[10] Over a decade after Nokia's departure, fantasies of wealth and discovery endure as the dispossessed are continually forced to contend with shattered pieces of home and community. Excised from prior urban core relationships, evictees also gain social and cultural stigmatization for nomadically living among waste. This denigration invokes centuries of anti-Roma racism which maps impoverished transience as chosen rather than as a result of banishment. As Enikő Vincze and George Zamfir contextualize, many of those wastelanded to Pata Rât today "have experienced a series of evictions from centrally located areas of the city, which were cleansed systematically of the remnants of a defamed 'Gypsy lifestyle.' Racist voices argue that these people would rather live in inadequate and insecure conditions and are undisturbed by the sight and smell of the Pata Rât garbage mountains."[11]

Yet amid this overt anti-Roma racism amplified by Siliconization, there has also been a proliferation of "digital nomads" arriving to the city—some self-ascribed as "digital Gypsies." These are primarily Western tech workers who engage in remote tech labor and who enjoy the freedom of leisurely travel, all the while financially bolstered by Western tech corporations, start-ups, and entrepreneurial capital flows. Digital nomadism as a term grew popular in the late 1990s amid the San Francisco dot-com boom, yet it was after the 2008 financial crisis and alongside the dawn of the sharing economy and Nokia's entry into Cluj that Romanian cities began attracting digital nomads. This was in part due to the country's exceptionally fast internet, its relatively low cost of living (compared to the West), its high safety index and English language proficiency, its recent accession into the EU, a plethora of coworking hubs, and recoded Orientalist myths that bleed wanderlust fantasies of "the East."

It was over a decade later, during the COVID-19 pandemic, that Romania adopted a formal digital nomad visa program, one aimed to amplify Romania's "brand" and compete with other countries offering similar programs.[12] Romania aimed to attract tech workers beyond the EU to stimulate the economy and capitalize on newly mobile "human capital" liberated by Silicon Valley's pandemic embrace of remote work. Today, Romania offers digital nomads who can prove gross monthly salaries of at least three times the national average a means of obfuscating otherwise tedious (and sometimes impossible) visa requirements—all with support from the Ministry of Research, Innovation, and Digitalization, the Ministry of Internal Affairs, and the Ministry of Foreign

Affairs. In this sense, the last decade has seen digital nomads migrate from a fringe identity mostly found in online forums, cafés, and tech coworking spaces to one institutionalized by the state.

Divorced from Roma materialities and identities, digital nomad fantasies uphold the individualism and wanderlust of nineteenth-century Gypsy novellas and poems—a literary trope penned by white male authors who allegorize Western European imperial fantasies through the deracinated figure of the Gypsy. These texts, from Prosper Mérimée's 1845 *Carmen* to George Borrow's 1851 *Lavengro*, exoticize the free and wandering Gypsy—an alibi that like today's digital nomad abstracts and mutilates Romani experiences of personhood and dispossession. Today's digital nomads allegorize Silicon Valley imperial desires by reproducing Gypsy fantasies, while the displacement of Roma residents makes way for the arrival of Western tech workers and firms. This gets at what I describe as *deracinated dispossession*, an analytic that I first conceptualized with Alex Werth and that I mobilize here to highlight how the loss of home transpires alongside the theft of personhood.[13] I continue to explore contexts of deracinated dispossession here in order to map desires and dispossessions brought on by Siliconization.

While new tech worlds materialize deracinated dispossession, anticommunist property restitution practices are also in play in postsocialist contexts. Restitution, as a form of reprivatization, enables descendants of presocialist private properties to reclaim homes made public during socialism.[14] Liberal anticommunist narratives obviate that despite its failures, state socialism did provide housing to those in need. Today, the very idea of social housing has withered from public memory, while those who were propertyless prior to socialism are made houseless once again along familiar racial capitalist lines. Factories that had been nationalized during socialism too are being co-opted by Western firms that construct outsourcing branches on the exoskeletons of socialist working-class labor. Digitally nomadic Silicon capital thus lands on an anticommunist urban palimpsest that has been attempting to wipe housing and labor justice histories of state socialism off the map since state socialism's collapse.

With a focus on postsocialist Cluj, this chapter studies how on one hand, digital nomads and technocapital conjoin in the appropriation of Roma personhood and housing. Yet on the other, Roma residents are made more precarious as a result of Siliconization. While today's digital redux discursively updates nineteenth-century imperial dreams, it also signals techno-imperium's geographic shift from Western Europe to Silicon Valley. By assessing these geographies of deracinated dispossession, in this chapter I also explore how prior Romanian property histories bleed into the Siliconizing present—from those of presocialist racialized housing regimes to those developed during socialism.

In what follows, I map interlocking stories and frictions, exploring deracinated dispossession from the wastelands of allegory, eviction, and banishment. First, I dive into speculative fantasies undergirding digital nomadism as well as their nineteenth-century underpinnings. Next, I turn to lived geographies of racial dispossession, eviction, and urban renewal, foregrounding the racial geographies underpinning presocialist Romanian property regimes now reanimated through restitution. In doing so, I draw on a digital multimedia storymap, *Dislocari*, that I coproduced with Căși Sociale ACUM! (Căși/Social Housing NOW!). *Dislocari* narrativizes the eviction routes of seven Roma residents now living in Pata Rât, each of whom has experienced a series of evictions from the city center following the collapse of socialism. These wasteland narratives unravel the enchantment digitally woven into nomadic mobility. They also suggest that other possible relationships between digitality and housing justice are possible.

Fantasy

As a phenomenon, digital nomadism is often attributed to Tsugio Makimoto and David Manners and their 1997 dot-com-boom-era *Digital Nomad* book, which presaged a future run by wealthy IT business professionals equipped with "digital toolkits" who could live a life of "location independence." But even decades earlier, science fiction writers such as Arthur C. Clarke envisaged the idea, speculating on a world in which "any businessman, any executive, could live almost anywhere on earth and still do his business."[15] As he elaborated, "In the global world of the future, it will be like if you're living in one small town, anywhere anytime, about a third of your friends will be asleep. . . . So, you may have to abolish time zones completely, and all go on the common time, the same time for everybody."[16]

Today's digital nomads rely on Clarke's "common time," and are often paid Silicon Valley salaries as they transit between "exotic" locales with high-speed internet. From the Latinx Mission District of San Francisco (more exciting than the suburban Silicon Valley located an hour south) to more distant and mysterious spaces such as Cluj, digital nomads freely traverse the globe, often acquiring capital along the way. In this sense, the digital nomad is what Annalee Saxenian has described as "the new argonaut," or high-tech commuters who have, through their global border crossings, made the United States wealthier.[17] Yet, few of these travelers use mythical Greek sailors as allegorical figures to represent themselves. Instead, they often prefer "digital nomad" and even "digital Gypsy." For instance, James Taylor, who identifies as an "award-winning entrepreneur" and a "white middle-class professional living in a first world country," wrote a 2011 blog post describing the rise of this new lifestyle. He and his wife transit between Europe and the United States, he writes, running an app-enabled autopilot business. In his words, "Being a Digital Gypsy is more a frame of mind than genealogy."[18] As his testimony suggests, this transnational digital figure is enabled by Silicon Valley technocapital and infrastructure, presaged by Clarke's "common time" fantasies.

Yet it was long before Clarke's science fiction and Makimoto and Manners's book that nomadic fantasies began indexing imperial consciousness. It was during the mid-nineteenth century—a zenith of numerous Western European colonial projects—that the Romantic Orientalist literary movement emerged, rife with Gypsy novellas, poems, and theater. This movement combined contemporary Romanticism—a literary, artistic, and intellectual movement positioned against industrialization, Enlightenment norms, and the logics of scientific rationalization—with Orientalism, a system that Edward Said nominated to describe the colonial rendering of exotic and haunting Oriental worlds juxtaposed to those of a progressive, mechanistic, and cold Europe.[19] While Said's focus was the Middle East, numerous scholars have since found purchase of the concept in Eastern Europe and the Balkans.[20] What I focus on more here though is how the romanticized literary figure of the Gypsy effectively became the workhorse of national movements across the continent. Standing in for peripheralized, less-than-European locales, it simultaneously legitimized the desires of the nomadic colonizer and what Said described as a "male power fantasy."[21] Indeed, Gypsy novellas often feature Western male protagonists whose countries were, at the time, engaged in colonial projects. Protagonists generally fall in love with sexualized, racialized Roma women, and then attempt miscegenation and "life as Gypsy." Frequently, male narratives end up tragically murdering their muses, so that "the dark passionate Gypsy woman" and her death, as Alaina Lemon suggests,[22] allegorize Western heteromasculine colonial desires.

The deracination endemic to these texts has also informed centuries of ethnographic "Gypsy lore" scholarship. This racist writing has rightfully been the subject of much Roma feminist critique. Ethel Brooks, for instance, suggests that the representations written by *gadjes*, or non-Roma people, speak to "an appropriation that mixes fantasies about and hatred of our actual existence."[23] Similarly, Carmen Gheorghe writes that through racist history making "regulated by political, hetero-normative and discursive regimes," Roma women have become "a transmitter of negatively charged social and cultural messages, almost obsessively so."[24] And in these racial, demonic, and romanticized portrayals of Romani peoples rendered through racial and imperial historiography, social imaginaries have formed of Roma people being hypersexualized, spreaders of disease, vagabonds, nomads, criminals, and more. Yet at the same time, scholarship on Europe's colonial legacies has largely obviated Roma experiences. Thus on one hand, "Gypsy lore" scholarship erases Roma feminist agency, not to mention far-from-monolithic practices of identification, theorization, narrativization, gender, race, refusal, border crossing, passing, and alliance.[25] On the other, as Ioanida Costache reminds us, leaving Roma people out of scholarship on European imperialism "has hindered the ability of European societies to understand the nuanced history of Romani people in Europe and its repercussions in the present."[26] With this in mind, here I focus on nomadic fantasy not to reproduce its harms, but rather to assess what it indexes of imperium—be it of the nineteenth century or of today.

In nineteenth-century Britain, Gypsy novellas and nomadic poetry gained repute for allegorizing territorial expansion.[27] Literary works used the figure of the nomad to narrate nostalgia for preindustrial landscapes on imperial, open-range topography. As the poet John Clare characterized in his 1825 "The Gipseys Song," Gypsies fantastically "pay no rent nor tax to none / But live untythd [sic] & free . . . In gipsey liberty."[28] By equating the Gypsy with premodernity, Clare allegorizes British nativism and colonial expansion alike.[29] This figure can magically traverse untouched frontiers, find shelter in the dwindling commons, and evade paying rent and tax (resonant with contemporary tech endeavors). Works by Clare and his contemporaries then inspired texts by authors in France, Spain, and beyond.

Like Clare, German Orientalist Wilhelm Jensen, in his 1868 *Die braune Erica*, associates Roma freedom with bucolic landscapes. His book tells the story of a restless German natural scientist longing for a rare plant, *Erica janthina*—itself a stand-in for a Roma woman, Erica, who entices him to leave his settled life. Transfixed by Erica's androgynous, racialized body, the scientist murmurs her taxonomical name one night while asleep, which she hears in her "natural language," drawing her to him. She then leads him to the rare moor-dwelling heather that he had been searching for all along. But then Erica is bitten by an adder and falls ill. Despite his Western knowledge, the scientist remains powerless to heal her, and so she accepts her death. However, when he reasserts his love, she magically heals herself by engaging in a wild, ecstatic dance. Although they marry and live a settled life on the margins of German territory, she eventually leaves him—an expression of the spontaneous and uncontrollable Gypsy spirit. Jensen does not posit Gypsies as possessing chiromancy, but rather as a foil to the confines of modernity. Gypsies are not a threat to German ascendancy, he infers, as ultimately, they are nonreproductive. Nicholas Saul contextualizes that in this way, Gypsies are written as "a diaspora paradoxically without a homeland, adapted neither to their alienation (the Occident) nor their homeland (the Orient). They therefore cannot transmit their inheritance."[30] Such texts then render Roma people both titillating to modernity's confines, yet unthreatening to imperial reproduction.

It was often encounters with Roma people on newly colonized lands that inspired these Orientalist works. This was the case with Alexander Pushkin's famous 1823 poem "Tsygany" (The Gypsies), based on the writer's engagement with Roma people on newly acquired Russian lands.[31] Yet at the same time, in many parts of Central and Eastern Europe, Roma communities had been long engaging with their *gadje* counterparts in ways that were neither romantic nor exceptional.[32] In Romanian regions, Roma had been enslaved for centuries, and much of the migration to Western spaces in which Gypsy lore was being crafted involved attempts to find better labor and land conditions.[33] This complexity gets overridden in contexts of nomadic fetishization.

As a movable racial figuration, then, the deracinated Gypsy maps the sexual, racial logics of imperial reproduction, but also the conflation of disparate geographies and histories. Yet from the figure's recurrent textual death and ongoing mutilation, different ghosts materialize—including today's digital nomad. However, there are immense differences between this nomad and that of the nineteenth century. Today's figure is not something that imperialists lust after; it is an identity that many Western tech workers believe they have already become through a more complete process of deracination. Unlike Orientalist caricatures in which Roma women contrast the rigidity of Western modernity and techno-industrialization, digital nomads understand technology not lacking in freedom, but rather as emblematic of it. Also distinct from their nineteenth-century predecessors, today's digital nomads have little reference for Roma people.

Yet nonetheless, just as Orientalist tales emerged from the heart of Western empires, so too do digital nomad fantasies of today. In digital nomad Daniel Kay's self-reflection, "Digital nomads are unintentional pawns in a new wave of economic imperialism."[34] This fantasy embodies Silicon Valley imperialism—a phenomenon in which the Valley materializes new nodes and edges to facilitate surplus capital accumulation at home in California. Yet the nomadic avatar—as an allegory for a highly paid worker or even a roving tech company like

Nokia itself—is conditioned by nineteenth-century colonial fiction. Reliant on location independence, they give up spatial rootedness for exotic locales, cheap living costs, and an ability to remain anchored in Western capital flows through remote labor and outsourcing. As a form of geographic arbitrage—in which commodities and labor are bought and sold in uneven markets to capitalize on better prices[35]—digital nomads such as James Taylor mobilize Silicon Valley platforms like Upwork to accumulate money while sleeping. As another self-proclaimed "libertarian nomad" from San Francisco living in Cluj explained, the idea of settling down is not at all appealing. The world is global, and success means being at home in the global world. "People used to brag about buying and selling real estate developments. I brag about developing my own apps while living in Airbnbs," he told me. In his analysis, apps, data, and the sharing economy hold more value than real estate. While this elides the materialities that digitality both necessitates and produces, from hardware mining to outsourced labor,[36] it also erases the dispossessions that digital nomads impart. As digital nomad Kay self-critiques: "This is gentrification at its simplest. This is globalization. . . . Every dollar we spend, every blog post we write, and every coworking space we patronize contributes to this inequality. . . . We appropriate places and lead trends, we go where life is cheap but hip, and we are a little bit in love with our own lives. . . . We have the economic potential to destroy communities."[37] As I continue to explore, the landing of digital nomads and nomadic firms reproduces nineteenth-century imperial desires while also materializing novel contexts of dispossession and exploitation.

Exploitation

Today the area surrounding Coastei Street where the 2010 eviction transpired is peppered with familiar signs of Siliconization. One only has to step outside to breathe in new construction particles and observe fiber optic cabling sticking out of buildings like alien tentacles, waiting to be connected. Former industrial socialist factories, from the Flacăra textiles factory to the Napochim plastics factory, are either being converted into tech plants for foreign firms like Bosch and iQuest or into fancier residential blocks. Nearby, the coworking ClujHub sits on the top floor of the Central Commercial Center, a socialist-era department store that opened in the 1970s. There, talks, gatherings, and meetups occur around the clock, mostly geared toward inculcating Romanian programmers with entrepreneurial skills. As Oana Mateescu writes, "With their clean lines, airy and light interiors, transparent and glossy surfaces, IT offices are a far cry from the socialist factories on whose ruins they are built. But the

FIGURE 1.1. New development in Cluj. Photo taken by author, 2018.

difference goes beyond design: it is a matter of workplace environment and corporate culture, imported from global hi-tech hotspots like Silicon Valley, oftentimes as a form of discursive dumping that mimics the inequalities of the outsourcing value chain which sustains it."[38]

Digital nomads often claim to find Romania attractive because of its Siliconized familiarity, not to mention its anticommunist values, English fluency, cheap housing, and exploitable labor. Citing Romania's fast internet alongside its emergent EU status, the Nomad Capital website brags, "Romania is one of the top countries in Europe to find outsourced labor on sites like oDesk [now Upwork], and you should be able to easily find relatively qualified technical gurus for as little as several hundred dollars a month."[39] The Transylvania Hostel ranks the best Wi-Fi in coffee shops for digital nomads, describing Cluj as a "cheap destination for digital nomads who look for quiet places where they can sneak in with their laptops and work on their revolutionary ideas."[40] Meanwhile, the travel guide Atlas & Boots ranked Romania as the third-best country for remote labor in 2022, after Portugal and Spain.[41] This coincides with Romania's digital nomad visa program, which was institutionalized through Law 22/2022 during the pandemic seeking to address "Romania's need to attract both human capital and financial resources and to better promote Romania in the eyes of foreigners."[42] According to Diana-Anda Buzoianu, the parliament member who introduced the program, the goal is to annually attract two thousand workers who earn at least three times the national salary to help Romania build the country's "brand."[43] In this sense, just as digital nomads find Romania attractive, the state itself places transient tech workers within a broader desire of Westernization and capital accumulation.

In addition to fast Wi-Fi, digital nomads often celebrate the availability of Western sharing economy platforms such as Airbnb and Uber—both embedded in processes of "tourism gentrification" in part because they transit Western familiarity.[44] As one nomad in Cluj has blogged, "The fact that we also landed a kick-ass Airbnb rental obviously helped us feel at home."[45] The tour guide Lonely Planet ranked Transylvania as the top "region" of 2016, promising: "Yes, horses and carts still rumble through the wooded countryside, but they'll soon share the roads with Uber cabs ferrying visitors to chic Airbnb lodgings."[46] Uber entered Bucharest in 2015, and Cluj in 2016, and in 2018 it launched the food delivery service Uber Eats. By 2022, it had become available in seventeen Romanian cities, sometimes ferrying anti-Roma racism in its wake.[47] Per a French digital nomad visiting Romania, "Before I arrived, I was told I would be chased by beggars and if I survived, all my belongings would be stolen by thiefs. The chief risk that you take by coming to Romania is to pay five times the real taxi fare. Before you learn how to spot a honest taxi, better use Uber" [sic].[48] This fear of beggars and taxi drivers alike is rooted in classist and racist histories. Not only are many drivers Roma, but I have also heard countless tales of people losing their jobs after 1989 only to find refuge in taxi driving. For instance, Ion, who trained to be an engineer during socialism, now drives taxis at night to afford groceries.

There have been numerous protests by taxi drivers in Bucharest and Cluj, and even lawsuits. Nevertheless, Uber, itself a digital nomad of sorts, continues to prey on tourists and the local aspirational culture of Western recognition. Meanwhile, Romania's own taxi app, Clever Taxi, was acquired by a German company in 2017. The Estonian company Bolt (formerly Taxify) then came onto the scene. When questioned, several nomads told me that they prefer Uber to other services, just because it's familiar. I've also heard Romanian developers laud its integration with Google Maps. This falls in line with a longer postsocialist trajectory of using tourism and IT to affirm Western values. Beginning in the mid-1990s, Romania began disavowing its socialist past through tourism, reimagining the now fully European country as "'reborn,' 'free' and having shaken off its totalitarian past," as Duncan Light observes.[49] Western technotourism functions as a vehicle of anticommunism, merging entrepreneurism and informality together.[50]

Romania's 2007 EU entry was in part preconditioned by Western imperatives that Romania fully embrace capitalism. This meant privatizing what had been state-owned enterprises and welcoming global capital through "Foreign Direct Investment."[51] Yet investment was relatively slow at first compared to that transpiring across the former Eastern bloc, in part due to the political turmoil and austerity imposed by disaster capitalism.[52] Things began to shift around 2004, when the European Commission acknowledged that Romania finally possessed a functioning market economy. The country then joined NATO, firming up a Western orientation. In 2005, a tax reform incentivized foreign investors even further. Then, in 2007, the year that the country joined the EU, Nokia, cast as a digital nomad, made its spectacular $110 million investment.[53] Soon after, companies including Hewlett-Packard, Huawei, Ericsson, and Gameloft came rushing in. Siliconization followed, paving the way for tourism and now digital nomadism.

Romania's portrayal as both safe and exotic, as freed from its aberrant past and yet not fully Western, continues to appeal to nomadic fantasy. During the winter of 2018, I sat down in a fancy coffee shop with a German digital nomad, Fabian, who founded a geospatial data firm in 2007 in Cluj, which has since expanded to San Francisco, Detroit, Berlin, and China. As he sipped a green tea latte, he described Cluj's appeal. After college, he began dabbling in Berlin politics but found it boring. He then realized that the one thing that would never bore him was entrepreneurship. Attracted to the "the wild east of Europe," he considered Romania, Bulgaria, and Ukraine. It became a toss-up between Cluj and Sofia, as he wanted to remain in the EU and as Bucharest was "too political." Cluj won because of the plethora of cheap flights between the city and Berlin. While his employees didn't earn much at first, now they make three times as much as doctors in the region, competing within an international market. His international travels are nonstop, and he even owns an apartment in San Francisco that he rarely visits. It's a great life, but he's thinking of selling his share and starting something new soon, just for fun.

While Fabian's office sits in a new IT tower called The Office (formerly a textiles factory), other digital nomads prefer cafés or coworking spaces. There are dozens of these in Romania today,[54] and in 2023, according to the ranking site HomeToGo's "Workation Index," four Romanian cities are featured as the top 150 European destinations (Cluj and Bucharest sitting within the top twenty) for digital nomadism due to the large number of coworking spaces per capita, along with internet speed and vacation rental prices.[55] While coworking spaces serve as places of sociality and labor for digital nomads and Romanian tech workers alike, they also attract Western entrepreneurs who lead trainings on project acceleration and incubation and where firms sponsor events such as TechFest, Techsylvania, Startup Transilvania, and TEDxCluj. Such events function as technologies of inculcation, where Romanian tech workers absorb Western values and desires and even celebrate outsourcing. As the CEO of a Cluj-based software company adamantly explained, though 1989 was disastrous, transition created new opportunities. "The multinationals, they really ended up saving us," he proffered, suggesting that foreign investment was necessary for future development. As of 2019, foreign-owned companies generated 43 percent of the country's GDP, with up to 90 percent of banking owned by foreign capital as early as 2016.[56] The country also boasts the highest percentage of foreign control of computing and software enterprises in Eastern and Central Europe.[57]

Over the last decade, dozens of software recruitment agencies and global capital firms have been ranking countries according to their outsourcing strengths, and Romania generally finds its way into top counts. McKinsey & Company, for instance, notes that between 2017 and 2022, the tech economy grew as much as 8 percent each year, with digital commerce growing 17 percent annually.[58] Tech services currently account for 6 percent of the country's GDP, though McKinsey predicts it being nearly 15 percent by 2023.[59] TopCoder, which aims to "unlock the power of the global workforce," lists Romania as twelfth in its list of top countries.[60] Meanwhile, the International Trade Administration suggests that Romania is Europe's leader and ranks sixth internationally when it comes to the number of certified IT specialists, noting the presence of Amazon, Hewlett-Packard, IBM, Microsoft, and Oracle.[61] Continuing, the agency notes that Romania's top fifty tech companies have quadrupled their teams as of late, IT rescuing the GDP from COVID-19 pandemic levels. It also praises Romania's cybersecurity excellence and the country's fast internet, fixed broadband, and prolific 5G networks. Interestingly, it also notes gender parity in tech, with Romania ranking third in the EU regarding women in IT.

The short-term technical recruiting company YouTeam also names Romania as one of the most favorable destinations for outsourcing due to an array of factors including a rising GDP, but also affordable skilled software developers who charge less than those in other Eastern European countries, such as Poland and the Czech Republic.[62] Yet the firm cautions Western consumers to beware that Romanians are "a bit more risk-averse as a result of decades of oppressive communism. Within the software development industry context, this sometimes means that Romanian developers lack an innovative approach."[63] Nevertheless, Romania still serves as an ideal outsourcing alternative to India, the firm notes, largely due to competitive costs, English fluency, proximity to Western Europe, outstanding education system, and government-backed economic security. The government also allows tech workers in Romania an income tax exemption status, incentivizing the sector.[64]

Romania's first IT recruiting agency, Brainspotting, takes a different approach to YouTeam and suggests that socialist-era informatics history is actually a reason why Romania maintains heightened status as a top service delivery location.[65] For instance, the country has excelled in the International Math and Informatics Olympiads since 1958, the agency notes.[66] Similarly, Softech, a Cluj-based software development agency that provides outsourcing (or what they refer to as "nearsourcing") to the United States, Germany, the Netherlands, Canada, Switzerland, France, and more, explains: "Romania has a developing economy and still has one of the lowest living costs in Europe. On the contrary, the pool of talented and skillful software developers is one of the best in Europe. Therefore, software development outsourcing contracts with Romanian partners resulted as a legacy of the former regime's education system oriented toward science and technical excellence."[67] In fact, the gender parity that the International Trade Administration noted is also a socialist legacy. During socialism, the Communist Party favored science and technology education for all genders, in part to supply factories with workers. As Andrada Fiscutean writes, "'Equal work, equal pay' was a catchphrase at the time. It was drawn from the 1948 Constitution, which stated that women and men should be paid equally, provided they had the same job."[68] Much of this work entailed cloning Western products such as cars and computers (as described in chapters 4 and 5), crafting affordable products for the Romanian market.

While economists understand the country's tech boom to be driving economic growth today,[69] much as was the case during socialism (albeit differently), IT usage and infrastructure vary dramatically. Romania maintains the highest rate of poverty and social exclusion in the EU,[70] but has a steadily rising number of people employed in computer programming, with more than 20,000 tech companies, over 140,000 tech professionals, and up to 8,500 annual graduates.[71] In Cluj, where tech is considered the second largest professional sector, the number of firms has quadrupled over the last decade, now numbering over 20,000.[72] Rents have topped Bucharest's, with one in three employees a professional.[73] As Mateescu writes, "IT companies compete in offering attractive benefit packages to their turnover-prone employees: high salaries (relative to the Romanian average, close to 700 euros in 2020), private health insurance, gym, pool or sauna subscriptions, and countless opportunities for learning (in hard and soft skills but also 'life skills' such as yoga, meditation, etiquette, wine tasting, etc.)"[74] Of tech graduates from Cluj universities, Google is the top desired employer, followed by Emerson, Endava, Bosch, and Microsoft.[75]

Most work conducted in these firms is far from glamorous, and involves monotonous and repetitive tasks. Less technical work is increasingly sourced not from tech schools, but from liberal arts programs. But even this work is considered desirable. Per Mateescu, "Slaving away on the night shift at the service desk—on a meager salary but with the imagined promise of potentially spectacular advancement—is preferable to picking strawberries in Spain, harvesting asparagus in Germany or caring for the Italian elderly," common employment sources for poor diasporic Romanians.[76] Tech work is also more secure than gig work, which grew more popular throughout the COVID-19 pandemic.[77] As couriers for companies such as Uber and Glovo, delivery workers are not digital nomads, but rather pawns of companies themselves fantasizing unrestricted "Gypsy-like" transit across the pandemic planet. A tech job then means finding a bit more job security, but also, often enough, aligning with Western promises.

Cluj's city administration continues to capitalize on such promises to attract foreign investment, digital nomads, and tourists. In this vein, the city placed a bid in 2016 to become the 2021 European Culture of Capital. While it was unsuccessful (instead going to Timișoara), the bid was critiqued as an attempt to legitimate Western becoming and simultaneously mask the city's own dispossessory practices.[78] Not only did the bid flatten a cornucopia of differences into a singular narrative of European culture, but had it been successful, it would have instantiated a whole new wave of gentrification. This of course would only have worked if Eastern European difference was properly defanged from socialism enough to be rendered both exotic and benign.

Propertylessness

It is not only Silicon Valley and technocapitalism to blame for contexts of racial disposability and local exploitation. While nineteenth-century Romantic Orientalist fantasies are informative, so are centuries of propertied violence in what is now Romania. This is a history that has seen, over the course of hundreds of years, coordinated efforts to exterminate, expel, and exclude Roma and Jewish people, and to deny them property. It has also witnessed the targeting of nomadic Roma, who have long been seen as "in the way" of private property's logics. Given this, here I explore a genealogy of presocialist propertied histories in very broad strokes to help make sense of the gentrifying ground on which today's nomadic avatars land.

Slavery (*robia*) in the principalities of Wallachia and Moldova can be traced back to the 1241 Mongol invasion, initially applied to Tartar war prisoners.[79] Roma people then arrived as slaves per common war practices of the time or were taken as slaves later in the fourteenth and fifteenth centuries. Some of these practices bled into fifteenth-century Transylvania, where serfdom anchored labor practices. In the centuries that followed, Roma were made property of the state, the church, nobility, and wealthy boyars (landowners) throughout what became Romanian lands.[80] During this time, it was generally accepted that while not all enslaved people were Roma, that all Roma people were enslaved.[81] When it came to property, then, being Roma came to imply being others' property and being unable to own land or housing oneself. Given that racialized slaves "were treated as commodities, being sold and bought, or exchanged for animals and things,"[82] and given that many were highly skilled in various craft-based professions, their labor supplied the coffers of the wealthy. In this way, while slavery served as a technology of racial capitalism, Roma labor made property ownership a lucrative business model.

Despite the fact that racialized slavery intimately shaped centuries of land and labor practices across the region, knowledge of it rarely makes its way into history books. As Anca Parvulescu and Manuela Boatcă write, "Romani populations in East Europe remain a paradigmatic and often neglected example of a double practice of erasure and appropriation."[83] On one hand, labor histories tend to focus on urban working-class exploitations rather than those transpiring in agrarian contexts. On the other, historians of slavery tend to focus more on transatlantic slave trade than on East European contexts. As Parvulescu and Boatcă put it, "The Roma fell through these temporal and spatial cracks in Europe's politics of memory, which remains incomplete without a consideration of anti-Romani racism and the legacy of Romani enslavement in Europe."[84]

Such consideration necessitates investigating conflicting imperial struggles as well as emerging configurations of race and ethnicity alongside evolving nationalist and capitalist developments. This is in part why conditions in Transylvania (which the Habsburg Empire took over from the Ottomans in the early eighteenth century and which later became part of Hungary until becoming part of Romania in 1920) were different from those in Wallachia and Moldova (which remained under uneven Ottoman suzerainty until the 1859 unification as Romania). Yet there were also connections. For instance, while slavery was formally abolished in 1783 in Transylvania, an agreement with Moldova guaranteed the province the return of any runaway slaves.[85] The Habsburgs, meanwhile, attempted to curb Roma movement and migration. Nevertheless, conditions in Transylvania were generally better for Roma people than they were farther east in Wallachia and Moldova, where slavery endured into the mid-nineteenth century. While some Roma itinerant labor was protected in Transylvania, there was nevertheless a concerted effort to "civilize" what were described as "savage" Roma people, which meant banning traditional customs including the Romani language. Much of this was referred to as Roma colonization (*colonizarea țiganilor*), and was intended to obliterate what were described as "backwards," "idle," and "savage" practices associated with nomadism.[86] As Heinrich Grellmann wrote in his *Dissertation on the Gipsies* in 1787 (widely circulated in Transylvania), it was time to "humanize a people who, for centuries, have wandered in error and neglect; and it might be hoped, that, while we are endeavoring to ameliorate the condition of our African brethren, the civilisation of the Gypseys [*sic*], who form so large a portion of humanity, will not be overlooked."[87] With an Enlightenment-inspired paternalism reflective of broader colonial discourse, difference was to be domesticated. Yet despite such efforts, segregation policies endured.

Jewish inhabitants of Transylvania were also prohibited from owning land in the early modern period, and were even encumbered with a "tolerance tax."[88] While many restrictions were eventually lifted, robust assimilation efforts to eliminate Jewish difference took their place. Jewish emancipation was declared in 1867, meaning that finally Jews could acquire property. Yet following the path of racist Enlightenment aftermaths globally,[89] anti-Semitism endured alongside anti-Roma racism. Often each group was pit against the other, creating strategic perceptions that Jewish-Roma solidarity would remain impossible. Such solidarity, Parvulescu and Boatcă write, would have "upended both the colonial and the imperial matrix of power into which all groups were woven at the time."[90]

The Enlightenment also played a role in luring Moldova and Wallachian thinkers into new fantasies of Westernization—ones in which they could disavow their so-called Oriental pasts. This line of thought first inspired the nineteenth-century codifications of slavery, and then, in 1855–1856, its abolition.[91] Yet racism endured. Ciprian Necula has estimated that the Romanian state owes Roma people more than 247 billion euros for the labor they performed during slavery.[92] Yet material reparations were empty promises, and instead landlords received financial compensation for their own loss of slave labor. Of concern to the state wasn't Roma freedom, but rather conscripting Roma people into "dependent peasants."[93] Like sharecroppers in the United States, dependent peasants were obligated to pay state taxes and perform tasks for their landlords, and were denied land and tools. Because of this, very few Roma were eligible to receive property during the major land reform of 1864, which marked the end of legal serfdom (and which conveniently contained no mention of slavery).[94] Many people began leaving Romania in what became known as a "great migration" to Ukraine, Russia, Poland, and Western Europe,[95] where their deracinated lives became fodder for Orientalist tales.

For Roma who remained in Romania, racism continued. By the dawn of the twentieth century, most still lacked property.[96] A land reform of 1918–1920 led to some new Roma organizations and civil rights groups forming, yet this came to a sharp halt after Marshal Ion Antonescu proclaimed Romania to be a National Legionary State backed by eugenicist understandings of Romanian "ethnic purity."[97] Nomadic Roma were considered especially dangerous for the nation, with nomadism itself functioning as a racial signifier.[98] In 1934, nomadic Roma became policed per a governmental directorate.[99] Similar denigrations transpired across the region, with laws passed in Czech lands seeking to criminalize vagrancy and semi-migratory labor.[100]

The Romanian government also passed what became eighty anti-Semitic *Romanization* laws during this time, including those that forcibly expropriated Jewish homes and farmland and that prohibited Jews' employment.[101] A 1941 census (powered by IBM calculators that I further explore in chapter 4), and then a more refined survey, located Jewish and unsettled people in an effort to fascistically "cleanse the ground." Up to 40,909 Roma people were demarcated as "problems," including 11,441 nomadic people and 13,176 sedentary but "dangerous and undesirable" people.[102] Roughly 11,000 Roma people who were rounded up perished in Transnistrian death camps plagued by a lethal typhus epidemic.[103] Romanian authorities also murdered between 150,000 and 250,000 Romanian and Ukrainian Jews in Transnistria. An additional 135,000 Jews living under Hungarian control were killed in Transylvania.[104]

Anti-Semitism was officially banned in Romania in 1944, but Jewish stolen property was never returned. This in part foreshadowed the continuation of anti-Semitism under state socialism, during which many Jewish socialists were purged from the Communist Party and fled to Israel.[105] Homes of Jews who were murdered or who fled, as well as excess homes of the presocialist bourgeoisie, were collectively nationalized per a state effort to urbanize, industrialize, reduce housing inequality and under-occupied shelter, and eliminate homelessness.[106] As many as 241,068 previously privately owned dwellings (not just Jewish homes) were nationalized via Decree 92 in 1950.[107] A series of laws were passed after 1965 regulating landlord and tenant relations, interpreting housing as a field of consumption rather than production. Up to 4.4 million new apartments were also built.[108] The landlessness status that many Roma communities found themselves in during this time rendered them prime recipients of nationalized and thus public housing. Beginning in the late 1970s, many families moved into poor-quality nationalized buildings. Therefore, although racism endured throughout socialism (with Roma assimilation for instance remaining on the national agenda and with Romania's history of anti-Semitism and anti-Roma racism rarely mentioned), and though homelessness was criminalized, housing was better provided to those in need. Labor-intensive jobs in heavy industry and agriculture also enabled upward social mobility for many Roma people.[109]

These provisions were eviscerated after 1989 per neoliberal, anticommunist property restitution processes incentivized by EU mandates of transitional justice. While some of this was incentivized by reparations efforts for Jewish homes stolen before state socialism—in part because of the inability to make such demands during socialism[110]—anticommunist restitution rhetoric quickly began conflating the presocialist fascist period with the socialist one. Despite this conflation, one championed by Westernization imperatives and liberal takes on anticommunisum, the undercurrents of fascism began to grow. A 1995 poll revealed that 62 percent of Romanians maintained a favorable opinion of Antonescu, who was bestowed a half dozen statues, twenty-five streets and squares, and even a cemetery in Iași.[111] These fascist afterlives continue to inform new Romanian parties today such as the Alianța pentru Unirea Românilor (Alliance for the Union of Romanians), which gained parliamentary representation in 2020 and which reveres the fascist interwar Legionnaires. Yet fascist afterlives also gain strength through processes of property restitution (restituire), which seek to restore presocialist private property regimes under the auspices of transitional justice as I continue to explore. Restitution here is not enacted to account for anti-Semitism, but rather it mobilizes liberal language to restore property relations marked by racial capitalism. In doing so, Roma communities are dispossessed from homes that many have been living in for generations.

Restitution

When it comes to property, 1989 shook the ground across Romania, from cities to farmlands. Laws were passed enabling "sitting tenants" in buildings constructed during socialism to purchase their state-owned homes at relatively cheap prices,[112] in part to quell revolutionary dissent. This is in part why it is estimated that 98 percent of Romanians today are said to own their homes (though there is a mass undercounting when it comes to those living informally or those not recognized on leases, not to mention those living in squats, shelters, or unsanctioned homes). As Sophie Gonick puts it, the "idea of homeownership as a fix to quell the rabble is something that a lot of leaders come up with. . . . Property offers this solution: if you are concerned about your house and your home, there is not much time to attend things like union meetings and get organized."[113] This tactic has been deployed across a range of locales beyond Romania, from post-Franco Spain to postsocialist Russia.[114] According to George Zamfir, Romania's housing landscape is often rendered as a "super homeownership" society—which, while partly true, erases how housing security vanished for hundreds of thousands of people after 1989 under the premises of "post-communist social healing."[115] After all, despite such high rates of homeownership, Romania contains the EU's highest poverty rate, with 34 percent of the country at risk, and many people living precariously.[116] This is especially the case for Roma people, which Roma activists, organizations, and scholars have repeatedly pointed out.[117]

There has been more attention allocated to the strange properties of property itself throughout transition, which admittedly has been, as Katherine Verdery marks, contentious, to say the least.[118] In the mid-1990s, past communist leaders known as the *nomenklatura* became what she describes as "entrepratchicks," or former party elites who became entrepreneurs overnight.[119] Entrepratchicks, at least at first, didn't want to sell the country to foreign investors in order to guard their own financial interests. However, when possibilities of Romania joining the EU were first considered in 1999, things began to change. Many who capitalized on "fuzzy property rights" following transition ended up exploiting popular trust in Western institutions such as the EU and NATO. Utilities soon became privatized per an EU mandate in order to "promote the principles of market economy," resulting in countless people losing heat while transnational companies began forming new monopolies.[120] Thus as Emanuela Grama suggests, "The process of Europeanization could be viewed as a form of gentrification on a continental scale: the constitution of a union of European states aimed to engender flows of capital, people, and goods has been accompanied by an intensification of border control and international surveillance meant to identify those who do not have the right to move freely and evict them."[121]

While transition saw homeownership become an option for many living in apartments constructed during socialism, things were quite different for tenants living in presocialist property that had become nationalized, many of whom were Roma. Property restitution policies sought the return of what had been expropriated and nationalized by the Communist Party in the 1950s to the presocialist heirs. Restitution policy materialized in 1995 after heirs began filing claims with the European Court of Human Rights. It then was augmented in 2001 through Law 10 as a Bretton Woods incentivized EU-accession precursor. Through restitution, buildings can either be returned in kind through eviction (*in natură*) or through financial compensatory measures (*compensare*). Romania maintains one of the highest rates of in-kind restitution in the former Eastern bloc, meaning that evictions are rampant. They play a role not simply in clearing land for new market-rate and luxury development, but also, as Zamfir writes, in punishing those unable to acculturate into the upper echelons of capitalism.[122] Joanna Kusiak terms this process "dispossession-by-restitution."[123]

Restitution has been a wildly transformative process, functioning alongside anticommunist transitional justice lustration laws written to prohibit former high-ranking officials in Romania from holding office.[124] Neda Atanasoski describes such processes as techniques of post–Cold War US imperialism, during which "a global human rights regime based in liberal law increasingly monopolized notions of justice and facilitated the spread of free-market economies."[125] This has had everything to do with property. As Verdery writes, "If we see the transition as a project of cultural engineering in which fundamental social ideas are resignified—including not only democracy, markets, and private property, but also ideas about entitlement, accountability, and responsibility—then the (re)creation of private property is evidently a critical locus for this cultural project."[126]

Before restitution evictions began slipping out of national consciousness as they largely have today, mainstream television in the 1990s and early 2000s began broadcasting them on primetime news.[127] Media stories often focused on postsocialist tensions between non-Roma Romanians and Roma, portraying the latter as subhuman. This led to a slew of racist pogroms exploding across the country that targeted Roma homes and communities, often with government impunity.[128] In 2013, legislation was passed prioritizing in-kind restitutions and relegating law enforcement for evictions. By 2017, over 202,000 court cases for restitution had been filed.[129] Over a third of these restitution claims still remained unresolved as of 2021, meaning that thousands of buildings have not yet faced eviction but may soon. While some claimants have been Jewish descendants seeking to remedy fascist-era dispossession, others are heirs of the presocialist bourgeoisie. Either way, claimants aspire not to move back into the crumbling homes of their parents and grandparents now occupied with "inherited" families, but rather to demolish old buildings and construct luxury apartments, hotels, office space, art galleries, coffee shops, private kindergartens, and tech hubs in their wake. This, often enough, requires eviction.

Up to 30 percent of the country's housing stock was nationalized during socialism, but less than 2 percent of housing is public today.[130] This means that the very concept of social housing has been gentrified out of the public imaginary—but not for all. Upon restitution, many evictees advocate for social housing alternatives. This, they argue, would be better than winding up houseless or in a shelter. While shelters are better than nothing, they often segregate families by gender and sever communities. There are also far too few. Irina Zamfirescu and Liviu Chelcea observe that in Bucharest, there were 22,000 applications for social housing in 2017, but only twenty apartments available.[131] Contexts such as this have animated the political strategies of housing justice collectives such as the Frontul Comun pentru Dreptul la Locuire (FCDL/Common Front for the Right to Housing) in Bucharest and Căși Sociale ACUM! in Cluj,[132] both advocating for dignified social housing production and against racist restitution evictions.

Dislocari

To trouble the pervasive notion that those residing in Pata Rât remain there by choice, and to better illustrate the accumulation of evictions engendered in postsocialist spatiotemporality, in 2016 I collaborated with members of Căși Sociale ACUM! and in particular its founder Enikő Vincze to create an interactive digital storymap, *Dislocari: Rutele Evacuărilor spre Strada Cantonului (1996–2016)* (Dislocations: Eviction Routes to Cantonului Street [1996–2016]). The map, which became a collaboration between Căși Sociale ACUM! and the Anti-Eviction Mapping Project (a countercartography collective that I cofounded in San Francisco in 2013),[133] follows the eviction routes of Roma residents— Ioanică, Leontina, Babi, Sandu, Ligia, Katalin, and Gelu—all of whom reside on Cantonului Street in Pata Rât alongside 160 neighbors, all in small makeshift homes. Many have been there since a wave of restitution evictions in the late 1990s. The map embeds video horror stories in which residents narrate routes of what Ananya Roy refers to as "racial banishment," or the forced displacement of subaltern residents to the city's end.[134] Today, some of their former homes are now redeveloped into IT offices; others have been razed and are now filled with a messy array of vegetation. As Vincze and Zamfir write, "Since the overwhelming majority of Cantonului dwellers evicted from the city are Roma and stigmatized as inferior, their dislocation comes as a racialized administrative act supporting the redevelopment of the city without providing alternative homes to the impoverished evictees thus relegated to a socioeconomic and cultural status of inferiority."[135]

The storymap begins with Ioanică, who lived in a former state-owned building on Turzii Street in the early 1990s. Numerous families were legally living there, most of whom were working in nearby factories such as Clujana and Carbochim. Ioanică had been a street cleaner. But his building was not maintained, and one day, he "woke up with the ceiling on the floor." Rather than repair the building (which today remains an empty lot), the city moved Ioanică's family to Croitorilor Street. The new apartment was nice, but soon, a man from a different city restituted it and evicted them without compensation. Similarly, Ligia received a restitution notice on Eroilor Street in 2011, although her contract was good until 2014. She had been paying rent on time, but the new owners wanted hundreds of euros a month, which she could not afford. "So, they threw us out on the streets—we had no other choice," she articulates. "I asked how is this possible, and they said it was because these were their houses, and they wanted them back."

Ioanică's former home now functions as a pharmacy, and the rest of the area has been converted into IT buildings. As he questions in the film: "I have no idea why more office buildings are built for companies, and not apartments for people. Years have gone by, and now you wake up with so many offices for rich people. The authorities care about one thing—to evict people without legal documents so that they can reclaim buildings, pushing people to the outskirts of the city." Restitution urban renewal processes pave the way for new tech development, now considered the largest driver of office development.[136] Much of this is facilitated by ever-mutating planning laws, which have changed at least sixteen times over the last thirty years. Often the city incorporates the private sector through the language of "participation," but only as a form of what Bianca Wylie has described as "engagement theater" in which corporate projects capitalize on selective and often tailored means of involvement.[137] Indeed, Ioanică was never invited into any conversations about the future of his home.

While the current mayor, Emil Boc, has welcomed Cluj's Silicon Valley status and the new tech development it welcomes, it was the prior mayor, Gheorghe Funar, that Vincze argues "created a favourable space for capital accumulation in the hands of local entrepreneurs without completely excluding foreigners."[138] Between 1990 and 2004, Funar averted regulations, preparing "the ground for the further development of Cluj—under neoliberal governance—as an entrepreneurial city or a 'competitive city.'"[139] This coincided with a two-part national Private Sector Adjustment Programme executed in 1999 and 2000 to privatize state-owned companies such as Romtelecom, the Romanian Bank for Development, the Dacia automobile company, and the Felix computer factory. These all got swallowed up by Western firms and divided into stocks and sold. In addition to privatizing state-owned companies, real estate developers began absorbing peripheral orchards, agricultural land, and forests. In 2005, urban plans were drawn in Cluj enabling foreign real estate developers to build new apartments.[140] Another plan was crafted in 2014, auguring developers and foreign investors to turn from peripheral zones to industrial zones in the city center. It was then that buildings such as the old Arbator butchery, the Flacăra textile factory, the Ursus beer factory, and the Napochim furniture factory became converted to tech firms and luxury real estate developments.

While unions organized against privatization, they faced heavy repression. Numerous engineers lost their jobs, as did laborers in heavy industry and agriculture, many of whom were Roma. Although the number of wage earners in formal and informal sectors decreased dramatically in 1989 aftermaths, the trend continued for decades, mostly attributed to out-migration. In Cluj, the number of employees in 2010 was 73 percent of what it had been in 1990.[141] Today, Romania maintains the fifth largest diaspora globally, though the greatest rate of migration transpired earlier, between 2005 and 2010.[142] Such contexts were starkly intensified after Romania and Bulgaria joined the EU in 2007.[143] This is highly racialized, with the ratio of those who remained versus those who emigrated 13 percent for non-Roma between 1991 and 2011, and 32 percent for Roma.[144] Such statistics speak to postsocialist contexts of anti-Roma racism within workplaces, but also the raciality of property restitution.

Siliconization has only fed these contexts of racial dispossession. Throughout 2019, for instance, there was an ongoing eviction fight on Stephenson Street in Cluj, right across from Liberty Technology Park—a complex that hosts tech companies including the German Siemans, the Austrian Impact Hub (a well-regarded coworking space for digital nomads), as well as Romania's own Spherik Accelerator. Developed by the Swiss company Fribourg Development, the park champions innovation and entrepreneurship, bragging of being "the first technological park in Romania, a park for creative ideas built in a revolutionary place designed to offer exceptional growth and quality environment for companies in the IT&C and R&D domains, all in one unique area both conceptually and architecturally."[145] Yet the space is hardly new at all. Known as the Libertatea Furniture Factory during socialism, the building itself goes back much earlier, to 1870, when a Viennese craftsman built pianos in the space. It was in the 1970s that residents moved in across the street, paying formal rents. Over time, the residents, mostly Roma, grew their families and community, and built informal homes next door. All had been going relatively smoothly until Libertatea became Liberty in 2013. Suddenly, neighbors began calling the police on the Roma families who had been living there for decades, complaining about the laundry they were hanging on their clotheslines outside. Washed as they were, the hanging clothes were deemed too unsightly for emergent visions of Siliconization.

Narratives of racial cleansing permeate *Dislocari* stories as well. After being evicted from Croitorilor, for instance, Ioanică moved to "the NATO block." His building was smoky and derelict, and the ground floor was home to refuse and animals. "No one picked up the garbage because the people living here were Roma," he explains. "The children named this block NATO. It was back when our country got into NATO, and we said, okay, this is the NATO block." While entry into NATO and the EU has been heralded by anticommunists as progress, the block lacked running water, electricity, and toilets. There, residents formulated their own critiques of EU accession and its empty promises. "Instead of electricity, we used candles. We made fire with wood. It was very smoky. Some people had jobs, some people were picking up garbage, exactly as it is now," Ioanică laments, referencing the informal labor that many in Pata Rât partake in. He recollects peering out from his glassless windows during Christmas, enviously viewing people in other buildings watch TV in the burgeoning Silicon Valley of Europe.

Because NATO residents had no formal contracts, the military police raided their home. It was then that Pata Rât became the last resort. While many presume that people reside near the dump because of poverty, Ioanică blames the city hall for never offering his community guidance on how to apply for social housing. As he described in *Dislocari*, since then he has remained in Pata Rât with his two adolescent daughters, crammed into a sixteen-square-meter barrack and lacking a sewage system and electricity. In 2015, the community was granted two portable toilets, but before that, they had none. As Leontina, also featured in *Dislocari*, bemoans: "They didn't bring us toilets, they didn't bring garbage containers, they didn't care about us. As if we were already dead, and they already put us under the ground, and that's it. We were put in the garbage dump and that's it. It's worse for us than it is for the rats." For Leontina, postsocialist transition and the influx of global capital has forced her into what Neferti Tadiar describes as the "exit zones of abandonment."[146] That Silicon Valley imperialism and its avatars fetishize nomadism simply adds insult to injury. As Vincze and Zamfir write, "Those who cannot catch up with such developments are expected to leave the city. Alternatively, they are forced to move to its underdeveloped margins, working to serve (in sanitation companies, but not only) the lifestyle of the more privileged."[147] And, often enough, residents are not provided with basic amenities like sanitation.

Racial Transits

In the summer of 2016, I planned to attend a gathering in one of the city's new coworking spaces, ClujHub, hoping to learn more about nomadic fantasies. I already knew that some of its regulars, such as Victor, Berlin based but a weekly visitor to Cluj, believe that tech is big in Romania because of foreign language skills—a sentiment that he and many others attribute to the influx of unsubtitled US television in the 1990s. I also had already met the development manager, Danny, who grew up in London and works for a software company there. Similarly, Andre works for a Cluj start-up partnered with a German Microsoft-funded company, and builds smart home security devices. These devices are gaining popularity in the West "with this new immigrant problem," he explained, failing to acknowledge that, especially since Romania's 2007 EU accession, many of these immigrants are Romanians.

My roommate, curious about ClujHub, decided to attend the gathering with me. But when we arrived, we were greeted by a fifty-lei fee (US$12). While for Westerners this isn't much, for my roommate it was laughable. "On a normal Cluj salary, that's ridiculous. Most people could buy all the food that they needed for a week on that. It's extreme," she scoffed. Thus, we changed course for Fabrica de Pensule, once a paintbrush factory and now a collective art space that, over the last year, has been partly displaced by new tech companies. On arriving, rather than a hefty fee, we encountered a multimedia piece curated by Claudiu Lazăr entitled *?uropa*, a critique of Eastern European experiences of hostility when migrating to the West. As Angéla Kóczé argues, while Western migrants are considered expats in East Europe, Easterners in the West are interpellated as pariahs.[148] This has long been more visceral for Roma migrants than non-Roma, from postemancipation migration waves to the present.

I happened to be living in Belfast in 2009 when members of the fascist group Combat 18 (the "18" standing for Hitler's enumerated initials) attacked a recently arrived Romanian Roma community. Windows were smashed and copies of *Mein Kampf* were stapled on doorways, while graffiti demanding that "Romanian Muslims Go Back to Romania" was penned on brick walls (even though most Romanian Roma are Christian). Even more uncanny was that many of the attackers waved Israeli flags, marking their opposition to the Palestinian solidarity that anticolonial Northern Irish Republicans espouse. Many of those whose homes were besieged and who fell victim to a new iteration of deracinated dispossession did return to Romania, yet many expressed feelings of being caught in between two genres of anti-Roma racism—one amplified in contexts of postcoloniality, the other in contexts of postsocialism. Meanwhile, many non-Roma Romanians living nearby strategically distanced themselves from their Roma neighbors in an effort to espouse newfound Europeanness. Such forms of disavowal recruit postsocialist subjects into what Alyosxa Tudor and Piro Rexhepi describe as "the ongoing racial, classed and gendered (geo)politics of EU borderization,"[149] in which non-Roma Eastern Europeans imagine that they might stand a chance of assimilation as long as they are not Roma.

I first met Marian in 2011 on a train in Romania. Fluent in over a dozen languages, including numerous Indian dialects due to their similarity with Romani, Marian aspires to help other Roma people uncover their Indic roots. Yet he has long been unable to find steady work in Bucharest due to pervasive racism, having also been expelled from school. One sweltering August day, years after we first met, we reconvened in an air-conditioned McDonalds café. He had just returned from France and wanted to tell me about his trip. Or rather, his trips. He had been traveling to France numerous times over the years, not because he enjoys traveling and the freedom that EU accession affords but because there are camps on the outskirts of Paris where he can make a bit of money. It's far from dignifying work though, and in fact, "It's like hell." Camp life lacks toilets, food, everything. There, he encounters not only anti-Roma racism from Westerners, but also what he describes as anti-Blackness, "a double crime." Blackness for him refers to a form of colorism within Roma worlds in which he faces stigma for having darker skin than other Roma people. This also reflects, per Kóczé, a transnational anti-Blackness that affixes itself to Roma people and that has only metastasized in neoliberal times.[150]

Yet despite this, Marian was going back and forth to France to take advantage of a French policy in which the government at the time was giving Roma 100 euros if they would return to Romania. "They were even sending Bulgarian Roma to Bucharest just because they assume all Roma are from Romania!" Marian laughed. He made the trip a few times that summer, but he was always relieved to return home to his family and friends. He, like hundreds of people with whom I've shared cheap European airplane flights to and from Bucharest, is far from an expat or digital nomad. Yet always scattered on these plane rides are also tourists, entrepreneurs, and digital nomads. Unlike Marian, they are driven by imperial fantasies powered by geographic arbitrage rather than by precarity, racism, and sheer survival.

At the same time, there are also fancier planes transiting a newer digital nomadic iteration into Romania. These are epitomized by figures such as the

American-British internet personality Andrew Tate. Notorious for his explicit racism and misogyny, Tate also maintains status as the ultimate digital nomad due to his possession of seven passports, fifteen driver's licenses, and residencies in thirty countries, including Romania. After being apprehended by Romanian authorities on account of his role in an exploitative webcamming criminal ring in 2022, he has continued to maintain a following among young digital nomads subscribed to his membership platform. While in many ways he can be understood as an extreme example of digital nomadic fantasy, his continued fame reveals a significant aspect of nomadic desire. This is only emboldened by digital nomad visa programs, so long as one's practices are less overtly violent than Tate's. Yet less public violence pervades everyday life in the form of deracinated dispossession, essentially protracting nineteenth-century nomadic fantasy into local contexts of gentrification.

To Whom Does the Smart City Belong?

Despite the ongoing violence of deracinated dispossession as it compounds Silicon Valley imperialism, Orientalist fantasy, and presocialist property geographies, the fight against racial banishment endures. Over a decade after the 2010 Coastei Street eviction, residents are still wastelanded in Pata Rât. In December 2021, amid the COVID-19 pandemic and increased housing precarity, Căși Sociale ACUM! convened another of what have become annual commemorations of the Coastei Street eviction—this one specifically highlighting the incongruities of Cluj having been branded a smart city. A banner and light displays were hung from Elisabeta Bridge, spelling out, "I miss social housing," and "Me too." An "online march" was also convened entitled, "To whom does the smart city belong?" Tenants and activists were encouraged to share photos on social media about the smart city's failure to address housing. Hundreds participated, displaying photos of signs being held with messages questioning: "To whom does the smart city belong, if public interest is only for profit?" "To whom does the smart city belong, if hundreds of people live without electricity and hot water in Pata Rât (near the landfills)?" "To whom does the smart city belong, if it is allowed to evict the most vulnerable ones?" "To whom does the smart city belong, if in the last five years there have been less than ten social housing units allocated (each year) for several hundred applications?"[151] A group of activists gathered next to a new "smart" bus stop on Memorandumului Street, holding a placard questioning, "To whom does the smart city belong, if you need to leave the city, because you cannot afford a home?" Indeed, among the hollowed-out Siliconized city, marked by the tower-

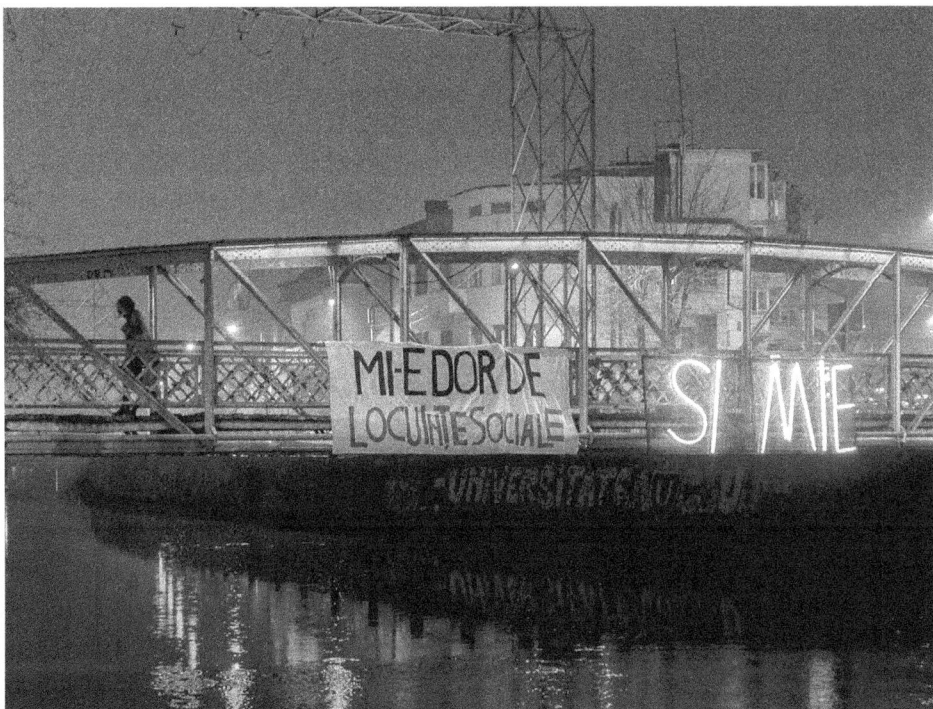

FIGURE 1.2. "To Whom Does the Smart City Belong" light installation on the Elisabeta bridge reading: "I miss social housing. . . . Me too." Photo by Căși Sociale ACUM!, 2021.

ing NTT Data tower, new luxury condos, and now even a Wizard of Oz nursery where the Coastei Street home used to be, to whom does the smart city belong?

Reflecting on what it's like to visit Cluj's city center after being racially banished from it, former resident of Coastei Street, Silviu Zsiga, reflects,

> When I come here and look at everything that is here and what is around now, honestly, I have to say that it is beautiful, clean, it smells good. But what is not so beautiful is that everything that has been done, has been done on the suffering and on the tears of others. But that's the way people are, they only look after their own well-being, even if they push others out of the way. They don't care who was left behind in tears, who was beaten. These things could have been done in a different way, not necessarily with the suffering, sorrow and tears from so many people. They could have come and tell us, we don't like how this place looks like, we want to clean it, but we are also moving you to a place where you will be well, not to suffering and torment.[152]

Righteous anger backed by experiences such as Silviu's fueled an ensuing flash mob at the smart city protest in which organizers held a large photograph of young Coastei Street children happily squeezed onto an outdoor couch prior to their eviction. "Unde au dispărut copiii de pe canapea?" (Where did the children from the couch go?), bold red letters questioned on the image. Căși Sociale ACUM! went on to propose that an Eviction Monument be built exactly where the couch used to sit.

Holding a sign in support of eviction memorialization, Roma feminist activist Linda Greta Zsiga questioned, "To whom does the smart city belong, if in Cluj there is no Roma monument?" Reflecting on the absence of memorials for the dispossessed and racially banished in Siliconized San Francisco, Nancy Mirabal writes: "There is no place for remembering the recently displaced and excluded. Instead, the memorials are embedded in a re-scripted historical memory of space and time that extends far beyond recent events and experiences. They cull safe memories and operate as historical anecdotes ready for tourist consumption."[153] Tourists don't want to confront the violence of contemporary dispossessions, she infers. Rather, like digital nomads, they embrace Romantic Orientalist fantasies of freedom to consume dispossessions so deracinated they appear safe. In other words, it is easier to fetishize the fanciful wandering Gypsy and to embrace digital nomadic ontology than to acknowledge the racial violence that imperial freedom dreams impart. What might it do to digital nomadic desire to confront the dispossessions manifested through the Siliconization that one transits? How might fantasies of smart city urbanization shatter when confronted by those racially banished to the wastelands of urban renewal in order to restitute capitalism? Yet, as Mirabal writes, despite a lack of commemoration for people forced from their homes, there is "a seething presence, a haunting if you will, that travels and moves through space, resting in the cracks of the sidewalks and waiting for what comes next."[154] Here too, in the ruins of Siliconized Cluj, where, per Căși Sociale ACUM!, "the real estate chaos is suffocating us" and where the "smart industry" amasses profit,[155] a seething presence persists. As Karen Barad writes, "Attempts at erasure always leave material traces: what is erased is preserved in the entanglements, in the diffraction patterns of being/becoming."[156] Nestled into pavement cracks, bolstering the very infrastructure that the becoming Silicon Valley requires, the seeds of a very different urban technofuture have already been planted.

Postsocialist Silicon Valley

Canoes gently glide through Mission Creek past the redbrick National Guard Armory building while rich plant life sprouts up amid chinampas, or the floating gardens of Tenochtitlán that are still practiced in Xochimilco in Mexico City. We are not in Xochimilco, but rather in San Francisco's Mission District as depicted by Fernando Martí, a local artist and longtime housing organizer who spent years fighting his own eviction amid Tech 2.0 geographies marked by apps, start-ups, and the so-called sharing economy. I myself took part in a couple of demonstrations intended to pressure his tech start-up landlords into rescinding the eviction threatening to displace him and his family. Yet in his *Futuros Fugaces: Armory Chinampas*, a giclée digital print created with pencil, watercolor, and Photoshop, Martí imagines a different Mission world, one informed by Latinx futurism, queer ecologies, and housing and racial justice. By unearthing a mythical layering of Mesoamerican imagery, Martí mobilizes past imaginaries to connect stolen Ohlone lands and Aztec histories to a future cosmic time. As he questions, "Will our streets become canals, traveled by colorful lanchas, the sidewalks farmed in chinampas wherever the old creeks and marshes, now paved over, return to their watery state?"[1] Or will they remain the playgrounds for the technocapitalist elite, many of whom masquerade liberal grammars of progress and sharing?

Martí writes that he first conceptualized the image in the late 1990s, when the Mission Anti-Displacement Coalition crashed a party that the mayor was holding to celebrate transforming the crumbling, dilapidated National Guard Armory into a server farm to house dot-com-boom technologies. First erected after the devasting 1906 earthquake that eviscerated its predecessor in Western Addition neighborhood, the building served as an arsenal and armory famously having facilitated the suppression of the San Francisco General Strike in 1934. Military personnel gradually trickled out of the building, but then rushed back in 1966 during the height of the Cold War to suppress the Hunters Point Uprising—a racial justice rebellion that sparked after a white police officer shot and killed Matthew Johnson Jr., a Black seventeen-year-old.[2] The uprising formed as people across the city surrounded the Armory to thwart repressive troops. As John Ross recalls, it became a battle between "Mission Rebels" and over four hundred military personnel equipped with bayonets.[3] While there was hope that new solidarities would grow, Chris Carlsson notes that "automatic weapons, portable artillery, and federal troops, i.e., military occupation, offered a vivid demonstration of how far San Francisco would go in the attempt to contain black rage. . . . Meanwhile, the Hunters Point Uprising itself disappeared down the memory hole."[4] Today, amid new uprisings against police violence and gentrification, the urgency of learning from past uprisings weighs heavily.

Yet gentrification functions by erasing emancipatory histories and dispossessing those who remember them. A decade after the uprising, the Armory building closed, and several spaceship scenes were filmed inside for the Cold War–era Star Wars film *The Empire Strikes Back*. Yet the building was not well maintained, and the city began discussing the possibility of turning it over to the community. But instead, then-mayor Gavin Newsom gave it to his rich tech investor friends, who transformed it into a dot-com-boom server farm. Yet the farm didn't last, and instead the brick castle became home to the San Francisco–based pornography producer Kink.com. Kink had a decent stint until 2018, when the building was sold to a realty firm. And so go the trends of real estate speculation amid post–Cold War tech booms, where anticommunist experimentations laid the foundations for new intimacies between technocapitalism and real estate speculation in its aftermaths. Yet such theatrics are also informed by pre–Cold War histories of spatial violence, including eighteenth-century Spanish colonization, the gold rush, and ensuing US empire. Even in

FIGURE 2.1. *Futuros Fugaces: Armory Chinampas*, by Fernando Martí, 2020.

the aftermath of the COVID-19 pandemic, with an economic recession leading to new waves of eviction and houselessness in San Francisco and beyond,[5] there is also an ensuing artificial intelligence (AI) boom being likened to the first dot-com boom and gold rush alike.[6] As tech booms come and go, then, dispossession accumulates alongside acts of rebellion.

In this chapter, I focus on how the commodification of land, housing, public space, data, and infrastructure recodes colonial, racial capitalist, and Cold War logics in the post–Cold War Siliconized Bay Area. This process emboldens what I describe as racial technocapitalism—or the means through which technocapitalist growth inheres raciality. Upon this landscape, data harvested, mined, brokered, and stolen from people globally and locally accumulates massive wealth for companies such as Facebook/Meta, Google/Alphabet, Apple, Twitter/X, Amazon, Netflix, and more, not to mention a huge swath of start-ups, venture capitalists, and private equity firms. Real estate speculators and local governments capitalize on this Siliconized imperial geography, all the while appropriating the liberal language of sharing. Manissa M. Maharawal describes such processes as those of techcolonialism, whereby the tech industry's spatiality operates through "colonial logics of racialized dispossession and materially extend and reproduce the colonial present," and in which "technology companies enclose the 'commons,' operate above laws, invest surplus capital in speculative urban racialized property regimes, and treat governments themselves as merely outdated and archaic institutions to be 'disrupted.'"[7] Tech colonialism also gets at much of what I describe as Silicon Valley imperialism, as both analytically point to technocapitalist logics updating those of settler colonial dispossession. Silicon Valley imperialism also, for me, signals the geographic and epistemic weight of Silicon Valley itself, which remains both an aspiration and epicenter, and which transits globally and unevenly—merging with yet diverging from US empire all at once. At "home" in Siliconized cities such as San Francisco, Silicon Valley imperialism manifests racial dispossession and capitalist accumulation upon stolen and enclosed land. Today, AI-powered robots roam sidewalks near the Armory to patrol the unhoused, while the city becomes a laboratory for Waymo (formerly known as the Google Self-Driving Car Project) and Cruise driverless "robotaxis." Airbnb, Uber, and Lyft, all birthed in the city, meanwhile promulgate fantasies of sharing economies, despite what has been over a decade of pushback for their gentrifying effects and exploitative labor practices, built upon the logics of private property.[8]

These sharing economy imaginaries, alongside social media discourses of public forums owned by private companies, highlight a novel aspect of Silicon Valley imperialism in which racial capitalist processes are cloaked by technoliberalism. By technoliberalism, I invoke Neda Atanasoski and Kalindi Vora's critique of a postracial and postgendered version of universal humanity enabled by technology, one in which fantasies of progress for the liberal rights-bearing subject mask colonial mechanisms of seizure, exploitation, appropriation, and degradation that technologies reproduce.[9] Technoliberalism also gets at how, amid the fourth industrial revolution and second machine age, not only have racialized and gendered differentiations been accelerated, but also sharing economy grammars have appropriated socialist understandings of communalism in order to advance capitalist expropriation. Postsocialist analytics rooted in an understanding of multiply existing social and communal projects that exceed confinement by state socialist spatiotemporality help elucidate the mechanics of this predation.

While technoliberal and imperial processes indelibly inform the present, so do stories of refusal. As Rachel Brahinsky and Alexander Tarr write of the gentrifying Mission, despite the totalizing powers of tech companies and their narratives, neither a Google map nor a focus on Google's hegemony can "show you what it feels like to hear infectious K-pop beats coming from a second-floor dance studio that was saved from eviction by community protests, while you eat your lunch in a local taqueria where conversations still take place in Spanish."[10] By only seeing the world through Google, or by solely focusing on its destructive powers, other worlds that defy Silicon Valley's own overdetermination are erased. Indeed, the Bay Area today is all at once cacophonous, contradictory, and uneven, particularly when it comes to experiences of living upon a tech-boom palimpsest.

After all, other technofutures that predate the formation of Silicon Valley inform the present. Property itself has long functioned as a technique of dispossession, one that colonial projects have long found requisite for establishing capitalist markets. While racial capitalist land grabbing predates the colonization of the Americas having been alive and well in places such as Eastern Europe prior (as described in the previous chapter), Brenna Bhandar writes that the "transatlantic slave trade, and the appropriation of indigenous lands that characterized the emergence of colonial capitalism on a worldwide scale, produced and relied upon economic and juridical forms for which property law and a racial concept of the human were central tenets. Scientific techniques of measurement and quantification, economic visions of land and life rooted in logics of abstraction, culturally inscribed notions of white European superiority, and philosophical concepts of the proper person who possessed the capacity to appropriate (both on the level of interiority and in the external world) worked in conjunction to produce laws of property and racial subjects."[11] In the Bay Area, this has materialized the bloodstained bedrock beneath Native Ohlone lands first fictionalized as cities such as San Jose and San Francisco during Spanish colonization, and then as the region of Silicon Valley during the Cold War. During this process of Siliconization, one marked by weapons manufacturing, cybernetics, computation, and data accumulation, San Francisco, Oakland, and San Jose were made laboratories of pacification techniques to quell anti-imperial, communist, and racial justice organizing.[12] Much of this organizing was connected to decolonial and racial justice movements such as the American Indian Movement and the Black Panther Party.[13] While one might imagine technologies of anticommunist pacification to have abated with the collapse of the Berlin Wall, instead, Silicon Valley technologies were adapted for consumeristic and carceral use while afforded new global transits. On one hand, this helped grow Silicon Valley imperialism and the US security state; on the other, it consolidated the conditions for the 1990s dot-com boom and its aftermaths.

Although the Cold War is well understood as a temporal node for apprehending the Siliconized present, postsocialism—as an analytic normally reserved for mapping out geopolitical contexts in the post-1989/1991 former Eastern bloc—rarely makes its way into the framing. In this chapter I unmoor postsocialism from its long calcified spatiotemporal location to better apprehend anticapitalist visions, organizing work, and abolitionist dreaming informative of Bay Area social life despite the concreteness of Silicon Valley imperialism. Looking at socialist legacies and presences connected to anticolonial organizing and commoning work, Atanasoski and Vora postulate that postsocialism can be "both an analytic and a plural condition," one that foregrounds "how historical political imaginaries connected to the advent of the Cold War and the independence of formerly colonized nations simultaneously undergird and trouble contemporary ethical collectivities."[14] Inspired by J. K. Gibson-Graham's theorization of already-existing postcapitalist politics and their insistence of capitalism itself being a diverse set of practices,[15] Atanasoski and Vora propose that socialism, as well as its various posts, be dehomogenized. As they aver, just as there was never one singular socialism, neither is there one universal postsocialism. The "post" in postsocialism signals not socialism's demise, but rather "an epistemological shift that makes evident how the Cold War imposed a false historical binary, delimiting both socialism and capitalism as singular visions and practices."[16] It also marks anticapitalist desires and practices that existed long before and will continue to endure beyond formal Eastern European and Soviet state socialism. Postsocialist temporality thus refutes Francis Fukuyama's "end of history" spatiotemporal enclosure,[17] and in turn reignites the heterogeneity of socialisms that both predate and today exist in excess of the Cold War.

Inspired by postsocialist possibilities as they inform technofutures beyond the confines of capitalism, in this chapter I offer postsocialism as a conceptual purchase for mapping out the violence of racial technocapitalism in the post–Cold War Bay Area present—as well as apprehending various forms of anticapitalist pasts, presents, and futures. Looking to Bay Area anti-eviction organizing work, some of which I have been a part of, I study political worlds being crafted that refute Silicon Valley imperialism practices and epistemologies. But first, I map out some of the spatial and racial violence that Cold War technologies inherited before exploring post–Cold War consumerist transformations. This then allows me to place housing justice organizing within the time-space of postsocialism.

Palimpsest

There are cumulative Bay Area histories of dispossession and resistance that laid the groundwork for the Cold War becoming of Silicon Valley. While most working-class people living in "Silicon Valley" don't refer to it as such and instead call it by names such as the South Bay, San Jose, Santa Clara County, Palo Alto, and San Francisco, these names too reflect different moments of imperiality. Between 1776 and 1833, twenty-one Catholic missions were erected across California, transforming stolen Native lands into various Mission Districts. In Santa Clara, now home to the Intel Corporation, missionaries reported being awed and stupefied that the Ohlone living there were simply "poor creatures of the forest" lacking reverence for "superior" colonial technological systems.[18] Backed by colonial logics, complex ecosystems were ransacked while Native peoples were forcibly baptized, contaminated with European diseases, and worked to death. In what had become the state of California, the Ohlone lands of Ramaytush, the Tamien Nation, and the Confederated Villages of Lisjan became divided into colonial cities. At least five thousand Ohlone and Miwok peoples were buried in San Francisco's Mission Dolores Cemetery alone.[19] As Julian Brave NoiseCat puts it, "Today's land rush is nothing new. For more than 200 years, there has been a run on Bay Area real estate—a relentless wave of colonization, then urbanization and now gentrification that left the Ohlone, the Bay Area's first people, landless."[20] In other words, one cannot understand the co-optation and privatization of Bay Area space today without taking into account violent imperial histories. At the same time, there is a long practice of anticolonial organizing, including early Ohlone practices of resisting "recruitment" into Spanish missions.[21]

Spain ruled Alta California until 1821, after which it briefly became a part of Mexico until 1846, when Anglo settlers and the US Navy fought against Mexican rule. By 1847, US control had been achieved, only to become solidified in 1848 with the Treaty of Guadalupe Hidalgo, which ended the Mexican-American War. California's statehood took hold in 1850, protracting US imperial rule to the Pacific coast. Yet it was really with the 1849 gold rush that cities like San

Francisco saw huge settler population booms and that Native people, lands, and natural resources were murdered and plundered at unprecedented rates.[22] It was also with statehood that the 1850 Act for the Government and Protection of Indians was passed, essentially sanctioning genocide and enslavement.

Anglo settlers rushing in for profit largely couldn't fathom that rather than engaging in accumulative agriculture based on private property techniques, heterogeneous groups of very different Ohlone groups engaged in seasonal migration patterns that responded to abundance rather than scarcity. While settlers ignorantly interpellated this as laziness and derogatorily described Natives as "diggers," Ohlone practices were astute, sophisticated, and varied.[23] Miner councils meanwhile excluded Native people and immigrants from gold claims, mobilizing a white logic that informed the incipient Golden State government.[24] For instance, the 1850 Foreign Miners' Tax Act authorized racialized systems of rent, enclosing stolen land and excluding non-white land and rights claims. This gets at what Cheryl Harris describes as "whiteness as property"—a US legal doctrine in which whiteness and the right to own property are rendered synonymous.[25] In this sense, racial technocapitalist spatial understandings became rapidly affixed to people, land, labor, and law.

While Native peoples fought back against genocidal practices, state-sponsored genocide did ensue.[26] California's first governor, Peter Burnett, made his 1851 state address one specifically stoking elimination politics. In his words, "The white man, to whom time is money, and who labors hard all day to create the comforts of life, cannot sit up all night to watch his property; and after being robbed a few times, he becomes desperate, and resolves upon a war of extermination." This war against "unskilled" Natives, he suggested, "will continue to be waged between the races until the Indian race becomes extinct."[27] As his words inferred, white men were made the bearers of wisdom, property, and futurity. As war was waged, militias guarded and controlled water sources and forced Ohlone communities into conditions of slavery while settlers massacred people by the hundreds, supported by the federal government.

During this time, unceded lands quickly became divided and mapped through imperial techniques such as surveying—a practice derived from sixteenth- and seventeenth-century England during which manorial officers and overseers ritualized the demarcation of "real property."[28] It was no accident that original English surveying practices emboldened the privatization of the English commons—a practice that targeted nomadic Roma and Irish Traveller communities whose cultures transgressed British epistemologies of private property.[29] It was during this period that landlordism, Poor Laws, debtors' prisons, and forced displacement—all of which Marx would later describe as a process of primitive accumulation—replaced feudal systems.[30] As Cedric Robinson historicizes, from the get-go, racism was built into this process, having already seeped into the medieval feudal order throughout the expansion of European Christendom at the expense of countless peoples along Europe's growing borders.[31] For instance, in Eastern European lands where Roma slavery was widespread (as explored in chapter 1), practices of racialized labor and property making had deeply informed racial capitalist formations.[32] Anti-commoning practices were then exported to Africa, the Americas, and Asia through Western European colonialism.[33] They were then reinterpreted by the United States as the nascent empire began swallowing up Native nation after nation as it expanded west.

US imperialism mobilized new property technologies of surveillance and dispossession as it grew. This process turned the colonial gaze into a technoscientific weapon that proclaimed, as Felicity Amaya Schaeffer writes, "the power to 'see' and 'unsee' land and bodies."[34] This project aimed to discredit Native sciences and scientific understandings of land, rendering such practices as barbaric, savage, and in need of salvation. Land was delivered to speculators, cattle farmers, railroad companies, loggers, miners, and infrastructure projects—all protected through technologies such as guns, militia, and the police.[35] In the Bay Area, ancient redwood old-growth forests were privatized and destroyed for timber, while grizzly bears, sea otters, beavers, tule elk, and several species of whales encountered near extinction. The gold rush and hydraulic mineral extraction introduced novel toxicities into the water systems, while at the same time, water companies claimed what had previously been a public good.

This era saw the evolution of what Malcolm Harris describes as the "California engineer," a frontier entrepreneurial scientist who made the state its laboratory and whose extractive techniques and technologies soon were exported globally. As he writes, "The Wild West was the model for a new world, an integrated sphere of value and labor flows arranged according to white power and generic accumulation."[36] Richard Walker similarly notes that it was California "irrigation engineers, machinists, and plant scientists" whose innovations soon transformed the region into an agricultural hub and epicenter of global technocapitalism.[37] Merchants, industrialists, and robber barons, including Stanford University founder Leland Stanford, made their way west with haste, also finding opportunities with the Central Pacific Railroad Company of California. Stanford, who had already served one term as governor, saw the railroad's completion in 1869—an act that completed the transpacific infrastructure and that allowed capital to flow with newfound speeds across the United States. As part of what Manu Karuka describes as "railroad colonialism," this expansion, alongside a series of Homesteading Acts that facilitated white settlement, attracted settlers in the East to buy "unimproved" land surveyed and owned by the railroad.[38] Railroad companies even had "colonization offices" in Nordic European countries to recruit Western frontier occupiers, yet all the while depended on the labor of Chinese immigrants who were denied newly enclosed land.[39]

Stanford and his associates' business practices involving the railroad, but also the government, quickly became monopolistic. As Harris writes, Stanford "developed a stranglehold on economic and political life in California," indicative of a "strange new species of corporation."[40] Indeed, a cartoonist of the time, G. Frederick Keller, anthropomorphically mapped out the state's industries as an octopus, one in which agricultural industries, mining and infrastructural industries, and transportation industries were all connected, held together in the cephalopod's body that contained Stanford's face in its right eye.[41] As the 1882 "Curse of California" cartoon inferred, California's economic future was to be dictated by those who controlled the puppet strings of both technocapitalist innovation and government. Today, venture capitalists such as angel investor Ron Conway have followed this path well, funding tech-friendly elected officials and policy initiatives, and investing in tech start-ups such as Airbnb.[42] Conway has also invested seed funding in social media platforms such as Twitter/X, which masquerade as unbiased digital public squares yet are anything but public and unbiased. Martí too has built upon the tradition of using octopi to depict technocapitalist power in the Bay Area with his *Speculation Stole Our City* illustration created in collaboration with the San Francisco Anti-Displacement Coalition displaying the tentacles of gentrification including real estate speculation legal loopholes and short-term rental platforms.[43] As Keller's "The Curse of California" reveals, Silicon Valley projects of controlling politics behind the curtain of "openness" and "free speech" have historic precedent in the Bay Area.

This new monopolistic species of corporation depicted by Keller, like technocapitalist ventures that came before it, continued the tradition of exploiting racialized laborers who were denied land. From Mexican Americans who had lost citizenship as their homes were enclosed by US empire to Chinese immigrants who after being driven out of mining camps found work through sharecropping and performing stoop labor in strawberry fields and orchards, racial dispossession was prolific. In urban areas, Chinese and Japanese workers were prohibited from owning land via the Gentlemen's Agreement of 1907 and the Alien Land Law of 1913.

Yet, as David Pellow and Lisa Sun-Hee Park chronicle, these racialized practices of land and resource enclosure in what would later become Silicon Valley were not met without militant and strategic rebellion.[44] From Japanese labor strikes in the early 1900s to post–World War I labor conflicts between agricultural immigrant-led unions and largely Anglo-American management, struggles were prolific. This involved groups such as the Wobblies, the Teamsters Union, the United Farm Workers, the Cannery and Agricultural Workers Industrial Union, and more. In San Francisco, union organizing among longshoremen, seamen, and teamsters led to the 1934 General Strike, when 150,000 workers protested the police murdering two protesters and wounding hundreds during the West Coast Waterfront Strike.[45] At the time, the police had been sheltered in the same Armory building that Martí depicts in *Futuros Fugaces*.

Many union organizers of mid-twentieth-century San Francisco and beyond explicitly embraced socialist politics, mobilizing against prolific toxicity, injury rates, long hours, and exploitative technologies. As Curtis Marez writes, agribusiness technologies in the Central Valley and also in what would become Silicon Valley (yet at the time was an epicenter of fruit production) were determined to manufacture a white futurity, one that fetishized "new technology in an effort to eliminate resistance and subordinate workers of color to the machinery of production."[46] Yet at the same time, farm workers and unions crafted and mobilized technologies from below. In doing so, they crafted complex technocultures of resistance including visual documentation of abuse, speculative art projects, and technological appropriation. In Marez's words, "forces of rebellion and anti-imperial resistance have often appropriated technologies of time–space compression for their own ends."[47] All of this would continue to foster anticapitalist and anti-imperial dissent into and despite the Siliconized Cold War. While orchards became microchip foundries and Native lands were converted to white suburbs, organizers continued to mobilize against the racialized privatization of labor, land, and technology.

Cold War Silicon Valley

Haunting Cold War Silicon Valley were not only imperial pasts, but also the growing US war machine. Prior to World War II, the electronics industry was largely centered in the Midwest and the Northeast, where vacuum tubes and other goods were manufactured. After, companies such as IBM, the Food Machinery and Chemical Corporation, and numerous defense industry manufacturers turned toward San Jose and Santa Clara County. Stanford University soon became the recipient of numerous defense grants. In 1946, Bay Area financiers and university officials launched the Stanford Research Institute to accelerate industrial and defense research. Thus, as the 1947 National Security Act presaged the dawning of the Cold War, a conglomerate of higher education, military defense, and scientific research was already gaining funding. Government support for scientific freedom and the "Cold War multiversity" was only bolstered post-Sputnik as the Eisenhower administration endeavored to not fall behind in the space race.

While East Coast universities such as MIT were making short lobbying trips to Washington, DC, to secure support, the geographically distant Stanford University realized that setting up a Washington office would be more expedient than cross-country commuting.[48] In 1951, the Stanford Industrial Park was founded to lease land to tech companies. Much of this was overseen by Stanford's first dean of engineering, Frederick Terman—one of the "Fathers of Silicon Valley." Terman (whose father had been a champion of eugenics), convinced his former students William Hewlett and David Packard to start their own company. Hewlett-Packard, along with Lockheed Martin, General Electric, and more, soon settled into Stanford Industrial Park.[49] Terman's Silicon Valley coparent in this process was Stanford professor William Shockley, the Nobel Prize–winning creator of the transistor, who in 1956 established the first semiconductor laboratory in Mountain View. Shockley also became well known for his scientific racism and "retrogressive evolution," a eugenicist concept through which he framed Black people as less intelligent.[50] He even went so far as to advocate for sterilization of the "genetically disadvantaged."

The development of Silicon Valley eugenicist technoscience coincided with a broader US plot to employ scientists and psychologists to study the possibility of global dissemination of the democratic mind, merging science and politics to cultivate new anticommunist epistemologies of universal humanism. Norbert Wiener, theorist of human–machine interaction and coiner of "cybernetics," and Lyman Bryson, a champion of "scientific humanism," argued that democratic nations must utilize science and technology to construct social spaces in which individuals could obtain maximum freedom through the negation of communism.[51] A cohesive narrative was thus spun up in which the white capitalist man would triumph through technology. Meanwhile, economists such as Milton Friedman and Friedrich Hayek were hard at work scheming up neoliberal futures antipathic toward the social state.[52] These economic ideas would soon also inspire Silicon Valley economics as well.

In 1957, the defense industry experienced its first slump since 1939. In response, the government sold a huge bill of goods promulgating "arms for peace." American televisions began flooding viewers with anticommunist tropes such as "Beat the Russkies with nuclear physics" and "Better living through chemistry," producing what Ruth Wilson Gilmore describes as "the cultural and economic preconditions for Star Wars."[53] In 1958, the National Defense Education Act was passed, with science and engineering students being given near-free loans to advance anticommunist technoscientific research. By 1971, what had been previously known as "the Valley of Heart's Delight" for its abundance of orchards (built on the exploitation of racialized labor) was officially reconstituted as "Silicon Valley" in reference to the extracted mineral relied on by semiconductor companies to produce transistors and integrated circuit chips. Yet the electronics industry too relied on racialized, gendered labor in toxic conditions transpiring behind the smokescreen of white-collar scientific accomplishment. Pellow and Park have thus reframed the Valley of Heart's Delight to "the Valley of Toxic Fright."[54]

While it was largely immigrants laboring in high-risk hardware manufacturing environments, the figure of the white suburban scientific hero grew. Because the federal government worried that large urban centers would become easy Soviet atomic targets, urban planning practices of geographic dispersal coupled with widespread white flight sparked "slum" denigration, incentivized funding for suburban development.[55] The US Army erected prefabricated housing to attract and house this new resident in Silicon Valley—not so dissimilar from how real estate speculators in San Francisco today rebrand neighborhoods and properties to attract Google, Apple, and Facebook engineers.[56] Stanford's Board of Trustees meanwhile heralded the emergence of a post-Fordist "light industry of a non-nuisance type" that would "create a demand for technical employees of a high salary class that will be in a financial position to live in this area," or in other words, "a better class of workers."[57]

The framing of clean, light industry and its white suburban residents was set into relief against cities such as San Francisco and Oakland, which had, like many cities of the era, been plagued by white supremacist redlining along with policies of divestment and segregation fueled by the real estate industry. In San Francisco, the redevelopment of the predominantly Black neighborhoods of the Fillmore and Western Addition between the 1940s and 1970s saw tens of thousands of the city's Black community displaced, as the city became a testing ground for Cold War "urban renewal" and "slum clearance."[58] Japanese and Filipinx neighborhoods suffered similar fates, though Black neighborhoods were hit the hardest.[59] Marie Harrison—interviewed by the Anti-Eviction Mapping Project for the countercartography collective's *Black Exodus* zine[60]—recalls the devastation of seeing whole blocks get razed in the Fillmore: "It was like they came down overnight. It was like you're boarding up all of these units and moving everybody out. And there are people who are literally about to be homeless."[61] Many business owners who left the neighborhood intended to come back and reopen their shops, but then couldn't afford the new rents which seemingly tripled overnight. Many people relocated to Bayview-Hunters Point, where soon after, the Hunters Point Uprising was sparked in reaction to the white supremacist police violence that residents began to face upon relocation.

But police violence wasn't the only source of strife in Hunters Point—toxicity due to contaminants from the nearby shipyard began wreaking havoc. Upon relocation, Marie first obtained a job in the neighborhood's shipyard, unaware that the "little white stuff" from ship sandblasting drums scattered on her clothes, hair, and community was carcinogenic asbestos. As she describes, "A lot of people, upon the hill, have died from one thing or another. From asthma, cancers, you name it. Our asthma rates, our cancer rates, our heart disease rates, the premature babies—there's something going on that's not right.... On my block alone, on Quesada ... before my husband died, there had been eight men who died from two types of cancer."[62] Marie soon after became one of Bayview-Hunters Point's fiercest environmental justice advocates, organizing with groups like Greenaction against environmental racism before passing away due to the carcinogenic particles she began breathing at the age of seventeen.

In what is often portrayed as one of the most progressive, technologically advanced, and environmentally friendly US cities, health is only afforded to those who can purchase or rent from some of the country's most expensive properties. This is in part why Savannah Shange describes San Francisco as a "progressive dystopia" or "a city where industry and state development schemes collided to produce a racialized, uneven distribution of life and death."[63] Cold War visions of progress and renewal posit technology as a remedy for spatial improvement, but only for those already privileged through the ongoing project of enclosing the commons for those worthy of private "non-nuisance" space.

Yet, as the Hunters Point Uprising of 1966 reveals, this era wasn't only marked by loss. Rebellions in fact were taking place left and right. To name just a few, there were the Brown Berets in San Jose militating against the Vietnam War, the Free Huey rallies in Oakland and San Quentin Prison against the incarceration of the Black Panther Party (BPP) leader Huey P. Newton, the Third World Liberation Front strikes in Berkeley, the Filipinx-led I-Hotel campaign against racialized evictions in San Francisco, the American Indian Movement's reclamation of Alcatraz Island, Weather Underground organizing against US racial and imperial violence, and numerous campaigns for rent control and tenant protections in cities across the region. Many of these groups espoused genres of Marxism, and most were engaged in political work to collectively craft anticapitalist futures despite repression from US imperial forces.

There were also antiwar movements that specifically mobilized against Silicon Valley nuclear technologies. Student movements across the country meanwhile found targets in military-industrial labs on their college campuses, such as the Applied Electronics Laboratory at Stanford.[64] There was also Computer People for Peace (CPP), whose "Project IBM" protested the police use of IBM computers to track Black people in Apartheid South Africa (not so dissimilar from IBM'S punch card project used in the racializing of Roma and Jewish people in presocialist Romania, as I describe in chapter 4). Project IBM also grew out of CPP'S attempts to raise bail funds for BPP member Sundiata Acoli, who had been a computer programmer with NASA for twelve years prior to becoming politicized by the murder of Martin Luther King Jr. In 1969, after having become finance minister for the BPP, he was arrested as part of the Panther 21 case, in which BPP members were framed for acts later revealed to be linked to undercover agents.[65] As CPP cofounder Joan Greenbaum recounts of bail-raising tactics, "We talked about racism wherever we went, including computer conferences, demonstrations and discussions inside the companies we worked for."[66] She notes that much like today, tech companies of the time were feudalistic, with women and people of color often relegated to menial tasks such as keypunch operation. Part of the CPP goal, then, was to build feminist, antiracist, and anti-imperial power within the companies themselves in order to transform technoculture. Such tactics continued to inspire organizing efforts against racial technocapitalism in Cold War aftermaths.

Dot-Com Boom

With defense cutbacks following the end of the Cold War, questions arose as to the trajectory of Silicon Valley technologies. This coincided with the dawn of the internet and the World Wide Web, which became intricately woven into post–Cold War landscapes. While the internet was on one hand conceptualized to be "anti-spatial" and composed of a "negative geometry,"[67] it was anything but anti-spatial in technocapitalists' ongoing quest to grab, enclose, and accumulate land and data—building on Cold War imperiality. Yet for fifteen years before its commercialization, tens of thousands of small-scale computer networks had been created by amateurs across the country. As Kevin Driscoll documents, these were maintained by dial-up bulletin board systems operated by a range of modem aficionados, from HIV/AIDS activists to radio operators.[68] These networks, not capitalist in nature, laid the groundwork for corporations such as Netscape, Cisco, Hewlett-Packard, 3Com, and Intel to build on and exploit.

This new consumerist-based tech era was guided by what David Scott describes as "smugly confident liberalism," accumulating momentum by "re-territorializing power to roll back what was now perceived as the 'moral evil' of communism."[69] This is the period in which Michael Hardt and Antonio Negri wrote their seminal *Empire*, in which they illustrated how local territorial rule was being replaced with decentered and deterritorial global flows.[70] This, they suggested, effaced the tripartite geography of Second and Third World divisions, and coalesced something wholly new and interconnected. The Web and Silicon Valley were theorized as intricately part of this new social order, constituting the United States' "soft power" fueled by internet capitalism—the offspring of Cold War informatics but also the co-optation of what had been more of an internet commons.

With the collapse of the Iron Curtain, Silicon Valley technocapitalists delighted in the prospect of ingesting the former Second World's land, data, and infrastructure to further its imperial mission. Apple's former CEO and visionary Steve Jobs had already visited the Soviet Union, desirous of expanding business. Intel, the world's largest producer of semiconductor computer chips, similarly fantasized global scope with a caption below a 1977 photojournalistic piece reading, "The Sun Never Sets on Intel," mimicking the former trope acclaiming the scope of the British Empire.[71] Yet these Cold War fantasies proved difficult to actualize until the fall of the Berlin Wall. Not only did the West abet in engineering socialism's demise in countries such as Romania by disseminating anticommunist programs like Radio Free Europe,[72] but it then rushed in to co-opt socialist informatics infrastructure and create new consumer markets.

As Silicon Valley imperially began to seep past former Cold War borders, it quickly began to amass immense capital "at home." During the last quarter of the twentieth century, the Valley's housing prices rose more rapidly than anywhere else in the United States, totaling a 936 percent increase.[73] Left and right, the city encountered what Stephen Graham and Simon Guy call a "dot-com invasion" of entrepreneurs and internet industries espousing heteromasculine "omnipotence fantasies."[74] Former infrastructure, such as the Armory building depicted in Martí's illustration, also became repurposed as a data farm. As Richard Walker chronicled: "Obscure little South Park, once a refuge for a small black residential block, is now a popular eating spot for the denizens of Virtual valley, the new hot spot for multimedia electronics and computer magazine publishers."[75] During this time, evictions grew by 400 percent, with the Mission becoming a displacement epicenter.[76] Newcomers arriving to the Mission to work in tech were oftentimes hostile from the start, buying up buildings and evicting residents, even installing surveillance cameras to spy on their working-class Latinx neighbors. Yet, as Martí also alludes, direct action and organizing against this invasion fomented with groups such as the Mission Anti-Displacement Coalition fighting back and keeping people housed.

To combat multiple forms of resistance, post–Cold War Silicon imperial strategies began to encompass those of sublation. During this time, the Silicon suburb mutated into what Brian Chung describes as a "trans-Pacific hub of Chinese high-tech business," in which it became commonly ridiculed that "'Silicon Valley is built on ICs'—not integrated circuits but Indian and Chinese engineers."[77] On one hand, such proclamations of Asian inclusion produced techno-Orientalist fictions of Asians being simultaneously technologically superior but intellectually primitive, and thus in need of Westernization.[78] On the other, technoliberal Silicon Valley culture was pictured as one of meritocracy, multiculturalism, and postraciality. As Jobs suggested in 1997, racial difference does not matter; "What matters is how smart you are."[79] That same year, *Business Week* asserted that Silicon Valley was the "immigrant gateway" or "the quintessence of the American Dream," where "any good idea in a garage can turn into a gold mine" with "no pedigree required."[80] Yet anti-Asian racism flourished as the dot-com boom came crumbling down, with articles such as "No More Mr. White Guy" and "War Surplus Job-Market Misfits" blaming Asian domination on white job layoffs.[81] Yet the myths of digital meritocracy and technocratic colorblindness continue to pervade Silicon Valley thinking, which, in Safiya Noble and Sarah Roberts's words, "suppress interrogations of racism and discrimination even as the products of digital elites are infused with racial, class, and gender markers."[82]

As US empire continued to grow amid dot-com-boom advances and the newfound war on terror, Silicon Valley imperialism and US imperialism continued to coevolve. Amy Kaplan helpfully conceptualizes US empire as "a network of power relations that changes over space and time and is riddled with instability, ambiguity, and disorder, rather than as a monolithic system that the very word 'empire' implies."[83] She looks at how overseas US interventions and conquest have not only transformed global geopolitics but also domestic culture "at home." Although Kaplan's understanding of US imperialism is one that too easily brushes aside the continuity of settler colonialism, it is useful in theorizing how Silicon Valley imperialism abroad is tethered to Native conquest.

Take US military technology such as the "Apache helicopter," named after Southwest tribes that settlers first attempted to wipe out before appropriating the name with a military technology used to eradicate "illiberal" others overseas. There is also the open-source Apache Software Foundation, which cofounder Brian Behlendorf named in homage of "the last tribe to give up their territory," which for him "almost romantically represented what I felt we were doing with this web-server project."[84] This imperial ethos of "playing Indian" to grow Silicon projects has continued to protract past the dot-com boom. It informs figures such as the "digital nomad" (discussed in chapter 1), along with "white utopic" festivals such as Burning Man—well known for Native appropriation.[85] As Felicity Amaya Schaeffer historicizes, Indians have long been "romanticized as fiercely independent and thus ideal subjects exemplifying a rebellious individualism antagonistic to industrialized docility but were also considered a dangerous impediment to manifest destiny and thus to settler wealth and security."[86] This is why Native intelligence inspires US military technology projects today—ones that reproduce imperial violence in order to void Native sovereignty, and that remain materially tethered to growing Silicon Valley infrastructure and capital.

Tech 2.0 and the Sharing Economy

The dot-com boom busted shortly after it began due to overconfidence and failed investment strategies (perhaps something akin to the mass tech layoffs transpiring at the time of this writing in 2023). While the crash led to a decrease in rental and home prices in the Bay Area, it also impelled the restructuring of surviving companies into more robust capitalist machines led by Apple, Cisco, and Intel. Google and Facebook became rising stars, and then—in the aftermath of the foreclosure crisis which wrecked the slow gains made by people of color to build equity and secure stable housing across the region—Airbnb, Uber, Lyft, and sharing economy start-ups headquartered in San Francisco blossomed overnight. Twitter/X also launched in San Francisco, nestled into what soon became known as the Twitter Tax Break Zone, where tech companies avoid paying city taxes. As Wendy Liu offers of Tech 2.0 dreams:

> Silicon Valley is more than a region in northern California that has become synonymous with the high-tech industry. It is a dream. It is the dream of a world with new rules and new rulers, based on the principles of meritocracy and efficiency and hacking your way to the top. It is the dream of the win-win: innovation that generates profit through frictionless experiences

and synergistic efficiencies, not exploitation. It is the dream that a hacker playground with unimaginable wealth and minimal outside supervision is indisputably making the world a better place. But what may be a dream for a select few is steadily becoming a nightmare for everyone else.[87]

Welcome to the nightmare of the Tech 2.0 boom, where sharing economies and hacker playgrounds prosper yet where companies go out of their way to avoid paying for public goods. This technoliberal fervor protracts the technocapitalist imperative to deracinate socialist projects and imaginaries for profit.

As in prior eras, technocapitalist appropriation of socialist space has not been met without dissent. In 2014, for instance, what became known as the "Dropbox Dudes" video went viral. Titled "Mission Playground Is Not For Sale," the homemade YouTube clip features a group of white Airbnb and Dropbox employees mostly new to the city attempting to kick out Black and Latinx youth from the public Mission Playground to hold an informal corporate match.[88] At the time, Dropbox was in the process of expanding to a space large enough to hold an indoor soccer field, while Airbnb, also headquartered nearby, was facilitating the transformation of long-term affordable housing into short-term profitable vacation rentals under the veneer of "Fair to Share" marketing. In the viral video, the corporate employees pressure youth of color, most of whom had been playing pickup soccer in the playground for years, to abdicate the field. One of the youth, Kai (who has been evicted multiple times in the city), attempts to negotiate with the white men. One man, donning a Dropbox T-shirt, claims that the tech employees have the right to the field because his friend, Conor, reserved it through a new app. After some suspense, Conor enters the scene and waves a printed permit obtained through the app in the air as if it were a colonial flag. Generously, one of Kai's friends attempts to educate Conor that people have played soccer on that field without a permit for years. It makes no sense that they are now being asked to vacate the park because of an unheard-of app. As it turns out, the app had been created through a public/private partnership between the Recreation and Park Department and the City Fields Foundation run by the Fishers from the Gap company and the global capital firm, Charles Schwab. The app hadn't been made public yet, but it was available for tech companies such as Dropbox and Airbnb to test. Their access to the app—as privileged users effectively able to displace those foreclosed from being able to download it—highlights the contradictions of technoliberalism whereby technologies wedded to liberal conceptions of universality and freedom are applied only to those already benefiting from racial technocapitalist innovations.

That the app was made to capitalize on the concept of sharing public space—perhaps a step above Airbnb's marketing strategy of "sharing" the intimate private space of one's home—speaks to the anticommunism imbricated within technoliberalism. Technoliberalism, as Atanasoski and Vora write, "appropriates collaboration, sharing, and the commons to announce capital's unprecedented liberatory potential, while divesting the concepts it uses from an anticapitalist politics and ethos."[89] Liberal futurity and its technologies thus require the predation of anticapitalist ideals. Whereas Silicon Valley firms co-opt socialist-era infrastructure in cities such as Cluj to grow "little Silicon Valleys" abroad (as explored in chapter 1), technoliberal impulses assimilate spaces not yet enclosed through Siliconization into the laboratories of empire under the guise of equality.

The Mission Playground has been far from the only public space experiencing enclosure amid Tech 2.0 ascriptions of who is and who is not human. "Google buses," a vernacular stand-in for private luxury limousines contracted by companies including Google, Facebook, Apple, and Netflix, emerged during this time as well. Described by some as "alien overlords" crawling through city streets,[90] double-decker white luxury buses unavailable to the general public began shuttling white-collar workers from "cool, hip" urban centers to pastoral suburban tech campuses. The gist was that this program would incentivize techies to move to the Bay Area and work in Silicon Valley without having to actually live in the insipid suburbs. The program enabled private buses to co-opt public bus stops via a secret "handshake" agreement with the municipal transportation agency. Fallout from the program was widespread, for instance public buses being delayed due to the clogging up of their depots by private luxury vehicles. But also, real estate speculators found property proximate to the bus stops lucrative, and began listing apartments as "two blocks from the Google bus stop," "three blocks from the Facebook bus stop," and so on. As the Anti-Eviction Mapping Project illustrated at the time, rental prices and eviction rates followed suit, piling up around the co-opted, once-public depots.[91]

In response, tenants began orchestrating "Google bus blockades," many of which I helped organize with the direct action mutual aid collective Eviction Free San Francisco. While our blockades generally included pickets and speakouts in front of buses by tenants facing eviction, other groups such as the Heart of the City Collective featured festive, carnivalesque demonstrations.[92] On the other side of the Bay, anarchist groups in Oakland stylized blockades by weaponizing vomit, decorating hearses, and dropping banners with captions such as "Capitalism Is the Driver; Gentrification Is the Vehicle; Techies on the

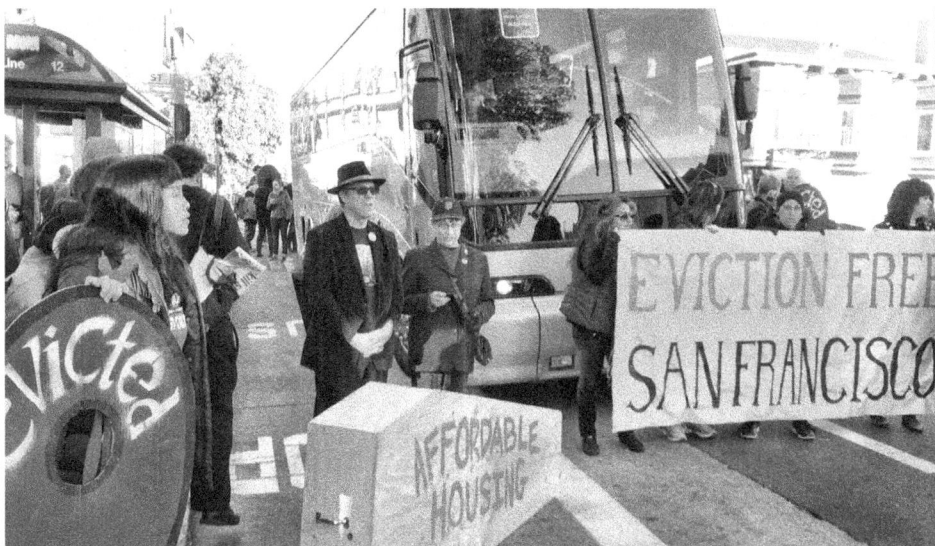

FIGURE 2.2. Housing organizers blockade a tech bus in San Francisco's Mission District. Photo by Kurtis Alexander, 2013.

Bus." The solidarity network, Defend the Bay, pleaded for "all Bay Area residents to take action against the tech takeover's many manifestations: increased rents, exclusive access to transportation, and the intensified police repression that accompanies gentrification, which is literally killing Black and brown residents in their own neighborhoods."[93]

Google bus blockades, while powerful and transformative for tenants facing eviction, were quickly portrayed as neo-Luddite, "anti-tech," and out of joint by liberal media. For instance, in 2015, *San Francisco Chronicle* writer Kristen Brown penned a story chastising a Google bus blockade that had taken place days before, characterizing it as anti-tech, juvenile, and unproductive.[94] This blockade wasn't organized to stop a particular eviction, but rather the replacement of teacher parking at the public Spanish immersion school, Fairmount Elementary School (now Dolores Huerta Elementary School), with a Google bus stop. The teacher who led the blockade, Claudia, was in the midst of fighting an eviction by Google's then head of e-security, and so she was already well versed in organizing blockades. Unlike some of the larger and more planned demonstrations against tech-induced displacement, this one was impromptu and small, though powerful for Claudia and those of us there.

While Brown's article chastised the demonstration due to its relatively small turnout, the point of this protest hadn't been one of spectacle-making, but rather to create an ephemeral moment in which to express anticapitalist worldmaking and collectivity. Maharawal, in reflecting on the Google bus protests, writes of how "affective transformation of feelings of disempowerment into sources of collective political action" was for those overwhelmed by feelings of dispossession and neglect.[95] Even if the bus blockades only thwarted global flows of capital for sporadic moments, by putting our bodies on the line in what was supposed to be public space, feelings of power and fearlessness became palpable. During the blockade at Fairmount, Claudia remarked that she no longer felt afraid in the overwhelming presence of gentrification. This gets at what Eric Stanley refers to as an "affective commons," which analytically highlights "how negative affect, or bad feelings, produce psychic bonds and collective energies in the practice of queer worlding."[96] By coming together and joining forces around a feeling of rage against the dispossession being viscerally experienced, a new commons is generated—one less tethered to making available colonized land and more rooted in "the irreducible friction of togetherness, the constriction of the 'we,' and its transformative potentiality to open to another world."[97] This new commons produces a genre of speculation antithetical to that of the real estate industry. It also weaves together a space of collectivity unassimilable to technoliberal impulses. Instead, this affective commons is rooted in the tradition of anti-imperial worldmaking, spatial justice, and anticapitalism.

Paralysis

Throughout the summer of 2014, the San Francisco Mime Troupe toured the Bay Area region with its satirical musical comedy *Ripple Effect*, written by Eugenie Chan, Tanya Shaffer, and Michael Gene Sullivan. The piece depicts familiar tensions on the city's gentrifying landscape where revolutionary potential gets swallowed by Siliconization, yet resistance ensues. Much of the comedy emerges aboard a small vessel named the *Distant Horizon*, which traverses the waters surrounding the peninsular city. The boat's paranoid captain, Deborah, is a former member of the BPP. Since the 1960s, she has been searching for a lost partner disappeared by COINTELPRO (the Cold War–era Counterinsurgency Program intended to surveil, infiltrate, and disrupt domestic political organizations). Onboard her ship are two passengers: Jeanine, an anxious, overstimulated app developer from Nebraska working for a tech giant, Octopus; and Sunny, a Vietnamese immigrant and defender of the American dream also traumatized by the Vietnam War. She runs a beauty salon in Hunters Point while also monitoring her daughter with a surveillance app invented by the uneasy Jeanine. Ironically, Sunny is now facing eviction because Jeanine's company is acquiring new office space in the gentrifying neighborhood. And so go typical technocapitalist geographies of San Francisco.

As the story unfolds, we learn that Deborah's partner was not disappeared, but rather he went underground, only to reemerge as the CEO of Octopus, Jeanine's boss. The play reaches its apex as the women realize that the only way to dismantle the panoptic Octopus is for all three of them to collaborate, dismantling its systems through a backdoor Jeanine had coded into the surveillance app. At first Jeanine is reticent, complaining to the adamant Deborah that she is not political, and that she does not know how to fight the Silicon empire. To this, Deborah dramatically retorts, "There is no such thing as not political!" much to the crowd's delight. Later, Deborah interrogates Sunny's middle-class identity, vehemently shouting, "There is no middle-class; there is only the working-class!" As Sullivan later confided, the performance was meant to intimate that growing working-class consciousness is integral in fighting the power of tech giants.[98] The performance concludes with the women acknowledging that together, through direct action, they can keep Sunny and her daughter housed. Anticapitalist and anti-imperial politics thus resurface in the struggle against Silicon Valley imperialism.

Months before the performance, Eviction Free San Francisco was asked by the Mime Troupe to participate in their 2014 debut in Dolores Park in San Francisco rallying the audience after the protest. Just a block away from the performance was Claudia's home, where she and her neighbors were facing eviction from Google's then head of e-security. The Mime Troupe had envisioned that following the performance's rallying cry, audience members would be inspired to take action. But instead, people seemed generally too committed to their artisanal picnics to crawl up Dolores Street to Claudia's home. In this sense, what Gary Wilder describes as a "politicotemporal paralysis" took over, whereby imaginaries of freedom have been eclipsed by those of markets and in which alternatives to liberal capitalist democracy appear foreclosed.[99] In addition to Silicon Valley imperialism, some of the *Distant Horizon*'s biggest obstacles are the pervasive powers of politicotemporal paralysis and techno-liberal dissolution. Such an affective foreclosure to commonist possibilities, alongside the monopolistic future-making portended in G. Frederick Keller's 1882 "Curse of California" cartoon,[100] haunts the present heavily. Is there any ability to find freedom from technocapitalist tentacles that span centuries? Or does its weight paralyze possibilities of dissent?

Paralysis here collapses sharing economy logics and anticommunist historiography into end-of-history futurity. It galvanizes imaginaries that common spaces are simply those for entertainment and artisanal picnics rather than stages for organizing. Perhaps this has to do with how understandings of common spaces themselves are so often divorced from decolonial politics and histories. It also reflects how technoliberal initiatives co-opt these commoning acts and spaces for capitalist use. As Stanley elaborates, "As a place, a structure of feeling, and an idea, the commons provides refuge in the ruins of capital's totality, yet its liberatory promise is betrayed by the abstraction of Indigenous land, which is to say the imposition of settler-sovereignty, that allows it to be imagined in the first instance."[101] By remaining hypnotized by settler fantasies of common land for the taking, communalism is evacuated of anti-imperial potentiality and instead made available for artisanal picnics, Dropbox-Airbnb matches, and Google bus stops.

Artificial Enclosure

The Tech 2.0 economy experienced a massive plummet during the COVID-19 pandemic—one that at the time of this writing San Francisco has not yet recovered from. Its own paralysis is often blamed on a combination of it having "put all of its eggs" into one tech basket, the numerous economic effects of the pandemic on the tech industry, and perhaps most significantly, the ongoing lack of adequate protections for renters, the unhoused, and communities bearing the brunt of racial capitalism's crises. On one hand, dystopian media analysis has been fixated on portraying the "failed" city as a harbinger of "dangerous" unhoused people and abandoned shops, one that requires renewed carceral securitization through police and surveillance technology.[102] On the other, the Silicon Valley economy continues to flourish and amass power for white-collar tech elites, in part due to widespread investment into AI products such as ChatGPT. The market has begun to compare this new AI boom with the early-1990s dot-com boom when Wall Street bet on internet companies such as Cisco and Oracle.[103] Others are calling it the new gold rush.[104]

While media portrayals of San Francisco are currently filled with doom and gloom, in part to encourage racial capitalist investment in securitization techniques, a number of tech elites are also reifying a narrative of the portending AI apocalypse. This account portrays a bleak future in which AI-powered programs will take over the world and render human labor and life obsolete. Strategically, this tale has been used to spin up a new genre of investment in "ethical AI," "open AI," and "effective altruism"—all initiatives based in elite tech spaces such as Stanford University. These seek to reform algorithmic programs "for good," rather than heed calls that racial justice organizers and scholars have long made to abolish violent tools.[105] Reform here serves as a liberal guise, with effective altruists such as Sam Bankman-Fried proposing to purchase the entire nation of Nauru to build a bunker and "wait out the end of the world."[106] In this overt exemplar of Silicon Valley imperialism and technoliberalism alike, survival on a planet poisoned by the toxins of technocapitalism is only safeguarded for those profiting from it upon colonized space.

Strategically, these dystopic AI conversations also obviate that it continues to be corporations rather than magical machines amassing technocapitalist power and reanimating decades-old computing techniques. In the words of Meredith Whittaker and Lucy Suchman, "The term 'artificial intelligence' is widely recognized by researchers as less a technically precise descriptor than an aspirational project that comprises a growing collection of data-centric technologies."[107] In this sense, conversations about the AI boom fictionalize that something new is at play rather than acknowledge that companies such as Google, Microsoft, Amazon, and Facebook are continuing to amass computation power even if masqueraded in openness.

The AI apocalyptic storyline thus produces an artificial enclosure, circumscribing technological future-making possibilities within the ever expanding domain of those who promulgate its narratives. Such accounts reify what Atanasoski and Vora describe as "the surrogate human effect," in which by mediating racial logics of differentiation, categorization, and elimination, technological innovation becomes a surrogate for the liberal subject.[108] Put differently, conversations about automated futures become activated as surrogates to an imagined postracial and postgendered universal future freed from degrading forms of human labor. Surrogate humanity in this way "stretches from the disappearance of native bodies necessary for the production of the fully human, through the production of the fungibility of the slave's body as standing in for the master, and therefore also into the structures of racial oppression that continue into the postslavery and post–Jim Crow periods, and into the disavowal of gendered and racialized labor supporting outsourcing, crowdsourcing, and sharing economy platforms."[109] Thus, technological apocalypse visions and resultant calls to invest in "good systems" obscure technocapitalism's racial logics of dispossession. Ignored are the histories of degrading racialized forms of labor that have long powered technological innovation in the region. Also omitted are the multitudes of anticapitalist and abolitionist political projects crafting other techno urban futures—ones that refuse technocapitalism's artificial enclosures, and that in doing so, live beyond the end of the world.

Commons beyond the End of the World

While the Armory building that Martí illustrated no longer houses military personnel, servers, or porn production equipment, it does still sit squarely in the middle of the Siliconized Mission District, distinctly out of joint and haunted by imperial pasts and presents. Martí reflects, "Today, with National Guard troops mobilizing around the country to quell uprisings, the building had a different resonance." Produced in the aftermaths of the killing of George Floyd by Minneapolis police and the resultant uprising for Black lives, the Hunters Point Uprising seeps into the present. But also bubbling below the brick building is a natural spring connected to the nearby Mission Creek. Every rain floods the basement with water, connecting its catacombs to waterways that precede the colonization of the Mission and subsequent racial violence. Per Martí, "I originally imagined it sitting on a lake, with squatter shacks hanging off its walls like the hills above Guayaquil or Caracas. But as I thought more of rising seas and adapting to the new climates we will all be facing, the image that stuck was of the chinampas, the floating gardens of Tenochtitlán, still practiced in Xochimilco." In this sense, Martí gestures to technological practices that connect the past to the present, and that help carve out emergent technofuturist ecologies and solidarities beyond technologies of the police, the military, and property. These futures, he writes, "will contain hints of the dystopias we're already living through, and they will contain the messiness and contradictions of our cultures, a collage of *rasquachismo* (an underdog, working-class Chicano aesthetic sensibility),[110] rooted in a reclamation of ancestral traditions and collective memory to urban land struggles and queer ecologies."

Here Martí gestures toward technologies of worldmaking and collectivity that while cognizant of imperial technological violence also find hope in emancipatory technological possibilities. Nick Estes describes this technological conjuncture well:

> Technology is interesting because its value is socially constructed. For Native nations, technological progress is usually top-down. It's usually something that's forced on us. More generally, capitalism as a social process has devastated our communities. It has ensured that we don't have self-determining authority over the means of production that are located on our land. . . . At the same time, I would say that Indigenous ontologies and ways of being are social systems that value different things than settler ontologies, so our technologies look different. Indigenous technology gets cast as primitive, like it may have been useful in

the past but no longer has any relevance. But that's not true. Assembling communal life is in itself a technology.[111]

Thus, despite the impending doom of Siliconized dispossession, anticapitalist and anti-imperial technologies of communing continue to blossom in pavement cracks, jutting out beyond the shadows of sterilized condos. In their work theorizing "postcapitalism," J. K. Gibson-Graham suggest that postcapitalist politics focuses on a rich landscape of already-existing capitalist refusals.[112] These emerge locally and often autonomously, not necessarily rooted in state revolutionary models. Building on this, Atanasoski and Vora offer that in crafting postsocialist politics, it is urgent to consider "the relationship between the afterlives of distinct, if interlinked, socialisms, and the politics of revolution as a mode of social transformation."[113] Such a repositioning allows us to account for the multiple socialisms already alive and thriving, and to understand commoning projects beyond state enclosures that thrive despite feelings of paralysis.

Rethinking socialisms as they interlock anticapitalist spaces and dreams also updates communist futures past. As Peter Linebaugh historicizes, in the 1840s, communism was used to express the revolutionary dreams of proletarians.[114] "The commons," meanwhile, was apprehended as a vestige of the past from an attempt against feudal destruction (though brought into the future with the Paris Commune). Nevertheless, Linebaugh suggests that today, "the semantics of the two terms seem to be reversed, with communism belonging to the past of Stalinism, industrialization of agriculture, and militarism, while the commons belongs to an international debate about the planetary future of land, water, and subsistence for all. What is sorely needed in this debate so far is allegiance to the actual movement of the common people who have been enclosed and foreclosed but are beginning to disclose an alternative, open future."[115] Common people today are after all actively opening futures for anti-imperial collectivities. This is not done in the cramped space of the sharing economy, but rather in affective worldmaking spaces of bus blockades, playground demonstrations, and anticolonial speculation. Even amid the driverless car frenzy of 2023, as automated robo-taxis appear on practically every San Francisco street—often accidentally glitching out, stalling other vehicles, and occasionally running into pedestrians per Silicon experimentation—frustrated residents have found affective solace in the ability to temporally blockade cars by placing traffic cones on their hoods, in turn confusing their algorithms.

While this book's other chapters bring into focus commoning struggles in formerly state socialist space, this chapter instead theorizes postsocialist commoning projects antipodally. Here I build on Ruth Wilson Gilmore's vision of "small-c communism," or communism without a party, one committed to the broader project of abolishing the prison industrial complex and its claims on private property.[116] Or, as Rinaldo Walcott puts it, "Abolishing property and creating new meanings for understandings and relationships around the things that make life livable and enjoyable is central to all abolitionist claims."[117] For him, the first step in abolition begins by fostering a communalism that draws on Indigenous perspectives of land and lifeworlds. This speaks to what Nik Heynen has illustrated as practices of re-Earthing, which involves "working in common on common land" in order to materialize a politics of reparation.[118] As he critiques, throughout the last centuries, it has mostly been white men discussing property and the commons rooted in English and German contexts, mobilizing Western Eurocentric frameworks that ignore colonial, white supremacist, and patriarchal uneven power relations.[119] Much of this scholarship has negated feminist, Indigenous, and marronage defenses of common spaces within and beyond the West.[120] Recovering an unpublished speech that Clyde Woods delivered in 2009, Heynen quotes Woods:

> The commons is not just a pre-capitalist formation. It's creating the idea, by the people who are displaced by this process, it's creating the idea that there are new alliances to create new commons, but it's also creating new commons themselves, on the margins, in the swamps, as they say in New Orleans, but through a number of different ways by working class communities. . . . So, a plantation can be a commons, a ghetto can be a place of refuge and resistance, affirmation, so this commons is created both theoretically but also in fact by the very process of the extension of capitalism and is the original extension of its reproduction.[121]

Learning from Woods, then, commoning practices can be understood as both active praxes of recovery, reclamation, and rematriation, but also, sometimes, as those generating emancipatory anticapitalist, anti-imperial worlds in the midst of empire. Commons can be found within and despite geographies of Siliconization, not through the sharing economy but instead in active spaces of dissent carved out by common people.

It was such a vision that inspired Martí's *Futuros Fugaces*, in which Indigenous technologies of regeneration nurture the lands and water surrounding and flowing through the Armory building—despite its prior role in quelling racial justice uprisings and in fostering Silicon Valley imperial topographies. In another of his illustrations, *On Indigenous Land*, Martí further reflects on decolonizing commonist work. He had been asked to reflect on the commons yet was troubled by liberal conceptual commonist frameworks deracinating the commons from Native lands. As he writes, "Here in San Francisco where I live and work, I am constantly aware of development and the modern city being built on stolen land, the rising new skyscrapers downtown that are built over an erasure of history."[122] While portraying this history of dispossession, Martí also depicts native plants, a California condor, and Ohlone canoeists traversing the San Francisco Bay with the Siliconized city skyline blocking out the background.

This refusal of Siliconized overdetermination was conceptualized in collaboration with the Sogorea Te' Land Trust, an Indigenous feminist rematriation project working to reclaim Ohlone land and culture. As the first urban Indigenous women-led land trust, their ongoing project is one of decolonizing and commoning. Cofounder Corrina Gould (also the tribal spokesperson for the Confederated Villages of Lisjan) suggests that this work requires a recognition of belonging to the land itself. Such a commonist relationship, she notes, has been under threat for over 250 years not only by Spanish missionaries, the Mexican government, and then the US government, but also by contemporary gentrification.[123] Yet the very being of the Sogorea Te' Land Trust and its project of rematriating the village of Lisjan (which sits within the territory of Huchiun in the heart of deep East Oakland) counters the dispossessive impulses of Silicon Valley imperialism and its attempts to co-opt space, sharing, and the future. It aligns with what Estes and others have been championing as the Red New Deal, a plan that centers land decolonization and "the caretaking economy," or a system that "seeks to live in a correct relation with each other as human beings and nations, as well as a correct relation with the nonhuman world."[124] This is not an economy that is Siliconizable, as its orientation is anticapitalist. Aligned with practices of weaving together both affective and antiimperial commons, it reaches for a future that, in Stanley's words, "might help chart a politics after the political, or a way to survive the unsurvivable present, and remain beyond the end of the world."[125]

The Technofascist Specters
of Liberalism

It was during the throes of the COVID-19 pandemic that the Alianța pentru Unirea Românilor (Alliance for the Union of Romanians/AUR) party gained parliamentary power in Romania. AUR, which translates to "gold" in Romanian, celebrates the Iron Guard Legionnaire movement, the populist presocialist fascist force that endeavored to cleanse the country of its Jews, Roma, queers, deviants, and communists. Legionnaires were also called "Greenshirts" given their standard green uniform, a nod to Hitler's "Brownshirts" and Mussolini's "Blackshirts." Their power was amassed during the region's so-called golden era, during which Bucharest was considered "the Little Paris of the East"—an aspirational bourgeoisie fantasy of Western recognition today being updated through liberal fantasies of Siliconization. This desire to return to presocialist golden times is thus shared between advocates of liberal Westernization and fascist nationalists alike.

While small nationalist and far-right groups have existed in Romania throughout the postsocialist period, until AUR's ascent the country had been one of the few in Eastern Europe "liberal enough" to keep an overtly fascist group out of parliament. Prior, the Partidul România Unită (United Romania Party/PRU) had unsuccessfully attempted a bid, reflecting "phoenix populist" tendencies, whereby far-right parties ritualistically reemerge in new forms.[1] Similar to AUR, the PRU espoused "regaining Romania for Romanians," inferring desires to cleanse the country of Roma people who they termed "assisted people"—a burden on the welfare system.[2] As PRU leader Cristian Diaconu had alleged, "Perhaps Romanians have had enough of these assisted [people], whose only illness is not wanting to work, of these minorities who want to rule the country, to have a state within a state."[3] He also invoked presocialist anti-Semitism, during which the Legionnaires based their genocidal logics on allegations that Romania had become colonized with Jews. AUR updated these sentiments, also stoking widespread COVID-19 pandemic-era racism in the region, which framed Roma people as vectors for viral spread. Vocal party member Sorin Lavric described Roma people as a "social plague," while mass media and social media alike targeted people returning home from the diaspora.[4]

While much of the early AUR movement relied on Facebook channels,[5] it also developed on the backdrop of liberal Light Revolution protests in which tech workers and those committed to preserving the golden era mobilized Siliconized technoculture to grow a populist anti-corruption movement. Gaining fame for the utilization of smartphones, lasers, and light technology, the Light Revolution was largely led by middle-class millennials upholding capitalist fantasies of Westernization along with architects hoping to preserve interwar cultural heritage. Espousing anticommunism, demonstrators made their enemy the ruling and corrupt Partidul Social Democrat (Social Democratic Party/PSD)—a neoliberal party which, due to its former, albeit weak, connection with the former socialist-era elite, has become the subject of ongoing red baiting. While undoubtedly the PSD is corrupt, the anticommunist Light Revolution failed to acknowledge the corrupt nature of the country's other neoliberal parties, not to mention the Western disaster capitalism that has drained the country of labor, land, and lifeworlds following the end of state socialism in 1989. Yet Light Revolution logics reduce socialism from a pluralistic political field to a corrupt neoliberal party—one cast as requiring Western salvation.

Such spatiotemporal tension is the subject of this chapter, which examines the technofascist possibilities that liberal anticommunist spaces of protest and urban renewal foment. By technofascism, I reference the mechanisms and technological fantasies through which fascist conditions of possibility materialize. Rather than fall into stereotypical liberal invocations of Romania and Eastern Europe as historical and geopolitical sites from which to theorize the prefiguration of illiberalism, authoritarianism, totalitarianism, and fascism in a post–Trump era West, I instead ask: What can Eastern European anticommunist movements teach about the contradictions of Euro-American liberalism made apparent in its recent crises? As I show, ongoing Western liberal allegations of Russia, China, and Eastern Europe political worlds responsible for the rise of Trump and his Make America Great Again (MAGA) movement not only obscure the deep history of white supremacist imperial violence constitutive of the United States, but also take for granted the post–Cold War other as the nexus of illiberalism. This obfuscates the role that liberalism has played in emboldening fascism in both the East and West, which has had everything to do with anticommunist spatiotemporality and the ongoing hold of Enlightenment dreams of Western modernity in both.

The recirculation of "Cold War" as a frame of reference for geopolitics today rehearses the terms of Cold War liberalism in its binary logics to conflate capitalism with democracy, transparency, and accountability, often to the detriment of those who bear the burden of disaster capitalism. Kristen Ghodsee writes, "Just as the popular stereotype of communism is rarely uncoupled from the state repression of the twentieth-century experience of it, today . . . the democratic ideal is becoming inseparable from the social chaos neoliberal capitalism has wreaked in its name."[6] In this chapter, I push this coupling further to question how the democratic ideal in fact necessitates the grotesque coupling of socialism with corruption, in turn emboldening racial capitalism and fascistic power to grow. This coupling is endemic to Western characterizations of much of Eastern Europe since transition, protracting Cold War structures of illiberal enmity into the twenty-first century. In 2008, conservative Eastern European politicians and intellectuals went as far as to sign the Prague Declaration, equating the victims of state socialism with those of Nazi Germany, demanding justice from EU governing bodies. Throughout Romania today, there are monuments dedicated to anticommunist resistance, like the one in Cluj's Central Park adorned with a Romanian and EU flag. Here, communism and fascism are interpreted as one and the same—the evil, fascistic monster that liberal capitalism will cure. This gets at what Lilith Mahmud critiques as the spectral powers of fascism, which are summoned as an imminent threat that liberalism must stand up against.[7]

While liberalism does often enough oppose fascist grammars, it also often marginalizes antifascist organizing and anticapitalist positions in order to preserve capitalism's reign. This was made evident during the rise of Mussolini and Hitler, but also Antonescu in Romania.[8] As Clara Zetkin contended in a 1923 speech to the Enlarged Plenum of the Communist International's Executive Committee, fascism emerged out of "the imperialist war and the accelerated dislocation of the capitalist economy" with a goal of suppressing the growing Comintern International "for the exploited of all races."[9] Put differently, liberal capitalism, as she saw it, had fostered conditions for fascism to spread by not actively supporting the plight of those racially exploited by it. This has long been germane within but also beyond Europe. As W. E. B. Du Bois once reflected, "Hitler and Mussolini were fighting communism, and using race prejudice to make some white people rich and all colored peoples poor. But it was not until later that I realized that the colonialism of Great Britain and France had exactly the same object and methods as the fascists and the Nazis were trying clearly to use."[10] Du Bois and Zetkin, along with anticolonial contemporaries such as George Padmore, Jawaharlal Nehru, and Aimé Césaire,[11] made clear that anticommunism consolidates the powers of empire, racial capitalism, and fascism alike transnationally.

During the Cold War, the US project of statecraft cast Soviet totalitarianism as its strategic enemy, which according to Nikhil Pal Singh, became the "primary explanatory terrain" regarding post–World War II European geopolitical stratifications.[12] The very theory of totalitarianism thus grew as a legitimating force of US empire, which discursively consolidated power by framing its monstrous double abroad as evil. This also worked at home, where communist uprisings led by groups such as the Black Panther Party, the United Farm Workers, the Weather Underground, and the American Indian Movement were framed as illiberal.[13] Liberal futures were posited as ones void of these anti-imperial Marxist movements. Alyosha Goldstein and Simón Ventura Trujillo offer, "Fascisms call attention to how the elevation of a Euro-American liberal antifascism continues to serve as a domesticating intellectual and cultural force, one that casts the horror of European fascism and Soviet totalitarianism as the foil against which the militarized and carceral expansion of the warfare-welfare state would be pursued as freedom."[14] Put differently, the collapsing of fascism, illiberalism, and communism together has fueled US imperial technologies such as carcerality and militarism.

In the wake of Trumpian illiberalism, some scholars have begun to wonder whether postsocialism finally has something theoretical to offer the West due to its ability to theorize illiberalism. These ideas often hinge on anticommunist Western media hype that reify interwar and Cold War fascist specters in order to keep US liberal empire alive. As Dace Dzenovska and Larisa Kurtović argue, "A quick overview of interventions made by or on behalf of (post)socialist subjects in the Western media at the moment reveal that there are at least four dimensions to the newfound public audibility of the (post)socialist subject: (1) knowledge of totalitarianism/authoritarianism; (2) knowledge of fascism/

nationalism; (3) knowledge of Russia; and (4) prefiguration of the future of the West."[15] As they elaborate, that which made the postsocialist subject irrelevant to Western knowledge production in the past is precisely that which tenders its relevancy today. However, it is not because the postsocialist subject understands the perils of fascism that makes postsocialism germane, but rather postsocialism's ability to theorize the perils of liberalism. In the words of Neda Atanasoski and Kalindi Vora, "The dominance of present-day liberal politics, which collapse political notions of freedom with the unrestricted spread of free markets, and justice with liberal rights-based outcomes, beg for an extended exploration of the aftermaths of the social, political, and cultural disappearance and subsequent reconfiguration of a socialist political imaginary."[16] If there is any prefiguration to be done in postsocialist space, liberalism rather than illiberalism might be the more politically salient object of critique.

In this chapter, I examine spaces of Romanian protest over the last decade, not to prefigure illiberal futurity, but rather to assess the workings of liberalism in postsocialist contexts. I focus on the suppression of anti-imperial and anticapitalist organizing, looking at how emancipatory spaces become corrupted by Silicon fantasies, which then facilitates footholds for fascism to root. I begin by mapping out the antimining Salvați Roșia Montană (Save Roșia Montană) protests of 2013, throughout which tens of thousands took to the streets in protest of extractive mineral technologies being enacted by a Canadian gold mining company. While initially anticapitalist in its framing, the protest movement became increasingly liberal, adopting what might be understood as an "all protesters matter" ethos. In doing so, it began failing to attend to the racial technocapitalist dynamics undergirding the mining project itself. By disavowing anticapitalist organizers in favor of a politically open stance, a space of populist uprising created the conditions for the Light Revolution and its Silicon Valley aspirational politics to fester. These, I show, have expressed a specifically postsocialist spatiotemporality characterized by desires to return to the golden past on one hand, but to gain Silicon status on the other. To better theorize this conjuncture, in this chapter I also look to the role of a cultural heritage movement that backed Light Revolution Enlightenment golden era fantasies. As Veda Popovici argues, "These networks didn't see themselves as right-wing but they were accommodating the self-described right-wing groups who were more palatable for the liberal taste,"[17] thus laying the groundwork for today's fascist turn.

While examining these geographies of liberalism mapped onto populist spaces of dissent, I also look to a protest that never came to be—that against the multinational IKEA company. Over the last decade, IKEA, much like mining companies, has seen Romania as a site of resource extraction. Yet its role in exploiting local forest worlds is not rendered as problematic as Canada's stake on Romania's minerals—in part due to the aspirational status that IKEA bears in urban space. Not only is IKEA furniture indexical of affordable Western modernity for many, but also, the company plays a significant role in the development of Bucharest tech office space bearing promises of Siliconization. This in part explains why so few people have organized forest defense, while hundreds of thousands continue to protest government corruption and communist ghosts. Might it be that these anticommunist desires incarcerate real possibilities of dissent, ones necessary in combating a growing landscape marked by Silicon Valley imperialism, racial technocapitalism, and technofascism alike? I conclude by turning to the rise of the MAGA movement in the United States, assessing how it has become emboldened by an apocryphal fear materialized by liberal denigrations of communism.

Blood Gold

Roșia Montană (Red Mountain), a part of the Apuseni Mountains nestled into Transylvania's Carpathian mountain range, has long been scarred and bloodied by extractive mining techniques. Since the Roman Empire, imperialists have set their eyes on what is today the continent's largest gold deposit.[18] The socialist state also took advantage of the mountain's riches, yet it has been in postsocialist times through land privatization practices that the mountain has been made vulnerable to global capital. This has been supported by the project of Westernization, which heralds anticommunist imaginaries of post-1989 "cleaner" and "lighter" technologies necessary in liberating Romania from heavy industry and gray polluted landscapes endemic to socialist industrialization.[19] EU and Bretton Woods incentives also support land restitution practices, or the reprivatizing of forests and agricultural property that had been rendered a public good during socialism. In 2006, when the European Parliament's Foreign Affairs Committee voted on reports concerning Romania's entry into the EU, it was suggested that the country "speed up the processing of claims relating to the restitution of properties confiscated by the communist regime" and that it should make further efforts in protecting the environment from "large-scale mining projects having substantial environmental implications, as in the case of Rosia Montana."[20]

State socialism did indeed play a role in the mountain's ecological devastation. The Communist Party took control of Roșia Montană in 1948, and then maintained underground and open surface operations into the 1970s.

During this time, the regime sought to reduce debt and foreign dependency, from reliance on Polish copper imports to the Soviet Union's COMECON economic assistance project. Local mining was one of many means to economic independence. As many of the gold-bearing veins had been exhausted by the 1970s, and as the regime tripled its debt between 1974 and 1979, the state turned to strip-mining, forever altering the landscape. This wasn't unique to Roșia Montană. Nearby, for instance, the abandoned village of Geamăna haunts the region as a ghost town physically under red water. It was in 1977 that four hundred village residents were displaced after the state discovered a massive copper deposit nearby and decided to create an artificial catch basin for the mine's contaminated cyanide sludge. Its cinematic effects linger to date, having subsumed the local houses, church, and cemetery, pooling toxic red cyanide into domestic spaces and the graves of former miners. A church steeple still floats above the crimson waterline as if a tall, thin sailboat on the horizon.

But projects such as these pale in comparison to those speculated on by Gabriel Resources, which entered the scene in the rubble of socialism's collapse and the rampant state austerity that followed. The Canadian company's speculative Romanian project actually began in Austria in 1995 when the London-based Romanian-Austrian businessman Vasile Frank Timiș launched Gabriel Resources NL Austria. Timiș was already renowned for his brutal iron ore mining operations in Sierra Leone, which had led to the displacement of local villagers and earned him the nickname, "Emperor of African Resources."[21] That same year, the Romanian state-owned mining company Regia Autonomă a Cuprului began searching for a private company to partner with to mine precious metals from both Roșia Montană and the nearby Gurabarză-Brad. The Eurogold Resources joint venture thus formed, financed in large part through Timiș's gold exploits. Lingering financial problems led to his regrouping under Gabriel Resources Limited in 1996, sheltered in a Jersey tax haven. Through elite connections, Timiș found access to various Romanian mineralogy research databanks and hired research scientists from the topographic department of the Romanian Ministry of Defense who "discovered" gold, silver, and other valuable minerals in the region. The state-owned Minvest was also pulled in, soon becoming a partner of Gabriel's Roșia Montană Gold Corporation (RMGC), which only allocated the state company a small portion of its shares.

Early on, RMGC furnished two "Urbanism Plans" to slate the region into an industrial playground for extraction forty times the size of the state socialist operation. Romania, once dubbed "the granary of Europe," seemed to have been discovered by a new genre of capitalism hungry for a new type of grain. This involved the exploitation of three hundred tons of gold and 1,600 tons of silver, along with the eradication of three villages and four mountains, not to mention the replacement of two thousand people with a forty-five-hectare tailing pond. The sludge basin was slated to be built on the Corna River and would require a six-hundred-meter-wide dam that would change the river's direction.[22] This would not only pollute nearby rivers and destroy the ecosystem but would also threaten the health of six thousand people and countless other species living downstream. While cyanide and sulphocyanide-rich sludge were the main toxins of concern, the extraction project would also unearth toxic minerals such as germanium, tellurium, arsenic, lead, and zinc. Gabriel's project also threatened ancient monuments of the area, much to the chagrin of heritage preservationists as well as the Ministry of Justice, which argued that the project would violate Articles 44 and 136 of the Romanian Constitution on the right to private property and modalities of state expropriation. Even the Romanian Orthodox Church came out in opposition. Others observed the absurdity that Romania was projected to only benefit from 6 percent of Gabriel's profits.[23]

All of this was fodder for antimining organizing from local villagers. In 2000, farmers formed the NGO Alburnus Maior and prepared to enter legal battle. Two years later, they launched the Salvați Roșia Montană campaign. Then in 2004, activists held the summer Fân Fest festival in the mountain, building up collective ecological and anti-imperial solidarity. So, when in September 2013 the PSD government conceded to Gabriel's lobbying pressures and permitted mining authority, there was already a large base from which to build resistance. A series of local and national protests were sparked under the banner of Salvați Roșia Montană and Uniți Salvăm (United We Save). At the time, these amounted to the largest series of protests since 1989, with thousands of protesters taking to the streets each Sunday. Solidarity actions also took place in Western cities, with demands that Romania sever all ties with Gabriel. Over five thousand activists meanwhile held a gathering nearby in Câmpeni to present a declaration demanding the prohibition of cyanide and hydraulic fracking, the declassification of government relations with Gabriel Resources, criminal investigations into supporters of the project, and Roșia Montană gaining inclusion on Romania's UNESCO World Heritage site list.

Predictably, the PSD prime minister at the time, Victor Ponta, sided with Gabriel, accusing antimining activists of extremist behavior. In response, protesters cited Ponta's own political corruption—an accusation that would continue to grow in upcoming years. They also critiqued Gabriel for having purchased $5.4 million in ads, many of which depicted antimining advocates as being vagrants, drug users, and minions of George Soros.[24] Gabriel also denounced the "dirty" socialist-era mining practices of the past, mobilizing the language of "sustainable development," "environmental sustainability," and "corporate social responsibility" to justify extraction. Additionally, Gabriel invoked a 2006 film that they had funded, *Mine Your Own Business*. In it, the mining project is positioned as freeing locals from poverty and propelling Romania into Western technological futurity. It features a local twenty-three-year-old unemployed miner, whose chance of working for Gabriel becomes thwarted due to the rowdy antimining campaign orchestrated by foreign environmentalists. As the film's codirector, Phelim McAleer (who has been behind several far-right conspiracy documentaries), put it, the film is one of human rights: "The human right to a job, the human right to have your children educated, the human right to see your child reach their first birthday."[25] While the antimining organizers are portrayed by the film as foreign agitators, what is ignored is that Gabriel was the real outsider on the scene.

Contrary to Gabriel's cinematic portrayal, the early Salvați Roșia Montană campaign was led not by foreign agents but by local anti-imperial activists attentive to the deadly effects of disaster capitalism. In part, they built on the tenor of 2008 anti-NATO protests that fostered the conditions for housing justice collectives, alternative library projects, and antifascist, feminist, and anarchist social centers that have grounded my own experience and education in Romania. Many of the early organizers spewed an explicitly anticolonial framework, noting how Timiș's operations in Africa laid the groundwork for his co-optation of postsocialist space. While portrayed as outside agitators by Gabriel, journalists meanwhile depicted them as incomprehensible to the generation which overthrew the communists. Their parents were blamed for "failing to give their children a pro-capitalist view."[26]

While anticapitalist Salvați Roșia Montană organizers were attacked by the media and also at times by police (as they had grown accustomed to throughout prior anti-NATO and anti-austerity marches), they soon also found themselves targeted by liberals who had begun opening doors to far-right participants. When my close friend publicly confronted a Roșia Montană leader about the increasingly cramped space from which to articulate anticapitalist and anti-imperialist politics, she was told, "The beauty of the movement is that you'll see a homophobe holding hands with a homosexual." It also helps with the numbers, she was told. Yet when nationalists began attacking her and other antifascist friends, my friend retreated, thereby decreasing numbers. Others were later pushed out of a Roșia Montană summer camp for espousing "too much" "Jos Capitalismul" (Down with Capitalism) messaging, revealing the limits and pitfalls of liberal notions of inclusivity.

In the 2018 documentary film *Portavoce* (Megaphone), directed by Ruxandra Gubernat, Marcel Schreiter, and Henry Rammelt, the Roșia Montană and Light Revolution protests are woven together to make sense of postsocialist protest politics. I was able to watch the film as it debuted in Romania's 2018 One World Romania film festival in Bucharest with friends who had been part of the early iterations of Salvați Roșia Montană. Yet unlike the queer antifascist organizers I attended the screening with, thirteen out of fourteen people interviewed in the film were men, and most were DJs or musicians in rock and alternative bands such as Luna Amară and the Amsterdams. Others were engaged in creative capital ventures such as Street Delivery, a project aimed at "delivering" culture to Bucharest's streets, and which has been critiqued for abetting processes of gentrification and by effectively celebrating the arrival of Richard Florida's "creative class."[27] As Gubernat suggests, the film effectively defines Romanian protest culture as "recreational activism."[28] When comparing Romanian protesters with those of Western Europe, she finds lower levels of commitment, increased flexibility in ideology (though most espouse anticommunism), and less importance placed on formal groups. Many activists work for multinational corporations and creative capitalist ventures, and desire to disaggregate their "patriotism" from communist nationalism by embracing the "new Romania." Also important to protesters is the "concept of a scene," Gubernat explains. This characterization aligns with media descriptions of Salvați Roșia Montană as the "protest of hipsters"[29]—illustrative of how far the movement migrated from an anticapitalist revolution against predatory global capital to one run by gentrifying creative class hipsters working for multinationals.

By voiding anticapitalist organizing and critique from the space of protest, ignored are those living in Roșia Montană in Gabriel's wake whose homes have been threatened and eradicated. Instead of an anticommunist politic, many of the dispossessed look back on state socialism with nostalgia. As local farmer Eugene described, "If they try to forcefully relocate me, I'll go to Ceaușescu's grave, light a candle, and say: 'Comrade Ceaușescu, you were a dictator, but I'm sorry we killed you.'"[30] Speaking to Gabriel's determination to dispossess over 1,800 people living in 740 homes, and even to exhume and relocate the dead, he espouses a familiar sentiment among those rendered disposable amid the ruins of disaster capitalism. As an employee of the Catholic Church paid by Gabriel to recruit locals to work for the corporation frustratingly explained of her job after being interrogated by local Cluj activists, "I toll the bells for the dead." Such sentiments destabilize anticommunist notions of anticapitalism being the domain of aberrant, militant urban youth, and instead reveal its multiplicities.

As Gabriel slowly turns Roşia Montană into a ghost town, not all people have been equally impacted. Disproportionately, Roma have been faced with contaminants, invoking the familiar color lines of environmental racism. Unlike other mountain villagers, many live in Gura Roşiei at the bottom of the valley, previously having worked for the state mining company. Residing in abject conditions, many are unemployed and without adequate utilities. As an older woman from the region described, yes, the cyanide tailings from the dam outside her house have been toxic for some time, but at least during socialism, she and her community had jobs. In 2012, her friend died after a ten-year battle with cancer, having had no access to employment since socialism's demise. Everyone around her is sick, or, in Julie Sze's words, "technologically polluted."[31] Many would work for Gabriel in a heartbeat, but institutional racism has denied them employment.

In this way, not only are the region's Roma communities foreclosed opportunities by postsocialist racializing technologies, but further, they are classified as pollutable by global capital. Their homes have become what Traci Voyles describes as "wastelanded," a racial and a spatial signifier that renders racialized bodies and their lands pollutable.[32] Yet, it is liberalism and the politics of individual rights that are galvanized by Gabriel and films such as *Mine Your Own Business*, which elide the environmental racism undergirding the region. In this sense, the rights and futures that Gabriel espouses foreclose Roma people from the future, and from the realm of the human. As Sylvia Wynter's work teaches us, throughout modernity, the universal "Man" of humankind has claimed universality while utilizing race to foreclose many from its domain.[33] Yet Gabriel is far from the only Man failing to account for those who live beyond the pale of a liberal politics of rights. The transformation of anticapitalist space into one of creative capital and "all protesters matter" is instructive regarding the foreclosures of revolution that liberalism produces.

Despite the movement's failures to address the lethal effects of waste-landing, after months of protesting and successfully overcoming a media blackout, in the spring of 2014, public pressure worked. The state took a stance against Gabriel's exploitations, which was met in return by the multinational taking Romania to World Bank arbitration court. Yet Roşia Montană protests died down around this time, with many activists considering their work successful. Others organizing with Alburnus Maior drafted a petition to afford Roşia Montană the status of a UNESCO World Heritage site, which it was tentatively granted. When news later erupted that Romania had stymied heritage status allocation given that inclusion might negatively impact the lawsuit, small demonstrations ensued, not against free trade, but rather opposing local politicians deemed corrupt. This tendency to displace critique of global capital for that of local corruption has become the status quo of liberal politicking since, informing movements such as the Light Revolution while keeping actual revolutions at bay.

The Light Revolution

In February 2017, Romania's streets and cities lit up as nearly one million protesters gathered to demand an end to political corruption. Building on Salvați Roșia Montană rhetoric, demonstrators equated the ruling Social Democratic Party (PSD) to the "Red Scare" of socialist endurance. Known as the "Light Revolution" due to the widespread utilization of digital, smart, and light-emitting technologies, the movement was also called #Rezist in homage to the United States's anti-Trump #Resist movement. Hundreds of thousands of smartphones lit up Bucharest's Piața Victoriei (Victory Square) on February 6, nationalistically choreographed to display the country's red, blue, and yellow flag. Lasers projected gimmicky GIFs on government buildings, depicting the PSD as old and corrupt, and its leader, Liviu Dragnea, as poor and with rotten teeth. As one protester's sign read, in English, "FEAR OF THE DARK(nea)." Above him, EU and US flags undulated in the breeze amid professionally printed signs appealing to the West for salvation from the lingering Red Scare. Some spelled out "Save Us" and "Help Us" in English, while hashtags circulated on social media such as #WorldAgainstCorruption. Romania's technological prowess, protesters demonstrated, is light years ahead of the decrepitude that still occupies the allegedly still-socialist government (despite its neoliberal politics). Demonstrators expressed that by expunging the communist specters polluting the government, the country could finally catch up to the West.[34] Consolidating what Konrad Petrovszky and Ovidiu Țichindeleanu describe as an imagined Eastern "ontological time lapse behind the authentic present of the Free World," the Light Revolution helped propel Romania along its never-ending "transition to 'normality.'"[35]

Indeed, a Cold War narrative structure has endured throughout an endless transition, one that straightjackets the horrors of the authoritarian leader Nicolae Ceaușescu onto the entire communist project, and that imposes a continual demand for Romanians to prove they have left their backward past behind. In this way, Romania—as geographically a part of but still not quite a part of Europe—is read, as Maria Todorova elaborates, as Europe's "incomplete self."[36] By appealing to the West for salvation, and by utilizing digital technology, Light Revolutionaries attempt to restage the death of Ceaușescu, imagining that this time, they can finally lustrate socialist retrogression. As one man's placard in Piața Victoriei boldly spelled out, also in English, "WE WILL STAND OUR GROUND LIKE OUR PARENTS DID IN '89." This desire to finish what the 1989 revolution attempted—a merger with Western spatiotemporality— has been an ongoing quest since that year. In 2003, for instance, the artist Dumitru Gorzo stenciled images of Ceaușescu across Bucharest with the text "VIN ÎN 5 MINUTE" (BACK IN 5 MINUTES), alluding to a fear that the former leader would return despite his execution.[37] In 2010, the Ceaușescus' bodies were unearthed for DNA testing, just to make sure they were truly dead. The Light Revolution is thus the newest layer of an unending postsocialist lineage of disinterring socialist remains to ensure that the past is truly dead.

Anxieties of socialist returns are not unique to Romania, having transpired alongside similar reburial performances across the region, from Slovenia to Bosnia. Sometimes fears align with antiauthoritarian and anticapitalist politics; other occasions have seen paranoia posit conservative regime change as the solution. As Alexei Yurchak argues, narratives of corruption also have the power to divorce a country from its geopolitical contexts, "reducing it to a zone that is subjected to its own internal logic of authoritarianism."[38] In Romania, where more politicians have been jailed for corruption over the past decade than in all of Eastern Europe, these logics are a driving force. In 2005, the Direcția Națională Anticorupție (DNA) was founded by an EU directive to ensure their power in order to secure capitalist futurity. The Light Revolution then erupted after Dragnea introduced a bill that would decriminalize bribes up to $48,500—a move that sparked outrage among a corruption-obsessed population. While of course government-supported bribery is antidemocratic, anti-corruption politics hinge on the idea of socialism itself as evil. Yet those profiting most through corruption are not allegedly socialist politicians, but rather global capital firms such as Gabriel Resources. According to Alexander Clapp:

One of the great successes of the DNA has been its ability to use middle-class protests to control Europe's vision of Romania today. Those who join the street movements admire it out of a mixture of naivety and fear of what Romania has been. It is a generation whose memory of communism is that of the austerity decade into which they were born, and who were raised in the wild-turf capitalism of the 1990s. Not only has their prosperity come from the influx of multinationals, whose CEOs now take to the streets with them in protest; so have many of their progressive values.[39]

Or, as an anonymous writer in CrimethInc. more succinctly put it, "Anti-corruption discourse has served to rally people to coordinate their own colonization and exploitation by Western capitalists in the name of anti-communism."[40]

Much of the anti-corruption sentiment against the PSD reached a fever pitch a couple years before the Light Revolution in 2015, when an accidental and deadly fire erupted in the nightclub Colectiv. Protesters blamed then-PSD prime minister Victor Ponta for dodging permit regulations, which could have prevented sixty-four deaths. While the PSD is undoubtedly corrupt, mafiaistic, and neoliberal at its core, so is the rival party that many #Rezist protesters support—the National Liberal Party (Partidul Național Liberal/PNL), also the party of the president, Klaus Iohannis. If anything, the main difference between rival parties is that the PSD enjoys most of its support from rural, poor, small-town, and senior populations, while the PNL is backed by urban millennials and global capital. This is not to say that the PSD represents the poor—far from it—but at times, it has worked for a patriarchal system of redistribution that partially benefits them.[41] Meanwhile, the PNL is understood as "more European," parading a president that many speculate won the election based on his ethnic German background. Fast forward to the early days of the Light Revolution, and Iohannis himself participated in opposition to the PSD at this point led by Dragnea (instead of Ponta).

While anti-corruption demonstrators berated Dragnea by mobilizing anti-communist and classist imagery, Rezistors were largely praised for their positivity in the media. Many worked for multinational corporations, which gave their employees time off to attend. The Jandarmeria, Romania's military police, was made famous for holding heart-shaped balloons, and even the head of Raiffeisen Bank attended a demonstration in Cluj with his family. McDonald's offered protesters free tea so they could stay warm and rehydrate, and at one point, a US State Department representative described the protests as a "sea of humanity" to a cohort of US Fulbright students, myself among them. There was nothing anarchistic about the demonstrations, he declared proudly, noting that even though Piața Victoriei where the protests took place is surrounded by big banks, none of them had their windows smashed in, and everyone respected the police.

On my way home from observing one of the protests, I passed through an underground crossing near the metro in Piața Universității (University Square) where I found a bunch of printed pages strewn across the ground. I picked up a couple to find that one was titled "Cum Să Fii Cetățean Model" (How to be a model citizen). Made by Educație Civica (Civic Education), a platform of "Funky Citizens" funded by the Romanian-American Foundation, the goal of the flyers was to coax Light Revolutionaries into becoming "civically fit."[42] According to the foundation's website, this entails using smart technology, visualizations, and infographics. Aligned with the Romanian-American Foundation's mission of propelling Romanians into the technology and innovation sectors, the program is aimed at fostering entrepreneurial skills and competition.[43] To this end, it funds coding camps, an entrepreneurial university program, and innovation labs, while also partnering with the Fulbright office to expose Romanian professors to US models of entrepreneurialism. Writing of a parallel utilization of entrepreneurial dreams in neoliberal India, Lilly Irani suggests that "the figure of the entrepreneur has been a dynamic tool used by policy and industry elites to legitimize liberalization and explain how development ought to proceed in shifting political economies."[44] This figure, she shows, extends citizenship rights to those in the middle class who fit liberalism's molds, effectively remaking development. Silvia Lindtner has traced similar liberalizing techniques in China, whereby "the colonial project of prototyping a certain way of life (and demanding that others model themselves after that particular image) endures through the ideals and practices of technology innovation. It lives on in the construal of Silicon Valley's methods, instruments, and ideas of technology design and engineering as universally applicable."[45] This prototyping experimentation draws on what Lisa Rofel describes as a "postsocialist technology of the self."[46] While in Romania, model citizenship projects are often implemented in IT firms, tech conventions, and coworking hubs, they also bleed into underground metro spaces and Light Revolution protests where crumpled flyers dispel apocryphal promises of becoming Silicon Valley.

Romania's Light Revolution helped advance US understandings of civic progress while creating a safe space for police, banks, nationalism, and even the president. Yet it did not create any semblance of safety for antifascist organizers, many of whom have been sidelined in anti-corruption demonstrations since Roșia Montană. Their marginalization has led to increased breathing room for banks and police, but also for far-right members of the Noua Dreapta (New Right) and the homophobic Coaliția pentru Familie (Coalition for the Family)—both of which slowly crept into the public square. Perhaps then it should be no surprise that one of the popular chants crooned during Light Revolution protests was "PSD-Ciuma Roșie" or "PSD-Death to the Red Plague." As it filled the air around us, a friend explained that the same recitation was crooned in the 1930s by fascist Legionnaires targeting Jews, Roma, and socialists. "It's beyond disgusting," comrades affirmed back in the Macaz Bar Teatru Coop (Macaz Bar Theater Cooperative) after we regrouped from a collective ethnographic venture, shaking melting snow from our boots.

During the summer of 2018, a new wave of protests began to percolate in the blistering Bucharest streets. These, while supported by Light Revolutionaries, also became known as the Diaspora demonstrations. Provoked by ongoing PSD corruption, they embraced Western values and technology even more so than the original Light Revolution protests of the year prior. They were ignited in part when a Romanian living in Sweden, Razvan Stefanescu, drove to Bucharest with new license plates fastened to his Audi spelling out, "Muie PSD" (PSD cocksuckers). *Muie* is technically a Romani word meaning "mouth" and inferring deception, but non-Roma Romanians have been using it for decades as a perversion, often deracinated from its Roma origins. Upon arriving in Romania, Stefanescu was pulled over by the police, who confiscated his license plate, claiming its invalidity. But according to Sweden, the license plate was valid throughout the EU, which includes Romania. The confiscation generated outrage among Romanians living in Romania and in the diaspora, inciting a new wave of demonstrations.

The first Diaspora protest invited Romanians living abroad to return to Bucharest to demonstrate their anti-PSD angst. Roughly seventy thousand people showed up in August outside Piața Victoriei, some with hypermasculine and heteronormative signs depicting protesters raping the government. Others wove flags from their new countries, mostly from the United Kingdom and the United States. These flags were interspersed among recycled insignia from prior Light Revolution demonstrations denouncing the Red Plague. Someone even paraded a cartoon poster depicting the evolution of communists, from Marx to Lenin to Dragnea (the latter of course far from communist). Other signs depicted PSD members in white-and-black-striped jail suits, celebrating carceral aesthetics.

Despite a celebration of carcerality, demonstrators ended up getting teargassed by the military police early in the night, injuring 450 people. The internet subsequently exploded, mostly with people rebuking the PSD. The Jandarmerie's Facebook page meanwhile was flooded with one-star ratings made in disapproval. Social media thus framed protesters as technologically advanced members of the diaspora while the PSD was again portrayed as retrogressive. Another image circulated on Facebook of a screenshot of Google's Waze mapping application, in which the tile of the web-map had been hacked to spell out "Muie PSD" near the city of Iași. The caption below the screenshot read, in Romanian, "So I'm talking with the Taxify taxi driver about tomorrow's protests outside of the government, and he invites me to look up Carrefour in Iași with Waze. I zoomed in on the map. Priceless. Here's how Romanians

FIGURES 3.1–3.2. Two Light Revolution protesters with signs, one in the Bucharest metro conflating corrupt neoliberal politicians with Marx and Lenin, and one suggesting that smartphones and Facebook will help fight corruption. Photos taken by author, 2017 and 2018.

are good at IT." Techniques of entrepreneurial citizenship can be expressed in numerous ways.

The Light Revolution and its Diaspora offshoot can be theorized as an outcome of Silicon Valley imperialism and its golden era fantasies, which, when stitched together, galvanize dreams of Western liberal recognition to erase anticapitalist alterity. The PSD, neoliberal to its core, is scapegoated as socialist, while the materially damaging impacts of global capital are acquitted. Building on the ruins of Salvați Roșia Montană, which through liberal inclusivities crafted populist space for fascist imaginaries to root, the space of protest itself has become a frontier of liberalism. As Anna Tsing suggests, frontiers are "not just discovered at the edge; they are projects in making geographic and temporal experience."[47] Building on this, Lindtner observes that in the case of China's Siliconization, the country was "'remade' in the broader tech imagination as a place to dream, to see the future 'again,' precisely as the future was being called into question."[48] Siliconized techniques of Western proximal revanchism coopt the space of revolution into one of capitalist futurity. This dangerously opens the door for establishing anticommunist footholds in which fascist imaginaries simmer.

The Heritage Movement

While there are numerous anticommunist pathways to be traced in understanding the Light Revolution, from Salvați Roșia Montană inclusivities to incursions of entrepreneurial citizenship, also at play was a growing heritage movement intent on restituting Romania's presocialist past. It was during the interwar era that Bucharest saw the "golden age" of urban development, becoming known by many as the "little Paris of the East." This was also the age of intensified fascism, marked by anti-Semitism and anti-Roma racism. The Communist Party in part arose to nullify the fascist movement and the classism that backed it. Of the party's many initiatives, one was an intensive urbanization project that included housing nationalization. Owners of multiple properties gave up excess units to the state, which then moved new residents in, including the racialized poor (as described in chapter 1). Much of this occurred in older city centers, while new socialist modernist buildings were erected in the semiperipheries.[49] Decades later, after transition, EU-supported urban housing restitution policies were implemented to return formerly nationalized buildings to descendants of prior owners and heirs. Forestlands, agricultural terrain, and mountains too have been reprivatized, leading to new land grabs by multinational corporations such as Gabriel Resources. Interpreting socialism as an aberration, property restitution laws have thus facilitated the reclamation of former wealth while making room for new frontiers of global capital. In cities, this has incited a widespread trend of racialized dispossession and evictions,[50] but also an emergent architectural heritage movement invested in the value of interwar heritage buildings. Their politics, too, helped inform the Light Revolution.

In the late 1990s, real estate speculators framed the transition-wrecked Bucharest as an easily exploitative space, and soon after, unofficial development became orchestrated beyond official city plans. Ioana Florea studies how architects, planners, and proponents of postsocialist urban beautification understand this as "derogatory urbanism," positing new development projects as slated to annihilate golden era architecture.[51] Architects and students, some of whom formed NGOs, launched a "cultural heritage movement" backed by expert architectural knowledge of the interwar era. Soon, conservative and nationalist groups desirous of reinstalling presocialist urban identity joined, and by 2008, the Association to Save Bucharest (Asociatia Salvați Bucureștiul/ASB) party emerged. Small protests outside the parliament became frequent. Some took the shape of mock funerals intended to mourn the loss of historic buildings; others chastised corrupt officials with development ties. Rather than mourn those being dispossessed from their homes through property restitution practices, the heritage movement displayed more concern with presocialist buildings and their symbolic capital.

This came to a head in 2010, when Bucharest's city hall obtained the right to construct a "North–South middle line" cutting across the city, a throughway first conceptualized in the 1930s intended to connect the government at Piața Victoriei to the parliament farther south. This would mean widening the streets along the Berzei-Buzești corridor. When implemented in 2011, ninety-eight buildings were destroyed, and one thousand people in the Matache neighborhood, most of whom were Roma, were racially banished. While some residents did rise up to fight evictions, most of the resistance to the development project was instead led by the heritage movement, which instead focused on the destruction of the one-hundred-year-old Matache market building. In 2018, filmmaker Dragoș Lumpan debuted his *Matache 2.0*, a documentary of the Matache demolition. While an homage to the neighborhood's loss, the film only mentioned those displaced by development peripherally. Rather, prominently featured were architects and planners bemoaning the razing of beautiful interwar buildings. Most blamed the corrupt mayor at the time, Sorin Oprescu, who, along with the planners who implemented the destruction, were described as "little Ceaușescus." In a screening of the film that I attended, Lumpan made similar remarks, grieving the loss of the marketplace while referring to those displaced with brazenly anti-Roma and homophobic language. Also berated were the sex workers who had long found employment in the area, and whose lives have been made more precarious through redevelopment.

In reflecting on the value that ruins differentially inhere, Ann Laura Stoler describes how the restoration of World Heritage sites has historically dispersed and redistributed people.[52] Similarly, Yukiko Koga writes of the "colonial inheritance" of Japanese imperialism in China, in which colonial building remnants are capitalized on.[53] While the Matache neighborhood was not fully restored to its presocialist past, the heritage movement does indeed aspire to restore architecture from a period marked by widespread racial capitalism. This tension reached another apogee in 2012, when an old building in the city center, Carol 53, was bestowed historic value and granted restitution and restoration. The heir, a famous architect and senior member of the heritage movement, evicted a large Roma family who had been squatting there for years. He then handed the building over to a collective of young artists and architects, who proceeded to launch a "cultural" co-living/working project. Describing themselves as "squatters," they soon began giving presentations and tours of their new building. Florea argues that Carol 53 flawlessly signals the brutality of the heritage movement: "With 'Little Paris' being negotiated as its identity symbol and its vision of what is valuable, the movement found itself in a process of excluding all those groups not fitting into or not adhering to this cultural value system—such as the poor, the Roma, the uneducated, the less educated, the less urbanized dwellers."[54] In this sense, the creative class cannibalized the homes and personhoods of those racially banished in the name of presocialist preservation.

After Carol 53, the ASB transformed into the Union to Save Romania (Uniunea Salvați România/USR) party, led by mathematician Nicușor Dan, who would go on in 2020 to become Bucharest's mayor. By the time of the 2017 Light Revolution, it had become the second most popular party in Bucharest after the PNL. Anti-corruption and anticommunism became two of the party's central tenets, and numerous USR supporters comprised Light Revolution constituents alongside those of the PNL. While the USR has been framed as "left-ish," Adina Marincea argues that it is first and foremost anticommunist, never actually having worked toward social justice.[55] Throughout the Light Revolution it indeed transited anticommunist messaging into Piața Victoriei—a plaza incidentally now more connected to the parliament due to the Berzei-Buzești corridor, but also to the West, thanks to the ocean of smartphone lights beaming outward. Yet also plugged into the Light Revolution circuits, thanks to the heritage movement, has been the presocialist past and its fascist incantations.

IKEA

While the Light Revolution sits a world away from actual revolution, and while it is more inclined to rehearse post-1989 revolution fantasies of Westernization than early Salvați Roșia Montană anticapitalist organizing, it is instructive in mapping out revolution's political terrain in postsocialist times. In order to better apprehend this, here I engage in a counterfactual exercise to examine a postsocialist revolution that never came to be. I focus on the Swedish furniture company IKEA, which could have been the subject of mass dissent and protest in Romania but never was. This failure, I suggest, has everything to do with the company's interpellation as progressive by those seeking Western recognition despite the fact that it materializes a similar genre of violent resource extraction as Gabriel Resources. In studying a protest that never came to be, one that could have been as loud and powerful as the early Salvați Roșia Montană movement had capitalist desires not gotten in the way, the antirevolutionary powers of liberal light revolutions glow in the dark.

Today, Romania contains 70 percent of Europe's virgin forests and the continent's largest brown bear, lynx, and gray wolf populations. While much of Europe was deforested during the industrial era, Romania was not, with state socialist land nationalization projects a technique for protecting the country's forests from capitalist land grabs and global export markets.[56] A major wave of ecological destruction took place after 1995, and then another after 2005, correlating with property restitution legislation. Romania's 2007 entry into the EU then created a large and liberated market for Austrian and Swedish firms, as well as providing cheap surrogate labor to power new techniques of extraction. By 2009, up to 45 percent of previously national forests were restituted and privatized.[57] As Alexander Sammon writes, Romania's forests have "been referred to as the Amazon of Europe, a comparison apt and ominous in equal measure, because of the speed at which it, like the Amazon itself, is disappearing."[58] He attributes this "delirium of deforestation," in which between a half and two-thirds of the country's forests have been lost since 2007, to property restitution and global capital as well as to the astronomical growth of the fast furniture industry which thrives on Romanian beech and spruce trees.[59]

Corruption does also come into play, though not in the ways recognized by Light Revolutionaries. Investigative journalists Daniel Bojin, Paul Radu, and Hans Strandberg blame "crooked businessmen and dirty politicians [who] seized the moment, forging documents and claiming forests that had never belonged to them or to their ancestors."[60] Indeed, there have been many cases in which stacks of forged paperwork are mobilized by those aiming to peddle land off to foreign companies for lucrative returns. Some of this gets at what Katherine Verdery has described as post-1989 "fuzzy property rights," whereby there may be an "idealized image of exclusive private property," but "from the point of view of privatization programs such as those being implemented in the post-communist states, the rights appear fuzzy because of their complex interrelations and the multiplicity of actors holding them."[61] This partly explains why over half of Romanian timber harvesting between 2013 and 2017 was conducted illegally.[62] Per Sammon, "Every link in that chain makes the wood's point of origin fuzzier. Depots in particular are notorious for stacking illegal and legal logs together behind fencing or inside warehouses, where they become indistinguishable."[63] Yet multinational lumber companies, the Orthodox Church, and real estate mafia groups alike continue to benefit from the fruits of restitution and Europeanization. And despite IKEA's reputation for its sustainable harvesting, there are numerous cases proving its dependence on illegal harvesting obtained from third-party contractors. There have also been a number of high profile attacks, murders, beatings, and even poisonings against forest protectors, and not much done in remediation.[64]

As has been the case in restituted and renewed urban spaces such as Matache, Roma residents have borne the brunt of forest restitution far more than those non-Roma. Not only were Roma people dispossessed from collectivized agricultural and industrial projects after 1989, but further, under the pretext of land shortage, many were denied the half a hectare of land otherwise gifted to socialist collective farm employees.[65] While Roma residents had been working in the forests for generations in regions such as Dragomirești in Dâmbovița, they received neither agricultural nor forest land. In 2003, many began illegally cutting large timber (rather than simply gathering underbrush for broom making and firewood as they had been doing previously), selling it to wholesalers in southern Romania for meager profit. In response, the new forest owners mobilized racist tropes, going so far as to declare that Roma "should be killed since they are not good for anything else but stealing our forest."[66] Roma residents scraping to get by amid reprivatization's violence are thus accused of stealing forest space, while, as I continue to explore, a Swedish furniture company monopolizes land without much pushback.

IKEA was founded in 1943 by the seventeen-year-old Ingvar Kamprad, who named it after his initials as well as his childhood farm (Elmtaryd) and village

(Agunnaryd). That same year, Kamprad became the 4,014th member of Sweden's fascist Socialist Unity Party. An enthusiastic Nazi sympathizer, he went on to recruit and fundraise for the party even after World War II ended, and continued to maintain ties with the Swedish fascist leader Per Engdahl.[67] Although he publicly renounced his affiliation in 1994, over a decade later, he still maintained Engdahl's greatness.[68] By the time Kamprad died in 2018, he was considered one of the world's wealthiest people, with capital built on fascist materialities.

Since its origins, IKEA has been in a state of expansion. As of 2022, it owned and operated 474 stores in sixty-four countries.[69] It is the largest individual consumer of timber globally, insatiably devouring on average two million more trees each year.[70] This means that the company uses 1 percent of the global wood supply each year—10 percent of which comes from Romania—to produce roughly one hundred million pieces of "smart" furniture.[71] Like many global franchises, IKEA offshores its financing through complex networks, having managed to avoid paying one billion euros in taxes between 2010 and 2016.[72] It also owns TaskRabbit, the start-up company founded in San Francisco in 2008 by a former IBM software engineer in the name of "revolutionizing the world's labor force."[73] TaskRabbit workers perform an array of odd jobs for users, for instance assembling IKEA furniture.

While IKEA's ventures into Romanian forestlands only began in 2015, the story begins earlier, when Harvard University set its eyes on Romanian forestlands. In 2004, the university designated Dragoș Lipan as its representative to begin purchasing newly restituted lands through various shell companies.[74] Though many of his purchases were made through dubious restitution claims, by 2010, Harvard became the largest private owner of forests in Romania and found itself managing over $100 million worth of investments through the Boston-based tax-exempt Phemus Corporation. Eventually, some of Lipan's fuzzy dealings surfaced as illegal, and so in 2015, Harvard brusquely sold the majority of its property to IKEA in what became its largest transaction in raw forest, valued at $62.6 million.[75] By 2018, IKEA owned ninety forests in twenty-one Romanian counties, totaling thirty-three thousand hectares of trees.

While Romanian forests and labor feed global supply chains, many Romanians too enjoy IKEA furniture. In 2018, Bucharest began building its second IKEA store, already maintaining a popular one near the airport. That said, most of Romania's IKEA-owned trees are slated to become furniture not for locals, but for the West. While during socialism, furniture production and sales were for the most part domestic affairs, today forests are for export. Nevertheless, IKEA was no stranger to Romania during socialism. Declassified files have revealed that the Swedish company maintained a 1981 agreement with the Romanian timber company, Tehnoforestexport, to have Romanian Securitate secret police utilize a special foreign trade company, ICE Dunarea, to skim capital from the transactions.[76] A 1986 memo from the Ministry of Interior marked "Top Secret, sole copy," elaborates that the "Scandinavica currency collection operation" functioned by "over-billing the payments made in the contract between ICE Tehnoforestexport with IKEA of Sweden, valued at 97m Swedish crowns (13.6 million US dollars)."[77] IKEA claims to have seen the transaction as a sort of commission,[78] a corrupt practice that Light Revolutionaries today might rally against.

However, unlike the Light Revolution, and unlike Salvați Roșia Montană that preceded it, there have been no large-scale protests against IKEA's exploitative past or present. While Greenpeace as well as Cluj's activist-based Eco Ruralis Association have been actively fighting IKEA in courts, and while journalists have conducted important research uncovering its predations, there is no massive movement aimed against the smart furniture monopoly. Several environmental activists have told me that lack of widescale organizing around forest restitution and land-grabbing more broadly can in part be attributed to the large concentration of anticapitalist activists in urban centers. Others have blamed the love affair that Romania has with IKEA, observing that the company's smart furniture is read as a barometer of urban savviness. This materializes and dematerializes particular futures from taking place. For instance, in 2018, I attended a book launch in Bucharest's famous bookstore, Cărturești Carusel. There, attendees dressed in nice clothing and snacked on appetizers, excited to take home their own copy of the book being debuted: IKEA's annual catalog.

Even if IKEA is not offering Romania reparations for stolen trees, it nonetheless peddles the aesthetic dream of Western modernity online and in urban retail stores. In Bucharest, I've heard countless tales of people taking the long trip to the Otopeni store by riding the 783 airport bus just to hang out and eat a meal, and maybe to buy something small downstairs (though now there is a train line as well). One middle-aged man told me that he loves going to the store because his family had no furniture options during socialism, and now he can transform his socialist-built flat into any interior style he so chooses. Such aesthetic fantasies make one hard-pressed to imagine the possibilities of a mass movement against the company. There is just as much to learn about liberalism from revolutions that never came to be as there is from those that have been assimilated into the realm of global capital.

Beyond offering Western modernity in middle-class aspirational homes, IKEA also renders possibilities to Romania's urban fabric. Beginning in 2008, the Inter-IKEA Group and the Inter-IKEA Property Division (founded by Kamprad in 1989) established the Interprime Properties investment fund, with eyes fixed on Romanian socialist-era industrial sites that it hoped to redevelop into high-end office buildings. In 2014, it rebranded itself as Vastint Romania SRL, a subsidiary of Vastint Holding B.V. "Vastint" is technically an abbreviation for "Vastgoed Internationaal," meaning "International Real Estate" in Dutch. Today, the Swiss Interogo Foundation owns both Vastint and the IKEA group, which Kamprad secretly created in 1989 to secure his company's assets.[79]

In 2010, Interprime Properties purchased the fifty-three-thousand-square-meter plot that was once Bucharest's Timpuri Noi (New Times) Industrial Platform and Metal Works for 34.6 million euros. First established during the second half of the nineteenth century, the Timpuri Noi factory was once an industrial stronghold. During socialism, it produced compressors, pumps, plant materials, and the country's only small- and medium- capacity compressors.[80] Bucharest's first metro line was opened in 1979 specifically to connect Timpuri Noi with Semănătoarea, which at the time was the city's industrial agricultural hub. But both Timpuri Noi Metal Works and Semănătoarea struggled to survive post-1989. There were 2,700 employees working for Timpuri Noi in 1990; in 2011 there were only 130 remaining.[81] Withering, the factory relocated to Jilava, forty kilometers outside of Bucharest, leaving the crumbling lot to Interprime. Semănătoarea meanwhile transformed into Sema Park, a bustling IT office complex mostly for outsourced tech labor. With Interprime's arrival, the area began to follow Sema Park's direction. It is now known as Timpuri Noi Square, where the Vastint logo flashes on one of its tall glass towers. By 2018, the complex had reached a 90 percent occupancy rating, housing over three thousand IT specialists and companies such as GoPro, Sephora, and Impact Hub.

Having lived nearby the complex in the working-class Vitan neighborhood, I witnessed the region's dramatic transformation daily. As newer, fancier residential housing complexes sprung up, food trucks began appearing outside the Vastint buildings during lunch. No longer do working-class factory workers queue up for canteen meals as had been the case during socialism, but rather middle-class aspirational tech workers with lanyards and badges line up for boutique fast food. Rents have gone up in the neighborhood, while the lawn across the square maintains a manicured, out-of-joint aesthetic guarded by a placard reading *proprietate privată* (private property)—an emblematic sign of liberal times in which the square is no longer public. Perhaps this too is the trajectory of Piaţa Victoriei, the site of the ongoing anti-corruption protests

FIGURE 3.3. Vastint development in Timpuri Noi. Photo taken by author, 2018.

where capitalist rather than commonist interests are espoused under the banner of Westernization.

Although there is ample evidence of IKEA's role in urban gentrification and forest clearcutting, both of which employ racial capitalist logics, here what I am interested in is why cultures of dissent against the multinational corporation have been minimal at best. The loss of Timpuri Noi did not invoke a cultural heritage movement, and the forest dealings between IKEA, Harvard, and the state have largely commenced under the radar. Outside of a handful of activists, I have never heard widespread critique of IKEA, its history, nor its involvement in Siliconized gentrification predicated on the restitution of private property regimes. This highlights the authority of liberalism in casting revolutionary possibilities, or the lack thereof. While the Roșia Montană protests began as anticapitalist, they slowly and strategically transformed into spaces of liberalism. Meanwhile, the Light Revolution was inspired by entrepreneurial citizenship dreams alongside racist understandings of presocialist preservation. Here, revolutionaries cast corrupt politicians rather than global capital formation as the enemy to be eradicated through Siliconization. On this movement's shoulders, there was no space left to organize against transnational capital led by companies such as IKEA. To understand and organize against Western exploitation, a movement would have to be willing to give up Siliconized promises and take up organizing against technologies of racial capitalism. It would take such an anticapitalist politic to thwart fascist tendencies seeping into the public square today.

Back to Europe

While the West continues to look eastward to prefigure illiberalism, liberal fantasies of Westernization are left uninterrogated. Yet we need not look eastward to encounter ample evidence of how liberal logics of inclusion open the door for fascist predation. Writing of the twentieth century, Cedric Robinson suggests, "Many of the radical Black intellectuals who witnessed the rise of fascism in Europe . . . were convinced that whatever its origins, at some point fascism had become an instrument of capitalists with the objective of destroying working-class movements."[82] With this in mind, Alyosha Goldstein and Simón Ventura Trujillo suggest pluralizing fascisms in order to account for the contemporary political conjuncture in which fascists continue to mobilize capitalist imperatives in order to destroy working-class movements.[83] Lilith Mahmud argues that this takes place under the banner of liberalism, which functions as a transatlantic cultural category anchored in Enlightenment epistemologies of Occidental superiority.[84] Theorizing the rise of Trump and his international cohort, she writes, "rather than focusing on the neofascist politician or the illiberal agenda of the day, we turn our gaze to liberalism itself." Thus, despite a proliferation of Occidentalist takes and solutions to keep fascism at bay, it is movements born out of crisis and rooted in anticapitalism and anti-imperialism that set the parameters for the antifascist revolutions we need.

In the infamous January 6, 2021, US Capitol insurrection led by Trump and his MAGA supporters, many spectators rebuked overt linkages between US homegrown white supremacy, settler colonialism, anticommunism, and what appeared to be a European genre of fascism. Trumpian demonstrators waved confederate flags and pro-police "Blue Lives Matter" banners, all the while "playing Indian" by appropriating Indigenous imagery—a historic settler trope. One man whose photograph spread like wildfire wore a shirt spelling out, "Camp Auschwitz: Work Brings Freedom." By this he paid homage to 1930s fascist movements in the United States such as the Silver Legion of America, the Amerikadeutscher Volksbund, and the Crusader White Shirts, as well as to Nazi Germany. Another MAGA sign spelled out, "The real invisible enemy is communism," evoking historic and contemporary anticommunist politics undergirding fascist formations. After the attempted coup, and evidencing the longevity of Cold War enmity-making, some liberal pundits sought to blame the East. It was UC Berkeley Chancellor's Professor of Public Policy Robert Reich who tersely responded with "Putin won,"[85] recasting the Cold War alibi of the "communist-illiberal" to legitimate US moral superiority. Similar lines were drawn after Trump's 2016 electoral victory, with blame awarded to Russian hackers for election meddling rather than homegrown US white supremacism.

I conclude this chapter on the fascist possibilities that liberalism affords by suggesting that the West would be wiser to look to local fascist formations and their racial capitalist underpinnings over Eastern illiberalism. Some of this crystallized for me in 2017 during the so-called Battle of Berkeley, when the British "alt-right" commentator Milo Yiannopoulos (who rose to prominence during the misogynistic online "Gamergate" scandals of 2014) was invited to talk at UC Berkeley. While antifascists militantly organized to shut his speech down (in part due to a leak that he had planned to out undocumented students on campus in accordance with his right to "free speech"), liberal organizations such as the American Civil Liberties Union defended him. Though such tensions are far from novel regarding the First Amendment, and while they are not unique to the United States as this chapter has already illustrated, they do highlight the racial technocapitalist hospitality that liberalism affords.

It was during the 1960s and the dawn of the Free Speech Movement (FSM) that free speech was taken up by leftist organizations against repressive UC Berkeley power. Although the university housed communist political activism in the 1930s, by the 1950s, it had been pacified into what Don Mitchell appraises as "a laboratory for the creation of a new and more rational society."[86] It was also then that UC Berkeley was attempting to take over "blighted" southern sections of the city, predicating its own expansion as an epicenter of "liberal intellectualism" on technologies of dispossession.[87] These contexts, along with civil rights struggles and anti-imperial organizing against the Vietnam War, fomented discontent among anticapitalist student activists who saw the university itself as no better than an autocratic firm, one that liberalism would be insufficient in transforming.[88] This came to be particularly true as Ronald Reagan, then governor of California, launched his neoliberal career through leftist student suppression.

Years later, the neoliberal university sought to erase these past tensions by commodifying the FSM and naming a café after it, defanging its anticapitalist politics from its concrete afterlife. This gets at what Jodi Melamed describes as practices of racial liberalism, in which, "in contrast to white supremacy, the liberal race paradigm recognizes racial inequality as a problem, and it secures a liberal symbolic framework for race reform centered in abstract equality, market individualism, and inclusive civic nationalism."[89] Official anti-racism becomes sutured to liberal notions of freedom, welcoming some people into the realm of the human, but not all. Resonant with what Olúfẹ́mi Táíwò describes as practices of "elite capture," bourgeois institutions capitalize on mutilated renditions of radical political organizing to profit.[90] Such co-optation maps how, while revolutionary futures past can be assimilated into liberal historiography, those continuing to militantly organize for futures beyond those of capitalism cannot.

Today, fascist organizers have built on this trajectory, protracting free speech from the realm of capitalist cafés into projects intended to materialize racial dispossession, deportation, and erasure. While many describe this as a form of fascist regression, Wendy Brown advocates for a more nuanced reading.[91] It was in the early mid-twentieth century that theorizations of neoliberal economics were concocted in the Mont Pèlerin society, during which Austrian and Chicago economists espoused both a repugnance toward socialism, feminism, and the New Deal, but also toward Nazism. While their neoliberal theorizations may have been launched in opposition to fascism, their anticommunism and heteronormativity triumphed, going on to materialize fascist futures from Pinochet's Chile to Trump's America. Contemporary fascist movements in this way are the fruits of neoliberalism coming to bear. As Mark Forman describes, "The capital-F Fascism of authoritarian government is possible because of the lower case-f fascism that thrives in everyday life under capitalism."[92] This, he argues, is nothing new, as fascists have long marched "to war down roads that were paved by centuries of European colonialism and imperialism." This all gets at the importance of reading the contemporary fascist moment through an anticapitalist and anti-imperial perspective.

I attended several of the 2017 antifascist counterdemonstrations against Milo Yiannopoulos's Berkeley appearance with a Romanian friend who was visiting at the time. At one point, while being assaulted with bagels by members of the "chauvinist" Proud Boys and the Fraternal Order of Alt-Knights (in what we later understood to be an anti-Semitic gesture), we overheard other antifascist organizers begin yelling for the white supremacists to "go back to

Europe." My friend, perhaps the only one of us actually "from Europe" in the mix, looked at me in confusion as bagels flew toward us. All I could do was shrug amid what felt like a surreal expression of the 1989 Berkeley Systems screen-saver software "Flying Toasters," which featured winged toasters, toast, and occasionally bagels flying through flat dark space. Uncannily, users at the time could adjust the toast's darkness while listening to Richard Wagner's "Ride of the Valkyries," part of an anti-Semitic opera that pays homage to Norse figures who transport slain warriors to the mythical halls of Valhalla in preparation for apocalypse. The tune also made an appearance in D. W. Griffith's 1915 film *Birth of a Nation*, which celebrates the white confederacy and galvanized the second iteration of the Ku Klux Klan.[93] Paralyzed amid an onslaught of bagels, I began wondering how much this operatic tune and its cinematic iterations prefigured our current battle.

While many of the bagel wielders did vaguely resemble a duct-taped version of Nordic warriors paying homage to Aryan pagan mythology, and while some did belong to alt-right hate groups such as Identity Evropa (now rebranded the American Identity Movement), most of the free speech activists hadn't traveled far. Looking back, much of this was a rehearsal of sorts for the January 6 attacks made iconic with images of the so-called QAnon Shaman, a man who showed up adorned with horns and tattoos of various Norse symbols. Like the bagel wielders, he too hadn't arrived from Europe to get to the Capitol, although he worshipped Aryan origin myths. While some interpreted this as fascism "coming home" from Europe, fascist conditions have been brewing on US soil since the earliest days of US empire. In other words, despite its reference to Norse mythologies, the MAGA movement is far from a Western import; rather it is deeply informative of the ongoing histories and daily realities of US empire, which while primed by Western European colonial conceptions of race, capital, and the human, never vacated US imperial epistemologies after European colonial rule. As Lisa Lowe writes, "In the very claim to define humanity, as a species or as a condition," liberalism's "gestures of definition divide the human and the nonhuman, to classify the normative and pathologize deviance."[94]

By going "back to Europe" in this chapter, instead of centering the white Nordic Valhalla imagery embraced by Identity Evropa, I rather explored how the circulation of liberalism materializes fascist conditions of possibility. Contrary to attempts to prefigure the MAGA movement by looking eastward, I find more use in assessing the power of liberalism on both sides of the Atlantic as it forecloses anticapitalist revolution. However, and as upcoming chapters detail, anticapitalist and anti-imperial worldmaking projects continue to grow despite such foreclosure, sometimes in the cracks and crevices hidden from the liberalizing trajectories, sometimes more overtly. As Mahmud writes, "If it is fascism we fear, we would do better to take a page from the movements that have historically succeeded in resisting it and from the new movements of today . . . that were born out of crisis and have redefined the parameters of political dissent. Hint: they were not liberal either."[95]

PART II

Techno Frictions and Fantasies

The Most Dangerous Town
on the Internet

In a 2011 San Francisco tournament, two of *Jeopardy!*'s famously successful players, Ken Jennings and Brad Rutter, lost to IBM's Watson AI supercomputer.
Jennings was showing promise, but then a question was asked regarding an author inspired by William Wilkinson's *An Account of the Principalities of Wallachia
and Moldavia*. While all three players correctly guessed Bram Stoker, the author
of *Dracula*, Watson AI wagered more money, thus manifesting its victory. Watson AI, named after IBM founder Thomas J. Watson, runs on a supercomputer
powered by 2,880 IBM Power750 cores (computing brains) and fifteen terabytes
of memory. It relies on DeepQA, a software architecture that merges natural language with its own structured information. Many have noted that this
is a huge improvement from IBM's 1997 Deep Blue, which famously beat the
Russian chess master Garry Kasparov. As was joked after its *Jeopardy!* victory,
Watson may be on a path toward becoming "HAL," the computer of Stanley
Kubrick's 1968 Cold War film *2001: A Space Odyssey*.[1] Perhaps it was no coinci-
dence that HAL's initials sit just one letter ahead in the alphabet from IBM's.

In part, this chapter is interested in assessing how Watson AI knew about the Orientalist novel *Dracula*. While I am less interested in the architecture of the neural language processing and the human-algorithmic illegibilities from which algorithms are derived,[2] instead I look to the materialities and imaginaries that informed Watson AI's knowledge base. While Stoker wrote *Dracula* without ever having traveled to Romania, basing his vampiric depiction on Orientalist and gothic horror literary tropes of the era, it turns out that Watson had made the journey to Romania—Thomas J. Watson, that is. As I allege, it wasn't just algorithmic calculations that enabled Watson AI to win at *Jeopardy!*; IBM's role in Romanian technological worlds also has to be accounted for. While IBM rushed into Romania after socialism ended in 1989, absorbing Romania's computing workforce and its national Felix computer factory, IBM had spent plenty of time in Romania before socialism even began, assisting the engineering of the country's fascist 1941 census made to help materialize the annihilation of Jews, Roma, communists, queers, and more.

While companies such as IBM have wreaked havoc in postsocialist Romania, destroying lifeworlds and co-opting un-Siliconized technofutures, US liberal imaginaries position Eastern European hackers as an ongoing threat to liberal democracy requiring intervention. In the aftermaths of Trump's 2016 electoral triumph and the dawning of the "Trumpocalypse," Russian hackers quickly became the alibi for technologies of US white supremacy, one for Siliconized cybersecurity firms to root out. The framing of illiberal Eastern hackers and hacking geographies—from the Romanian hacker known as Guccifer, infamous for having hacked Hillary Clinton's emails, to the mountain town of Râmnicu Vâlcea, portrayed as "Hackerville" by the West—highlights liberal conjunctures in the postsocialist present. Today, Silicon Valley imperialism, or the modes through which Silicon Valley extends its material and imaginative scope, recycles Cold War Orientalist tropes to elide the violence it wields. As Alexei Yurchak suggests, in Trumpian times, proponents of Western liberalism reinvigorate the "temporarily forgotten figure of 'Red under the bed.'"[3] Red-baiting the illiberal postsocialist hacker obviates historic (and ongoing) technologies of white supremacy animating the present.

Following Neda Atanasoski's argument that postsocialism can be read as "a global condition that produces a social, economic and cultural ethic that builds on and disavows previous racial and imperial formations,"[4] here I focus on how Silicon Valley imperialism animates Cold War imaginaries while disavowing its own fascist past. By mapping out IBM's Romanian history before and after socialism, I aim to flip the anticommunist framing of Eastern European illiberalism on its head and redirect attention to Silicon Valley's technofascist underbelly. By technofascism, I signal the technologies, for instance eugenic technoscience, co-constitutive with fascist future making. Throughout this chapter, I draw on ethnographic and archival work related to Romanian computing histories, as well as close readings of Silicon Valley propaganda made by cybersecurity firms and Western media. I also dwell within a theater play made by the Bucharest-based playwright David Schwartz, which brings to the fore lived and imagined experiences of postsocialist technological transition.

Counting

In Romania, the word *computer* has traditionally been *calculator* (although now people often just say "computer"). The country's first computer, CIFA-I, was built by Victor Toma in 1957 in the National Physics Institute outside of Bucharest in Măgurele (today the institute is home to the world's largest nuclear laser project, ELI—Extreme Light Infrastructure, financed by the European Regional Development Fund). I was thus surprised when a friend of mine told me that she found mention of *calculatoare* (computers) in the Romanian National Archives from 1938. How could it be that there were computers being used then, years before the country's first computers?

On further investigation, I found the *calculatoare* that she mentioned to be actually written as *mașini electrice* and *electrocontabila*, what we might refer to as electronic calculators. I would have assumed that they were just simple counting machines made by the state, but what confused me was that in 1938 and 1941 they were being shipped to Romania's National Institute of Statistics by the Compania Electrocontabila Watson S.A.R., headquartered at 590 Madison Avenue in New York—the home of, yes, the International Business Machines Corporation. I found these records in the archives of Sabin Manuilă, who had been leading the National Statistics Institute during the interwar era when he was tasked with creating a national census. It was this census that was later used to geolocate Jews and Roma so that they could be shipped to camps for extermination.

While Manuilă was the census designer, the technofascist underpinnings of the census were not his alone. Manuilă had been a former student of the infamous eugenicist Iuliu Moldovan, creator of Cluj's School for Hygiene, who helped lay the infrastructure for transforming Cluj into the "biological capital" of Transylvania. His aim was to limit the spread of venereal disease, alcoholism, and tuberculosis. While his vision was short lived, his school continued, publishing works such as the *Bulletin for Eugenics and Biopolitics*. Moldovan also authored the 1926 book, *Biopolitica*, which Maria Bucur has described as "a manifesto that called for the total eugenic state based on biological princi-ples—an entirely new way of organizing politics in Romania."[5] Inspired by Mol-dovan, as well the broader eugenicist movement, it was Manuilă who argued that Jews were not a racial, but rather an economic and "sentimental" prob-lem. Wary of miscegenation, he supported Jewish segregation laws, and even proposed creating a "Superior Council for the Protection of the Race."[6] He also worked to criminalize sex work. But Manuilă's most extreme views were directed toward Roma people, who he asserted were subversive and dysgenic, constituting "Romania's racial issue" and requiring sterilization.[7] But how to implement his technofascist future? As he determined, a census was needed to determine where racialized and sentimentalized bodies were located. As it turns out, IBM was instantly ready to assist him.

The creation of census-counting machines to implement eugenic utopia is part of IBM's own origin story. It was in the late nineteenth century that US census worker Herman Hollerith came up with the idea of punch cards for the production of reliable demographic census data, leading to the creation of the German Deutsche Hollerith Maschinen Gesellschaft, or Dehomag. The com-pany sold the punch card license to the US industrialist Charles Flint, who had launched the Computing-Tabulating-Recording Company (CTR) led by Thomas Watson.[8] Soon after, Watson took over the company, rebranding it In-ternational Business Machines (IBM) and designating Dehomag as its subsid-iary. After Hitler rose to power in 1933, Watson quickly established a business relationship with him. As Edwin Black tracks, Watson saw Nazi Germany as a lucrative business opportunity and began what would become semiannual excursions to Germany.[9] In 1937, he received a medal from Hitler for his role in abetting fascist purification. Soon after, Watson was granted Dehomag pow-ers in other Nazified countries, such as Poland.[10] Not only were IBM's punch card machines used for censuses, but also for tracking and coordinating freight train routes to concentration camps. Up to two hundred million punch cards were used to materialize train routes where millions of people were brutally enslaved and murdered in the name of technofascism.[11]

It was not only Nazified Germany and Poland where IBM made its imprint. IBM's other subsidiary, Compania Electrocontabila Watson, was established in Bucharest in 1938. There it claimed $240,000 in equipment, leasable machines, and punch cards. The subsidiary primarily worked with the Communications Ministry, statistical offices, local census bureaus, and the railroad company. IBM Europe fulfilled Romania's orders, with IBM New York closely monitor-ing all developments. Soon, Compania Electrocontabila began printing over twenty million punch cards annually on its Swift Press machine.[12] This infra-

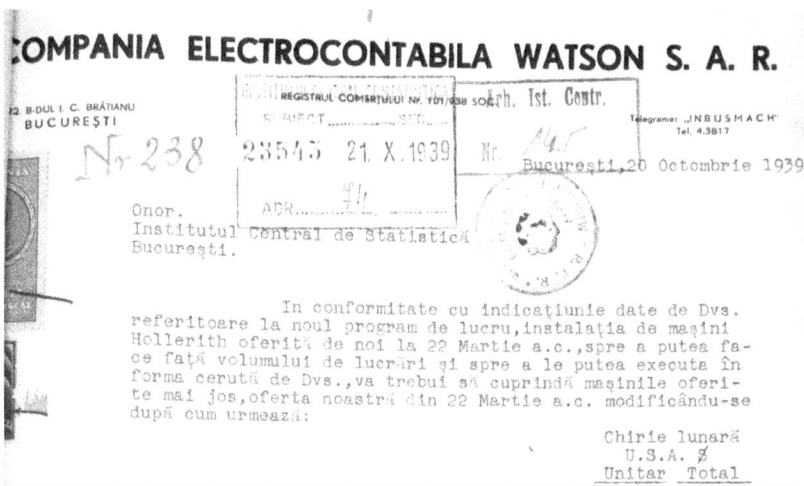

:OMPANIA ELECTROCONTABILA WATSON S. A. R.

12, B-DUL I. C. BRĂTIANU
BUCUREŞTI

REGISTRUL COMERTULUI Nr. 701/938 SO.… rh, Ist. Contr.

S…/…ECT……………SEC…

Telegrame: „INBUSMACH"
Tel. 4.3817

Nr. 238   23545 21. X.1939   Nr. /4 …

Bucureşti, 20 Octombrie 1939

Onor.   ADR……… 44
Institutul Central de Statistică
Bucureşti.

        In conformitate cu indicaţiunie date de Dvs.
referitoare la noul program de lucru, instalaţia de maşini
Hollerith oferită de noi la 22 Martie a.c., spre a putea face faţă volumului de lucrări şi spre a le putea executa în
forma cerută de Dvs., va trebui să cuprindă maşinile oferi-
te mai jos, oferta noastră din 22 Martie a.c. modificându-se
după cum urmează:

                                      Chirie lunară
                                       U.S.A. ǿ
                                   Unitar Total

FIGURE 4.1. Details of an offer written in 1939 for IBM to supply Romania with counting machines. Photo taken by author from the Romanian National Archives, 2018.

structure inspired Manuilă to launch his lofty census endeavor, which would go on to span ten days and employ twenty-nine thousand census takers to take inventory and map all people, property, assets, and even animals. IBM designed its questions and hired specially, trained enumerators to determine whether someone was Jewish even if they were not overtly "Jewish-seeming." Roma were also counted, and it was specified that even if someone was perceived as Roma but declined to admit Roma ancestry, the census taker should write "Ţigan."[13] The accumulated data was then handed over to the fascist military leader, Marshal Ion Antonescu, who, right before Romania joined the Second World War in 1941, demanded lists of all Jews, communists, and sympathizers throughout the country. He also called for the shipping of all Jews between the Siret and Prut rivers to concentration camps on already-scheduled trains, and worked with his Second Section intelligence unit and three statistical offices to oversee this deadly roundup. At least 270,000 Jewish and ten thousand Roma people were brutally murdered in Romania during this period.[14] After the war, blame for Jewish and Roma extermination across the continent was for the most part placed entirely on Germany, obviating the role that Romanians played. But also, the US tech company was let off the hook. IBM even filed compensation claims for machine damage.

Not everyone employed by the National Institute of Statistics to conduct the census project shared IBM's sociotechnical vision. While in some ways, all who did participate in it engaged in what Hannah Arendt describes as the "banality of evil,"[15] some stories contain important nuance. One of the men powering Manuilă's census endeavor was Sterian Pompiliu, who is currently over one hundred years old and is considered the oldest blogger in Romania.[16] Mostly he chronicles happenings at the Moses Rosen Senior Center, an assisted living home for Jewish elders located on the far edges of Bucharest and named after the city's chief rabbi during socialism. I have had the pleasure of meeting Mr. Pompiliu at the center, where seniors regularly have collaborated with the Macaz Bar Teatru Coop (Macaz Bar Theater Cooperative), cocreating anticapitalist plays about political futures past and those yet to come. Most members of Macaz identify as antifascist, as do the Moses Rosen seniors with whom they collaborate.

Pompiliu's own politics grew out of his experiences growing up in 1920s Bucharest, during which he enjoyed working on abacus calculators in school. After graduating, he enrolled in the Bucharest University of Economic Studies, but he was soon expelled per an order that banned all Jewish students from university courses. Soon after, laws were passed to expropriate Jewish property, and Pompiliu, suddenly homeless, was forced to sleep on a straw bed in a makeshift lean-to. It was then that he began working at the National Statistics Institute to help power the 1941 census. But, unlike many of his coworkers, because he was Jewish he was never paid. He had no idea at the time, he later recounted, that his employment was part of an endeavor to decimate his own community. Today, there are thousands of Romanians whose cheap labor is exploited by Western firms via outsourcing, many of whom are paid just a fraction of their Western counterparts, and few of whom are provided information about the material effects of the technologies and companies that their surplus labor enforces. In Romania, IBM maintains outsourcing firms in Bucharest and Brașov. While IBM's role in outsourcing in Romania is far from novel, its historically layered role in exploiting Romanian labor is.

When it comes to census data and the science of the state, it helps to think through what Katherine McKittrick and Alexander Weheliye describe as "commodification and dispossession through accounting."[17] The dispossession and death that the census project inhered facilitated IBM's own data accumulation. While IBM lost some machines after its European exploits, the company has continued to prosper through its past and ongoing data-grabbing techniques in which racialized people's bodies, lives, communities, and homes have become fodder for accumulation. Meanwhile, Watson's name was barely tarnished despite widespread liberal disavowal of the technofascist project. In 1949, shortly after its European affairs, Watson initiated the IBM World Trade Corporation to manifest imperial ambitions, many of which took place throughout Latin

America.[18] In Chile, IBM's interventions were explicitly anticommunist in nature, in part by sowing the seeds for Pinochet's brutal dictatorship. In 1952, IBM began operations in South Africa, importing electronic tabulating machines for their census.[19] It would go on to provide guidance for a discriminatory panoptic national ID system instigating mass anti-Black police brutality. By 1965, during the height of the Cold War, IBM World Trade maintained a gross income of over $1 billion.[20]

While the company's Cold War imperial ambitions have undoubtedly informed the economic architecture of Watson AI's deep learning powering in postsocialist times, this gets whitewashed through liberal understandings of technofascism, which today glom onto the figure of the illiberal Eastern European hacker rather than US technocapitalism. In a way, Watson immortalized himself and IBM's genocidal inheritance in the form of his *Jeopardy!*-winning Watson AI. This algorithmic entity is not only the result of 2,880 politically neutral IBM Power750 cores; the materiality of its machine learning is also fed by a technofascistic past woven into its robotic DNA. These cores continue to be powered by the bodies of those incinerated, shot, and worked to death at the behest of the US company's global exploits. They are also maintained by those engaged in surrogate labor in Romania and beyond working for fractions of the cost of what white-collar tech workers make. To assess this conjuncture, I continue to explore both socialist and postsocialist computing landscapes.

No Such Thing as a Free Lunch

IBM was largely absent in the Romanian tech scene during socialism, apart from the haunting of its technofascist computing ghosts. Yet computing and technological development became a crucial part of the communist project. As was the case throughout the Eastern bloc, the figure of the engineer itself was understood as a socialist cyborg of sorts,[21] intended to propel the region into modernity. Projects of electrification and industrialization meanwhile grew. These projects did not inhere assimilatory drives into liberal democracy, but rather the sustenance of a dialectical post-Enlightenment future, one premised on industrialization, urbanization, and centralization.[22] People were moved into cities undergoing rapid development, while dormitories were built around factories to house workers—the cyborgs of socialist futurity.

Technological growth in socialist Romania developed in part due to the country's maverick status with both the West and the Soviet Union. The Romanian Communist Party (known as the Romanian Workers Party or Partidul Muncitoresc Romîn until 1965, when it became the Partidul Comunist Român) had refused to fully align with the Soviet economic bloc COMECON, which had stipulated that each nation maintain an economic specialty, Romania's being agriculture.[23] But with technofuturist visions of collectivization as a precondition for industrialization, the Communist Party wanted to develop technology rather than supply food to the rest of the bloc. Scientists at the Atomic Physics Institute built Romania's first computer in 1957, CIFA-1, making Romania the eleventh country to manufacture one. After CIFA-1, an array of models erupted, from MARICA, DACICC, and CET in Cluj to MECIPT in Timișoara. For the most part, these machines were crafted to further scientific inquiry and to advance techno-urban centralization, for instance optimizing sugar beet harvesting and public transportation timetables.[24]

Having spoken with computer scientists involved in these early endeavors, nostalgia and wistfulness characterize many of their memories, as does a form of paternalism for having been the first or best at this or that. Vasile Baltac, one of the early makers of the MECIPT models, is a professor at Bucharest's National School of Political Science and Public Administration and the CEO/cofounder of software companies SoftNet.ro and Novatech. These are headquartered in the same building on Floreasca Boulevard that centralized national computer research during socialism. In the winter of 2017 he met with me there, eager to share photographs of times past when he and his colleagues led some of the country's most valorized technological missions. Unlike software company headquarters in Silicon Valley, the building is old and cracked, yet alive with technological futures past woven into concrete and cables.

As Baltac recounted, back in 1967, the government launched a program to promote computational industrial development and introduce computers into the national economy. Although third-generation computers were imported from the West, Romania successfully produced and exported its own by cloning Western models. France offered Romania the license for IRIS-50 medium-sized computers, which Baltac and his team transformed into the Felix C-256. An entire Felix family was cloned, with over 650 mainframes and many HCs (home computers) such as PRAE and CoBra. While Communist Party leader Nicolae Ceaușescu determined HCs to contravene party ideology for being too consumerist, their manufacturing continued beyond his purview.[25] Yet determined that Romania excel in informatics, polytechnics, and cybernetics, he developed research centers throughout the state. These specialized in hacking Western products and licenses. Over twenty-five official computer models were crafted during socialism, many of which were exported to the People's Republic of China, the Czechoslovak Socialist Republic, the German Democratic Republic, the Polish People's Republic, Syria, Egypt, and Iran.[26] By the time of the regime's collapse in 1989, Romania was exporting the most computers in the Eastern bloc.

This computer development project crumbled after 1989, at least the official one (I explore the unofficial one at length in the following chapter). But for the purposes of assessing Silicon Valley imperialism and IBM's role in gentrifying Romanian technoscapes, Felix's death is significant. In 2003, the company was privatized by special state order. Five days later, a board of directors with no computer background was established. The next year, roughly half of the factory's shares were auctioned and divided into joint stocks. Some went bankrupt in 2006, selling their land and buildings to real estate speculators who determined that the twenty thousand square meters on which the factory sat was worth more than the factory itself. It was then that IBM swept in and absorbed Felix workers, all the while delivering messages to Romanian IT managers about the technological merits of capitalism and the backwardness of socialism.

IBM's post-1989 technocapitalist messaging was part and parcel of an onslaught of Siliconized campaigns at the time. For instance, in 1990, a *New York Times* article proclaimed Romania technologically "20 years behind" due to communism's "crippling legacy," and thus requiring Western salvation.[27] In 1995, Malcolm Penn, representing a British think tank, gave a talk in Romania encouraging Romanians to embrace a new market opportunity while also warning of some potential "Key Issues" in a PowerPoint slide. These included "Lack Of Capitalist Culture/Work Ethic" and "Jealousy Risk When Sense Of Envy—Overtakes Sense Of Entrepreneurialship" [sic].[28] In other words, Penn suggested that unless Romanians fully embrace capitalism, failure will abound. As he continued: "Capitalism Is Not Perfect But, Like It Or Not, That Is The Way Of The World. The Challenge Is To Learn How To Exploit Its Benefits & Make It Work To Your Advantage . . . Just Like Everyone Else Has To!"[29] Later in the slideshow, he suggested that for Romania to move forward and avoid what he described as "colonisation" by the West, partnership with firms such as his was requisite.[30] Thus, in one fell swoop, he erased the entire history of Felix and Romanian computer production, positioning the country as technologically retrograde due to its anticapitalist alterity. At the same time, he rehearsed a trope that numerous colonial projects have perfected across the globe: cooperate with us or be decimated by us.

Throughout the 1990s, the promises of Western salvation were just mirages and false promises strewn about throughout Romania. These are woven together in David Schwartz's 2017 theater play *'90*, which chronicles the disenchantment and alienation experienced by everyday people unprepared for transition. Disillusionments included anticommunist "moral purity," entrepreneurial enthusiasm and disappointment . . . illusions of freedom . . . the closure of mines in Jiu valley . . . the legal restitution of houses once taken by communists to the more "correct" people . . . the degradation of the lives of workers and state employees . . . lives played at Caritas [the Ponzi scheme that took over Romanian lives between 1992 and 1994 before going bankrupt, leading to US$450 million in debt], CAR [Casă de Ajutor Reciproc—the mutual aid assistance program of the socialist era that served as a type of non-bank financial institution and that lost its power with socialism's collapse], [and] pawnshops.[31]

I first watched Schwartz's play in an anticolonial summer camp in the Romanian village of Telciu, surrounded mostly by millennials who were in tears by the end of the play, recollecting how much these false promises decimated their parents' lives. These promises get at what Lauren Berlant describes as "cruel optimism," or the unattainable fantasies of upward mobility that endure despite the reality that liberal-capitalist societies are unable to provide opportunities that make lives "add up to something."[32]

It was during this era of cruel optimism that English-language proficiency, along with the abundance of socialist-trained informatics workers, became fodder for Western firms looking to launch a new Eastern European outsourcing market. While these jobs offered opportunities to some, many people with whom I have spoken recount having lost, rather than gained, employment in the 1990s. Others meagerly pieced together an array of undignified gigs. In 1988, computer production was valued at ten billion lei, but in 1991 it sunk to three billion, with hardware production ceasing.[33] Florin, founder of an IT company, recounts the number of IT workers dropping rapidly and a Canadian firm swooping in to extract a team of two hundred people. In Cluj, the production of HC386 computers was halted, and "everything just shut down," he woefully remembered while pointing out that there are only four HC386s left in the country today. As factories crumbled, malls appeared. As small grocery stores vanished, Mega Image and Carrefour hypermarkets manifested from Western Europe. Casinos and gambling venues erupted with chain venues such as MaxBet. Between 2003 and 2014, the number of slot machines quadrupled in Romania, reaching sixty-two thousand.[34] Today these gambling venues are still filled with working-class people trying to win at a capitalist game rigged against them.[35]

Cristian, a friend and local DJ, works for a multinational in Sema Park, adjacent to the Polytechnic University. One cold winter day, he met me there to show me around. As we began walking by teams of tech employees with badges hanging from lanyards worn around their necks waiting in queues for food trucks, Cristian began reminiscing about his own rootedness there. His father had been a cyberneticist, having studied at the Polytechnic University in the 1980s. While his father got a good job upon graduating, it was made obsolete after 1989. So instead, he resorted to driving taxis and working odd jobs throughout Cristian's childhood. After high school, Cristian was able to study economics in the United Kingdom. He then managed to get a job for Hewlett-Packard in Romania. Now he does technical writing for a different firm, here in Sema Park.

During socialism, Sema Park had been an agricultural industrial center, connected by metro with Timpuri Noi Metal Works (now also a growing tech epicenter explored in chapter 3). But today Sema Park lives as a jumble of high-tech glass towers and old socialist-era warehouses. There are still canteens that serve the same traditional Romanian food that they served to socialist agricultural workers, but now they've rebranded their exteriors with brick and glass, having changed their names to hipster-sounding titles such as Cactus. "They're just doing what they have to do to keep up," Cristian told me. There are also new food trucks that sell burgers and coffee, and a fancy café surrounded by a tropical botanical garden inside the glass building where he works. Nearby is a sports center and bowling alley called IDM, with a logo mimicking IBM's. It has been there for a while though, and, having bowled there myself, I can attest that it is far from bourgeois inside. "It's more in the Western simulation style of the 1990s and early 2000s," Cristian told me. "This is what everything was like in the '90s—I miss it," he said, pointing at a crumbling, empty lot next door. He used to come here to go clubbing back when it was cheap, he told me, his voice trailing off.

The Most Dangerous Town on the Internet

Not everyone engaged in postsocialist technoculture is employed in Silicon Valley surrogate labor. Nor is everyone engaged in Silicon mimicry. On the contrary, a rich cyberculture beyond Silicon Valley developed underground during socialism, only to balloon in postsocialist times. Yet most Western imaginaries of Romanian computing culture today portray the region as seeping with dangerous hackers operating underground, threatening to rip out the heart of the free world. These imaginaries displace attention from technofascist computing ventures such as IBM's, and instead focus on Eastern Europe as the harbinger of illiberalism. This obviates not only the role that companies such as IBM have long played in Romania, but also the violence of Silicon Valley imperialism.

In 2018, the Romanian-German television series *Hackerville* made headlines as HBO Europe's first co-international production. The series features a German-Romanian detective who returns to her Romanian hometown of Timișoara to track down a ring of dangerous cybercriminals. As is revealed, some of these criminals are just kids having fun and trying to make fast money, while others are embedded in a nefarious international criminal network. Created by Ralph Martin and Jörg Winger, the series also explores repressive socialism histories in Romania. However, "Hackerville" as a geographic descriptive generally refers not to Timișoara, but rather the smaller mountain city of Râmnicu Vâlcea, which in 2011, *Wired* famously described as "Cybercrime Central."[36] Not mentioned in the article is that capitalist injections into the local Râmnicu Vâlcea economy have been largely disastrous, with former state-owned factories such as Râmnicu Vâlcea Chemical Works collapsing and inciting widespread unemployment. Hacking developed there as one of many means of postsocialist survival.

Perhaps inspired by the *Wired* article and precursor to *Hackerville* in 2015, the Silicon Valley cybersecurity firm Norton Security and director Sean Dunne debuted a film about dangerous Romanian hackers. In it, they rendered Râmnicu Vâlcea as the "Most Dangerous Town on the Internet."[37] Similar to *Hackerville*, Norton depicts Romanian cybercriminals in socialist-era decrepit buildings, threatening to hack the entire planet. But unlike the HBO series, Norton's video features actual hackers, many of whom have since been apprehended, some of whom were offered plea deals to work for cybersecurity firms. Centrally featured are Guccifer (who famously hacked Hillary Clinton, George W. Bush, Colin Powell, and more), Iceman (who hacked NASA), and Tinkode, the most wanted hacker of 2012, ill-famed for having hacked the Pentagon, the US Army, YouTube, SUN Microsystems, Google, NASA, Facebook, and more. While Guccifer stands by his cyber activity, driven by anti-US imperial and anticorporate politics, Tinkode, after being apprehended, was offered a plea bargain to work for Western cybersecurity experts. This trend of flipping sides was relatively common during the 1990s in the West as "the hacker" transformed from an underground, subversive status to one of professionalization applauded by the media and even politicians.[38] Yet in Eastern Europe, it wasn't until the 2000s that the figure of the hacker became synonymous with corruption and therefore a target of cybersecurity co-optation.

Throughout Norton's film, cloaked hacker figures are juxtaposed with harrowing police narratives, the ramblings of a somber priest, and the authoritative voice of Norton's all-knowing head of security, Kevin Healy. As captions ominously warn in the beginning, "Last year, over a billion dollars was stolen by Romanian hackers. Everyone knows what is happening, but *omerta*, the code of silence, is the norm."[39] As is inferred, the Silicon Valley cybersecurity company is here to save innocent Americans from the most dangerous town on the internet and its code of silence. Abetting this plot, Nicolae Stănculescu, a former Râmnicu Vâlcean authority figure during socialism, attempts to contextualize the city's proliferation of hackers. "The legacies of communism are complex," he warns. "Many of the burdens from that regime still dominate aspects of people's lives. Important changes took place, especially in the 1980s and 1990s when Romania went crazy resulting in the creation of the so-called new human." Mădălin Dumitru, a Romanian IT security specialist and founder of Cyber Smart Defense, offers, "Because under communism, we were quite limited. We didn't have so many gadgets. We didn't have so much access to technology. And since 1989, since the Romanian revolution, Romanians started to have access to this technology, and they started to develop more and more. They were hungry for IT and for technology." Aligned with Siliconized anticommunist narratives in which everything that transpired during state socialism was retrograde, these anticommunist narratives equate capitalism and liberation.

Much of the film centers around an interview with Guccifer (Marcel Lehel Lazăr), who fashioned his portmanteau to conjure "the style of Gucci and the light of Lucifer."[40] He first made headlines in 2013 after hacking into the accounts of nearly one hundred American politicians and celebrities, including that of Hillary Clinton's former adviser, highlighting the Secretary of State's illegal use of a private email server while in office. Guccifer was later caught and extradited to the United States, where he has since admitted to having executed his hacks in Romania while using proxy servers in Russia. Shot in the cold, stark winter, the film is made to sensationalize the bleakness of Romanian cybercriminality and the durability of undying communist ghosts materially and virtually haunting the "free world." Other hackers are filmed against crumbling socialist buildings, wearing hoodies that obscure their identities. Yet viewers are offered hope. After watching the film, they can easily navigate to Norton's web page to purchase a security plan, thereby ensuring that their digital life will never be hacked by a Romanian cybercriminal from the internet's most dangerous town. Silicon Valley securitization has thereby mobilized a Cold War narrative just to produce a purchasable antidote—the ultimate technocapitalist plot!

Norton is not the only Silicon Valley cybersecurity firm to profit through Cold War renderings of Romania's hackers. After Trump's victory in 2016,

US liberal pundits began blaming Eastern and Russian hackers, rather than acknowledging the Democratic Party's own failings or homegrown white supremacy. While hacking did indeed abet Trump's win, Eastern blame created the perfect narrative structure to reanimate the Cold War. The hack was first claimed by an individual with the moniker Guccifer 2.0, who asserted Romanian origin but who cybersecurity firms Russophobically named Fancy Bear and Cozy Bear. One such cybersecurity firm, ThreatConnect, concluded their investigative report by invoking the 2005 speculative film, *Star Wars: Episode III—Revenge of the Sith*.[41] The space opera, which was first released during the height of the Cold War in 1977, chronicles struggles between enlightened Jedi knights and the evil Emperor Palpatine. It is Palpatine that ThreatConnect latched onto, suggesting that for the United States to remain enlightened and free, it must defeat the dark Russian/Soviet enemy. Silicon Valley imperialism in this way justifies its technological intervention by mapping fictive battles between good and evil onto geopolitical sites of intervention.

While Norton's film strategically fails to capture the violence of disaster capitalism in Romania, never mind the role of Western firms such as IBM in engineering it, there are other media pieces that bring this relationship into focus. In 2018, David Schwartz debuted another of his plays in Râmnicu Vâlcea's National Theater, *Portofele Virtuale: Proiect Generația Y* (Virtual Wallet: Generation Y Project). Based on interviews with the city's youth about their hacking experiences during transition, he portrays a version of the town's hacking culture unrecognizable through cybersecurity advertisements and films. Several acts are staged in progression in which it becomes clear that hacking in the internet's most dangerous town emerged not through malice, but rather through a combination of play and survival amid a faltering economy. Scams and schemes devised in internet cafés and bedrooms alike, Schwartz illustrates, offered young people some sense of hope, but also kinship and sociality.

One evening after the play's debut, Schwartz told me about how amazed he was that the bulk of the hackers he interviewed were just kids. Many of them had parents who left to work abroad in the West, and who by engaging in informal and occasionally formal language training were able to deceive Westerners online. For instance, the opening act of the play "Primul Jaguar" (The first jaguar) begins in 2004 and features two then-ten-year-old friends, Ștefan and Cătă, from a quiet neighborhood known as Tic Tac. Ștefan's mom works at the Tricotextil factory, owned by an Italian firm. His dad is a bodyguard at the Coca-Cola plant. Cătă's mother meanwhile lives in Italy and sporadically sends money back home to her poor family while his father works at a local construction site. It was during that era that internet cafés began popping up in Tic Tac. As Ștefan and Cătă chronicle their exploits in Tic Tac's early internet cafés on stage, youth surrounding me in the audience clearly familiar with the neighborhood's histories began laughing hysterically. Amid the laughter, Ștefan and Cătă recount that their main objective then had been to play games such as *Counterstrike*, a US- and Microsoft-funded first-person shooter game. They also note that vehicles began appearing in the streets around this time, including a Jaguar owned by Ștefan's upstairs neighbor Viorel. It was then that Viorel began asking Ștefan for help with online translation. Ștefan barely knew how to translate, but soon, by enlisting language support from his friends, he began making more money than he had ever dreamed of. Yet, at the time, he had no idea what a "hacker" even was. "I know the word, in English, but what is a hacker?" he rhetorically poses to the audience in Romanian.

The play then fast-forwards seven years, to a summer evening in Tic Tac during which Ștefan recounts sitting outside, sipping on a Radler beer. The neighborhood has completely fallen apart by then, despite the presence of scattered Mustang cars and other frayed luxury objects. That evening the police swarm Tic Tac, searching for Viorel. Ștefan feels like he is in a really bad video game, one infused with machine guns and masked officers. It is only after Viorel gets incarcerated that Ștefan discovers that his upstairs neighbor was one of the city's first hackers. Somehow, through an online scam that Ștefan had unknowingly abetted in, Viorel had profited from the sales of two million helicopters without even having really sold one. And so goes a typical hacking account of the early 2000s from the most dangerous town on the internet, where characters such as Ștefan, Cătă, and Viorel engaged in online scams not to take down the free world, but rather for play and survival amid a crumbling economy. Writing of scammers in postcolonial Jamaican contexts of joblessness, Jovan Scott Lewis suggests that the scam functions as a form of "reparative seizure," whereby scammers "exploit the local's long engagement with the global, where seizure finds its ethical virtue in the claims of the poor."[42] As an extralegal form of remediation, the scam and the hack each vindicate capitalist consumer-based logics championed by companies such as IBM, all the while reshaping what is possible within its enclosures.

Vampires

The so-called end of history following the collapse of the Cold War was ruptured not only by postsocialist cyber deviance, but also by the West's need for a new enemy that liberal values could be reconsolidated against. This built on the Cold War inimical, a monstrous figuration of the dangerous other inspired by imperial Orientalist and gothic vampiric imaginaries. As Jill Galvan argues, Stoker's *Dracula* was originally an allegory of British imperial fears of racial contamination amid imperial expansion, particularly regarding Russian military intelligence and Indian rebellious communications.[43] These fears were mobilized along Europe's ambiguous Eastern borderlands, amplified by the aftermaths of the Crimean War. With this in mind, Neda Atanasoski suggests that instead of calcifying a hardened "boundary between European modernity and its others, the imperial Gothic frame and its political afterlife exemplify how knowledge and technology are constituted through the very horrors they seek to subjugate."[44]

While Orientalist and gothic imaginaries informed US Cold War readings of the dangerous Third World,[45] it also consolidated fears against the Second. Alaina Lemon writes, "In nineteenth-century Britain we also find the fear of automation expressed via suspicion of materialism—a suspicion that would carry over into the ideological enmity between socialism and capitalism in the next century."[46] Imperialist British anxieties of Russian and Indian communication channels thus sowed the seeds for US Cold War fears of vampiric communist mind control and influence. The Cold War other thus gets revived in Cold War aftermaths by the figure of the vampire. The Cold War vampire, marked by what Atanasoski describes as "an interior difference of belief," then lives as "a testament to modernity's unfinished project, which has kept the West ever vigilant of 'others' who might reemerge from the dead to strike at civilized lifeworlds."[47] In her words, "The racialized specter of Communist unfreedom became a repository for anxieties surrounding the limitations of liberal reforms to account for ongoing inequality in the nation."[48] This inspired US counterinsurgency militarized campaigns against communist organizing across the world while also attempting to win hearts and minds at home and abroad with, as Nick Estes puts it, humanitarian aid becoming "the empire's bargaining chip."[49] This salvific sentiment helped engineer a Cold War victory and continued post–Cold War Western intervention. Yet now this Western vampiric obsession has become recoded through the figure of the hacker. This vampiric hacker speaks to the incomplete project of the Cold War, but also to the Western imperialism that predates it. An unremitting stream of Silicon intervention is thus framed as requisite in order to bring about history's long-awaited end.

While the gothic hacker hooks into Cold War 2.0 fears and fascinations, one could also argue that in fact it is Silicon Valley imperialism sucking the blood from undead socialist-era computing infrastructure and technological prowess. This was after all the case when IBM rushed in to absorb the ex-socialist workforce after 1989. It was after all in *Capital* that Marx employed the allegory of the vampire to describe the violence of capitalist economics, scribing that "Capital is dead labour which, vampire-like, lives only by sucking living labour, and lives the more, the more labour it sucks."[50] Comparing exploitation in the US factory system with that of prior peasant appropriation by landowners, Marx looks to Romanian provinces for exemplification: "For Moldavia the regulations are even stricter. 'The 12 corvée days of the Règlement organique,' cried a boyar, drunk with victory, 'amount to 365 days in the year.'"[51] The boyar (a wealthy landlord) in Marx's account happens to be none other than fifteenth-century Vlad the Țepeș, or Count Dracula.[52] It was during this period that racial capitalist practices began to emerge in which Roma lives and labor served as technology fodder for boyar racial technocapitalist wealth (as explored in chapter 1).

Marx's capitalist vampire metaphor has continued to transit across time. Franco Moretti writes that "like capital, Dracula is impelled towards a continuous growth, an unlimited expansion of his domain: accumulation is inherent in his nature."[53] Donna Haraway describes the vampire as "the marauding figure of unnaturally breeding capital, which penetrates every whole being and sucks it dry in the lusty production and vastly unequal accumulation of wealth."[54] Thus, similar to the reliance on monsters in Orientalist and Cold War tales alike, anticapitalist analysis has fulfilled allegoric enmity through the figure of the vampire.

That a Romanian medieval count is used to allegorize the violence of capitalism for Marx, on one hand speaks to the central node that Eastern Europe played in early racial capitalist exploits. But on the other, it underscores the West's long-standing exoticization of and paranoia and squeamishness about the East, even in economic science. While read through Marx's own metaphors, Silicon technologies of predation are vampiric. Yet arguably, his very concept of *vampiric* is vampiric in and of itself, sucking the blood of an already appropriated figure to articulate the violence of extraction. This double appropriation helps delineate the longue durée of Western interpretations of the East, including today's obsession with the undead cyborgian Cold War other. The hacker vampire, like vampires of the past, violates classifications and taxonomies, enabling, as Haraway suggests, categories to travel.[55] Is the vampire the Eastern hacker plotting to take down Western democracy? Or is it companies such as IBM that profited not only from presocialist technofascist counting machines, but also by rushing back in after 1989 to suck the remnants of socialist-era technological prowess while inculcating societies with capitalist fantasies? Is it a bunch of working-class Romanian teenagers scamming US shoppers to have fun and vindicate consumer-based logics, or is it the cybersecurity firms justifying US intervention to thwart Palpatine's ongoing quest?

Today, the notion of hacking has had its own blood sucked through Western liberalism, with corporate hackathons a mainstay of corporate technoculture.[56] Most, if not all, of the so-called hackathons that I have attended in Romania still resemble Penn's 1995 slideshow edifying the merits of capitalism. I have sat in on countless of these sessions in coworking spaces, conferences, and tech hubs alike, where after an hour or so, the whole thing becomes dizzying. . . . In Bucharest, a German CyberGhost entrepreneur delivers talks on the benefits of outsourcing and geographic arbitrage in Romania. "My company could never have succeeded had I gone to Silicon Valley," he exclaims. Romania is where it's at. Then, Uber's Pierre-Dimitri Gore-Coty arrives in Cluj for the first time and delivers a talk on the need to innovate old industries in Bucharest's TechHub to a room packed full of nicely dressed workers. "Bus stops are too analog!" he excitingly exclaims, promoting Uber's new driverless cars. Pizza is delivered, and the aroma of hipster coffee seeps through the air. . . . Two days later, I find myself in TechFest nearby, where a man from a small Cluj-Berlin start-up markets the company's new smart home security device, which is becoming especially popular in Western Europe with "this new immigrant problem." No one in the room seems to mind, or to consider that it is often Romanians perceived by the West as part of this problem to be technologically solved through surveillance. He goes on about how the device can detect the gender of voices, so that if you are a woman and ask to watch a movie, it will go through "chick-flick and rom-com" options first. Applause. Yet the security device, while produced in Romania, only recognizes English and German. More artisanal coffee. No, the code is not open source, as they must run a business after all. . . . I could be in San Francisco. But I'm in Cluj's new IT building, unironically called "The Office." Sitting on the ruins of a socialist-era textiles factory, one would be hard-pressed to imagine the former mode of production in the now glimmering glass building. Rents have gone up around it, and the food court and wine bar underneath boast prices comparable with Silicon Valley.

While the salaries of "Office" IT workers are not commensurate with those of Silicon Valley, tech workers are still paid much more than their working-class neighbors.[57] As Maria, a tech worker from Brăila living in Cluj and working for a Florida start-up, describes, "Sure, we're paid less, but I'm still making more than any of my friends, and I can travel to these digital nomad meetups and work from home." But others are not so optimistic. Alexandra, who once was a programmer, now can't find a job nor achieve freelancer status. Instead,

FIGURE 4.2. The Office in Cluj advertising a tech festival. Photo taken by author, 2018.

she bemoans that tech companies are so behind the West in understanding proper management. She is now looking to leave the country and find a job in Western Europe, "anywhere but here." Andrei, on the other hand, likes the stability of his job working for a Silicon Valley company while living in Bucharest with his friends, but he's forced to work night shifts answering calls, and finds his moods altered due to lack of sleep. Many people I have spoken with who are employed as outsourced tech labor articulate aspirations of working for bigger and better Silicon Valley companies, either in or beyond Romania. As Megan Moodie writes, aspirations of upward mobility, when studied ethnographically, often reveal how particular groups of people weather "transition from an era of state-backed protections to an era of contract labor."[58] For instance, Oracle, now housed in Pipera near the Felix factory's ghosts, seems to be the end goal for those who wish to remain in Bucharest. Yet many people answering calls and writing boilerplate emails for large companies articulate boredom at work. For them, it's just a job. Iulia, an undergrad gender studies major in Bucharest who supports herself by working for Oracle during evenings and weekends, tells me that the only thing redemptive about her job is that she can sneak in YouTube videos on breaks between monotonous tasks.

For those like Iulia untrained in software development, the only real requirement for tech call center work in Romania is English fluency. While this has everything to do with US empire, it also has roots in socialist and transitional histories. During socialism, people were mostly restricted to watching one to two television stations made available by the Communist Party. But eager for more, people began illegally streaming neighboring countries' channels and thereby learning foreign languages, from Bulgarian to Serbian—perhaps another form of vampiric reparative seizure. Following 1989, Western programming flooded the channels, and many people, already accustomed to learning languages through TV, quickly mastered English. "Now they teach English to all the kids at school," a friend observed, "but our generation, we learned from the Cartoon Network." Iulia mentioned that it was by watching US television that she learned how to smile like an American and feign a US genre of enthusiasm, one largely absented from service work in Romania but necessary for outsourced labor.[59] Prior to Oracle, she worked for a US company for two years, where she was forced to smile even while writing emails to clients "who could tell." Meanwhile, those with coding skills are praised by their employers for "being so damn good at programming," Alex, who works for a small Seattle-based start-up affiliated with Amazon, told me. But he is only paid a small portion of what his US contemporaries are. "It's beyond patronizing," he shrugged. Yet his peers herald Western companies such as IBM as salvific, he told me over a beer after work one evening in a bar that would soon be shut down in the gentrifying neighborhood.

It was in the aftermath of the Cold War that customer service became restructured transnationally as US imperialism augmented its scope. Toll-free "1-800" numbers for US callers proliferated, each reaching a call center in the Global South and East staffed by workers around the clock. Jan Padios maps a mass proliferation of call centers in the Philippines during this time oriented toward capitalizing on "Filipinos' ability to speak with light or 'neutral' accents, their intimate familiarity with American media and ways of life, and their abundant affective capacity."[60] These capacities, she writes, have everything to do with the affective and emotional labor that US and Spanish imperialism required in the Philippines. While Romania was not colonized by the United States per se (though its lands were ruled by a slew of empires over time from the Ottoman to the Austrian), there are connections to be made via post–Cold War Silicon Valley imperialism and the Orientalist imaginaries it has upheld. There are also connections to be made with the incursion of presocialist predatory companies like IBM when Pompiliu, houseless, slaved away on the technofascist census for no pay. At the same time, technocapitalists such as Malcolm

Penn rushing in to co-opt Romania's microelectronics industry in the 1990s suggested that unless the country cooperated with the West, it would be colonized.

Despite this predatory history, Romanian tech workers today are not without agency. Through hacks and scams, many have found techniques to subvert Silicon Valley's imperial control. One of *Portofele Virtuale*'s more comical acts, for instance, features two bored British tech workers, Paul and Dennis, based in England. In their five-minute break between monotonous tasks, they turn to eBay. Paul, excitedly landing on a beautiful shirt for sale, asks Dennis if he's ever heard of an "I-E." When Paul explains that it's a handmade traditional shirt from Romania, Dennis replies, "From Romania? I thought they only exported scroungers and cheap labor." Paul protests, to which Dennis laughs, "What? Oh, I forgot I'm with Mr. Liberal at the office." Paul goes on to explain that his girlfriend's friend just came back from a Romanian business trip, where she picked up a lovely handmade blouse with red and blue flowers stitched around the neckline.

Unbeknownst to Paul and Dennis, two Romanian scammers, Roxana and Marius, are trying to sell this exact type of shirt on eBay. While one can buy a traditional Romanian *ia* blouse (*ie* is the plural) for less than a few euros in Romania (although handmade ones are indeed expensive), Roxana and Marius began selling them online for forty-nine euros. They carefully note that the organic objects are handmade from a tiny, traditional village, and that the pattern around the neck marks "the walk of life." Coming across their eBay post, Paul enthusiastically exclaims, "Wow, look at this, it's proper fancy. I am telling you Dior has a collection inspired from these 'yiaaahs.' They say it's from a northern village in 'Mermoores' . . . 'Mairmures.' They say this area of Romania, the Carpathians, benefits from one of the most powerful energetic shields of the planet." (Everyone in the audience familiar with the *ia* blouse and the region of Maramureș is at this point giggling hysterically.) Continuing, Paul turns to Dennis: "Mate, I'm not joking. Apparently, there are places that have this kind of energetic charge, places where the earth vibrates." Elated, Dennis then asks if Paul can buy ten, since they're so cheap. By playing into the Western fetishization of the East, Roxana and Marius are able to scam Silicon Valley imperialism and the Orientalism it peddles to materialize reparative seizure. As post–Cold War cyborgian vampires, they refuse to be confined to outsourced surrogacy. Rather, nestled in the internet's most dangerous town, they are able to trick the algorithms of exploitation undergirding Watson AI's materiality. In doing so, they weave together new digital relations that in refusing the mandates of Siliconization, create technofutures unrecognizable to Thomas Watson's algorithmic ghosts.

Corruption, *Șmecherie*, and Clones

There are about a dozen of us hovering around a table in the Macaz Bar Teatru Coop (Macaz Bar Theater Cooperative) in downtown Bucharest on Moșilor Street, where the artists Veda Popovici and Mircea Nicolae are convening one of several workshops as part of their project *Istoria (Nu) Se Repetă*, or *History (Does Not) Repeat Itself*. As workshop participants, we are tasked with devising objects that can be used to depict a future past from Romania's postsocialist transitional period—one that could have happened after 1989 but never did. As the artists describe their project:

> From darkness to light, from authoritarianism to freedom, from com- munism to capitalism—these tropes form the greatest narrative of re- cent history. This narrative casts collective experiences of solidarity and resistance in the footnote of history. The dreams and projections of the 1990s and 2000s, the post-revolutionary desires of a truly better world for all, remain buried under *caritasuri* (financial pyramid schemes), *mine- riade* (miner-led protests), and migration. In *Istoria (Nu) Se Repetă*, these

are returning fragments and imperfections in the narrations of possible but lost worlds: feminist trade unions, radical housing movements, collaborative economic projects or awareness raising campaigns on the dangers of capitalism.[1]

These counterfactual stories encompass an array of sites, from the Coop Bank and public information campaign entitled "Money Is Not Made through Work," to the Union of Women Workers of Romania, who occupied their Suveica factory and who now own their own homes in Floarea Albă (rather than the San Francisco–based Coldwell Banker real estate firm, which currently owns the 900-unit apartment complex). And the list goes on, filled with places and stories that could have been, but due to the decimating impacts of shock therapy during Romania's transition to capitalism, never were.

As *Istoria (Nu) Se Repetă* project participants, we have convened in order to imagine these critical fabulations and to fabricate their materialities. A few of us are excited about one space in particular: the building on Calea Victoriei that in the mid-1990s headquartered both the Roma rights association, Romani Criss, and the LGBT organization, Accept. During the 1990s, these two groups did indeed share space, forging what could have been rich and sustained space of anticolonial, anti-racist, anticapitalist, and queer futurity had liberal NGO-ization and capitalist imperatives not severed them. But in Popovici and Nicolae's future past, the two groups continue to grow together and build a Free School. As workshop participants, we opt to draft a syllabus for the school, and among other topics, we decide that hacking should be included in the curriculum. As one participant offers, "Yes, we all learned computer programming during the 1990s, and before that during socialism. And everyone hacked or knew someone who did. What would have happened if hacking could have really kept Romania from getting swallowed up by global capital?" Another bemoaned, "Romania had such a strong informatics program during socialism, and DIY tech stuff too—but it all got cannibalized by the West after 1989." "Look around, it's like Silicon Valley has taken over," another muttered. "*Șmecherie*—is alive and well in hacking here," another suggested, utilizing a Romanian word with Romani roots that connotes a form of street-smart ingenuity.[2] "Shouldn't it have been able to help us keep from being Siliconized?" Why wasn't Romanian computing culture better able to resist Siliconization? Is it too late?

By Siliconization, workshop participants refer to the practice of *becoming* Silicon Valley, or the concrete materialities caught up in dreams of techno-Westernization. Aligned with what Saidiya Hartman describes as "critical fabulation"—or the writing of speculative histories marked by violence and institutions on one hand, but also "desire and the want of something better"[3]— *Istoria (Nu) Se Repetă* fabricates a postsocialist transitional culture that could have been more emancipatory than it was. This genre of fabrication can be understood as queer, in that it refuses Fukuyama's normative end-of-history inevitability and what Elizabeth Freeman critiques as "chrono-normativity," or the temporality that capitalism inheres in order to reproduce its futurity.[4] Rather, it embraces possibilities often elided in liberal humanist institutions by following what Lisa Lowe describes as the past conditional or "what could have been."[5] Neda Atanasoski and Kalindi Vora build on this in theorizing postsocialism as a "queer temporality, one that does not reproduce its social order even as its revolutionary antithesis."[6] This aligns with Bogdan Popa's theorization of queer postsocialist politics, whereby queerness "emerges from desires that constitute a surplus in relation to the normal circuit of exchange value."[7] In dreaming up technofutures past, *Istoria (Nu) Se Repetă* participants don't aim to recuperate or reinvent state socialism, but rather to queerly pave the way for new anticapitalist futures.

Antithetical to normative socialist and transition technonarratives, *șmecherie* signals a form of deviancy and excess beyond capitalism's scarcity logics. This framework maps onto Anjali Arondekar's description of abundance as a queer archival paralogic freed from dominant trappings of historical recovery predicated on archival dearth.[8] What if the archive of computing knowledge beyond Siliconized frameworks is far from empty? There are after all countless tales of *șmecherie* untethered to Silicon Valley—the latter having become an unnecessary synecdoche for all things computational. Other computing stories, as Kris Cohen and Scott Richmond suggest, beget exploration of complex computational personhoods, how they came to be, how they "might have been otherwise."[9] They narrate "how people excluded from intelligible forms of being computer subjects have improvised lives and made worlds out of (but not always inside of) the strictures of computation."

Indeed, as *Istoria (Nu) Se Repetă* workshop participants agreed, socialist and transitional Romania maintained a rich cyberculture—one often erased in normative computing narratives. Victor Petrov suggests, "The conventional narrative of Eastern European communism is one of technologically backward states that failed to enter the information age, locked behind an impenetrable Iron Curtain that prevented both people and ideas from circulating."[10] Yet during the 1970s and '80s, Romania excelled in informatics, having cloned Western licenses in order to produce unique models such as the Felix and CoBra. Meanwhile, underground, technologists, hackers, and playful youth cloned and produced their own unique computers and networks, practices that endured and even flourished into post-1989 transition. Similar stories can be found across Eastern Europe, often having to do with contexts of making do, play, and sociality in ways that engender new forms of kinship, piracy, and commoning.[11]

In this chapter, I look beyond Siliconized strictures, weaving together ethnographic participatory work conducted in feminist, anticapitalist spaces such as Macaz with studies of Romania's socialist and postsocialist cybercultures. In conjoining these worlds, I look at how desires of both becoming and unbecoming Silicon Valley render differential retrospective, and also at times, speculative, technocultural accounts. Methodologically, I take up Alexei Yurchak's practice of attending to retrospective accounts of socialism and transition produced in their aftermaths.[12] I am interested in the differences between state tech projects and those produced in what he calls "deterritorialized milieus" outside, yet in relationship to, those of the state.[13] By not taking "the West" nor the state as technocultural origin points, yet by tracing their roles in the project of Siliconization, this chapter aligns with the ongoing political work of anticapitalist collectives such as Macaz committed to conjuring and recoding deviant relationships whitewashed in anticommunist transitional narratives.

Corruption

Amid the contemporary onslaught of liberal capitalist programming worlds, imaginaries surrounding the practitioners of șmecherie, particularly regarding the Cold War figure of "the hacker," are often interpellated as corrupt. Corruption here emerges through an anticommunist equating of socialist-era technicity as a viral threat to "end of history" operating systems. This operating system programs Silicon Valley imperialism as an anti-corruption antidote, inculcating Romanians with dreams of becoming Siliconized. While this takes on countless forms, perhaps it is most overtly visible in the high concentration of Western outsourcing firms that have taken over the country since 1989. Colossal glass IT offices and coworking spaces gentrify Romanian urban centers today, often sitting on but obscuring the exoskeletons of socialist-era factories. Hidden from view is the socialist-era cyber deviancy which provided the prowess and skills that Silicon Valley firms later co-opted and absorbed when they rushed in after 1989. Yet Siliconization is also corrupted by the dark technoworlds that it cannibalizes, but that which at any moment resurface in a number of forms ranging from pesky computer viruses to antigentrification organizing.

Liberal populist movements today are also corruption obsessed, rendering their enemy the corrupt and lingering ghosts of communism that need to be exorcised to augur in neoliberal futurity. As explored in chapter 3, much of this came to a head during Romania's 2017–2018 Light Revolution, marked by anti-communist demonstrators' use of "light technology" to chastise government corruption. Supported by big banks, tech firms, and neoliberal politicians, the idea was to overcome lingering socialist specters through Siliconization. While political corruption does exist profusely throughout Romanian governmental worlds, it also runs amok within global capital firms preying on Romanian resources and labor. Anti-corruption protests strategically turn a blind eye to capitalist corruption, instead focusing on the deals, bribes, and backroom channels mobilized by politicians—many of whom are depicted as the undying authoritarian specters of state socialism. While state socialism, particularly in the 1970s and 1980s, was marked by increased repression, austerity, elite control, surveillance, and nationalism, anti-corruption protests reify a Cold War discursive strategy that renders anticapitalism the real enemy.

Anticommunist-skewed understandings of corruption materialize in spaces of protest but also in computer programming. Take the following scenario from *Black the Fall*, a Bucharest-based, Japanese-backed video game: Everyone is watching. It's dark—it's always dark—and Black is trying to escape unnoticed from the repressive regime that is communist Romania. Black, a nut and bolt factory worker, has to deceive guards, smuggle goods, and manipulate people—all without getting caught in the cold, industrial never-ending dystopia. Black, a video game character in *Black the Fall*, has only one friend—an abandoned robot. On screen, Black, a humanoid perhaps more machine than human himself, is hard to make out against rows of identical figures. These are either bicycling to power the machine that was state socialism or listening to the censored Radio Free Europe—a Cold War US-backed media propaganda machine designed to instill anticommunist sentiment within the Eastern bloc.[14] As Black sneaks past a sea of coffins arranged in a half-collapsed building, an overseer blocks a forgotten room filled with old portraits, a vestige from the good old presocialist days when Bucharest was "the Little Paris of the East."

To the game designers writing code in "the Silicon Valley of Eastern Europe," this aristocratic era is a fond historical memory, a time when kings still meant something—a time before socialism and its aftermaths corrupted promises of Western enlightenment. In the game, even after "the wall" comes down in what is understood to be 1989, blackness persists. According to game creator Cristian Diaconescu, this is due to the specters of socialist corruption. As he puts it, "We called the character 'Black' because that's the word that captures how communism was for us."[15] In his words, while communism's ghastliness haunts the present, "The game is less about the horrors of communism, than it is about us." Fittingly, if one makes it to the game's end, a photo of Diaconescu's design team at a Light Revolution protest appears, the team disavowing communism's stubborn specters.

While corruption in computer programming and data storage refers to processes in which errors and malware alike compromise data integrity and lead to system crashes, in postsocialist Siliconized contexts, socialism and its remnants are rendered as corrupt. In the game, Black's robot friend is coded as clumsy, tired, and dark, nothing like portrayals of Siliconized clean, light technology of today. In this way, Siliconization ensures its futurity by straightening temporally corrupt cyberculture. Shannon Woodcock suggests, "Just as the homosexual is born into his/her closet and needs to develop in order to 'come out' into the world of heterosexuals, the 'post-socialist' East exists in Western capitalist discourse in order for EUrope to benevolently bestow recognition on its other."[16] This framework of recognition understands that to escape its socialist-era ghosts, Eastern Europe must become Silicon Valley and disavow the bleak past, shuttling "the Little Paris of the East" into "the Silicon Valley of Eastern Europe"—both periods of Western aspiration and mimicry.

Yet it was during socialism that mimicry was materially practiced in the realm of computer cloning. Many former hackers, scammers, and DIY technologists alike recall these past exploits not as a means of "catching up" with the West, but rather as experiments of *șmecherie*. Though few of these hackers identify as queer (or as part of Roma culture), they are woven into the deviant and cunning worlds that *șmecherie* (as it has been popularized in Romanian poor and working-class culture) gestures toward. While state-sanctioned cloning can be linked to Romania's own desires to catch up and simultaneously feed the machinery of state surveillance,[17] underground cloning, hacking, and cabling were rather implemented to instantiate kinship and connectivity amid conditions of rampant austerity and disconnection.

As *Istoria (Nu) Se Repetă* seeks to investigate, what would it mean to queer these anti-corruption accounts and also dream of futures past that could have kept post-1989 Siliconization at bay? By queering and aligning with queer theory, this inquiry diverges from reading queerness as an identarian code, but rather sees it as a field of inquiry and set of interpretative strategies meant to elucidate the relationality of socialist and transitional technoculture. This is in part what Popovici gets at with her analytic of "queer as corrupt," in which corruption breaks free from normative capitalist trajectories.[18] Queering thus signals computational coding acts that transpire in excess of official state histories and Siliconized Cold War victory narratives alike. Queer retrospective and speculative practices then point to how postsocialist technoculture hasn't just become the property of Silicon Valley and its anti-corruption narratives; there are other stories circulating in and out of transitional imaginaries and materialities.

Socialist Şmecherie

In her musings on cyborgs, Donna Haraway describes these entities as the "illegitimate offspring of militarism and patriarchal capitalism, not to mention state socialism."[19] However, "illegitimate offspring are often exceedingly unfaithful to their origins. Their fathers, after all, are inessential," she writes.[20] Cyborgs then, like technomonsters and algorithmic entities alike, while reflective of their makers' worlds, also bear their own accounts and computational worlds.[21] Many of these reflect little of their makers' intentions, having taken forays and sorties far beyond the state.

Tibi, who now lives in the United States where he works at a software company, grew up in Bucharest in the 1980s. There, he learned programming from his cloned Spectrum. The ZX Spectrum was built in Britain in 1982 and was soon copied and produced throughout Eastern Europe. Tibi explained Spectrum details to me one morning over a Skype call when I was living in Bucharest. The 8-bit HC ran a BASIC interpreter, making it relatively easy to use as long as you had a TV set and an audiocassette for external program memory, he recalled. "If you pressed 'i' it would be 'if,' 'e' it would be 'else,' so you could type BASIC pretty quickly." Most people he knew with computers in the 1980s had Spectrum clones, he told me, grinning. Although the Communist Party cloned the Spectrum to create the CoBra aboveground, these machines were enormously expensive and difficult to obtain. This inspired the proliferation of underground DIY hardware assemblage.

While Tibi doesn't remember where his family bought their computer, he does recall it being an unusual purchase. In the 1980s, CoBras cost thirty-five thousand lei, about half the price of a Dacia car.[22] Black market clones were much cheaper (and therefore more popular), sometimes going for twelve thousand lei. That said, clones were still five to six times the cost of the average Romanian salary at the time.[23] Tibi recounts having to buy Russian audiocassette tapes so that he could store information and load programs on his computer, since it lacked storage. Underground markets emerged, with people trading cassettes and parts. Rather than playing games like his peers, Tibi used these computers to learn software and programming. "I remember that at one point

I was using my computer to read a very precise scale that was measuring the input of a drop of water to show how it evaporates—even with 32k of memory," he reminisced. Soon after, Tibi joined his high school's computer club, which was unofficially organized by two professors who were into computers. There was one computer class taught in his school, but it was very simple, based on FORTRAN—a fast and efficient computer language developed by IBM in the 1950s. "You can still see traces of the past today," he explained, referencing how FORTRAN and BASIC are still used. Specters from Spectrum times.

Meanwhile, Bogdan Tîrziu, a retro-computing expert, is trying to archive these Spectrum times by creating a computer museum in Cluj. As he elaborated one afternoon in a downtown bar, every Thursday at midnight during socialism the party-sanctioned TV station would pause regular programming to instead emit an hour of code. It sounded like a fax machine, he described, mimicking its mechanical buzz. Bogdan's brother would fight the family for use of the television during this time, so that he could record the code on one of his floppy disks plugged into his cloned computer. He would then spend the week decoding it. "It wasn't some fancy key to some government secret—nothing like that. Sometimes it was just information about the airport, sometimes an announcement from a big shop, sometimes games and free software. This was how we began to learn BASIC programming," he smiled. His friends would come over to play the games, resulting in ten adolescents hovering around one computer.

This sort of cyber community became prolific among youth of the late socialist period. Bucharest's Polytechnic University became a hotbed of cloning, with students engendering all sorts of deviant computer practices, sometimes creating entire supply chains. As Andrada Fiscutean has well documented, sometimes parts were scrapped from other computers; sometimes they were flown in with the help of airline pilots.[24] Dealers would come to campus with electronics, parts, LEDs, and resistors, selling them in bulk to the students. Often, they would meet at a nearby campus pub. There was even this guy they called "the American" who sold transistors right in front of legitimate electronics stores, somehow getting away with it. Soon, everyone at the university had these șmecherie homemade machines, each made with about two thousand solder joints and a sea of wires. About 90 percent of the Romanian computer industry was built on reverse engineering in the 1980s, I've often been told. No two machines were ever the same. Even their cases varied, depending on what was available underground. The keyboards contained keys polished one at a time with a nail file, on which professional-looking paper letters and numbers were glued thanks to a friend's paper business, one man told me. Overall, the purpose was to learn and to have fun, never to engage in corporate profiteering.

Might these cloned computers—derived from smuggled and stolen parts alike—queer anticommunist narratives that map socialist technologies as impoverished accomplices to *Black the Fall* dystopian narratives? The Spectrum hybrid, a perversion to the West, was not produced by the West, nor by the socialist state. Its past is muddled and unattached to pure origin tales. Its materiality depended on illicit connections, disassembled motherboards, and forbidden border crossings—objects and events that *Istoria (Nu) Se Repetă* participants imagine might have led to futures beyond Siliconized overdetermination.

Scamming Transition

Sitting around the table at Macaz, across from a list of anti-racist, anticapitalist, and feminist politics stenciled on the wall, *Istoria (Nu) Se Repetă* participants began recounting stories of 1990s technoculture and its various perversities. What if these could have somehow staved off the dawn of post-1989 technocapitalism? "No, it would have been impossible to fight back," another ventured. "The West and its technologies were too powerful." With that, one workshop participant began detailing how much she remembers transition itself being informed by technology, particularly media. Not only was the 1989 revolution itself the first revolution televised, but the broadcasting of the event was staged by the West to justify Western intervention.[25] But on top of that, she recalls, "People just started watching TV. Western TV. Or Romanian TV modeled on Western programming. But either way, TV was the truth teller." Here I continue to explore the complex and often perverse relationship with the West that Romanian technoculture found itself in during transition.

After 1989, Felix found itself in a messy relationship with the actual IBM, the former suddenly supposed to produce hardware for the latter. And yet IBM's strategy failed, at least at first, as the company had to compete with a new underground market in which Romanians would assemble their own computers with uncertified IT parts from Hong Kong to Taiwan. On our Skype call, Tibi recalled, "In the early 1990s, I was interested in building my own PC. If you wanted to do an upgrade with some parts, it was cheaper to build your own. I was building for a couple of friends, even my brother." As in other peripheral locales, underground technocultures and practices sprang up just to make do with what was available. In doing so, new forms of kinship, connection, and *șmecherie* were engendered.

Tibi also remembered one of the first commercials to be released on Romanian television after 1989. It was a Felix computer commercial whose slogan went viral: *"V-am prins, vrăjitoarelor!"* (I caught you, witches!). "It was everywhere," he remembers. "Everyone knew it." But what might it actually mean? Today, people have different interpretations of the satiric commercial, which featured a man walking into a cave filled with witches preparing some potion for him. Were the witches Felix makers crafting socialist-era machines now liberated by capitalism, or were they Americans trapping corrupt Romanian technologists with their end-of-history alchemy? Then again, as witches are gendered and racialized in popular imaginaries in Romania (often invoking anti-Roma racism), might the ad have been conflating socialism with Roma people? If so, the ad renders Felix on a new Western journey away from its corrupt past. Or perhaps it was more of a prescient satire from the future, aware that despite the West's best efforts, Romanian computer perversion would continue to flourish—though maybe in internet cafés and computer labs instead of caves.

Indeed, despite the best spells cast by capitalism through Felix computer commercials and IBM co-optation alike, the specters of the Spectrum clone found their way into postsocialist times. This endurance, bypassed in Siliconized narrative structures, continues to bolster and pervert the present. While IBM was wreaking havoc in Felix worlds, Tibi and others continued to produce machines underground. Meanwhile, an array of computer magazines began circulating, saturated with computer construction manuals, software installation guidelines, code, and instructions for how to set up satellites and LAN networks. From backtracking methods to articles on virtual reality, technoskepticism, and "the hacker phenomenon,"[26] magazines such as *Open Tehnologia Informației* and PC *World Romania* blossomed throughout the 1990s.

Alexandra, a queer programmer who now works for a French tech firm in Bucharest, remembers learning to program and build computers from reading the magazine *Extreme PC*. It got big in the 2000s, replete with online chat rooms and support. She learned how to code in school during a weekly class and remembers learning more relevant coding in chat rooms, some of which are still active today. Meanwhile, apartments began setting up "decoders" to steal HBO, otherwise not available. "It was this funny little device that we all had on the back of our televisions," she recounted as we took a walk through an overgrown park on the outskirts of the city one blistering summer afternoon. If a decoder broke, everyone knew someone who would come and set up another, she laughed in remembrance.

FIGURE 5.1. Romanian computer magazines from the early 1990s, part of Bogdan Tîrziu's collection. Photo taken by author, 2018.

In 2014, Romania's piracy rate was twice that of the EU at 60 percent, but in 1996 it was as high as 86 percent.[27] Following socialism, there was little legislation protecting intellectual property, and the software market developed accordingly. MS-DOS was the first pirated operating system in the 1990s, and then OS/2, and later Windows, via Russia. At first, pirated software was largely not sold for profit, but rather was understood as educational material, building collective knowledge. As Alexandra contextualized the era, "We were just downloading things because we couldn't afford anything. In the US, you pay $15 for a CD. No big deal. But here, that's more than lots of people in the '90s were making in one day alone. It's not like CDs are less expensive here. It's the same." This was also the case with software, books, and games, she told me. In 2007, when Microsoft's founder Bill Gates visited Bucharest to celebrate the opening of a Microsoft outsourcing firm, then president Traian Băsescu expressed his own enthusiasm for 1990s-era Romanian piracy. As he declared, "Piracy helped the young generation discover computers. It set off the development of the IT industry in Romania. It helped Romanians improve their creative capacity in the IT industry, which has become famous around the world."[28] The workers supporting Microsoft's outsourcing in Romania, in other words, gained their skills through *şmecherie*.

Vlad, a queer performer from Râmnicu Vâlcea, also remembers this era well. It was then that a zillion internet cafés sprang up overnight. "It was hard to get into them because they were so crowded," he recalls. One of his neighbors invented a VPN to mask IP addresses, and soon everyone started paying him for VPNs so that they could hack from home. Vlad recounts that often people would make money quickly from some internet hack and then use the money to pay for personal *manele* (Roma popular music) concerts. Dimi, another former "hacker," recounts: "Before internet cafés, in the 1990s, Bucharest was a pretty dangerous place to just be walking around," he recalled. "It was sketchy. But maybe I was sketchy too!" he laughed. "But then the internet cafés popped up, and suddenly the hooligans who were roaming the streets jumped into the internet cafés to play games and hack." Others moved out of internet cafés in response to set up their own home networks. "It was super easy," he explained to me one evening while drinking beers in Macaz. "And it was really good internet. You would just string the cables, and voilà." Because the networks were local and small, it was easy to share music, games, software, and more.

It was home networks, however, where Dimi and his friends "became hackers." Accidentally, they discovered a burgeoning market of video chatting (a precursor to webcamming). Today there are least one hundred thousand models working in the industry in Romania, amounting to a billion-dollar industry granting it the title of the "webcamming capital of the world."[29] Its success is often attributed to the country's fast internet, English fluency, poverty, and the fact that webcamming is unregulated and not criminalized (though there have been some cases of criminalization, such as the 2022 arrest of digital nomad Andrew Tate for running an illegal business out of Bucharest). But it was nearly two decades earlier that Dimi and his friends found a way to hack US video chatting services. "The porn industry is divided between the US, Germany, and Japan," Dimi told me, matter-of-factly. "US porn watchers don't know anything about German or Japanese porn models as the worlds are contained, or at least were back then." And so, he and his friends found clips of a German porn model who they then collectively pretended to be—essentially all working together to become a composite Romanian webcammer in a US-based chat room. As a form of digital drag, they became her. "Back then, a lot of people didn't have microphones in their computers, so it was possible to just tell a client that the mic was broken and only use the text chat function. So we could really be the model." Dimi never actually texted with US users, but rather was in charge of crafting fake ID cards in Photoshop for the operation. "I was really good at this," he laughed. "Șmecherie!"

Dimi's friends would text with US clients, often suggesting that the client might want to see them do a certain thing, and then they would play the clip of the German model doing that thing. "See, hacking isn't so much about technology. It's about deception. Guccifer only made it to eighth grade, after all," he recounted of the infamous Romanian hacker known for breaking into numerous US email accounts (described in chapter 4). One of Dimi's buddies was really into US basketball, and so sometimes he would talk about basketball with the clients, who were always so impressed that a Romanian woman knew so much about US teams. "He'd get paid to type about basketball for hours!" Writing of Jamaican scammers and forms of what he describes as reparative seizure, Jovan Scott Lewis describes how youth "took on the persona they understand their victims would expect of a customer service agent, coupled with all of the sensed and observed qualities of Americana and Americanism that they have acquired over their experience living in proximity to Americans and their culture vis-à-vis tourism, media consumption, and first- and secondhand immigrant accounts."[30] While reparative seizure is analytically grounded in Black survival amid racial capitalist contexts, Romanian scamming practices converse with the logics of șmecherie in mobilizing technological cunning and impersonation to get by amid disaster capitalist contexts wrought by the West.

Dimi and his friends frequently got caught due to this "screenshot thing" that would monitor the chat room sites to see if the same images were used repeatedly. But then they would make new IDs and do it again. Through this they made a ton of money and even forced the United States to change its video chatting regulations, apparently. "I think the US was obsessed with us then because they're obsessed with vampires. They think we're sucking the blood out of their businesses," he proffered. Yet it wasn't that Dimi and his friends wanted to suck the blood of the West. They were just getting by, having fun, and experimenting in digital deception collectively. "The West hacked us after 1989; we just hacked back," he suggested. Yet their scamming acts were less about revenge, and more playful attempts of hacking transition.

The Xennials

Eventually, Dimi and his friends were forced to cease their scamming endeavors, in part because everyone transitioned to webcamming from online text chatting. But also, the independent intranet networks they had strung together to avoid internet cafés became rendered an extractable commodity for larger internet companies. Seemingly overnight, firms such Romania Data Systems (RDS) came in, promising better and faster services. Threatened by independent networks, RDS began collaborating with building administrators to force residents to tear down their cables, intimidating tenants with citations regarding minor technicalities having to do with the size or length of the wiring. Sometimes RDS would just cut cables. This predation gets at how Silicon Valley imperialism does not mean the manufacturing of new IT infrastructure from scratch, but rather the co-optation of what was already there.

Yet for a while at least, independent networks such as Dimi's were strung throughout neighborhoods, building the backbones of what became one of Europe's fastest internet connections. This wasn't the experimental project of state socialism intended to improve central planning and economics; it was more an organic decentralized network intended to connect and share information, music, movies, tools, games, and software among neighbors. Because internet dial-up packages were expensive, and because of the intense poverty incited by transition, generally, one person would buy internet and then share or sell it to people in their building, wiring cables haphazardly. As people had already been pirating and sharing satellite stations, and as magazines and chat rooms taught wiring techniques, stringing cables across apartments and blocks of flats "was really no big deal," I've been told. Today still, telephone poles from Cluj to Bucharest are adorned in a massive array of cables too woven in to detach. The first time I pointed these out to a friend visiting from the United States, she asked if it was an art installation. And yet, as people are always quick to remind me, today's cabling is nothing compared to the early 2000s when it was commonplace for telephone poles to crash with the weight of the cables, sometimes smashing cars parked beneath.

Bogdan set up a similar network in Cluj, connecting twenty-four people in his block. It was 2004, and he had no internet cable but somehow managed to use TV cable. "We all had Intel 486 computers then, the new generation," he told me. They had sixteen kilobytes, used routers, and it took five minutes to transfer a picture. You could never shut down your computer once it was connected because you didn't want to be bumped off. Setting up this network was just one of his many DIY computer projects of the era. For him, it all began in grade school when he would cut class and hide in the attic. There, he discovered an old broken MII8B computer from the 1970s. Curious, he came back the next day with a screwdriver. It was the late 1990s, and there was no Google or Yahoo to tell him how to fix it. But there were smoky internet cafés where he could ask questions. So, he began. Two years later, he won a math competition and was awarded an old Intel 486 computer that the national television

FIGURE 5.2. Telephone poles in Bucharest displaying an array of entangled wires. Photo taken by author, 2018.

station was discarding. Eventually, he saved up money from his job at the local newspaper to buy the parts to make it work and to install Windows. Hardware became cheaper after 2002, he remembers, and it became easier to pirate the operating system. Soon after, he began to visit the Oser flea market every weekend to pick up older broken models. Before long, his entire room was crammed with computers. It was then that he began to build his neighborhood network, eager to share and pirate new software for his growing collection.

But then, RDS entered the scene and began cutting the wires, and "everything went to hell." Eventually, Bogdan's network came down. Nevertheless, one stubborn cable remains strung up today. "No one says anything about it—I think people think it's part of a spy network!" he laughs. Today, Bogdan maintains a day job with Amazon but spends most of his time finding discarded and broken computers, cleaning and repairing them, turning them into specters of their former selves. He is also trying to implement a local computer museum in Cluj but has not yet received support from city hall. Official computer memory, he suggests, has become devoured by Siliconization as well. But Bogdan offers another insight useful in theorizing Silicon Valley imperial contradictions. "Contrary to what people think, the tech boom is not being led by firms, but by a particular generation of people, now in their mid-30s." This "Xennial" generation, occupying that interstitial space between Gen X and millennials, correlates with what Bogdan describes as the "x86 Generation," a reference to Intel's x86 microprocessor architecture conceived of in 1978 Cold War Silicon Valley. Since then, the x86 microprocessor has embodied numerous iterations, and still dominates desktop and mobile technology today.

In the West, Xennials are defined as being born predigital and then easily adapting to digitization in the 1990s. But in Romania, most Xennials were not able to afford Silicon Valley technology, despite the growing prevalence of Western firms and products. Instead, this generation had to learn how to create its own hardware and infrastructure. "It's really people in this generation that are creating all of the software and systems that the West wants today," he tells me. Unlike millennials, who grew up on digital technology platforms, the Xennials had to make the leap from analog to digital. It was Xennial technoculture and computing knowledge that the West came in to exploit. Thus, while Siliconization co-opts underground cyber worlds, it remains materially corrupted by, and dependent on, their existence.

Florentin, a member of the independent, free, and open-source software and hardware project Ceata, also remembers RDS sweeping in. His own father worked at the state-owned Romtelecom (now Telecom and connected to T-Mobile). Romtelecom, along with C-Zone, was bought up by RDS, he remembers. Meanwhile, UPC, another large corporation, bought up the smaller firm, Astrid. Florentin got his first computer in 2000 before this consolidation, but he never got to use an independent network because he couldn't find one in his Bucharest neighborhood, Drumul Taberei. "Maybe because everyone there was old," he questioned. There was a really cool network in Crângași where people battled for its control. Florentin wanted to set one up too, but he had no money to buy cables. His father had some extra telephone wires, so he tried to stretch them and use them in a ramshackle way, but it never worked. He recollects how slow the dial-up was in his block between 10:00 a.m. and 2:00 p.m., as this was when all the downloading and uploading would begin. He had wanted to start assembling computers independent from Microsoft operating systems, but to download other operating systems, you needed a fast connection. In a Silicon Valley imperial move, Microsoft had also set up an automatic update on his computer preventing him from downloading what he wanted.

Maybe it was this that got Florentin thinking about the importance of moving away from Silicon Valley and private software. Perhaps it was this that led him to Ceata. "The only way that you can maintain security is to have the right hardware," he explained. Today, Florentin creates new machines from spare parts, much like he and others did a decade earlier. His goal is to ensure that his computers aren't hacked by corporate tech. He and others from Ceata frequently visit other free software communities from across the globe, determined to string together a network of practitioners and users free from the corporate reins of Siliconization. Yet in post–Cold War Silicon Valley, fears of dangerous and illiberal Eastern European hackers accumulate. This imaginary often becomes internalized in Romania, reflected in *Black the Fall* imagery and Light Revolution protests alike. Nevertheless, technocultural deviancy persists, building on histories of informal infrastructure and subversive relationality.

Despite the fact that Romania maintains some of Europe's fastest internet today, when bringing up digital infrastructure in conversation, it is far more common to hear mundane tales of working for multinational firms or webcamming studios than it is to hear narratives about the DIY technoculture that laid the groundwork for the present. Meanwhile, when Romanian technoculture is brought up in the West, the most common motifs involve the country's dangerous hackers threatening to take down liberal democracy, or perhaps the well-documented authoritarian informatics and surveillance regime of the Communist Party.

Yet most hackers and scammers, for the most part, craft techniques to hack the inequities brought on by Silicon Valley imperialism, charging Western consumers for their internet skills and cunning. Most aren't trying to spark a global revolution, yet their everyday *șmecherie* cybercultural actions do create futures beyond and antithetical to Silicon Valley. This converses with what Amit Rai theorizes as *jugaad* in India, or "an everyday practice that potentializes relations that are external to their terms, opening different domains of action and power to experimentation sometimes resulting in an easily valorized workaround, sometimes producing space-times that momentarily exit from the debilitating regimes of universal capital."[31] Indeed, a momentary exit from the cramped space of technocapitalism is sometimes enough.

Space Invaders against Gentrification

In the spring of 2018, during a Light Revolution protest and also a far-right homophobic "Normality" demonstration, a third march crawled through Bucharest's streets. For the first time, the annual LGBTQ Pride parade was granted access to march through Bucharest's city center, rather than being confined to the urban outskirts. Also, for the second year in a row, IBM, Google, and Accenture pinkwashed the event, not dissimilar to Pride parades in

FIGURE 5.3. Bucharest's Pride parade, marked by both Google and anticapitalist imagery. Photos taken by author, 2018.

California's Silicon Valley. However, this year, a small group of anticapitalist protesters, many of whom were *Istoria (Nu) Se Repetă* participants, were prepared. Equipped with large banners against pinkwashing, racial capitalism, and fascism, we also brought "Fuck Off Google" stickers brought back from a solidarity action in Berlin where Google was attempting to establish a campus. A week later, comrades from A-casă, Macaz's sister social center in Cluj, replicated our messaging during their Pride march. Carrying a "LGBT and Space Invaders Against Gentrification" banner crafted in resistance to the tech gentrification, they invoked the 1978 Cold War video game. In doing so, they corrupted the Cold War 2.0 to queerly salvage robotic space invaders and fight the rising tides of Silicon Valley imperialism. Their reclamation was not one of history repeating, but rather one inaccessible to Cold War 2.0 reproductions of antithesis.

Unsurprisingly, liberals chastised anticapitalist messaging in both cities, reminding us that Romania was now finally free from socialism. How dare we corrupt that! As Veda Popovici recounts of the tensions, if progress can only be achieved through neoliberal complicity, "an anticapitalist position associated with queer and feminist positions becomes incompatible with the desired future of a Western becoming."[32] When a photo of one of the anti-pinkwashing banners began circling in a forum monitored by the then more mainstream LGBT group, Accept, rather than defend it, the image was deleted. It was "too far of a step to take, the anti-Google stuff," someone later explained. Accept in prior years had been known to appeal to the police and the US and German embassies to protect Pride.[33] This, of course, is a far step away from the speculative future woven by *Istoria (Nu) Se Repetă* participants, who counterfactually had imagined how Accept and Romani Criss worked together in the 1990s to corrupt Siliconization impulses and create a Free School with hacking classes.[34]

Had Ceata and others of the Xennial generation been committed to queer, decolonial future-making in the 1990s, perhaps a Free School could have come into being. In this speculative future past, *șmecherie* practices might have been able to corrupt early attempts at Siliconization. But instead, during transition, hacking practices were quite distinct from Accept and Romani Criss worlds. Nevertheless, Siliconization was resisted, even if mostly in tacit ways. As Robin D. G. Kelley has insisted, reserving the category of resistance for activists belittles everyday forms of resistance and subversion: "If we are to make meaning of these kinds of actions rather than dismiss them as manifestations of immaturity, false consciousness, or primitive rebellion, we must begin to dig beneath the surface of trade union pronouncements, political institutions, and organized social movements, deep into the daily lives, cultures, and communities which make the working classes so much more than people who work."[35] Along these lines, Saba Mahmood suggests that "the category of resistance impose[s] a teleology of progressive politics that makes it hard for us to see and understand forms of being and action that are not necessarily encapsulated by the narrative of subversion and the re-inscription of norms."[36]

While little *șmecherie* computing is intentionally revolutionary or explicitly political, technical orientations untethered to Siliconization can nevertheless be understood as a form of rebellion, one that need not be immediately redemptive. As AbdouMaliq Simone theorizes, "rebellion without redemption" can transpire quietly, tied up in daily collective life through underground infrastructural practices such as tapping into electricity lines—something he recounts being popular in the 1980s and 1990s among migrants in the Indian neighborhoods of Durban in order to power televisions in their shacks to watch football games.[37] Such techno acts may not be revolutionary, but they are rehearsals for militant sensibilities reflective of both "different kinds of uses but also about different imaginations of the technical."[38] Yet for militancy to eventually transpire, collectivity is integral—something that technologies of automation and alienation continue to threaten. As such, future rebellions necessitate "discovering new ways of sharing technical instruments and developing institutions of pedagogy and experimentation that establish cultures of knowledge production capable of effectively mediating the interpenetrations of the technical, collective, and human."[39] Such collective technicity can be found within socialist and postsocialist experimentations of șmecherie, as well as in the pedagogy being imagined and materialized by Istoria (Nu) Se Repetă participants.

Șmecherie technicity, despite its lack of overt politics, in this way subverts Siliconization beyond normative resistance frameworks. Deviant computer and networking practices created in excess of chrononormative cycles of capitalist reproduction carve out pathways. Rather than cloning liberal platforms of recognition, șmecherie thus exists in excess of Silicon Valley imperialism. It is this that perhaps Istoria (Nu) Se Repetă participants, along with Popovici and Nicolae, find hope in their dreaming and materializing of technofutures to come. José Esteban Muñoz writes, "To want something else, to want beside and beyond the matrix of social controls that is our life in late Capitalism, is to participate in this other form of desiring. Thus, the connection between queerness and utopia is most salient at this precise point—the desire for a new world despite an emotional/world situation that attempts to render such desiring impossible."[40] Queerness, as both perversion to capitalism and desire for something else, is not simply recasting socialist nostalgia or reproducing liberal imaginaries. Unattached to origin stories and processes of becoming Silicon Valley, queering here commits to speculating on other cyberworlds and friendships in order to code something new.

One might look back on the Free School as a future past that never materialized, yet there are spaces such as Macaz and A-casă, and more. Queer and anticolonial approaches to postsocialist temporality in this way suggest that just as Silicon Valley is always speculatively in a process of becoming, so are speculative processes of unbecoming. These acts of unbecoming are far from linear or repetitive, but rather are accumulative, recursive, and haunted. Routes of unbecoming are far from pure, and often involve corrupting Siliconized materiality for de-Siliconized means. Whether cloning Spectrum computers or wiring DIY intranet networks, processes of unbecoming Silicon Valley are messy, composed of șmecherie approaches to technofutures past, present, and yet to come.

Spells for Outer Space

Before 1989, there were two visions about the possible end of the co-existing histories of communism and capitalism which could not possibly fit into the same world. One imagined a global deflagration, a post-apocalyptical world of Mad Max. The other focused on the conquest of space, which was a third neutral space where . . . peoples could finally find peace. And maybe an ideal mode of co-existing. Twenty-eight years later, in places like this one here, of these two contemporary visions, memory retains only the apocalyptical vision. Yet it is very difficult to grasp, in what ruins are we here? What ruins are these? The ruins of which civilization? Of which historical period?

These words were spoken in Romanian by Ovidiu Țichindeleanu as part of a video arts piece, *Gagarin's Tree,* created by Romanian artists Mona Vătămanu and Florin Tudor.[1] It features Țichindeleanu, a scholar of postsocialist decol-onization, waxing philosophical while wandering throughout the halls of a former socialist youth center in Chișinău, Moldova, once known as Gagarin's

Youth Center. Dark pink magenta glass from now shattered windows, along with the deep forest green pines peeking into view from outside, create a rich palette in an otherwise abandoned concrete building. The film's scenes weave together the ruins of two futures past, one of state socialism and one of post-1989 disaster capitalism, both of which have now been made detritus in the wake of a more advanced stage of capitalism. It was during transition, in Țichindeleanu's words, that "the apocalyptic future from the Mad Max movies became the actual present in most of the neighborhoods and industrial cities from the former socialist bloc. The ruins that we are seeing here are not only the ruins of the communist dream. The signboard was put on the frontispiece of this building during the postcommunist transition . . . when a new order . . . became dominant and left their names on the building." But this first wave of transition could not sustain itself and now lies in the wreckage of a more advanced era of capitalism. Today, socialist and transitional infrastructure materially crumble together in the former youth center named after the Soviet cosmonaut Yuri Gagarin, the first human to enter outer space. The building was once adorned with rainbowed mosaics dedicated to cosmological agricultural visions of peacefully conquering space in order to inculcate a true communist utopia—a common communist aesthetic enveloped in dreams to "peacefully conquest the future." Today it is hollowed out and haunted.

I first wandered upon Vătămanu and Tudor's film about the center in a 2016 exhibit in Bucharest's Future Museum, an open curatorial platform for uncharted futures and theories. The film engages themes of socialist space exploration exemplified by socialist-era astrological and agronomical technological mosaics of farmers sowing the seeds of a true communist utopia among the stars and rainbows. As Țichindeleanu narrates, "The ploughman is . . . directly connected to the land, but also to space." This dream, he describes, "is not situated in a spaceship, or within a space station from another planet—this new dream is about space itself." Space in this regard is tied up in what Lisa Messeri describes as the "planetary imagination," which includes "scientific understandings of the planet and conceptions of planetary pasts and futures, as well as notions of what it would be like to be on and live on other planets."[2] The socialist-era planetary imagination was anchored by Gagarin's cosmological journey, but also one of anti-imperial utopianism. As legend has it, Gagarin even ferried acorns into the galaxy in order to cultivate this vision. These were then planted in soil on his return in order to cultivate a communist utopia back on earth, one of planetary peace.

Anti-imperialism was squarely a communist vision, though not state socialist practice per se. As scholars such as Bruce Grant, Francine Hirsch, Terry

what seems to be still alive is the power of that dream to bring people together and to create another history.

FIGURE 6.1. Still from *Gagarin's Tree* by Mona Vătămanu and Florin Tudor.

Martin, and Madina Tlostanova have all critiqued, the Soviet Union itself acted as an imperial power, having taken over and enfolded Eurasian lands into the Union of Soviet Socialist Republics (USSR).[3] The Principality of Moldova, after being a vassal of the Ottoman Empire for centuries, was split in two in 1812 during one of the Russo-Turkish Wars, with the eastern half, Bessarabia, annexed by the Russian Empire, and the western half later becoming a Romanian state—one that my own family was living in at the time. While Bessarabia later gained independence, becoming the Moldovian Democratic Republic and then joining with Romania, it was later occupied and reclaimed by the Soviet Union during World War II. It remained part of the Soviet Union until the withering of state socialism in 1991, after which it regained independence. (Today, amid Russia's violent occupation of Ukraine, many in Moldova fear that Putin will cast his eyes their way and make them his next target. Meanwhile, far-right nationalist groups in Romania still consider Bessarabia a lost territory of "Greater Romania.")

At the same time, in the aftermaths of the Russian Empire, it was Bolshevik revolutionary and Communist Party leader Vladimir Lenin who in 1917 published the Marxist book *Imperialism: The Highest Stage of Capitalism*.[4] In it, he renders imperialism the most advanced stage of capitalism, one in which labor, finance, and resource monopolies are required to sustain coloniality. In his words, "Capitalism has grown into a world system of colonial oppression and of the financial strangulation of the overwhelming majority of the population of the world by a handful of 'advanced' countries. And this 'booty' is shared between two or three powerful world plunderers armed to the teeth, who are drawing the whole world into their war over the division of their booty."[5] The only thing that could put an end to this plundering would be a revolution among the "thousand million people" of imperial colonies and semicolonies. This anti-imperialist vision in part set the tone for a growing Third World internationalism (despite the imperiality espoused by the USSR). But it also became reflected in galactic cosmological imaginaries in which immersion in outer space statelessness would sow the seeds for a communist utopia back on earth.

While one might dismiss state socialist outer space iconography imprinted on the ruins of the Gagarin Youth Center as simply reflective of the Soviet space race, Soviet imperialism, and the reification of cosmonautical heroes such as Gagarin, communist utopic and anti-imperial fantasies also need to be taken into account, as do their elisions. After all, the Bolshevik dream of creating "New Soviet Men and Women," or *Homo sovieticus*, also meant transforming peoples deemed "backward," nomadic, and arrested in the formative stages of the Marxist historical development timeline. Roma people in particular, it was inferred, needed to be sedentarized, assimilated, and deracinated, thereby eliminating the threat of the "wandering Gypsy menace" imposed on the socialist state. As Brigid O'Keeffe puts it, "Gypsies were stereotyped not merely as peripatetics, but also as parasites who produced nothing of economic value. In Bolshevik eyes, Roma jeopardized socialist modernity as a peculiar ethnic menace. Not only did they wander—they wandered aimlessly."[6] Indeed, Communist Party politics in countries like Romania and the Soviet Union alike were oriented toward eliminating this menace—not under the auspices of racial extermination per the prior regime, but rather through the logics of deracination and disavowal.

Today, astrosocialist utopian dreams of creating a *Homo sovieticus*, racial and ethnic assimilatory violence included, seem but a distant and out-of-joint fairytale amid the ongoing space race—one that reproduces spatial conquest fantasies from the perspective of the Cold War victors to embolden Cold War 2.0 imaginaries. It was the Trump regime that launched a new wave of nostalgia for past US lunar voyages such as Alan Shepard's cosmological trip (which transpired shortly after Gagarin's) and subsequent Apollo missions to the moon. This was revitalized in part to hedge US spatial and technological superiority amid growing competition with China, with Beijing implementing its first lunar voyage and creating its first space station (having been excluded from NASA's International Space Station). Cold War 2.0 discourse meanwhile began to frame outer space as the United States' ultimate vulnerability, as so much of the country's infrastructure and economy relies on satellites and GPS—itself a Cold War navigational infrastructure. As US Space Force General John Raymond declared in 2020, China and Russia "seek to stop US access to space, and they are developing capabilities that would negate the US advantage. . . . We've got to make sure that we stay ahead of this growing threat."[7] In this sense, China and Russia have become conflated as the dangerous Cold War East 2.0 that the West 2.0 must preemptively dominate.

Yet in the protracted aftermaths of the Cold War, it isn't the United States, but rather Silicon Valley leading the space race, with start-ups, entrepreneurs, tourism programs, and venture capital investing in the frontier of *NewSpace*. The term was coined in 2006 by the Space Frontier Foundation, an advocacy group driven by US libertarian visions of entrepreneurial space exploration and conquest. NewSpace ballooned in the aftermath of the 2011 retirement of NASA's Space Shuttle program, championed by Tech Boom 2.0 companies such as SpaceX (led by Tesla's CEO and multibillionaire Elon Musk), Blue Origin (led by Amazon's CEO and multibillionaire Jeff Bezos), and Virgin Galactic (led by billionaire and business magnate Sir Richard Charles Nicholas Branson). Musk's own Starlink satellite system employs over 3,000 satellites in low orbit.[8] With 6,700 of over 13,600 satellites deployed by private and public entities since the first Sputnik satellite was established in 1957, Musk currently controls more of the night sky than any other government or company (with plans to own 42,000 by 2026).[9] Indigenous advocates have described this satellite proliferation as comprising a new form of "astrocolonialism" due to their impact on animals' migratory routes, light pollution, and numerous peoples' deep relationship to the night sky.[10]

Thus, today it is no longer two or three powerful states armed to the teeth fighting for the final frontier of outer space, but rather tech billionaires promulgating colonial extraterritorial missions often justified under the auspices of protecting "mankind" from being stranded on a dying planet—yet in fact benefiting the planet's richest men at the expense of everyone else. Their libertarian ethos, one often justified through fictive missions of helping save the earth from anthropocentric disaster through asteroid mining, solar energy harnessing, and colonizing Mars, has drawn harsh criticism far and wide from scholars and organizations committed to decolonial outer space ethics.[11] As some question, whose version of humanity is being posited as worth saving? As biologist DNLee writes, "With the language of proposed interplanetary exploration and settlement using generous references to Christopher Columbus and New World Exploration and British Colonization and US American Manifest Destiny I was halted. I'm not on board for this type of science adventure."[12] Or as Jeff Doctor, member of the Cayuga Six Nations of the Grand River Territory, has contextualized in response, "Tech culture has to think in terms of history, place, lands, people—all of these kinds of things—and it just doesn't."[13]

Just as the Manifest Destiny mythos informed the US Cold War project of global domination, so does it inform this new era of outer space conquest led by Musk and his cohort. As NewSpace advocate Rick Tumlinson proffers, NewSpace ventures are just "one giant leap for commercial space and one small step towards an open space frontier!"—a statement mirroring Neil Armstrong's utterance on first setting foot on the moon in 1969.[14] This implies a neoliberal progression along a Fukuyamaian timeline, in which, thanks to the West winning the Cold War, outer space is now the sole dominion of Western corporate speculation.[15] Yet the anti-imperial futuring scribed on socialist infrastructure, rather than informing Russian outer space travel or Moldovan technological development, remains buried in rubble.

In this chapter, I engage in a different genre of speculation, exploring why the communist vision of a peaceful anti-imperial galaxy crumbled against the crushing weight of capitalism, paving the way for Muskian fantasies to take root. While unearthing emancipatory socialist cosmological visions of non-alignment and anti-imperialism, I question why these desires never fully concretized terrestrially. While there are many ways to address this, here I home in on the limitations of astrosocialism, particularly its failure to account for anti-Roma racism on earth. This is not to deny that anti-Roma racism was much worse prior to socialism during contexts of slavery and eugenic technoscience than during socialism, nor to ignore the severity of anti-Roma racism in postsocialist times as explored in prior chapters, but rather to acknowledge that despite noble socialist anti-imperial intentions, racial justice was not tethered as strongly as it could have been to the astrosocialist project. What sorts of technofutures might such a tethering have produced?

Reflecting on the potentiality of the communist space dream, Țichindeleanu muses that it still bears the actuary potentiality to "bring people together and to create another history. This history remains to be written." Building on his provocation, here I question: What might this cosmological futuring work—this history yet to be written—look like by attending to racial justice worldmaking? What insights could be gained by drawing on what Roma feminist playwright Mihaela Drăgan coins as Roma Futurism, or "an artistic movement that creates the interaction between Roma culture and technology and witchcraft."[16] Roma Futurism, she elaborates, "combines science fiction elements, the history of Roma people, fantasy, Roma subjectivity, magical realism, creative technology with magical practices and healing rituals." It promulgates what she defines as techno-witchcraft, in which Roma witches rather than the Silicon Valley elite control technology. Drăgan's intervention is not only a reparative antidote to a millennium of anti-Roma violence lodged on the figure of the witch, but also to the limitations of socialist astrofuturism. Perhaps learning from techno-witchcraft, alongside ongoing anticapitalist organizing against tech corporations and their imaginaries, can help de-Siliconize the future—be it in the far reaches of NewSpace or here on earth.

Astrofuturism

Gazing beyond the framing of the screen amid the ruination portrayed in *Gagarin's Tree*, Țichindeleanu seems to see a future past not yet dead. Sitting there, gently tugging at old mosaic stones now loose in the wall, he is wearing the same black leather jacket that he has when I've spent time with him in Romania and Moldova. For a couple of summers in a row, I also attended a summer camp in the small Transylvanian village of Telciu that he co-organizes with other scholars dedicated to decolonizing postsocialism such as Manuela Boatcă, along with Cluj-based artists and local cultural workers. There, housing justice activists, anticapitalists, queer theorists, antiracist organizers, performance artists, and more, have been annually gathering to think through futures past and present unrecognizable to Western coloniality. Slowly, they are doing the work of developing a new consciousness to decolonize the future. Part of this revolves around understanding the socialist past and its utopian visions of antifascist nonalignment with Western imperialism.

During my first summer in Telciu, Țichindeleanu took a small group of us up into the county of Maramureș to visit the ruins of a sculpture built by Géza Vida. Géza, an antifascist Romanian-Hungarian sculptor, industrial worker, and communist militant, had "illegally" fought in the Spanish Civil War while engaging in antifascist work in Romania. He then got into socialist realism sculpting, for the most part funded by the state.[17] We had traveled to Maramureș in order to view one of Géza's outdoor sculptures, *Monumentul Eroilor de la Moisei* (The Hero's Monument of Moses), a cosmological monument that commemorates twenty-nine Romanian antifascists killed by Hungarian fascists in 1944. After asking a number of local villagers for the location, we eventually found the path to the sculpture, which was perched on a hill and hidden away in the encroaching forest. We then somewhat solemnly made our way to the forest clearing, as if we were reaching a sacred object or perhaps

FIGURE 6.2. *Monumentul Eroilor de la Moisei* (The Hero's Monument of Moses), by Géza Vida. Photo taken by author, 2017.

a spaceship. Originally designed as a sort of Stonehenge-like circle made of twelve sessile oaks carved into godlike figures, it has since been reconstructed with stone. While these stones aren't in ruins, they are largely forgotten, as is the rich history of socialist antifascism.

Similar agricultural cosmonautical embellishments permeate Gagarin's Youth Center. The center, built in 1972 by socialist volunteers,[18] was once an autonomous spatial experiment in communist social production. It was replete with a hall for political and cultural events, a concert hall, a café-bar, a restaurant, and rooms for sports, meetings, and youth arts collectives. Its library held twelve thousand books. According to local stories, Gagarin himself helped with its construction when he resided in Chişinău in 1966, also during the time that he famously toured a local wine cellar, promising to fill it with metals from the moon.[19] But then, with transition, these visions crumbled. The youth center briefly transmuted into a discotheque until the ownership changed in the late 1990s. Since then, it has sat idle, weathering Moldova's cold winters and hot summers alike. Similar infrastructural states can be found throughout the region, where abandoned monuments, sculptures, and even Black Sea resorts modeled after the planets are now abandoned skeletons. Even the emblem of the former Communist Party depicted grain, trees, an industrial tower, and a sun. Today, many of these socialist structures have changed meaning, symbolically but also in use value.

For instance, the Crişul Shopping Center in Oradea opened in 1979, with flowerlike cosmological figures engraved into the columns of its concrete facade. Today, the building is home to a number of new businesses and offices, mostly from the West. It also houses a McDonald's, or "Mac," which obscures the agro/astrosocialist imagery with the franchise's iconic red umbrellas and golden arches. And yet, like many idiosyncratic spaces of postsocialist transition, socialist imaginaries endure, peeking out beyond the cheapness of McDonaldization. Etched into concrete, the flowers remain. Or, take the numerous resorts erected along Romania's Black Sea coast divided into towns named after planets, constellations, and astral wonders. There had already been resorts along the coast before socialism, but they were largely for the bourgeoisie. This changed in the 1950s when the Communist Party expropriated them. The idea was that every worker deserved an annual trip to the seaside and/or to the mountains. Former resorts transformed, and new ones were built in towns renamed as Saturn, Neptun, Jupiter, Olimp, Luna, Uranus, and Cap Aurora (Aurora's Head). Some of the resorts shut down after socialism due to austerity and the loss of guaranteed vacations. Yet others still function, with sculptures of Neptune, Venus, and Saturn's rings scattered throughout.

Agro/astrofuturist aesthetics invoke a genre of what Curtis Marez describes as farmworker futurism, or "visual discourses and practices that promote 'utopian' images of distinct yet overlapping future worlds."[20] While Marez is interested in Latinx and Chicanx working-class struggles and emancipatory speculations amid fascist agribusiness technologies in California, there is much to assess here regarding the agricultural technologies and their contradictions. As he argues, farm worker futurisms are both antagonistic to but at times also sympathetic with agribusiness futurisms, the latter projecting corporate and biotech utopias in which labor is exploited and organizing is repressed through machinery. Much of this flourished in white science fiction works after World War II, but also in technofascist practice. Yet at the same time, technologies and speculative future work from below led by activists and artists alike also grew. Artist collectives such as the Royal Chicano Air Force led by farm workers and their children celebrated aeronautical imagery and developed work alongside the organizing work of the United Farm Workers. Esteban Villa's painting, *Third World Astro Pilot of Aztlán*, for instance, features a feminine astronaut, while Ricardo Favela's drawing UFW *Cooperative Space Station #Uno* imagines communal outer space agricultural futures.[21] These astrofuturist works illuminate how divergent agricultural technologies have been tied to acts of speculation globally, whether those intended to repress or abet working-class struggles.

These tensions saturate socialist-era speculations. As Țichindeleanu ruminates, "In Moldova, not even the dream of space conquest managed to distance itself too much from notions of plowing and sowing." Pointing to the mosaic, he suggests that the farmer's territory was space, represented by the common motif of the rainbow. A friend, Zsuzsa, has shown me the piles of children's books that her family still keeps in their home, filled with such rainbow imagery. Țichindeleanu continues, "The ploughman is thus directly connected to the land, but also to space. However, the dream is not situated in a spaceship, or within a space station from another planet—this new dream is about space itself, which is the territory on which the ploughman writes its history." The communist dream, he offers, was anchored by Gagarin's cosmological journey. This was not because Gagarin was able to enter space before the United States, but rather because he was able to bring communist visions with him into it. There, legends say, he launched the project of cultivating communist utopianism to be transmitted back to earth.

During and after socialism, people surrounding Gagarin's Youth Center took the project of cultivating communist utopia seriously. This in part was aligned with the project of Marxist humanism. Whereas Marxist dialectical materialism, more popular in the Soviet Union, emphasized real-world class, labor, and social dynamics per Marxist economic science, Marxist humanism has been rooted more in Marx's earlier philosophical works that theorized and sought to abolish alienation, a vision more connected to enlightenment. Marxist humanism emerged in 1932 after the postmortem publication of his *Economic and Philosophical Manuscripts of 1844*, and then became more popular in the 1950s and 1960s. It is now associated with numerous thinkers ranging from Walter Benjamin, C. L. R. James, Herbert Marcuse, Henri Lefebvre, Raymond Williams, and more. Marxist humanism became particularly popular in the former Yugoslavia in the 1960s with the formation of the Praxis School, which opposed Stalinism and Leninism, understanding them both as antithetical to Marxist thought. It also grew wings in Hungary, Poland, and Czechoslovakia, as well as in Romania and Moldova.[22] While less robust in the latter, it did manage to seep into local astral imaginaries along the way.

Throughout the Moldovan city of Chișinău, legends endure about "Gagarin's Tree." This mythical tree, likely planted or seeded by Gagarin himself, was the offspring of an acorn flown into outer space on the cosmonaut's first mission. People in the city have reported that there are many of these acorns that visited the cosmos and that they've grown into tall oak trees throughout the former socialist world. While it's true that after returning from space, Gagarin planted a tree near the Cosmonaut Hotel in Baikonur, home of the Cosmodrome spaceport in southern Kazakhstan (at the time the Soviet Union's and today leased to Russia). The first satellite, Sputnik 1, was launched from the Cosmodrome in 1957. A few years later, Yuri was propelled into the galaxy. Since his return and his planting of the first "Gagarin Tree," cosmonauts have carried on the arboreal tradition before their Soyuz departures in the "Cosmonaut Grove" where Gagarin's first tree stands the tallest.[23]

While it is clear where Gagarin's tree grows in Kazakhstan, it is less obvious where his other alleged plantings are rooted. As Țichindeleanu muses in the film, "Nobody knows exactly which tree it is. There are multiple versions of it, depending upon who you ask." Rumors do abound, even beyond Chișinău in other parts of Moldova. In the small village of Păulești, for instance, Alexander Filip claims to have planted one of the acorns. But not everyone in the village believes this to be possible. One local, Valery Demidetsky, discredits the actuality of this "because of the conditions of the flight," which include a slew of technical issues. "I also cannot imagine that in the first flight, which lasted only 1 hour and 48 minutes, that Gagarin managed to find time for fun with acorns," Demidetsky censures.[24] Indeed, Gagarin's Vostok 1 trip only completed one orbit around the earth, which he had described as fast and chaotic: "Everything was spinning. One moment I see Africa—it happened over Africa—another the horizon, another the sky."[25] While there were problems with his reentry, he safely made it back into the atmosphere and parachuted to earth, gently touching "the soft surface of freshly plowed dirt in an open field not far from the town of Engels."[26] Demidetsky finds it absurd that he would have been able to recover acorns. "Yes, the experiments with seeds and plants in space were set as part of long-term flights. . . . There was even a program in the USA in which tree seeds were flown around the moon and then were planted. Maybe I'm wrong, but it seems that this is how legends are born!"

Legends are born, yet Mr. Filip is adamant that his nearly sixty-year-old oak tree is beyond fiction. He planted it in a courtyard when he was employed by a local school, he explains. "I was then working as a school director, I went to the department of education, and Mr. Timothy Chebrucha gave me a pot with a seedling. He brought it from Moscow. They planted roses there on the one hundredth anniversary of Lenin, and then they were given these acorns, which Gagarin had taken to space."[27] Everyone knows where Filip's contested outer space tree grows, including the mayor, who sees it as a tourist attraction. But back in Chișinău, the location of Gagarin's tree remains a mystery.

Over half a century after Gagarin supposedly cultivated acorns with communist utopianism, they continue to enchant speculative imaginings. In this way, socialist-era speculative futures can be read as still entwining cosmological visions with life on earth. This vitality shatters the widespread fiction that "socialism failed," which as Michał Murawski offers, has become an overdetermined, "ingrained discursive form."[28] Among the ruins of Gagarin's Youth Center, birds melodically chirp outside, perhaps unaware of any failure. The center, the trees, and the spaceship in the playground are, after all, still there. And the privatization that came after, the transforming of the complex into a discotheque, was only short lived. Géza Vida's cosmological stones also still stand tall in Maramureș, protracting toward outer space, surrounded by old oak trees. As Murawski suggests, "One hundred years after the 1917 October Revolution, in an era of unprecedented urban privation and inequality, we may, in fact, have a lot to learn from the still-existing achievements and enduring legacies of built socialism."[29] Many of these live on within the ruins of ethereal dreamworlds.

Disavowal

Not everyone during socialism was dreaming of agrarian astrosocialism. In Romania and Moldova, such visions were contingent on sedentarism and deracination. Further, given that farm work was conscripted through the institution of slavery for centuries, it didn't necessarily bear the same fantasies for everyone. In Romania, after the genocidal era that targeted Roma and Jews and sent countless to their deaths in Transnistria, many survivors returned home to their towns and villages.[30] One of the first programs initiated by the communists after gaining control in 1946 was specifically to settle nomadic Roma. While many Roma had been sedentary for centuries (in part due to slavery), and while nomadic Roma were targeted for extermination under the Antonescu regime, some nomadic and seminomadic people had managed to survive the camps. The Communist Party sought to settle nomadic people on the fringes of existing villages and on the outskirts of cities—oftentimes to the resentment of non-Roma villagers.[31]

In 1951, the Ministry of Interior launched a program to split up newly settled Roma communities so that they could be more easily surveilled, and also, at times, assaulted by police during raids.[32] As Daniel Dimi, who would later go on to become president of the Gypsy Party in Covasna, recalled, "Under

Ceaușescu it was not uncommon for police to come into Gypsy communities and beat Gypsies, even kill them. No one cared about us. We were treated like animals."[33] Adam Cornel from Huedin similarly reported:

> We had frequent police visits to our area. They would enter into the houses without a warrant. They use to set off firecrackers to scare the children. They thought it was funny. They came to visit at night, usually once a week each month and they would go to different houses each time. They would break the lock on the door if we weren't at home and enter. If we were at home we never protested because we knew we would be taken to the police station if we did. The police didn't treat Romanians the same way, but we don't have any value as human beings in their eyes.[34]

Nonetheless, during the first few years of the Communist regime, many sedentary Roma did gain party employment, some finding jobs in the militia, and some even becoming small town mayors. This was not due to Roma assimilatory policies per se, but rather due to new efforts to support poor and working-class people—ideal party proletariats vis-à-vis the forging of *Homo sovieticus*, or a deracinated communist human. Many landless Roma meanwhile joined agricultural collectivization efforts and were forced to adopt sedentarism and renounce racial difference.[35] As one non-Roma woman reported, "It was as if Gypsies did not even exist. We all knew that they were here. We could see them. But as far as the Party went, they simply did not exist."[36]

While Roma political organizations flourished in the early days of socialism, they were short lived as assimilation efforts gained strength. The General Union of Roma in Romania, which had existed prior to the fascist Antonescu regime, briefly resumed under the leadership of Gheorghe Niculescu. Soon though, communist authorities disbanded it. Roma people meanwhile were elided in the list of "co-inhabiting nationalities" spelled out by the Romanian Workers Party when the communist Party took over in 1948.[37] This trend continued throughout the regime, during which they were denied official state recognition and therefore any semblance of institutional support. In the late 1960s, when the idea of minority representation was introduced by the state to support Hungarians and Germans, Roma residents were again overtly absent. In Ion Blaga's *Romania's Population* (1972), a book that tracked Romanian demographics, while Romanians, Hungarians, and Germans comprised 99 percent of the population, the category "other nationalities" included "Ukrainians, Ruthenians, Hutsulains, Serbians, Croats, Slovaks, Russians, Tartars, Turks, Jews, etc."[38] As a Roma man reported in 1991 to Helsinki Watch, "We weren't Gypsies at all. We were always 'and all other nationalities' or just 'etcetera.'"[39] In 1983, the Propaganda Section of the Central Committee of the Romanian Communist Party was tasked with evaluating assimilation policies and how well Roma had abandoned their "parasitic" ways of life.[40] National citizenship could only be achieved through disavowal.

Sedentarization policies continued into the 1970s and 1980s.[41] It was during the 1980s that authorities and militia cracked down harder, and the bulk of caravans that had previously migrated from village to village all but disappeared. This transpired alongside the project of "systemization," an urban planning process carried out under Ceauşescu, inspired by North Korean urbanization with the goal of propelling Romania into an era of modernization. This led to the razing of many settled Roma *mahala* hamlets and communities, which shattered community ties and incentivized migration to urban centers. There, many people were crammed into tight and poorly maintained housing. As Nicolae Gheorghe recounted after seeing Roma homes destroyed, "When I first saw such areas, I was literally shocked by the misery there. So many people are concentrated in such a small amount of space. The blocks of flats were built in bad condition. Water is not running. . . . The result is a deterioration of social life."[42] Yet other Roma families found housing in buildings that had been nationalized and made public during socialism, which saw 30 percent of housing nationalized (as discussed in chapter 1).[43] Others found homes that had been dispossessed of Jewish residents through anti-Semitic policies prior to socialism (as described in chapter 4). This saw Roma people who had never maintained stable shelter in Romania due to centuries of racial dispossession finally secure stable housing despite ongoing efforts of deracination. While stable housing is now being eroded through post-1989 anticommunist housing reprivatization efforts, benefits gained through these housing policies, deracinated as they were, have been vital in materializing twentieth-century housing justice.

Assimilation measures also entailed eradicating traditional Roma craft making, replacing cultural work with new professions ranging from heavy industry to street sweeping to seasonal employment in state farms.[44] Nevertheless, many Roma still found ways to maintain traditions and refute the mandates of assimilation, sometimes abandoning state conscripted work in favor of traditional crafts.[45] Communities that had specialized in brick making, woodworking, and brandy distillation continued perfecting their crafts. While many who refused state complicity were punished, sometimes sent to perform forced labor at the Danube–Black Sea Canal project, others did manage to slip through the cracks. Some were even able to refuse sedentarization mandates, which in part is why nomadic and seminomadic communities endure to date (albeit often having to maneuver between minefields of criminalization, stigmatization, and Western fetishization).

Friendship among the Peoples

While anti-Roma racism (performed both through racial violence and through forced assimilation) endured throughout socialism, deeply entangled with the communist project was the dream of multiculturalism. This was quite different from multiculturalism developing on the other side of the Iron Curtain, which Jodi Melamed has well charted as a technique of neoliberal expansion.[46] Yet in Romania and Moldova, the multicultural concept of *prietenia între popoare* (friendship among the peoples) was distinct. This vision was one of Second and Third World friendships and solidarities strong enough to endure despite the magnetic grasp of Western imperialism.

It was in 1957 that the Romanian internationalist magazine *Orizonturi* (Horizons), edited by philosopher Mihai Șora, collaborated with the *Présence Africaine* magazine to publish articles and poems by the founders of Négritude—the literary movement launched by French-speaking African and Caribbean writers critical of French colonial rule and its mandates of assimilation. The magazine also featured the Senegalese historian of African precolonial culture, Cheikh Anta Diop. Much of the periodical's text revolved around themes of militant resistance for Third World liberation. When Romania joined the "Group of 77" nonaligned developing countries in 1976, it went so far as to declare itself a Latin American nation, finding more in common with the Latin Southern Hemisphere than the North.[47] Țichindeleanu describes these aspirations as "neither aligned with the Western order, Anglo-Franco-German-American, nor to the Soviet order. A sort of descendant of the Bandung Conference of the late 1950s. A friendship amongst peoples was the concept that framed most of the efforts identified as efforts for world peace."

Romania was not alone in forging these early socialist friendships. The Soviet bloc had begun hosting South African dissidents as early as 1951, while independence struggles in Angola and Mozambique were supported by other Eastern European countries.[48] Chișinău's Casa Naționalităților (House of Nationalities) in Moldova, which also briefly enters the frame in *Gagarin's Tree*, also encompassed this ethos, dedicating space to struggles against slavery and its aftermaths in other countries. As James Mark and Quinn Slobodian proffer, "Both the Iron Curtain and the borders of the Black Atlantic were more porous than often assumed, offering contact zones for interconnection between the Eastern Bloc and the Global South."[49]

Yet this socialist-era friendship among the people and the contact zones it mapped didn't hold. In 2007, when Romania entered the EU, the country withdrew from nonalignment. As Țichindeleanu notes in *Gagarin's Tree*, today, over thirty years into the postsocialist era, there is no building nor institution that defends regional Eastern European or Second-Third World interests—only spaces of alliance mediated by imperial Western powers. As Florin Poenaru writes, the West has become "the norm par excellence, the only path to follow, the East being on the verge of starting a 'new (blank) page' of its history."[50] The Western civilizing mission enforced a tabula rasa, with all friendships before "inevitably perverted or unusable." Anticommunism filled and created this void, along with new forms of nationalism and a galaxy full of what Țichindeleanu describes as "liberal colonial enlargement."[51] Not only were future past alliances deleted, but even alliances between other Eastern bloc spaces were stifled. But how did this come to be?

The term *decolonization* was first utilized in the English language in the 1930s in order to prefigure the independence already achieved in Eastern Europe for that which might be gained in Africa and Asia.[52] It was during this time that Western imperial leaders analogized Eastern European geographies with those of other colonized places, a trend that had been building since the Enlightenment and its various instantiations of Orientalism.[53] For instance, in the late 1930s, the British considered offering Nazis authority over Central African territory in exchange for curbing their imperial ambitions in Eastern Europe.[54] Nevertheless, the communists that came to power after the Second World War rarely used the word, as they saw it as too Western and paternalistic.[55] Instead, the language of "common struggle" was favored, a struggle that would unite the so-called Second and Third World struggles, from Accra to Havana, from Hanoi to Bucharest.[56]

Despite the early intentions of the communists to censure Western imperialism, many organizers from Third World struggles were wary of forming alliances with Eastern Europe, and for good reason. During the Paris Conference of 1919, for instance, Czechoslovakian politicians had lobbied for land in West Africa and Kamchatka.[57] Leaders of the popular Polish Maritime and Colonial League also argued for colonies, claiming that it was their European right, much to the admonishment of Nigerian soon-to-be president, Nnamdi Azikiwe. But then, after fascism began to grow across Europe, things slowly shifted. Trinidadian anticolonial political leader George Padmore censured Germany's invasion of Czechoslovakia, offering an alliance.[58] Soon after, so did anticolonial intellectuals such as Cyril Briggs, Jawaharlal Nehru, and Rabindranath Tagore, all of whom supported the sovereignty of Eastern European nations.[59] Meanwhile, as socialist governments came to power in the Soviet Union and Eastern bloc, socialist economists became excited about the expansion of communism into the Third World, reifying a Marxist teleological approach to futurity.[60]

Nevertheless, many in the Third World continued to be suspicious of the Soviet Union for replicating Western imperial models, a fear that drove the Sino-Soviet split in the 1960s. As Sharad Chari and Katherine Verdery have asked, "What, if not accumulation by dispossession, were the nationalization and collectivizations the Soviets imposed on their satellites?"[61] Despite critiques of Soviet imperialism, not all Eastern European socialist spaces were the same. Yugoslavia, for instance, which had broken from Moscow in 1948, was accorded a special position in imaginaries of international solidarity, becoming one of the main architects of the Non-Aligned Movement.[62]

Romania was not as assertive as Yugoslavia in distancing itself from the Soviet Union, but it did reject the COMECON trade agreement, which had mandated that each socialist state maintain an economic specialty. Romania had been slated to be agrarian due to its long-standing peasant culture. But Gheorghiu-Dej's Communist Party, transfixed with Marxist-Leninist understandings of communist futurity, wanted to develop heavy industry and technology, which it did. Romania adopted a firmer anti-Soviet position in 1968, the same year that Tito enacted his final split from Moscow. It also became a special ally to China, exchanging architectural ideas, technology, and even computers. Meanwhile, Romania demonstrated solidarity with the anticolonial and liberation struggles in African nations such as Angola, Zambia, Mozambique, Ethiopia, Cape Verde, and Burkina Faso, while also actively supporting the abolition of apartheid.[63] In 1965, after Ghanaian revolutionary Kwame Nkrumah managed to dodge an assassination attempt, he opted to flee to Bucharest. Peripherally involved in Middle East peace processes as well, Romania maintained strong ties with countries such as Syria and Libya.

Yet, despite concrete entanglements between the Second and Third worlds during this time, the two were not the same. As Mark and Slobodian suggest, analogies between postcolonial and postsocialist experiences (as well as socialist and colonial experiences for that matter) have "often distorted as much as they revealed."[64] However, per Nikolay Karkov and Zhivka Valiavicharska, "The political and economic developments in postsocialist Eastern Europe from the last nearly thirty years—the unchallenged privatization of public infrastructure, the rise or escalation of neo-fascism, nationalism, and ethnophobia, and the re-entrenchment of patriarchal relations—should also be seen in light of the decline of the anticapitalist, anti-colonial, feminist, antiracist politics that the socialist countries helped forge in the global sphere during the twentieth century."[65] State socialism was, after all, an incoherent and contradictory spatiotemporality "fractured by the universalist, colonial, and ethnocentric paradigms of hegemonic humanism and the evolutionary developmentalism of socialist frameworks of modernization, social progress, and liberation."[66]

In her instructive work on the past conditional, or questions of "what could have been," Lisa Lowe offers trajectories to think through foreclosures of historical imagination accorded by imperialism and liberal humanist institutions alike. She looks at how Black radical Marxist thinkers such as C. L. R. James sought political agendas in excess of colonial foreclosures and even in excess of Western Marxisms. Looking back to these not only offers insight into historical anti-imperial and non-Western Marxisms, but also foregrounds "times of historical contingency and possibility to consider alternatives that may have been unthought in those times."[67] Following her lead, one can ask: what would have happened if Eastern Europeans could have learned from the violence of the World Bank, the IMF, and Structural Adjustment Programs in 1970s and 1980s West Africa? But perhaps even more germane to this chapter, what might have happened if the communists of state socialism had extended the same antiracist and anti-imperial gestures that they did toward those in the Third World toward those racialized at home in the Second? What genre of astrofuturism, or sustained friendship among the people, might have materialized?

The Chimerical Cold War

Chimeras are biological phenomena in which single organisms are composed of cells with distinct genotypes and that can result from grafting one plant onto another. While they have been featured in an array of ancient myths (for instance, the ancient Dacian and now Romanian nationalist symbol of Draco, a dragon-dog bearing several metallic tongues), Cold War polarization also created a chimera of sorts, one inhabited by both state socialism and liberal democracy. This aligns with Susan Buck-Morss's argument that during the Cold War, both the US notion of unlimited individual freedom and the Soviet dream of a classless community shared a genealogy of post-Enlightenment Western modernity.[68] Similarly, Vasile Ernu offers that the two economic systems required dialectically framing the other as both enemy and interest.[69] Here I am interested in how this chimerical entanglement can be cosmologically mapped, and what such a mapping says about astrofuturist imaginaries.

Even before the Cold War, the desire for contact between the two Cold War antipodes led to a number of translation projects, with Western science fiction works by Edward Bellamy, Jules Verne, H. G. Wells (who also wrote of chimeras in *The Island of Doctor Moreau*), and more Cyrillicized.[70] These were tales of Anglo-American outer space colonization that emerged following the so-called completion of "Manifest Destiny" in California. Outer space was posited as the next frontier, mirroring and codifying US imperial tropes.[71] Yet at the same time, communist speculative fiction, some influenced by the West and some also by Russian imperial pasts, began naming airplanes and bombers after Russian fairy-tale characters. Other writing came out of Bolshevik futurism prefiguring the 1917 revolution, with artist Vladimir Tatlin claiming that "events of 1917 in the social field were already brought about in our art."[72] In 1908, for instance, writer Aleksandr Bogdanov published his science fiction novel about a Bolshevik revolutionary and mathematician who discovers a communist society on Mars, free from the gravitational pull of capitalism.[73] Nikolai Fedorov meanwhile imagined a "moral universe transformed through social-utopian applications of science (cloud-seeding, solar heat, travel by electromagnetic energy)."[74] Some of this material was whimsical, some Marxist-Leninist, and then some more anarchist. Regardless, their imaginaries bore material futures. Konstantin Tsiolkovskii, the founding scientist of Soviet rocketry, was, for instance, one of Fedorov's greatest fans.

In Romania, anticapitalist futuristic work began percolating prior to the emergence of state socialism. In 1921, the anarchist-socialist Iuliu Neagu-Negulescu scribed his utopian *Arimania sau Țara Buneiînțelegeri* (Arimania, Land of the Goodwill) while in prison in Brăila.[75] He had been working to organize trade unions, but with little success, and had then been imprisoned by communists for his radical views. In *Arimania*, Neagu-Negulescu imagines a future in which property is socialized based on cooperative models, and in which air, water, earth, and sun are honored as public spaces. No one can work for more than five hours a day, and everyone receives a month-long vacation. This is especially important for Arimanians, who love nature and who only use sustainable energy. Patriarchy does not exist in this sex-positive feminist society, nor does the bourgeois family. People, rather, are supported by community. Children learn in communal schools, and he, in particular, recommends cinema as a technology of education. While Neagu-Negulescu was less popular than other speculative futurists of the time, his imaginary does reflect a growing anticapitalist planetary sentiment that was embraced by the socialist futurists, even though the early Communist Party was not his biggest fan.

Indeed, astro/agrofuturism and speculative utopianism came to play a large part of technological imagining throughout state socialism in the Soviet Union and Eastern bloc. Several years after Gagarin's cosmological trip in 1961, the

Romanian Adrian Rogoz wrote his science fiction novel *Omul și Năluca* (The Man and the Phantasm), which depicted a society of human-plants growing on Venus.[76] A visitor to the planet falls in love with one of these chimeras, only to manifest a fanciful new tongue in order to communicate beyond terrestrial borders of human/nonhuman. Other texts abounded throughout the country, depicting various utopias and boundary crossings in outer space. Ion Cârje composed *Irene sau Planeta Cea Mai Apropiată* (Irene or the Nearest Planet) about a social utopia in space, and Gheorghe Săsărman scribed his *Cuadratura Cercului* (Squaring the Circle) about twenty-seven urban utopias organized around a metaphysical axis.[77]

It was during the time of plant-planet fantasies that debates in the Eastern bloc began to highlight problems with the Communist Party ideal of intensive growth. It was theorized that the most developed Eastern socialist countries (Czechoslovakia, the Soviet Union, the German Democratic Republic, Hungary, and Poland) had reached certain limits of human and natural exploitation, and that it might be impossible to reach the cosmological year of 2000 if the current course was maintained.[78] People began looking to alternative development strategies in Third World spaces as possible ways out. In 1977, East German philosopher Rudolf Bahro proposed an alternative to state socialism, which would embrace a "cultural revolution" that would merge the socialist idea of social justice with Indigenous visions of connection with nature. In 1975, Francisc Păcurariu introduced the term "cosmovision" into Romanian literature, a portmanteau inspired by Latin-Americanist cosmologies and understandings of social justice.

In the Soviet Union, this eco/extraterrestrial speculative connection came to full expression in Andrei Tarkovsky's famous 1972 film *Solaris*. Based on Stanisław Lem's 1961 novel, the film rotates around an interstellar journey to an old space station in order to study the fictive planet, Solaris. The planet, much to the surprise of the cosmonauts, exudes consciousness and an ability to read the mind of the orbiting humans. Able to materialize their grief and loss, the planet leads the cosmonauts into believing that it is smarter than they are. The film's last frame features a small houseplant that a cosmonaut had transported from earth into space. Somehow, the plant can communicate with the planet in a way that the cosmonauts never could, causing Solaris's gaseous materials to mutate into earthlike substances and colors. As Alaina Lemon provokes, "Some viewers interpret these last scenes as occurring within the protagonist's broken mind; others see real planetary changes imperfectly catalyzed by human memories of home. But what if it is the plant who finally establishes a channel with the planetary mind?"[79]

As Lemon suggests, this little houseplant can be understood as offering an alternative vision to that of Cold War xenophobia, one of cross-border post-humanist friendships that "sprout and thrive across borders, but that look like untidy weeds to the paranoid perspective."[80] Similar to settler coloniality informing Cold War border formations in the United States, Soviet Cold War xenophobia also bore imperial genealogies, in this case, that of Russian imperialism. Both the United States and the USSR continued to build on imperial visions throughout the Cold War internally and externally, extending prisons and military practices into new terrains while terraforming a carceral and bordered planet. The fusing of plants and planets in outer space thus pointed to a utopian vision of decolonization, of undoing borders. If plants and planets could become chimeras in outer space, what else was possible back on earth? Of course, despite these utopic extraterrestrial visions of interterrestrial connection, both Cold War superpowers continued to concoct laboratories of paranoia. While Lemon is more concerned about the nuances of such contact and communication between the two worlds, here I am specifically interested in the speculative visions of the plant-planet chimerical utopian framings of outer space visitation.

But also, I am interested in if the outer space communist dream really was one of visitation open to anyone who might arrive. Or, following Derrida's distinction, was it only one of invitation open to those summoned? By this, I refer to his notion of hospitality and radical ethics of cosmopolitanism, which he bases on Jewish messianic concepts of a justice deferred.[81] He understands that unconditional hospitality toward the unexpected visitor, one who cannot be anticipated and one who is wholly other, is to be part of the work of justice. This is not the Christian liberal notion of tolerance, but rather one in which difference itself—be it that of the refugee, immigrant, Native, exile, and/or foreigner—is recognized and embraced. Such hospitality is predicated on the abolition of private property, with Derrida suggesting that "hospitality precedes property."[82] This signals how the host resides in a home "which, in the end, does not belong to him." Interpreting this through the lens of the sanctuary, Ananya Roy writes that his conceptualization of hospitality here "is ultimately a resignification of the meanings of host and guest, self and other, native and foreigner."[83] Hospitality, in other words, "proceeds not from the security of self-possession but rather from its lack." Perhaps then, the downfall of astrosocialism was its lack of radical hospitality for racial difference. Not all plants were considered housebound and worthy of chimerical planetary futurism; some continued to be ignored. Others continued to be wastelanded as weeds.

Not All People

Dragan and Gigi, parents of a good friend of mine, had both been engineers during socialism in the Romanian city of Timișoara. Dragan, who has long been unemployed since his job was effectively rendered obsolete after 1989, loves to regale company with stories of socialist-era internationalism. He himself bears Serbian heritage, as many people do in the city, which sits close to the Serbian border. One morning, sitting at their kitchen table while he was attempting to get me drunk on *țuică* before breakfast, he decided to share the story of "the lion." It was in the early 1980s, and he and a bunch of fellow engineering students were on assignment in the city. They were an international bunch, as Romania was a top university destination for many engineers in the Third World. One of the students was from the Congo. It had been a warm summer evening, and they were all sitting around playing cards with the window slightly ajar. Suddenly, their comrade from the Congo jumped up, yelling that he had just heard a lion outside. Dragan laughed at the man, as did everyone else there, "as we don't have lions in Romania." And yet, the Congolese friend was unrelenting. "He said that he grew up with lions, and he knows a lion when he hears a lion," Dragan continued. They all shut the window and went on with their card game, laughing at their international friend. Then, the next morning, when they turned on the radio, they were all shocked. A lion had indeed escaped from a local zoo and had been roaming the city overnight. "We thought we knew about all the cats in this city, but it turns out we didn't know a thing!" Dragan exclaimed. As he was cracking himself up, Gigi entered the kitchen laughing, and proceeded to tell me that they are still in touch with some of their former classmates from African countries. A friend from Burkina Faso would be visiting them soon for a big class reunion, she noted excitedly. "I wonder how it was for them, back then, here. There aren't as many people from Africa in town these days, just tourists really. Maybe still a few students, here and there," she thoughtfully drifted off.

Gigi and Dragan blame the Romanian Communist Party, as well as Western imperialism, for the crumbling of this past "friendship amongst the peoples." Indeed, the party became increasingly isolationist and authoritarian, as has been well critiqued. Perhaps the problem was the socialist embracing of the Marxist-Leninist teleological narrative. This codified progress within the terms of post-Enlightenment modernity. Such a vision pathologized other understandings of temporality, whether within Romania or beyond.

In addition, despite its emancipatory policies of housing nationalization, public education, guaranteed work, and even guaranteed vacations to the Black

Sea, the Communist Party never adequately addressed anti-Roma racism or anti-Semitism. "There was zero mention of the Holocaust in school," Gigi explained, echoing a familiar tale across the region. Indeed, during communism, the country blamed Nazi Germany for the genocide at best, denying its own engineering of Transnistrian death camps.[84] Romania was the second-largest perpetrator of death and dispossession during the Holocaust after Germany, yet during socialism, fascism was depicted as a German import rather than a Romanian technology. Meanwhile, Roma children were often kept out of certain schools, in part due to poverty and discrimination, in part due to school failures to teach in the Romani language.[85] That said, schooling was more available than had been the case prior to socialism. Meanwhile, as Michelle Kelso maps, "Postwar state-issued textbooks mentioned victims of the Antonescu regime; however, their identities were labeled as communists and/or Romanians rather than as Jews or Roma."[86] This framing not only absolved Romania of fascist crimes, but also rendered Nazi Germany the enemy. Much of this changed after socialism ended (although schools are still not taught in the Romani language and many Roma children face even worse discrimination in the education system). In 1998, legislation was passed mandating that the Holocaust be taught in seventh and eleventh grades (although generally only Germany's role was mentioned), and in 2002, legislation forbade Holocaust denial.[87] Yet the following year, the Romanian government once again denied Romania's role in the Holocaust. This in part inspired Kelso to become active in Holocaust education. As she found, teachers have often recalcitrantly resisted acknowledging any violence that the state perpetrated on Roma communities. When studying Romanian language in Babeș-Bolyai University in Cluj myself, I was horrified that my own teachers described Roma DNA as biologically inferior to that of other Romanians, and warned students to watch out for the "Gypsy thieves" surrounding the university building. As it was inferred, these were people who belonged on the wasteland outskirts of the cities among the weeds. Kelso places pedagogy such as this as a nationalist extension both of the fascist and socialist regimes.

Racism was experienced by Roma communities during socialism, but also by visitors. Many African students studying in Eastern Europe had grown accustomed to freedom of debate and ideas in African countries, only to find Soviet-style socialism stifling.[88] In 1963, between 350 and 500 African students fled Bulgaria after finding it unsupportive of Pan-Africanism.[89] Some critiqued the Soviet project as too similar to the Western one. As one Nigerian student assessed of his experience in Moscow: "Africans did not wish to replace western imperialism with eastern imperialism, no matter how well camouflaged it might be with seeming sympathy for African nationalism."[90] This is not to deny the revolutionary antifascist organizing that contoured early socialist visions in Eastern Europe. There were, after all, people like Ana Pauker, a Jewish Stalinist who served Romania in the 1940s and 1950s as the world's first female foreign minister. But in 1952, Pauker was scapegoated by Communist Party leader Gheorghiu-Dej in the name of de-Stalinization in a move that many consider anti-Semitic and sexist.[91]

After Stalin's 1953 death, new socialist imaginaries began to take hold across Eastern Europe, for instance Marxist humanism. However, during the 1970s there was a strange return to Marxist-Leninism, what some called neo-Stalinism.[92] This was particularly marked by Romanian Communist Party leader Nicolae Ceaușescu's 1971 speech "Tezele din Iulie" (July Theses), issued in the name of "social humanism." While his ideas were inspired by a visit to the People's Republic of China, North Korea, North Vietnam, and Mongolia, it manifested increased authoritarianism rather than transnational friendship. Yet opposition to Soviet imperialism was sustained, which solicited a subtle approval in the eyes of those critical of the USSR.

While Marxist humanism might appear more liberatory and conducive of international solidarity than Leninism, Stalinism, or Ceaușescu's social humanism, it also bore, as Karkov and Valiavicharska put it, a "constitutive 'dark underside.'"[93] This had to do with a post-Enlightenment adherence to the human, and reflected an ongoing aspiration of becoming Western, and white. Thus, "by the time of the collapse of the state socialist governments (and even a little earlier), the internalization of the logic of imperial difference and its epigonal aspiration to true Europeanness" would incite internal racial violence.[94] Despite its liberatory potential and opposition to Soviet imperial logics, then, Eastern European Marxist humanism never fully freed itself from Western epistemologies. It is partly due to this that Buck-Morss proffers both state socialism and democratic liberalism emerging as inverses of each other, each chimerically bearing post-Enlightenment understandings of modernity.[95]

Shu-mei Shih suggests that perhaps another kind of Marxist humanism could have "offered the possibility of conjoining the two terms socialism and humanism productively into a compound term, with consequences for both postsocialism and posthumanism."[96] This branch of thought would link with Frantz Fanon's "new humanism," which critiques Enlightenment humanism's complicity with colonial violence. While Fanon finds Marxist analysis useful, it also "must be stretched slightly when it comes to addressing the colonial issue," particularly due to the recursive and superstructural economic infrastructure of race in the colonies.[97] Eurocentric Marxist analysis, in other words, fails to take race into account when analyzing modes of production. This failure makes humanism difficult to grasp. As he famously puts it, "When I search for man in the technique and style of Europe, I see only a succession of negations of man, and an avalanche of murders."[98] Yet Fanon does not want to give up on humanism and its promises. Rather, he finds the postcolonial promise in creating "the whole man, whom Europe has been incapable of bringing to triumphant birth."[99] Sylvia Wynter has built on Fanon's thinking, theorizing what David Scott describes as "a certain ideal of humanism—dissonant, a non-identarian, but nonetheless a comprehensive and planetary humanism."[100] Indeed, Wynter's planetary proposal is "being human as praxis," which, crudely put, means conceptualizing and becoming human beyond the genre of the white, heteronormative, and European "Man."[101] In other words, to become human one must hack a master code informed by hundreds of years of dehumanization and rewriting its core programming. Becoming then opens up an array of emancipatory futures. As Alexander Weheliye questions, "What different modalities of the human come to light if we do not take the liberal humanist figure of Man as the master-subject but focus on how humanity has been imagined and lived by those subjects excluded from this domain?"[102]

To break the Western European–derived master code then means to shift one's vantage point. In doing so, astronomical perspectives transform as well, bypassing the cosmological myopias of outer space fantasies that dominated Cold War imaginaries on both sides of the Iron Curtain. After all, if not all people are considered human on earth, why would we expect them to be in the stars, utopic as the skies may appear? Yet, what would it mean to apply Wynter's line of humanistic hope upward? Indeed, astrosocialism's project could have perhaps materialized differently if it had moved beyond the chimerical *Homo economicus–Homo sovieticus* bifurcation and their deracinations in crafting galactic anti-imperial friendships among the people. How might a Derridean conception of hospitality have altered the astrosocialist dream, and perhaps built on antiracist and anti-imperial work already taking place transnationally?

For instance, the same year that Ceaușescu issued his July Thesis, in 1971, the United Nations had called for the "Year for Action to Combat Racism and Racial Discrimination." In accordance, Romania printed a postage stamp in this spirit, with three human figures, one colored in yellow, one white, and one Black, depicted raising their arms together.[103] Also in response to the antiracist call, Roma activists from across Europe gathered in London with a collaboratively produced flag celebrating transnational solidarities and alliances across difference and beyond borders.[104] In this sense, despite political-economic shifts transpiring governmentally, humanisms beyond and despite the state were also taking root. While these were not tethered to social humanism or Marxist humanism, they were certainly grounded in anticapitalist, antiracist, and anti-imperial understandings of international solidarity. Such humanistic futures also speak to the inspiration and solidarity that Roma feminists have continued to find in Black and anticolonial feminist scholarship and organizing while acknowledging specific contestations of empire, nationalism, capitalism, race, ethnicity, and gender unique to postsocialist times.[105] Questions remain as to what would it have meant to weave these Roma Futurist solidarities with humanistic critiques of racial technocapitalism within and beyond borders during state socialism. Might this have helped quell the impending doom of capitalist ruination?

Techno-witchcraft

It was during the Cold War and amid ongoing repetitions of white US imperial confinement that Afrofuturistic speculative fiction began to imagine other spatial futures. Much of this was engendered during and despite Cold War contexts of anti-Blackness and militarized imperialism. As jazz musician and Afrofuturist visionary Sun Ra aptly declared in 1979, "If you can develop an atomic bomb, I'm sure you can develop an altered destiny."[106] For Afrofuturists, the cosmos emerged as a place in which the violence of anti-Blackness could be unpacked, but also in which antiracist and transhuman possibilities could be cultivated. Building on this, Reynaldo Anderson and Charles E. Jones have set to task describing Astro-Blackness, or "an Afrofuturistic concept in which a person's black state of consciousness, released from the confining and crippling slave or colonial mentality, becomes aware of the multitude and varied possibilities and probabilities within the universe."[107] Astro-Blackness, they suggest, understands outer space and global technocultural assemblages as hospitable to Black futurisms.

While Afrofuturist and Astro-Black critique has done (and continues to do) important work assessing the racial violence of Cold War and colonial science fiction, it has also served as an inspiration for other futurisms. During an artist residency at Para Site in Hong Kong, where she dove deep into studying forms of witchcraft globally, Roma feminist playwright and founder of the Giuvlipen Theatre Company Mihaela Drăgan developed the framework of Roma Futurism in order to "reclaim the figure of the witch."[108] In her manifesto, written against an ossified Orientalist framing that traps Roma people as primitive and of the past, Drăgan offers, "The future belongs to the Roma witches who have already started the war against racism and capitalism."[109] Her remediation intervenes on primitivism, but also on what Wynter critiques as "techno-industrial Progress and national-racial Manifest Destiny" through which tech-nofuturity is enclosed within the domain of white supremacy and empire.[110] Rather than adhering to such a technofuture, Drăgan rebuts:

> To those who think that we are not able to use the new technologies or those who think that we are cut off from science, we inform them that we have always been the ones who invented the crafts that made our life easier. We were blacksmiths, kettle makers and cobblers; we knew how to process gold and we called ourselves goldsmiths, we trained bears and we were bear leaders. We made spoons and pots that lasted for generations and no one quite knew how to make them like we did. But then IKEA and other big corporations came to make them, offering low quality imitations of our craft, stealing our craft and leaving our people jobless. This is the reason why witches will always despise capitalism.[111]

And indeed, Roma people have long been Romania's technological creators, with many specializing in specific genres of craft and tool making. Yet, as explored in chapters 1 and 3, today in postsocialist contexts of reprivatization and property restitution, IKEA and other Western companies have bought up forests and exploited racialized Romani labor. Through this process, Roma people become banished to wasteland spaces while Western digital nomads become active players in urban gentrification, all the while transiting deracinated Orientalist fantasies of Gypsy freedom. Not coincidentally, it was Arthur C. Clarke who envisaged digital nomadism during the Cold War, presaging technologically savvy businessmen who can harness the prowess of global capital and thus Siliconize the world.[112] It was also Clarke who suggested that "any sufficiently advanced technology is indistinguishable from magic."[113] Referencing this dictum, Drăgan argues that "if a Roma woman were to say the same thing, she wouldn't be taken seriously."[114] Rather, Roma witchcraft is ridiculed and demonized—as it has been throughout Western modernity.

Not coincidentally, witchcraft demonization was integral to the formation of capitalism. In her *Caliban and the Witch*, Silvia Federici importantly maps the hedging of the commons by capitalists and the role that witch hunts played in some of the earliest processes of primitive accumulation during the transition from feudalism to capitalism.[115] In her words, this transformation necessitated killing the precapitalist body, which had been "a receptacle of magical powers that had prevailed in the medieval world . . . so that labor-power could live."[116] The targeting of this magical and queerly "unproductive" body also meant criminalizing it as mad, as Michel Foucault has also articulated.[117] Building on this, Federici suggests that by not working, witches threatened the nascent capitalist order. As such, between 1550 and 1650, witchcraft was rendered a female crime, though male "vagabonds, beggars, itinerant laborers, as well as the gypsies and lower-class priests" were also suspect, as were Jewish people—all targeted by witch hunts.[118] Designations of who got burned at the stake were thus gendered and racialized, reliant on early articulations of racial capitalism and the newfound age of "reason." That said, in Russia, it was often men accused of witchcraft, many of whom offered spells against czarist abuse.[119] They too were a threat to the growing capitalist order.

This new era saw a separation between what Federico Campagna differentiates as the technic and magic, the former belonging to conceptions of order, the latter living in the realm of mystery.[120] Given this, non-Western and antinationalist sciences, including Roma technologies, were both appropriated into capital by landlords and criminalized by the police. As Oxana Timofeeva writes, those interpellated as witches found respite in borderlands, in queer spaces on society's edges,[121] perhaps an early instantiation of what Ananya Roy describes as processes of racial banishment that push those dispossessed by capitalism to urban outskirts (as explored in chapter 1).[122] Yet these borderlands also became a site of strength where many so-called witches held the power to transform one thing into another, in part in response to the intolerability of the capitalist world. Recounting Baba Yaga, an untamed witch from Russian folklore, Timofeeva writes: "A witch's desire is ontological: it must be strong enough to transform something that is not into something that is, nonbeing into being (to trigger rain, to raise the dead). Such a transformation is a miracle."[123] She also suggests that Lenin's own grandmother, who too was accused of being a witch, inspired Lenin's own conception that "a revolution is a miracle"[124]— though this too may have been informed by Jewish conceptions of miracles and *Tikkun Olam*, or healing the world.

For Lenin and other revolutionaries of the time (and since), the miracle of revolution requires comradeship and solidarity across difference rather than persecution due to difference. Indeed, the communist project intended to create an alternative to capitalism and empire alike. One would imagine, then, that state socialism would have better thought through histories of witch hunts, anti-Roma racism, and anti-Semitism. Roma Futurism seeks in part to correct this, refusing to forget histories of witch-hunting which, Drăgan suggests, "intended to terrify women and make them accept a new patriarchal order in which their bodies, work, sexual and reproductive rights were now owned and controlled by the state and were therefore transformed into economic resources."[125] As a project, Roma Futurism thus pursues reparations for presocialist racial capitalist technologies and also for those of postsocialist contexts of reprivatization, which, as in times past, banish Roma people to the wastelands of modernity.

Yet the future is not destined to be one of premature death and dissolution. As Ioanida Costache contextualizes, Drăgan's work in fact seeks "to create a world that is not simply an erasure of the past, but rather a negotiation with it, tracing a path towards the longed-for-world via instruments of healing and rituals that enact true emancipation for Roma—emancipation forged in the cauldron of the witch and not in the chambers of parliament."[126] Roma Futurism thus is embedded in a decolonial and feminist framework that redefines how Roma are construed but also traces a more intricate relationship to the past. Continuing, Costache writes, "Instead of portraits honoring our ancestors or archives documenting Roma joy, official archives are full of SS officers humiliating Roma women or exoticizing illustrations of Romani encampments circulating westward on postcards." Roma Futurism instead refuses such imperial and dehumanizing narratives by crafting "new images, new symbols, new myths to replace the damage that [was] produced by the disaster that is enslavement and genocide."[127] Operating from a place of joy and of empowerment, it also crafts new technological relations that render emancipatory futures unrecognizable to Silicon Valley, technofutures that can counter the ravages of racial capitalism proliferating in postsocialist times.

Not coincidentally, amid postsocialist contexts of racial capitalist proliferation, new genres of witch-hunting have also gathered steam, highlighting just how threatening to the capitalist order those rendered as witches are. Romania passed a law in 2011 defining witchcraft as taxable work and created a penalty for fraud—a move specifically intended to criminalize Roma women through what Alexandra Coțofană describes as a "witch tax."[128] Later, in 2016, a law was passed in Serbia barring "superstitious practices." As Christina Novakov-Ritchey critiques, the "normalization of 'superstition' as a descriptor of magical practice denies epistemic sovereignty to those people who have practiced these forms of healing and divination for centuries."[129] Yet despite this recoded criminalization alongside newfound impositions of premature and social death, Roma Futurism endures.

By forging new and old technological relations alike with magic, Roma Futurism articulates justice. Through its spells, Drăgan suggests that a phone camera can exorcise evil while computer viruses contain powers to make someone ill. Computers themselves can develop cyborgian human consciousness, with "witchbots" able to "release us from the grip of an unjust world." The oeuvre of techno-witchcraft also includes curses against fascist leaders such as Donald Trump and Viktor Orbán. One particular spell conjures the Spirit of the Internet and the Cyber Sisterhood to infect "stupid white men" with "thousands of computer viruses." This spell aims to trap these men in a black hole of computer crashes and gain access to their data, consigning them to live amid the "electrified dust of cybernetic chaos coils . . . in devastating electromagnetic storms." Such techno-witchcraft seeks not to assimilate into the Silicon order but rather to corrupt it. It considers Roma and anticolonial understandings with land and with technology as scientific. Writing of a similar phenomenon along the US-Mexico border, Felicity Amaya Schaeffer describes Indigenous *sacredscience* as "a methodology of collective intelligence that regenerates ancestral knowledges to sustain sacred intrarelationality with land."[130] Sacredscience, as Schaeffer writes, confuses "the temporal fabrications and historical erasures that segregate tradition from science, the human from the nonhuman, the subject from the object, the local from the universal, the past from the future, and so on."[131] Similarly, techno-witchcraft reclaims technoscience by embracing other ways of knowing, seeing, and being.

Back amid the ruins of Gagarin's Youth Center and its cosmonautical communist mosaics poking out among overgrown vegetation, techno-witchcraft appears overtly absent. While racial difference was celebrated among Second World visions of internationalism when it involved anticolonial struggles in the Third World, Roma and Jewish differences were for the most part rendered something to be assimilated into the racelessness of *Homo sovieticus*—from Romania to Moldova and beyond.[132] But beyond representational dearth, what I want to speculate on here is that perhaps ruination would not have transpired in the first place had techno-witchcraft been better baked into and constitutive of the communist political project of "friendship amongst the peoples" rather than relegated to the extraterrestrial, weedy wasteland of modernity. Might this engagement have generated spells powerful enough to have kept capitalism from becoming synonymous with technology? As Timofeeva offers, "Comradeship creates a shield against the witch hunters who will try to catch us one by one, but who will never destroy the whole set of alliances that make up the Great Sorcery International."[133] Might techno-witchy spells, alongside ongoing projects of Third World internationalism, have protected those targeted by capitalism and dismissed by the state during socialism, creating a comradeship to keep NewSpace imperial enunciations from being the dominant ones of outer space? Aligned with Wynter's vision of a humanism worth fighting for, such a futurity thus reflects an emancipatory humanism both already here on earth, and yet to come.

Anti-imperial Space Making

I first visited Moldova in 2011 when visiting an international anarchist "Space Camp" in an abandoned park, Drochia Raion, located in Mendic. The park had originally been built in the nineteenth century by a wealthy Polish entrepreneur for his wife. It was then used during socialism as a summer camp for children, similar to Gagarin's Youth Center. And, like the youth center, it was left in a state of ruination and rubble following socialism. I arrived after a Romanian friend of mine, who at the time was studying fascism in Budapest, had convinced me to hitchhike with him there. The plan was to participate in what Space Camp organizers described as a "self-organized camp about the organization of free spaces." For Space Campers, space itself was not galactic, but here on earth, awaiting exhumation to collectively sprout anti-imperial futures.

On the way to Moldova, we had stopped in Cluj, shortly after three hundred Roma residents from Coastei Street had been evicted and sent to Pata Rât upon Nokia's uncompleted downtown office construction and the ongoing racial violence of property restitution, documented in chapter 1. There, we visited the wasteland and met with dispossessed and enraged evictees, opening my eyes to the violence of property restitution and Siliconization alike. We also attended an organizing session back in the city center led by activists such as Enikő Vincze, who would go on to cofound Căși Sociale ACUM! (Social Housing NOW!) and with whom I would later collaborate on mapping the Siliconization of Cluj, documented in this book's introduction. After this formative time in Cluj, we finally arrived in Mendic.

Space Camp's aim was to build new skills and share knowledge through a series of workshops and skill-sharing sessions on organizing, permaculture, free software, first aid, and more, and we proceeded to lead conversations about racial dispossession amid tech gentrification, inspired by housing justice organizing efforts in Cluj. Another goal was transforming the weedy park into a sustainable space in which a future of solidarity and mutual aid could be materialized. Amid the ruins of both socialism and transition, we together imagined that another future could be possible—one of racial, housing, and technological justice. In a sense then, the goals of Space Camp were similar to what *Istoria (Nu) Se Repetă* participants would later dream up as part of their free school from the future past in Bucharest, documented in chapter 5. Both Space Camp and *Istoria (Nu) Se Repetă* in this way align with the project of techno-witchcraft and its endeavors to dismantle the racism, sexism, and capitalism undergirding dominant technocultural imaginaries. These projects do not endeavor to forget the violence of the past, but rather to trace entanglements of various subjugations and struggles for justice in order to envisage emancipatory futures. As Ann Laura Stoler writes, "Making connections where they are hard to trace is not designed to settle scores but rather to recognize that these are unfinished histories, not of victimized pasts but consequential histories that open to differential future."[134]

Upon leaving Space Camp, I found myself on a small bus headed toward Bucharest. It was there that I temporarily moved into the Biblioteca Alternativă, a feminist, anarchist social center then located in a quiet residential neighborhood near the city center. While structurally falling apart, the building and its courtyard were warm and cozy, containing a library filled with zines and books. These were organized in categories such as sociology/anthropology, anarchism/social movements/direct action, gender/sexuality/LGBTQ, colonialism/militarism, repression/political prisoners, literature, and art/photography. I stayed there for a month or so, engendering friendships and community.

While there are many origins to the Biblioteca, none are inseparable from the 2008 anti-imperial resistance movement against the North American Treaty Organization (NATO). It was then, a year after Romania had joined the EU, that a repressive police regime was established in Bucharest in order to secure conditions for NATO's anniversary summit at the Palace of the Parliament. Increased militarization, along with a growing resistance to Western capitalism, incited a collective of resistance. Organizers rented a large industrial hall in Timpuri Noi (now being redeveloped by IKEA, as explored in chapter 3), with plans to organize demonstrations at the summit. As Razvan, an anti-NATO protester, described in a 2009 retrospective documentary: "I was shocked by the atmosphere of the city. . . . Flags everywhere, Romanian flags, NATO flags, flags of other NATO countries, and the streets deserted, empty of people, empty of cars. It was as if a theater play was being staged."[135] Yet the day before the summit, antiterrorist units caught and detained dozens of activists, severely injuring some of them. While many people were too traumatized to continue organizing, others did, fomenting a "critical alternative to the formal paradigm of NATO's existence, mission, and expansion."[136] The summit thus did commence, during which it was declared that both Ukraine and Georgia would eventually join the transnational Cold War pact. This, then, in part set the stage for the 2022 Russian invasion of Ukraine, during which, not coincidentally, the Ukrainian government has become reliant on Musk's Starlink satellites to stay connected.[137] Yet despite auguring in Cold War 2.0 militarization marked by private capital taking up the space of government programs, also sparked into motion were new translocal solidarities against global capital. Much like

Space Camp, these sowed the seeds for future anti-imperialist worldmaking possibilities.

Soon after my visit to the Biblioteca Alternativă, the collective splintered into different groups and projects, one soon starting a new social center, Clacă. There the collective held workshops, events, and clothing swaps. During my first visit, I led a workshop on mapping and organizing against evictions in San Francisco with the Anti-Eviction Mapping Project, engendering what would become an ongoing housing justice solidarity connection between the two locales. It was there too that the Frontul Comun pentru Dreptul la Locuire (Common Front for Housing Rights / FCDL) was formed in order to support Roma, feminist, anti-eviction housing justice struggles. The collective grew quickly, responding in part to a property restitution eviction on Vulturilor Street nearby, where, in 2014, 150 residents were forcibly kicked out of their homes with only what they could carry. One evictee, Nicoleta Vișan, helped lead the community in setting up an unprecedented protest encampment, refusing to be erased through reprivatization mechanisms.[138] The FCDL supported those living in tents on the sidewalks and streets in front of where their homes had been, helping to provide resources but also collectively fighting for social housing alternatives and helping to bring the violence of property restitution into public conversations. Much of this drew on a framing advanced in 2006, after restitutions dispossessed another Roma community in the Rahova-Uranus neighborhood, which also powerfully fought back.[139]

Unfortunately, the space that housed Clacă (and by default the FCDL) was adjacent to the Colectiv Nightclub, which accidentally caught fire in 2015. The tragic deaths of sixty-four people soon became fuel for a growing anticommunist, anti-corruption movement (also described in chapter 3). The entire area around the fire was left uninhabitable, and the wary and exhausted members of Clacă had to find yet another space. Nonetheless, members regained momentum to found the Macaz Bar Teatru Coop (Macaz Bar Theater Cooperative) on Moșilor Street in the city center—a cooperative bar, social center, theater space, and library known for leftist public events, queer dance parties, and political theater plays. The FCDL made Macaz its new headquarters, where meetings were held and solidarity was organized. Sometimes regional projects such as the Bloc met there, which includes housing, labor, feminist, and antiracist groups across the country including the FCDL and its sister organization Căși Sociale ACUM! in Cluj, as well as RomaJust Asociația Juriștilor Romi (Association of Roma Lawyers), a Roma law student association; Dreptul la Oraș (Right to the City), a nonhierarchical critical and direct action collective in Timișoara; and Asociația E-Romnja (Association for the Promotion of Roma

Women's Rights), a nonprofit founded by a group of Roma and non-Roma activists for Roma women's respect, dignity, and rights. Many of these groups speak to Roma feminist and housing justice movement work that has been planting seeds and growing power for decades now. As Carmen Gheorghe, Letiția Mark, and Enikő Vincze write, this collective movement "posits a systemic critique of capitalism, and fights to dismantle the intertwined structures of domination, as well as imagining a better world where gender equality is empowered by the broader regime of social justice."[140]

In 2019, Macaz, situated between a handful of buildings undergoing restitution evictions, was forced to dissolve due to landlord pressures. It relocated nearby, but then experienced rampant anti-Roma racism from neighbors at its new location. That, coupled with increased precarity due to COVID-19, forced the group to shutter its doors. The collective has endured despite this, now in the new social center Filaret. Meanwhile, its sister space in Cluj, A-casă, has also been relocating to a new location outside of the rubble of Siliconized development, shadowed by the flashing NTT outsourcing tower that appears to be shooting up into space.

For the FCDL, A-casă, the Bloc, and Space Camp alike, space is not waiting in the distant horizon for Elon Musk and Jeff Bezos to permit access. Rather, space is a place of organizing and of home, of international solidarity being woven together for anti-imperial, anticapitalist, and justice-based futures. While palimpsestic racist histories and imperial formations echo the doom of ruination and wastelanding, as the work of techno-witchcraft teaches, space and technology alike are not foreclosed. Rather, like seedlings that fight eradication, the work of spatial, racial, and technological justice finds room to grow in nooks and crevices unmapped by Google, uncharted by NewSpace telescopes, and unrealized by astrosocialism's project of deracination. These futures, rather, are cast by justice-based incantations for a different outer space—ones invoked through the legacies of Third World internationalism alongside Roma Futurism, a hospitality of visitation, and the daily work of anticapitalist spatial organizing. Located here on earth, these spells cultivate acorns not in a distant ethereal galaxy but rather in a politics of emplacement.

Unbecoming Silicon Valley

I had been to the Office in Cluj before, having attended a couple of tech meet-ups and corporate hackathons hoping to gain some insight into the workings of its now Siliconized infrastructure. Formerly a textiles factory, the Office's shiny glass iteration was erected in 2012 on Bulevardul 21 Decembrie 1989—a street named in recognition of the date that state socialism ended and a new era of capitalism came into being. Now, replete with numerous tech companies, fancy restaurants, banks, and cafés, it is difficult to imagine what the space might have been like in its socialist iteration. Yet it wasn't until meeting up with a colleague outside of the Office that I became aware of one of its offices that now I can't stop thinking about.

Caro had recently moved back to Cluj to be closer to her family while in the midst of finishing her dissertation on interwar feminist labor histories. Struggling to pay her expenses, she had managed to land a night shift job at an Office call center. She thought it was just some regular tech outsourcing firm from the United States. Soon though, she discovered that it was in fact the property technology firm, Yardi. Her job also entailed serving one of Yardi's major clients, Invitation Homes—the United States' largest landlord of single-family homes. A former subsidiary of the half-trillion-dollar multinational company the Blackstone Group, Invitation Homes owns over eighty thousand properties and has been rapidly expanding throughout the COVID-19 pandemic under the logics of crisis capitalism. It employs unique-sounding shell companies to purchase its properties, often making it impossible for tenants to even know who or what their landlord is.[1] Invitation Homes also mobilizes surrogate labor and digital platforms to perform property management, creating new technocultural and technopolitical abstractions for its tenants. At the same time, those working for Invitation Homes through Yardi struggle to understand who their employer actually is. "It's all confusing," Caro explained while we were having lunch one day. "I don't know, do I work for Invitation Homes, or for Yardi, or maybe for their clients? Maybe if Invitation Homes is Yardi's client, then I work for the clients of the client?" she puzzled.

Yardi first emerged in 1984 in California, yet, like much of the so-called proptech industry, it really blossomed in the aftermaths of the subprime crisis amid the rise of corporate landlordism.[2] Yardi is but one of countless proptech companies today reshaping the provision, consumption, and management of rental property. Proptech, or what tenants might better understand as "landlord technologies," includes everything from tenant screening software to biometric facial recognition building access systems, from landlord- and property manager–controlled rental payment platforms to automated eviction notifications.[3] Desiree Fields nominates this turn the rise of the "automated landlord,"[4] where corporate landlords effectively mobilize data capitalism in order to expand and manage their portfolios.

While scholars have begun to investigate landlord technologies as a site of concern, less work has investigated the exploitative, repetitive, and dull outsourced labor undergirding global landlord technological formations. Yet, in the words of Thomas Mullaney, "Every single thing that 'happens online,' 'virtually,' and 'autonomously' happens offline first—and often involves human beings whose labor is kept deliberately invisible."[5] As a rich body of feminist materialist work on the racial and gendered tedious labor powering fantasies of automation reveals, the humans operating behind the curtains of automation are not simply unpolitical mechanical actors, even when their job descriptions indicate that they are.[6]

The post-Enlightenment West has been long marked by desires for enchanted technologies that garb hidden unfree human labor with machine autonomy. In the words of Neda Atanasoski and Kalindi Vora, "The category of labor has been complicit with the technoliberal desire to hide the worker behind the curtain of enchanted technologies, advancing this innovated form of the liberal human subject and its investments in racial unfreedom through the very categories of consciousness, autonomy, and humanity, and the attendant categories of the subject of rights, of labor, and of property."[7] Surrogacy, they find, motors the very project of modernity, with the "slave standing in for the master, the vanishing of native bodies necessary for colonial expansion, as well as invisibilized labor including indenture, immigration, and outsourcing." Technoliberalism meanwhile seeks to resolve liberal modernity's contradictory obsession with race and overcoming racism by transforming Cold War fears of Soviet totalitarian automation with paranoia of white labor being replaced by robots. Thus, while white supremacist movements galvanize fears of Mexicans and Chinese workers stealing US jobs, a simultaneous and seemingly oppositional postracial fear has emerged of Cold War 2.0 robots replacing human labor. This tension, taut by the contradictory yet aligned pulls of white supremacy and liberalism, relies on racial capitalist grammars.

While grabbing lunch one summer afternoon with me in Cluj, Caro detailed more about how she began working at Yardi. "Well, you see, I was just looking for a night shift job to pay my living expenses," she began. She had a friend working at Yardi/Invitation Homes who invited her to a "bring your buddy to work day," after which she was immediately offered the job. "The only real requirement was English fluency," she shrugged. Unlike other tech jobs in the city, Caro doesn't see much middle-class aspirational technoculture at the call center. "It's just lots of students just trying to get by." She began by working in the sales and billing department in Center Point, a building adjacent to, but not nearly as extravagant as, the main office in the Office. Her shift begins at 5:30 p.m. and ends at 2:00 a.m. It's not so bad, but it does "mess you up a bit" due to the late-night schedule. Others have to begin even later and work all night, which would be worse. "They could at least have good lighting as it's the night shift," she complained. She has Tuesdays and Wednesdays off, which she prefers over a Saturday and Sunday weekend as having "less of a life" enables her to focus more on writing her dissertation.

Yet sometimes, the toils of her work haunt her homelife. Just the other day, a woman whose son was dying called from California. The woman was tired of Invitation Homes denying her Section 8 housing. Caro tried to sound compassionate to the caller, but the woman saw through all of her boilerplate responses. Frustrated, the caller hung up, muttering, "Have a nice life—my son is dying!" "It's hard to just smile and go on to the next call after things like that," Caro sighed. Other people stigmatize her and her colleagues for their Eastern European accents. Callers have no idea they're dialing someone outside the United States until they hear their voices. Most of them think they're just calling a local property management company wherever they live. "They really have no idea that their home is even owned by Invitation Homes, they just think it's a local company," she explained.

Caro is but one of five thousand Yardi employees working in thirty offices across several countries today, providing platforms and virtual property management systems to abet its clients. "Yardi Romania" is the company's third largest outsourcing firm, where it employs nearly five hundred workers. There, it contracts with Invitation Homes as well as PropertyShark, a real estate database used by speculators across the United States, which it purchased in 2010. The call center opened its doors in 2013 as a laboratory for landlord tech surrogacy. Today, it provides 24/7 support in English and in Spanish. "We all know English from TV and school, and then most of us know Spanish from the telenovelas we were glued to in the '90s," Caro laughed. They are all trained in "Basics of Telephone Etiquette," and "Hold Procedures—Putting the Customer on Hold the P.R.E.T.T.Y. Way." Rolling her eyes, Caro pulled training manuals from her backpack to prove that they are real.

A few weeks after learning about Caro's exploitative call center experiences, I met with one of her coworkers, Ioana, also a student at Cluj's Babeş-Bolyai University. Ioana immediately dove into a laundry list of complaints about her job, many of which revolved around how bizarre it is that US tenants don't have any concept of what it means to fix things themselves. "How could someone think that that broken dryer or air conditioner is an emergency! Here in Romania, we don't really have either of those things, dryers or air conditioners, and when something does break, we just fix it ourselves," she contextualized. But their US clients find emergencies in everything, she expressed with frustration. This illustrates some of the many frictions of outsourced transnational surrogate labor, where despite fantasies of frictionless automation, housing differences between the United States and Romania add gravel into the cogs of capitalism and cause stress for workers and tenants alike. After all, most tenants in Invitation Homes dwellings are forbidden from fixing broken house systems and appliances. And, while outsourced workers find frustration in "lazy" US renters, tenants are frustrated that their landlord is in fact a global capitalist venture.

While Ioana and those staffing Yardi's night shifts struggle to make sense of US property landscapes, what she finds most infuriating is that callers often think that she's a robot on the phone. "I start talking, and then they start yelling commands and pressing buttons, as if I'm AI (artificial intelligence). If Yardi or Invitation Homes does get robots to replace us, well the clients, they'll be making complaints about that too!" Continuing, "When they ask where we're located, we're supposed to divert the question." But sometimes the threads are laid bare, both through accents and through failures of property translation. "It's like, first they think we're robots, and then we're foreigners. And when and if it is revealed that we're Romanians, they just assume we're Gypsies. Or maybe vampires." While most of these call center workers are not racialized subjects within Romania, the conditions of their subjugation embolden the racial scaffolding of Silicon Valley imperialism. This merges Orientalist framings of "the Gypsy" with anticommunist grammars of automation.

It was prior to the Cold War and state socialism, in 1920, that the Czech writer and playwright Karel Čapek introduced the word "robot" with his popular interwar science fiction drama, *R.U.R.* (Rossumovi Univerzální Roboti / Rossum's Universal Robots). Appalled by the chemical weapons and mechanical advancements characterizing World War I carnage, his play draws on themes from Mary Shelley's *Frankenstein*, looking at artificial life that aspires for freedom and the godlike ability to control humans.[8] Not knowing what to call artificial workers, Čapek at first thought of the word *labøři* (laborers). Finding the word too literal, he then turned to *roboti*, or slaves. While both the Cold War and communist projects introduced new systems of automation, computation, and cybernetics, US fictions focused on Soviet totalitarianism and its "terrorist" technologies in order to justify intervention.[9] Yet in the United States, Siliconized automation espoused technoliberal fantasies of racialized robots helping good white workers overcome the unfreedom of daily work.[10]

Though *roboti* infers slavery in Czech, as a verb it means "to toil" in Romanian. This is exactly what Caro, Ioana, and their coworkers do each night as the surrogate laborers for the post–Cold War imperial landlord. By obscuring human decision-making processes and calculi, landlord tech surrogacy proliferates postracial imaginaries of seamless property management for the benefit of corporations that profit through the propertizing of both data and housing. Yet what aggravates Caro most is the racism of some of her Romanian coworkers. "We get calls from people trying to get Section 8 housing in California," she explained. "This one guy, he racially profiles the callers, and if someone is calling because they need certain repairs done but he thinks that they're Black, he decides that they're unworthy and doesn't log the complaint. So, they get no service." Yet another coworker performs an audio version Blackface when he profiles a caller as Black. He chooses a "Black-sounding" name for himself, just to have fun, she recounts lividly. When I asked her why she thinks this happens, she paused, and then posited, "Well, there's the media. They just assume all Section 8 residents are Black and therefore lazy." This, I pointed out, is a similar attitude that countless non-Roma Romanians maintain toward their Roma neighbors, to which she agreed. It also gets at new transits of anti-Blackness, which take place alongside global circuits of anti-Roma racism through which Ioana and her colleagues get interpellated as "Gypsies."

While transatlantic routes of technocapitalism collapse anti-Blackness and anti-Roma racism in novel propertied configurations, there is something quite old about these entanglements as well. Adam Bledsoe and Willie Jamaal Wright argue that anti-Blackness is not an effect of capitalist expansion, but rather its precondition.[11] Similarly, as Cedric Robinson's work teaches us, capitalism was a racial project from its start—one that relied on anti-Roma racism and built on the extractive technologies of landlords.[12] The Cold War protracted such technologies into new domains, ones that Cold War victors continue to capitalize on through outsourcing where English language knowledge (itself racialized given its higher availability to those who are not Roma) remains the only prerequisite for becoming a robotic landlord surrogate. Thus, landlord technological surrogacy and its games of geographic arbitrage seek to assimilate some, but not all, of Romania's workforce into its machinery. Landlord tech platforms are advertised as seamless and frictionless to clients such as Invitation Homes,[13] yet they are rife with frictions and contradictions.

In her studies of the frictions that globalization inheres, Anna Tsing warns: "The successes of corporate consolidation, free-ranging finance, and transnational economic standardization backed by military muscle have made it difficult for people all over the world to think beyond the story of neoliberal globalization. This story is not enough."[14] Indeed, as the story of Yardi Romania shows, we can blame not only US neoliberalism and AI for what is unfolding. Additionally, the ghosts of the propertied past from both sides of the former Iron Curtain continue to haunt the present, creating new zones of entanglement and raciality despite the powers of Silicon Valley imperialism. In this way, the figure of the surrogate landlord is just as much a fiction as is Siliconization itself; both remain incomplete imperial imaginaries caught up in the stickiness of entanglement.

After all, it is not only the West that heralds surrogate labor. In 2018, Cluj's mayor—the same man who authorized the evictions of Coastei Street residents in 2010, landing hundreds of people into the wastelands of urban renewal (as mapped out in chapter 1)—announced the introduction of a public robot named Antonia to herald the city's newfound status as "the Silicon Valley of Europe." Although Antonia proved only to be a computer algorithm, lacking the robotic stock image body displayed in the press, she, as the first "public robot mayoral servant," was nevertheless conjured as part of a widespread technofuturist vision reflected in Romanian infrastructure and imaginaries alike. In the Silicon Valley of Europe, this configuration sits on the ruins of other technofutures past—infrastructurally, epistemologically, and imaginatively.

While interested in the spatiotemporal layering of this configuration, here in this coda, I conclude by thinking about new possibilities of anti-imperial alliance building across both labor and property geographies. Despite the dispossessive contexts of property technology for those laboring in Yardi's call center and for those subjected to surrogate landlordism in Section 8 US housing, there are other propertied futures currently being crafted, and other entanglements transpiring. These inhere emancipatory relationalities of labor, technology, and housing. As I write amid the COVID-19 pandemic, marked by newfound levels of housing precarity but also novel deployments of landlord technologies,[15] housing justice organizing continues. From within the heart of Silicon Valley's empire, the Sogorea Te' Land Trust continues its work of ramatriating stolen Ohlone lands (as explored in chapter 2), proving that Silicon Valley is one of many imperial fictions mapped on Native space.[16] And here nestled within the "Silicon Valley of Eastern Europe," groups like Căși Sociale ACUM! are continuing to organize against racial banishment to the city's wasteland instigated by processes of Siliconization and the anticommunist reprivatization of property. Căși is now part of new networks such as the Bloc, which bring together housing justice collectives, Roma feminist organizations, and labor justice groups across the country dedicated to anti-imperialism and private property's abolition.[17]

By abolition, here I am thinking with the work of Rinaldo Walcott, who suggests that while an abolitionist future is not possible without the abolition of police, nor is one feasible without the abolition of property.[18] After all, it was the formation of private property that helped establish geographies of racial capitalism upon which racialized labor exploitation took place. The police were then required to concretize racial capitalist borders and logics, punishing those who transgressed its authority.[19] An abolitionist geography, as Ruth Wilson Gilmore conceptualizes, then "starts from the homely premise that freedom is a place."[20] This idea of abolition requiring unpropertied futures isn't entirely new, and in fact Marx and Engels once suggested that "the theory of the Communists may be summed up in the single sentence: Abolition of private property."[21] Yet, and as Fred Moten has critiqued, Marx did not theorize the abolition of slavery when writing this, as he could not imagine "the commodity who shrieked."[22] An abolitionist politic then needs to entail more than decommodification of things rendered as property, but also the abolition of worlds in which people can be owned, incarcerated, and exploited. It is one that stands up against racial technocapitalism, freeing land, housing, bodies, and data from dispossessory logics. It would also seek to, as Wendy Liu argues, abolish Silicon Valley, which for her means remaking the world outside of capitalist logics, "decommodifying essential goods while also radically transforming the way we think about work."[23] Unbecoming Silicon Valley is thus a worldmaking project committed to remapping Siliconized lands and labor through abolitionist and anti-imperial visions.

What then would such an abolitionist approach to landlord technology look like? For one, it would heed calls from housing movements to cancel rent and rematriate stolen property. It would also mean dismantling the surrogate forms of labor that dehumanize Caro, Ioana, and their coworkers as robotic Gypsy-like vampires of Eastern Europe. It would undo the very concept of landlordism itself, for the conditions of a world in which tenant lives, data, and homes can be possessed and profited from constitutes the very bedrock of racial capitalism—a practice that in many ways launched in feudal Eastern Europe by capturing Roma people and exploiting their labor and technologies. Abolition in this way would cast spells against private property.

I conclude here by reflecting on what bringing abolitionist and anti-imperial geographies together in postsocialist contexts can do. Just as global capital connections map the Siliconizing moment, other connections scaffold the very possibilities of unbecoming Silicon Valley. It is precisely in the space of collective alliance-making, organizing, and dreaming of a world in which property no longer functions as a technology of dispossession that the very project of Siliconization begins to unravel. While there remains much to be done to grow worker and tenant solidarities against dispossessions wrought by racial technocapitalism and Silicon Valley imperialism alike, anti-imperial visions, practices, and connections are already here. These seek to abolish the figure of the landlord and undo the fantasy of Silicon Valley, crafting space for other techno-imaginaries and materialities to emerge.

Notes

INTRODUCTION

1 Roy, "Dis/Possessive Collectivism."
2 Popovici, "Becoming Western."
3 Vincze, "Ideology of Economic Liberalism," 32–33.
4 Zamfir, "Countering Housing Dispossession."
5 Chelcea and Druță, "Zombie Socialism."
6 Verdery, *My Life as a Spy*.
7 Atanasoski and Vora, "Postsocialist Politics"; Taylor and Brehmer, *Commonist Horizon*.
8 Mahmud, "We Have Never Been Liberal."
9 Stoler and McGranahan, *Imperial Formations*, 8–9.
10 Stoler and McGranahan, *Imperial Formations*, 8.
11 Rofel, *Desiring China*, 22.
12 Fiscutean, "'Life Is Pretty Good Here'"; Petrovici, "Working Status."
13 Mateescu, "In the Romanian Bubble," 243.
14 Lowe, *Intimacies of Four Continents*, 150.
15 Linguistically, *șmecherie* is used by Roma and non-Roma Romanians alike due to the prevalence of Roma culture in poor and working-class space and exists without an exact English equivalency.
16 Lindtner, *Prototype Nation*, 5.
17 Hu, *Prehistory of the Cloud*; Larkin, *Signal and Noise*; Mattern, *Code, Clay, and Dirt*.
18 Tadiar, "City Everywhere," 57.
19 Barad, *Meeting the Universe Halfway*.
20 Willey, *Undoing Monogamy*, 3.
21 Tsing, *Friction*, xi.
22 Robinson, *Black Marxism*.
23 Federici, *Caliban and the Witch*.
24 Parvulescu and Boatcă, *Creolizing the Modern*, 67.
25 Costache, "Subjects of Racialized Modernity."

26   Rexhepi, *White Enclosures*, 10.

27   Todorova, *Unequal under Socialism*.

28   Rexhepi, *White Enclosures*, 19.

29   Mireanu, "Incriminarea Romilor Din Baia Mare."

30   Vincze and Zamfir, "Racialized Housing Unevenness," 452.

31   Wallerstein, *World-Systems Analysis*.

32   Aston and Philpin, *Brenner Debate*; Morozov, "Critique of Techno-Feudal Reason," 102.

33   Brenner, "Origins of Capitalist Development."

34   Marx, *Capital*, 1:915.

35   Marx, *Capital*, 1:348.

36   Harvey, *New Imperialism*.

37   Chakravartty and Silva, "Introduction," 368.

38   Chakravartty and Silva, "Introduction," 368.

39   Bhandar, *Colonial Lives of Property*, 4.

40   Bhandar, *Colonial Lives of Property*, 2.

41   Parvulescu and Boatcă, *Creolizing the Modern*, 7.

42   Parvulescu and Boatcă, *Creolizing the Modern*, 7.

43   Boatcă, "Counter-Mapping as Method," 253.

44   Bakić-Hayden, "Nesting Orientalisms"; Todorova, *Imagining the Balkans*.

45   Boatcă, "Counter-Mapping as Method," 254.

46   Atanasoski and Vora, *Surrogate Humanity*, 4.

47   O'Mara, *The Code*; Weiss, *America Inc.?*

48   Benjamin, *Race after Technology*, 13.

49   Walker, *Pictures of a Gone City*, 7.

50   Irani, *Chasing Innovation*.

51   Schrock, "Silicon Valley."

52   Ahmed, *Promise of Happiness*.

53   Berlant, *Cruel Optimism*.

54   Tran, Twitter post.

55   Byrd, *Transit of Empire*, 28.

56   Madley, *American Genocide*.

57   Harris, *Palo Alto*, 21–22.

58   Harris, *Palo Alto*, 22.

59   Harris, *Palo Alto*, 22.

60   Estes, *Our History Is the Future*, 363.

61   Roy, "Dis/Possessive Collectivism," 3.

62   Pellow and Park, *Silicon Valley of Dreams*.

63   Hoefler, "Silicon Valley, USA."

64   Wiener, *Human Use of Human Beings*.

65   Brown, *Undoing the Demos*; Turner, "Machine Politics."

66   Roy, Schrader, and Crane, "Gray Areas."

67   Atanasoski and Vora, *Surrogate Humanity*, 11–12.

68   Rule, "Reagan Gets a Red Carpet."

69   Wynter, "Unsettling the Coloniality," 296.

70 Wynter, "Unsettling the Coloniality," 296.
71 Wynter, "Unsettling the Coloniality," 317.
72 Fukuyama, *End of History*.
73 Anderson, "End of Theory."
74 Chan, *Networking Peripheries*.
75 Toyama, "Problem with the Plan."
76 Friend, "Sam Altman's Manifest Destiny."
77 Solon, "Elon Musk."
78 McKittrick, *Dear Science and Other Stories*, 109.
79 Many scholars have argued that postsocialism is a global condition. See Fraser, *Justice Interruptus*; Lykke, "Rethinking Socialist and Marxist Legacies"; Verdery, *What Was Socialism?*; Shih, "Is the *Post-* in Postsocialism?"; Suchland, "Is Postsocialism Transnational?"
80 Atanasoski and Vora, "Postsocialist Politics," 139.
81 Koobak, Tlostanova, and Thapar-Björkert, "Uneasy Affinities," 1–2.
82 Lowe, *Intimacies of Four Continents*, 150.
83 Lowe, *Intimacies of Four Continents*, 175.
84 Scott, *Omens of Adversity*, 2.
85 Derrida, *Specters of Marx*; Robinson, *Anthropology of Marxism*.
86 Atanasoski and Vora, "Conversation on Imperial Legacies," 34; Dussel, *Twenty Theses on Politics*.
87 Graeber and Wengrow, *Dawn of Everything*.
88 Müller, "Goodbye, Postsocialism!"; Müller, "In Search of the Global East."
89 Chakrabarty, *Provincializing Europe*; Roy and Bhan, "Lessons from Somewhere."
90 Tlostanova, *Postcolonialism and Postsocialism*.
91 Shih, "Is the *Post-* in Postsocialism?"; Rofel, *Desiring China*.
92 Verdery, "Faith, Hope, and Caritas," 35.
93 Koobak, Tlostanova, and Thapar-Björkert, "Uneasy Affinities," 2.
94 Dunn, *Privatizing Poland*; Humphrey and Verdery, *Property in Question*; Razsa, *Bastards of Utopia*; Verdery, "Faith, Hope, and Caritas."
95 Tlostanova, *Postcolonialism and Postsocialism*, 4.
96 Nolan, "Trevor Noah."
97 Buck-Morss, *Dreamworld and Catastrophe*; Yurchak, *Everything Was Forever*.
98 Groys, *Art Power*, 154–55.
99 Starosta, "Perverse Tongues, Postsocialist Translations," 205.
100 Scott, *Omens of Adversity*, 5.
101 Robinson, "Cities in a World"; Spivak, *Death of a Discipline*.
102 Ouředníček, "Relevance of 'Western' Theoretical Concepts," 547.
103 Sjöberg, "'Cases unto Themselves?'"
104 Gentile, "Three Metals," 1140.
105 Vilenica, "Who Has 'the Right to Common'?," 12.
106 Chari and Verdery, "Thinking between the Posts," 11.
107 Chari and Verdery, "Thinking between the Posts," 29.
108 Even when it comes to less emancipatory revolutions, for instance the industrial and AI revolutions, postsocialist frameworks are helpful in unpacking associated

understandings of the human, freedom, and futurity. See Atanasoski and Vora, *Surrogate Humanity*.

109 Cucu, "Acts of Collusion," 276.

110 Lemon, *Technologies for Intuition*.

111 Yurchak, "Trump, Monstration and the Limits," 1.

112 Brown, *Undoing the Demos*.

113 Robinson, "Fascism and the Intersections"; James, "After Hitler, Our Turn."

114 Morozov, "Critique of Techno-Feudal Reason."

115 Nahoi, "De Vorbă cu Ideologul AUR."

116 Chiruta, "Representation of Roma."

117 Codruţ, "O Stewardesă Ryanair a EXPLODAT."

118 Costache, "'Until We Are Able.'"

119 Hellström, Norocel, and Jørgensen, "Nostalgia and Hope," 2.

120 Imre, "Illiberal White Fantasies."

121 Böröcz, "Horror of Miscegenation."

122 Cinpoeş and Norocel, "Nostalgic Nationalism"; Tudor, "Partidul România Unită."

123 Cârstocea, "First as Tragedy."

124 Arendt, *Origins of Totalitarianism*; Polanyi, *Great Transformation*.

125 Singh, *Race and America's Long War*, 111–13.

126 Atanasoski and Vora, *Surrogate Humanity*, 40.

127 Robinson, "Fascism and the Intersections," 152.

128 Robinson, "Fascism and the Response."

129 James, "After Hitler, Our Turn," 325.

130 Mahmud, "Fascism, a Haunting," 143.

131 Mahmud, "Fascism, a Haunting," 143.

132 Mahmud, "Fascism, a Haunting," 144.

133 Pine, "Field Is upon Us."

134 Mahmud, "Fascism, a Haunting," 160.

135 Collier, *Post-Soviet Social*, 112.

136 Gould, "Ohlone Geographies."

137 Getachew, *Worldmaking after Empire*.

138 Bahng, *Migrant Futures*.

139 Amin, *World We Wish to See*.

140 Wilder, "Hasty Reflections."

141 Barad, "Transmaterialities," 406–7.

142 Subrahmanyam, "Connected Histories," 745.

143 Lowe, "Insufficient Difference."

144 Hart, "Relational Comparison Revisited," 372.

145 Roy and Bhan, "Lessons from Somewhere."

146 Haraway, "Situated Knowledges."

147 TallBear, "Standing with and Speaking as Faith."

148 Chen, *Animacies*, 234.

149 Lowe, *Intimacies of Four Continents*, 6.

150 McKittrick, *Dear Science and Other Stories*, 48.

151 Byrd et al., "Predatory Value," 10.

152 Nader, "Up the Anthropologist."
153 Drăgan, "Roma Futurism Manifesto."

1. DIGITAL NOMADS AND DERACINATED DISPOSSESSION

1 Coastei Street is now Episcop Nicolae Ivan Street.
2 In addition to Nokia's office, the "Octavian Goga" Cluj County Library was slated to be built, along with a series of mansions and new headquarters for the Faculty of Orthodox Theology based out of the city's Babeș-Bolyai University.
3 Zincă, "Grounding Global Capitalism."
4 Căși Sociale ACUM!, "Humanitarian, Ecological and Housing Crisis."
5 Voyles, *Wastelanding*, 15.
6 Pellow and Park, *Silicon Valley of Dreams*.
7 Popovici, "Becoming Western."
8 Miszczyński, *Dialectical Meaning*, 58; Zincă, "Grounding Global Capitalism."
9 Mireanu, "Security at the Nexus," 126–29; Raț, "Și țiganul este aproapele meu?"
10 Tsing, *Friction*, 74.
11 Vincze and Zamfir, "Racialized Housing Unevenness," 443.
12 Romania Journal, "Romanian Parliament."
13 By deracinated dispossession, I build on a concept that I first developed with Alex Werth in which we mapped out how Siliconized analysis in San Francisco gentrification has bled into Oakland, deracinating contexts of East Bay dispossession that predate and exceed Silicon Valley–induced gentrification such as the foreclosure crisis or Cold War–era policing of Black-owned music venues. See: McElroy and Werth, "Deracinated Dispossessions."
14 Lancione, "Politics of Embodied Urban Precarity"; Popovici, "Residences, Restitutions and Resistance."
15 Australian Broadcasting Corporation, "One Day."
16 AT&T Tech Channel, "Interview with Arthur C. Clarke."
17 Saxenian, *New Argonauts*.
18 Taylor, "Life as a Digital Gypsy."
19 Said, *Orientalism*.
20 Bakić-Hayden, "Nesting Orientalisms"; Lowe, "Rereadings in Orientalism"; Saul, *Gypsies and Orientalism*; Todorova, *Imagining the Balkans*; Zăloagă, "Professing Domestic Orientalism."
21 Said, *Orientalism*, 247.
22 Lemon, *Between Two Fires*, 37.
23 Brooks, "Possibilities of Romani Feminism."
24 Gheorghe, "Cu Fustele-n Cap," 140.
25 Bițu and Vincze, "Personal Encounters"; Costache, "Roma Futurism and Roma Healing"; Gheorghe, Mark, and Vincze, "Towards an Anti-racist Feminism"; Kóczé et al., *Romani Women's Movement*; Oprea, "Romani Feminism in Reactionary Times"; Roman, "'Neither Here, Nor There'"; Rucker-Chang, "Challenging Americanism and Europeanism"; Vișan and Frontul Comun pentru Dreptul la Locuire, *Jurnal Din Vulturilor*.
26 Costache, "Subjects of Racialized Modernity."

27 Duncan, "Wild England," 382.
28 Clare, *Poems of the Middle Period*, 52.
29 Sonneman, "Dark Mysterious Wanderers," 130.
30 Saul, *Gypsies and Orientalism*, 117.
31 Lemon, *Between Two Fires*, 47–48.
32 Mróz, *Roma-Gypsy Presence*.
33 Parvulescu and Boatcă, *Creolizing the Modern*, 69.
34 Kay, "Digital Nomad Deception."
35 Hayes, "'We Gained a Lot,'" 1954.
36 Mullaney et al., *Your Computer Is on Fire*.
37 Kay, "Digital Nomad Deception."
38 Mateescu, "In the Romanian Bubble," 247.
39 Henderson, "Best Cities to Live."
40 Bunici, "Best Work-Friendly Coffee Shops."
41 Atlas & Boots, "Best Countries for Remote Workers."
42 Romania Journal, "Romanian Parliament."
43 Turp-Balazs, "Romania Becomes Latest CEE Country."
44 Cocola-Gant, "Tourism Gentrification."
45 Zara, "Best Places for Digital Nomads in Cluj."
46 Lonely Planet, "Top Region to Visit."
47 Cristian, "Uber Reaches 17 Cities."
48 Morin, "Romania Is Not the Land."
49 Light, "Facing the Future," 1058.
50 Kahancová, Meszmann, and Sedláková, "Precarization via Digitalization?"
51 Pavlínek, "Regional Development Implications."
52 Miszczyński, *Dialectical Meaning of Offshored Work*, 27–29.
53 Miszczyński, *Dialectical Meaning of Offshored Work*, 21–23.
54 Colliers International, "Romania Research and Forecast Report," 18; Digital Nomads Romania, "Coworking Spaces in Bucharest."
55 Marica, "Cluj-Napoca and Bucharest."
56 Ban, *Ruling Ideas*.
57 Eurostat, "Foreign Control of Enterprises."
58 Filip, Kmen, and Tisler, "Digital Challengers."
59 Filip, Kmen, and Tisler, "Digital Challengers."
60 TopCoder, "Community Statistics."
61 International Trade Administration, "Romania."
62 Senycia, "Developers in Romania."
63 Senycia, "Developers in Romania."
64 N-iX, "Top IT Outsourcing Destinations."
65 Brainspotting, "Europe Technology Talent Map," 6–7.
66 Brainspotting, "Europe Technology Talent Map," 35; Brainspotting, "IT Talent Map," 4.
67 Softech, "Software Outsourcing."
68 Fiscutean, "In Romania."
69 Colliers International, "Romania Research"; Filip, Kmen, and Tisler, "Digital Challengers."

70 Eurostat, "People at Risk."

71 Brainspotting, "IT&C Talent Map"; Brainspotting, "IT Talent Map"; Brainspotting, "Europe Technology Talent Map," 35; Eurostat, "Annual Detailed Enterprise Statistics."

72 Petrovici and Mare, *Economia Clujului*.

73 Brainspotting, "IT Talent Map," 9.

74 Mateescu, "In the Romanian Bubble," 245.

75 Brainspotting, "IT&C Talent Map," 6.

76 Mateescu, "In the Romanian Bubble," 245.

77 Kahancová, Meszmann, and Sedláková, "Precarization via Digitalization?"

78 Florea and Popovici, "Complicities, Solidarities," 141; Vincze and Zamfir, "Racialized Housing Unevenness," 446-47.

79 Parvulescu and Boatcă, *Creolizing the Modern*, 70.

80 Achim, *Roma in Romanian History*.

81 Parvulescu and Boatcă, *Creolizing the Modern*, 72.

82 Anastasoaie, "Roma/Gypsies," 264.

83 Parvulescu and Boatcă, *Creolizing the Modern*, 67.

84 Parvulescu and Boatcă, *Creolizing the Modern*, 70.

85 Parvulescu and Boatcă, *Creolizing the Modern*, 77.

86 Parvulescu and Boatcă, *Creolizing the Modern*, 79.

87 Grellmann, *Dissertation on the Gipsies*, ix.

88 Parvulescu and Boatcă, *Creolizing the Modern*, 57.

89 Lowe, *Intimacies of Four Continents*.

90 Parvulescu and Boatcă, *Creolizing the Modern*, 62.

91 Achim, *Roma in Romanian History*.

92 Necula, "Cost of Roma Slavery," 37.

93 Achim, *Roma in Romanian History*, 113; Anastasoaie, "Roma/Gypsies," 266.

94 Parvulescu and Boatcă, *Creolizing the Modern*, 75.

95 Achim, *Roma in Romanian History*, 122-24; Anastasoaie, "Roma/Gypsies," 267.

96 Petrovici et al., "Racialized Labour," 7.

97 Anastasoaie, "Roma/Gypsies," 269; Turda, *Modernism and Eugenics*, 72-79.

98 Chelcea, *Țiganii din România: monografie etnografică*, 99.

99 Anastasoaie, "Roma/Gypsies," 267.

100 Hajská, "'We Had to Run Away.'"

101 Ancel, *History of the Holocaust*, 2.

102 Achim, *Roma in Romanian History*, 89.

103 Kelso, "'And Roma Were Victims, Too,'"; Achim, *Roma in Romanian History*, 89; Anastasoaie, "Roma/Gypsies," 270; Ancel, *History of the Holocaust*, 2.

104 Friling, Ioanid, and Ionescu, *Final Report*.

105 Ioanid, *Ransom of the Jews*, 93; Levy, *Ana Pauker*.

106 Lancione, "Politics of Embodied Urban Precarity," 4.

107 Florea and Dumitriu, "Living on the Edge," 193.

108 Vincze, "Ideology of Economic Liberalism"; Zamfirescu and Chelcea, "Evictions as Infrastructural Events," 6.

109 Petrovici et al., "Racialized Labour," 7.

110 Dean, Goschler, and Ther, *Robbery and Restitution.*

111 Shafir, "Varieties of Antisemitism"; Shafir, "Polls and Antisemitism," 415.

112 Chelcea, Popescu, and Cristea, "Who Are the Gentrifiers?"

113 McElroy, "Public Thinker."

114 Zavisca, *Housing the New Russia.*

115 Zamfir, "Countering Illegibility," 38.

116 Eurostat, "People at Risk"; O'Neill, *The Space of Boredom.*

117 Gheorghe, Mark, and Vincze, "Towards an Anti-racist Feminism"; Matache, "Biased Elites, Unfit Policies"; Vişan and Frontul Comun pentru Dreptul la Locuire, *Jurnal Din Vulturilor.*

118 Verdery, "Fuzzy Property."

119 Verdery, *What Was Socialism?*

120 Grama, *Socialist Heritage,* 177.

121 Grama, *Socialist Heritage,* 178.

122 Zamfir, "Countering Illegibility," 41.

123 Kusiak, "Legal Technologies."

124 Stan, "Roof over Our Heads."

125 Atanasoski, *Humanitarian Violence,* 17.

126 Verdery, "Fuzzy Property," 54.

127 Zamfirescu and Chelcea, "Evictions as Infrastructural Events," 7.

128 Rorke, "Eyes Wide Shut."

129 Florea and Dumitriu, "Living on the Edge," 196.

130 Vincze, "Ideology of Economic Liberalism," 32–33.

131 Zamfirescu and Chelcea, "Evictions as Infrastructural Events," 7.

132 Vişan and Frontul Comun pentru Dreptul la Locuire, *Jurnal Din Vulturilor*; Zamfir et al., "Housing Struggles in Romania."

133 McElroy, "Digital Cartographies of Displacement"; Maharawal and McElroy, "Anti-Eviction Mapping Project."

134 Roy, "Dis/Possessive Collectivism."

135 Vincze and Zamfir, "Racialized Housing Unevenness," 452.

136 Colliers International, "Romania Research and Forecast Report," 18.

137 Mattern, "Post-It Note City."

138 Vincze, "Ideology of Economic Liberalism," 41.

139 Vincze, "Ideology of Economic Liberalism," 42.

140 Vincze and Zamfir, "Racialized Housing Unevenness," 453.

141 Petrovici, "Working Status," 41.

142 Romania Insider, "Over 43% of Romania's GDP."

143 Van Baar, "Emergence of a Reasonable Anti-Gypsyism."

144 Petrovici, "Working Status," 51.

145 Liberty Technology Park, "Liberty Technology Park Cluj."

146 Tadiar, "Metropolitan Life and Uncivil Death," 320.

147 Vincze and Zamfir, "Racialized Housing Unevenness," 457.

148 Kóczé, "Race, Migration and Neoliberalism," 461.

149 Tudor and Rexhepi, "Connecting the 'Posts,'" 1.

150 Kóczé, "Race, Migration and Neoliberalism," 461.

151 Căși Sociale ACUM!, "To Whom?"

152 Căși Sociale ACUM!, "To Whom?"

153 Mirabal, "Geographies of Displacement," 30.

154 Mirabal, "Geographies of Displacement," 30.

155 Căși Sociale ACUM!, "To Whom?"

156 Barad, "Troubling Time/s and Ecologies," 76.

2. POSTSOCIALIST SILICON VALLEY

1 Martí, *Futuros Fugaces.*

2 Hippler, *Hunter's Point.*

3 Shaping San Francisco, "John Ross."

4 Carlsson, "Hunters Point Uprising."

5 Gray-Garcia, "Ending Eviction Moratoriums."

6 Daniel, "Top Tech Analyst."

7 Maharawal, "Tech-Colonialism."

8 Dubal, "Drive to Precarity"; Oppillard, "From San Francisco's 'Tech Boom 2.0.'"

9 Atanasoski and Vora, *Surrogate Humanity.*

10 Brahinksy and Tarr, *People's Guide,* 8.

11 Bhandar, *Colonial Lives of Property,* 6.

12 Pellow and Park, *Silicon Valley of Dreams*; Roy, Schrader, Crane, "Gray Areas"; Self, *American Babylon.*

13 Estes, *Our History Is the Future,* 169–200; Harris, *Palo Alto,* 301–59.

14 Atanasoski and Vora, "Postsocialist Politics," 143.

15 Gibson-Graham, *Postcapitalist Politics,* 2.

16 Atanasoski and Vora, "Postsocialist Politics," 144.

17 Fukuyama, *End of History.*

18 Spencer, "Long before Tech Bros."

19 Madley, *American Genocide,* 36.

20 NoiseCat, "'Taking Back What's Ours.'"

21 Pellow and Park, *Silicon Valley of Dreams,* 50.

22 Baumgardner, *Yanks in the Redwoods.*

23 Harris, *Palo Alto,* 15.

24 Shinn, *Mining Camps.*

25 Harris, "Whiteness as Property."

26 Madley, *American Genocide.*

27 Burnett, "State of the State Address."

28 Blomley, "Law, Property, and the Geography of Violence."

29 Hayes and Acton, *Travellers, Gypsies, Roma.*

30 Harvey, *New Imperialism,* 149.

31 Robinson, *Black Marxism,* 10.

32 Parvulescu and Boatcă, *Creolizing the Modern*; Robinson, *Black Marxism.*

33 Lowe, *Intimacies of Four Continents.*

34 Schaeffer, *Unsettled Borders,* 9.

35 Blanchfield, "Top Guns."

36 Harris, *Palo Alto*, 22.

37 Walker, *Conquest of Bread*, 152.

38 Karuka, *Empire's Tracks*.

39 Estes, *Our History Is the Future*, 132.

40 Harris, *Palo Alto*, 45.

41 Keller, "The Curse of California."

42 Anti-Eviction Mapping Project, *Counterpoints*, 369–72.

43 Martí, *Speculation Stole Our City*, 336.

44 Pellow and Park, *Silicon Valley of Dreams*, 50.

45 Carlsson, "General Strike of 1934."

46 Marez, *Farm Worker Futurism*, 11.

47 Marez, *Farm Worker Futurism*, 29.

48 O'Mara, *Cities of Knowledge*, 27.

49 Rosenberg, *Cloning Silicon Valley*, 15; Pellow and Park, *Silicon Valley of Dreams*, 60.

50 Saxon, "William B. Shockley."

51 Turner, "Machine Politics," 159–60.

52 Brown, *Undoing the Demos*.

53 Gilmore, *Abolition Geography*, 55.

54 Pellow and Park, *Silicon Valley of Dreams*.

55 Augur, "Dispersal of Cities," 312; Chung, "Exceptional Visions."

56 Maharawal and McElroy, "Anti-Eviction Mapping Project."

57 Findlay, *Magic Lands*, 132.

58 Hartman, *City for Sale*.

59 Lai, "Racial Triangulation of Space."

60 Anti-Eviction Mapping Project, *(Dis)location/ Black Exodus*.

61 Anti-Eviction Mapping Project, *(Dis)location/ Black Exodus*, 57.

62 Anti-Eviction Mapping Project, *(Dis)location/ Black Exodus*, 124.

63 Shange, *Progressive Dystopia*, 24.

64 Harris, *Palo Alto*, 345–49.

65 Grady-Willis, "Explaining the Demise," 380.

66 Greenbaum, "Questioning Tech Work."

67 Mitchell, *City of Bits*.

68 Driscoll, *Modem World*.

69 Scott, *Omens of Adversity*, 4.

70 Hardt and Negri, *Empire*.

71 Marez, *Farm Worker Futurism*, 171.

72 Petrovszky and Țichindeleanu, *Romanian Revolution Televised*.

73 Cavin, "Borders of Citizenship," 12.

74 Graham and Guy, "Digital Space Meets Urban Place," 372, 369.

75 Walker, "Landscape and City Life," 39.

76 Mirabal, "Geographies of Displacement."

77 Chung, "Exceptional Visions," 4, 45.

78 Roh, Huang, and Niu, *Techno-Orientalism*.

79 Reinhardt, "What Matters Is How Smart You Are."

80 Reinhardt, "What Matters Is How Smart You Are."

81 Chung, "Exceptional Visions," 31.
82 Noble and Roberts, "Technological Elites," 113.
83 Kaplan, *Anarchy of Empire*, 13–14.
84 The Apache Foundation, "Trillions and Trillions Served."
85 Lucia, *White Utopias*.
86 Schaeffer, *Unsettled Borders*, 5.
87 Liu, *Abolish Silicon Valley*, 8.
88 MissionCreek Video, *Mission Playground Is Not for Sale*.
89 Atanasoski and Vora, *Surrogate Humanity*, 56.
90 Solnit, "Diary."
91 Maharawal and McElroy, "Anti-Eviction Mapping Project."
92 Dreyer, "Google Bus Blockades."
93 Tiku, "Oakland Rebels."
94 Brown, "Is the Antitech Movement Obsolete?"
95 Maharawal, "Infrastructural Activism," 6.
96 Stanley, "Affective Commons," 491.
97 Stanley, "Affective Commons," 492.
98 Schiffman, "SF Mime Troupe."
99 Wilder, "Review of the Book," 196.
100 Keller, "The Curse of California."
101 Stanley, "Affective Commons," 489.
102 Bowles, "How San Francisco"; McElroy, "Landlord Tech and Racial Technocapitalism."
103 Lango, "AI Is Primed."
104 Daniel, "Top Tech Analyst."
105 Tiku, "How Elite Schools."
106 Ngila, "Sam Bankman-Fried."
107 Whittaker and Suchman, "The Myth of Artificial Intelligence."
108 Atanasoski and Vora, *Surrogate Humanity*, 4–5.
109 Atanasoski and Vora, *Surrogate Humanity*, 9–10.
110 Ybarra-Frausto, "Rasquachismo."
111 Estes, "Water Is Life."
112 Gibson-Graham, *A Postcapitalist Politics*.
113 Atanasoski and Vora, "Postsocialist Politics," 143.
114 Linebaugh, *Stop, Thief*, 212.
115 Linebaugh, *Stop, Thief*, 212.
116 Gilmore, "Abolition on Stolen Land."
117 Walcott, *On Property*, 95.
118 Heynen, "'Plantation Can Be a Commons,'" 105.
119 Heynen, "'Plantation Can Be a Commons,'" 106.
120 Bledsoe, "Marronage"; Du Bois, *Economic Co-operation*; Federici, *Caliban and the Witch*.
121 Heynen, "'Plantation Can Be a Commons,'" 108.
122 Martí, *On Indigenous Land*.
123 Young, "Transcript."

124 Estes, "Water Is Life."

125 Stanley, "Affective Commons," 492.

3. THE TECHNOFASCIST SPECTERS OF LIBERALISM

1 Soare and Tufiş, "Phoenix Populism."

2 Cinpoeş and Norocel, "Nostalgic Nationalism."

3 Tudor, "Bogdan Diaconu."

4 Costache, "Subjects of Racialized Modernity"; Costache, "'Until We Are Able.'"

5 Marincea and Popovici, "Calling Fascism by Its Name."

6 Ghodsee, *Red Hangover*, xviii.

7 Mahmud, "Fascism, a Haunting," 143.

8 Arendt, *Origins of Totalitarianism*; Polanyi, *Great Transformation*; Ioanid, *Holocaust in Romania*; Singh, *Race and America's Long War*.

9 Zetkin, *Fighting Fascism*, 34, 61.

10 Du Bois, *Autobiography of W. E. B. Du Bois*, 305–6.

11 Césaire, *Discourse on Colonialism*; Goldstein and Trujillo, "Fascism Now?"; Padmore, *How Britain Rules Africa*.

12 Singh, "Cold War," 68.

13 Estes, *Our History Is the Future*; Kelley, *Hammer and Hoe*; Marez, *Farm Worker Futurism*; Gilmore, *Abolition Geography*.

14 Goldstein and Trujillo, "Fascism Now?"

15 Dzenovska and Kurtović, "Future of Postsocialist Critique."

16 Atanasoski and Vora, "Postsocialist Politics," 152.

17 Marincea and Popovici, "Calling Fascism by Its Name."

18 While acknowledging a long history of Western colonization in what is now Romania here, I am not aligning my critique with Dacian nativism, which often reproduces anti-Roma racism and anti-Semitism.

19 Pavlínek and Pickles, *Environmental Transitions*.

20 Moscovici, "Report on the Accession of Romania."

21 Beyerle and Olteanu, "How Romanian People."

22 HotNews.ro, "Rovana Plumb."

23 Rise Project, "Documentele Confidentiale."

24 Forbes Communications Council, "Câţi bani a cheltuit Roşia Montana Gold Corporation?"

25 Hume, "Mine Your Own Business."

26 Ghilezan, "Genetica Protestelor Din Piata Universitii."

27 Popovici, "Livrarea Oraşului La Picioarele Capitalului"; Florida, *Rise of the Creative Class*.

28 Călinescu, "Protestele Au Devenit."

29 Ruse, "Define: Hipster."

30 Quoted in Kenarov, "Romania."

31 Sze, "Boundaries and Border Wars," 792.

32 Voyles, *Wastelanding*, 9.

33 Wynter and McKittrick, "Unparalleled Catastrophe?"

34   Deoancă, "Class Politics."
35   Petrovszky and Țichindeleanu, *Romanian Revolution Televised*, 42.
36   Todorova, *Imagining the Balkans*, 18.
37   Pusca, *Post-Communist Aesthetics*, 32.
38   Yurchak, "Trump, Monstration," 3.
39   Clapp, "Romania Redivivus."
40   Anonymous, "'Light Revolution.'"
41   Poenaru, "What Is at Stake?"
42   Educație Civica, "Despre Proiect."
43   Romanian-American Foundation, "Technology and Innovation."
44   Irani, *Chasing Innovation*, 24.
45   Lindtner, *Prototype Nation*, 5.
46   Rofel, *Desiring China*, 118.
47   Tsing, *Friction*, 53.
48   Lindtner, *Prototype Nation*, 17.
49   Chelcea, "'Housing Question.'"
50   Popovici, "Residences, Restitutions and Resistance."
51   Florea, "Ups and Downs."
52   Stoler, "Imperial Debris," 198.
53   Koga, *Inheritance of Loss*, 3.
54   Florea, "Ups and Downs," 74.
55   Marincea and Popovici, "Calling Fascism by Its Name."
56   Sammon, "IKEA's Race."
57   Ioraș and Abrudan, "Romanian Forestry Sector."
58   Sammon, "IKEA's Race."
59   It is speculated that the insatiable industry will climb from $564 billion in 2020 to $850 billion by 2025. See Sammon, "IKEA's Race."
60   Bojin, Radu, and Strandberg, "IKEA's Forest Recall."
61   Verdery, "Fuzzy Property," 55.
62   Romania Insider, "Romania's Environment Minister."
63   Sammon, "IKEA's Race."
64   Sammon, "IKEA's Race."
65   Stewart, "Deprivation."
66   Quoted in Sikor, Stahl, and Dorondel, "Negotiating Post-Socialist Property," 184.
67   Asbrink, "Fascist Sympathizer."
68   Asbrink, "Fascist Sympathizer."
69   IKEA, "About Us."
70   Sammon, "IKEA's Race."
71   Bojin, Radu, and Strandberg, "IKEA's Forest Recall"; Sammon, "IKEA's Race."
72   Chee, "EU Regulators."
73   Butler, "IKEA Enters Gig Economy."
74   Bojin, Radu, and Strandberg, "IKEA's Forest Recall."
75   Bojin, Radu, and Strandberg, "IKEA's Forest Recall."
76   Rosca, "IKEA Funds."
77   Rosca, "IKEA Funds."

78 Rosca, "IKEA Funds."

79 The Local, "IKEA Founder."

80 Chelcea, "Postindustrial Ecologies"; Moga and David, "Cea Mai Mare Tranzacte."

81 Cojocar, "Cum s-a Reinventat"; Moga and David, "Cea Mai Mare Tranzacte."

82 Robinson, "Fascism and the Response," 155.

83 Goldstein and Trujillo, "Fascism Now?"

84 Mahmud, "We Have Never Been Liberal."

85 Reich, "Putin Won."

86 Mitchell, "Iconography and Locational Conflict," 156.

87 Mitchell, "Iconography and Locational Conflict," 155.

88 Savio, "Sit-in Address."

89 Melamed, "Spirit of Neoliberalism," 2.

90 Táíwò, *Elite Capture*.

91 Brown, *Undoing the Demos*.

92 Forman, "Fascism Is Possible."

93 Kaplan, *Anarchy of Empire*.

94 Lowe, *Intimacies of Four Continents*, 6.

95 Mahmud, "We Have Never Been Liberal."

4. THE MOST DANGEROUS TOWN ON THE INTERNET

1 Takahashi, "It's Alive."

2 Amoore, *Cloud Ethics*.

3 Yurchak, "Trump, Monstration," 10.

4 Atanasoski, *Humanitarian Violence*, 23.

5 Bucur, *Eugenics and Modernization*, 83.

6 Turda, "Nation as Object," 438.

7 Bucur, *Eugenie Și Modernizare*, 333; Thorne, "Assimilation, Invisibility, and the Eugenic Turn," 185–87.

8 Black, *IBM and the Holocaust*, 33–44.

9 Black, *IBM and the Holocaust*.

10 Black, *IBM and the Holocaust*, 107.

11 Black, *IBM and the Holocaust*, 270.

12 Black, *IBM and the Holocaust*, 387.

13 Today, "Țigan" is often racistly used by non-Roma people in reference to Roma people, equivalent to "Gypsy." That said, it also gets used within Roma communities nonderogatorily. Its utilization by outsiders was less inherently racist at the time, though the census itself certainly was. Regarding the census, see Black, *IBM and the Holocaust*, 384.

14 Kelso, "'Roma Were Victims, Too.'"

15 Arendt, *Eichmann in Jerusalem*.

16 Matzal, "'Am Trăit Patru Revoluții.'"

17 McKittrick and Weheliye, "808s & Heartbreak," 32.

18 Medina, "Big Blue in the Bottomless Pit," 26.

19 Kwet, "Digital Colonialism."

20 Medina, "Big Blue in the Bottomless Pit," 26.

21 Haraway, "Manifesto for Cyborgs"; Petrov, "Socialist Cyborgs."

22 Buck-Morss, *Dreamworld and Catastrophe*; Collier, *Post-Soviet Social.*

23 Mureşan, "Romania's Integration in COMECON."

24 Popoviciu, "Contribuții ale Institutului de Calcul."

25 Industrial robots too threatened Ceaușescu, who worried that they would replace the working-class labor force. While the word "robot" was banished from the press, robotics research continued, supported by local authorities who decided to turn their heads. See Kovacs, "Implementing Robots."

26 Baltac and Gligor, "Some Key Aspects."

27 Greenhouse, "In Romania, Ceaușescu Is Gone."

28 Penn, "Romania in the Global Microelectronics World," 11.

29 Penn, "Romania in the Global Microelectronics World," 12.

30 Penn, "Romania in the Global Microelectronics World," 14.

31 Miciu, "Fabuloşii Ani '90."

32 Berlant, *Cruel Optimism.*

33 Docaş, "Ice Felix-o?"

34 Meseşan, "Romanian Roulette."

35 Verdery, "Faith, Hope, and Caritas."

36 Bhattacharjee, "How a Remote Town."

37 Dunne, *Most Dangerous Town.*

38 Goerzen and Coleman, *Wearing Many Hats.*

39 Dunne, *Most Dangerous Town.*

40 Bertrand, "Mysterious Hacker."

41 ThreatConnect, "Does a Bear Leak?"

42 Lewis, *Scammer's Yard*, 16.

43 Galvan, "Occult Networks," 444–49.

44 Atanasoski, *Humanitarian Violence*, 139.

45 Kim, *Ends of Empire.*

46 Lemon, *Technologies for Intuition*, 46.

47 Atanasoski, *Humanitarian Violence*, 6, 138.

48 Atanasoski, *Humanitarian Violence*, 22.

49 Estes, *Our History Is the Future*, 217.

50 Marx, *Capital,* 1:342.

51 Marx, *Capital,* 1:348.

52 Neocleous, "Political Economy of the Dead," 670.

53 Moretti, *Signs Taken for Wonders*, 94.

54 Haraway, *Modest_Witness@Second_Millennium*, 215.

55 Haraway, *Modest_Witness@Second_Millennium*, 214.

56 Coleman, *Coding Freedom*; Goerzen and Coleman, *Wearing Many Hats.*

57 Petrovici, "Working Status."

58 Moodie, *We Were Adivasis*, 15.

59 For more on this affective work, see Hochschild, *Managed Heart.*

60 Padios, "Exceptionalism as a Way of Life," 152–53.

5. CORRUPTION, ȘMECHERIE, AND CLONES

1 Popovici and Nicolae, "Istoria (Nu) Se Repetă."
2 Linguistically, șmecherie is used by Roma and non-Roma Romanians alike due to the prevalence of Roma culture in poor and working-class space, and it exists without an exact English equivalency.
3 Hartman, "Anarchy of Colored Girls," 470.
4 Fukuyama, End of History; Freeman, Time Binds.
5 Lowe, Intimacies of Four Continents, 150, 175.
6 Atanasoski and Vora, "Postsocialist Politics," 141.
7 Popa, "Trans* and Legacies of Socialism," 30.
8 Arondekar, "In the Absence of Reliable Ghosts."
9 Cohen and Richmond, "New Histories," 161.
10 Petrov, "Socialist Cyborgs."
11 Gutfrański, "Speed of Guccifer"; Haigh, "Downloading Communism"; Jakić, "Galaxy and the New Wave"; Petrov, "Socialist Cyborgs"; Stachniak, "Red Clones"; Švelch, Gaming the Iron Curtain; Wasiak, "Playing and Copying."
12 Yurchak, Everything Was Forever.
13 Yurchak, Everything Was Forever, 128.
14 Petrovszky and Țichindeleanu, Romanian Revolution Televised.
15 Fiscutean, "This Video Game."
16 Woodcock, "Short History," 66.
17 Verdery, My Life as a Spy.
18 Popovici, "Solidarity in Illegality."
19 Haraway, "Manifesto for Cyborgs," 4.
20 Haraway, "Manifesto for Cyborgs," 4.
21 See Amoore's Cloud Ethics for an exploration of algorithmic accounts of being.
22 The Dacia automobile manufacturer was famously founded in Romania in 1966, and then purchased by the French Renault group in 1999.
23 Fiscutean, "Underground Story of Cobra."
24 Fiscutean, "Underground Story of Cobra."
25 Petrovszky and Țichindeleanu, Romanian Revolution Televised.
26 Pleter, "Fenomenul Hacker (Hacker Phenomenon)."
27 Fiscutean, "Mix of Poverty and Piracy"; Reuters, "Piracy Worked for Us."
28 Reuters, "Piracy Worked for Us."
29 Barberá, "Global Lockdown a Boon."
30 Lewis, Scammer's Yard, 74.
31 Rai, Jugaad Time, 6.
32 Popovici, "Solidarity in Illegality," 56.
33 Popa and Sandal, "Decolonial Queer Politics," 5.
34 Since the time of this writing, Accept has grown increasingly aligned with anticapitalist future-making.
35 Kelley, Race Rebels, 3–4.
36 Mahmood, Politics of Piety, 9.
37 Simone, Surrounds, 117.

38 Simone, *Surrounds*, 116.

39 Simone, *Surrounds*, 118.

40 Muñoz, *Cruising Utopia*, 278.

6. SPELLS FOR OUTER SPACE

1 Vătămanu and Tudor, *Gagarin's Tree*.

2 Messeri, *Placing Outer Space*, 12.

3 Grant, *In the Soviet House of Culture*; Hirsch, *Empire of Nations*; Martin, *Affirmative Action Empire*; Tlostanova, "Between the Russian/Soviet Dependencies."

4 Lenin, *Imperialism*.

5 Lenin, *Imperialism*, 2.

6 O'Keeffe, "Roma Homeland."

7 Quoted in Huang, "US General Describes 'China Threat.'"

8 Marx, "Elon Musk Should Not Be in Charge."

9 Marx, "Elon Musk Should Not Be in Charge."

10 Marx, "Elon Musk Should Not Be in Charge."

11 JustSpace Alliance, "Resources"; Oman-Reagan, "Queering Outer Space"; Squire, Mould, and Adey, "Final Frontier?"; Wattles, "Colonizing Mars."

12 DNLee, "When Discussing Humanity's Next Move."

13 Ferreira, "SpaceX's Satellite Megaconstellations."

14 Quoted in Valentine, "Exit Strategy," 1046.

15 Fukuyama, *End of History*.

16 Drăgan, "Roma Futurism Manifesto."

17 Bodea, *Vida*.

18 The center had opened in 1972, built by money earned by Komsomol members on days of volunteer-based unpaid labor following the October Revolution, known as *subbotniks* and *voskresniks*.

19 Stevens, "Letter from Yuri Gagarin."

20 Marez, *Farm Worker Futurism*, 9.

21 Marez, *Farm Worker Futurism*, 27.

22 Soper, *Humanism and Anti-humanism*.

23 Kluger, "Here's the Russian Ritual."

24 Quoted in Vladimirskaya, "Так рождаются легенды."

25 Science Direct, "Yuri Gagarin Was a Hero."

26 Zak, "Vostok Lands Successfully."

27 Noi, "'Дуб Гагарина' в Калараше Вырос Из Жёлудя."

28 Murawski, "Actually-Existing Success," 908.

29 Murawski, "Actually-Existing Success," 910.

30 Achim, *Roma in Romanian History*, 189.

31 Helsinki Watch, *Destroying Ethnic Identity*, 18.

32 Helsinki Watch, *Destroying Ethnic Identity*, 18.

33 Helsinki Watch, *Destroying Ethnic Identity*, 29.

34 Helsinki Watch, *Destroying Ethnic Identity*, 29–30.

35 Achim, *Roma in Romanian History*, 190.

36 Helsinki Watch, *Destroying Ethnic Identity*, 18.

37 Achim, *Roma in Romanian History*, 190.

38 Blaga, *Romania's Population*, 91–92.

39 Helsinki Watch, *Destroying Ethnic Identity*, 17.

40 Helsinki Watch, *Destroying Ethnic Identity*, 20.

41 Achim, *Roma in Romanian History*, 190.

42 Helsinki Watch, *Destroying Ethnic Identity*, 23.

43 Vincze, "Ideology of Economic Liberalism," 32–33.

44 Achim, *Roma in Romanian History*, 193.

45 Achim, *Roma in Romanian History*, 195.

46 Melamed, *Represent and Destroy*.

47 Mark and Slobodian, "Eastern Europe," 6.

48 Popescu, "On the Margins of the Black Atlantic," 91–109.

49 Mark and Slobodian, "Eastern Europe," 15.

50 Poenaru, "Rîs, Lacrimi și Priviri Coloniale."

51 Țichindeleanu, "Socialist Romania."

52 Ward, "European Provenance of Decolonization," 237–40.

53 Todorova, *Imagining the Balkans*; Wolff, *Inventing Eastern Europe*.

54 Pedersen, *Guardians*, 343–45.

55 Mark and Apor, "Socialism Goes Global," 853.

56 Gildea, Mark, and Pas, "European Radicals"; Mark and Slobodian, "Eastern Europe," 2.

57 Mark and Slobodian, "Eastern Europe," 4.

58 Mark and Slobodian, "Eastern Europe," 4.

59 Makalani, *In the Cause of Freedom*, 38; Nehru, *Unity of India*, 273–74.

60 Engerman, "Learning from the East," 232.

61 Chari and Verdery, "Thinking between the Posts," 14.

62 Byrne, "Beyond Continents," 923–27; Niebuhr, "Nonalignment as Yugoslavia's Answer," 146–79.

63 Țichindeleanu, "Socialist Romania."

64 Mark and Slobodian, "Eastern Europe," 3.

65 Karkov and Valiavicharska, "Rethinking East-European Socialism," 19–20.

66 Karkov and Valiavicharska, "Rethinking East-European Socialism," 21.

67 Lowe, *Intimacies of Four Continents*, 150, 175.

68 Buck-Morss, *Dreamworld and Catastrophe*.

69 Ernu, *Nascut in URSS*.

70 Buck-Morss , *Dreamworld and Catastrophe*, 45.

71 Kilgore, *Astrofuturism*, 2.

72 Quoted in Chilvers, "Tatlin, Vladimir."

73 Adams, "'Red Star.'"

74 Buck-Morss, *Dreamworld and Catastrophe*, 45.

75 Neagu-Negulescu, *Arimania sau Țara Buneiînțelegeri*.

76 Rogoz, *Omul si Naluca*.

77 Cârje, *Irene Sau Planeta Cea Mai Apropiată*; Săsărman, *Cuadratura Cercului*.

78 Țichindeleanu, "Socialist Romania."

79 Lemon, *Technologies for Intuition*, x.

80 Lemon, *Technologies for Intuition*, xi.

81 Derrida, *Specters of Marx*.

82 Derrida, *On Cosmopolitanism and Forgiveness*, 45.

83 Roy, "City in the Age of Trumpism," 770.

84 Kelso, "'And Roma Were Victims, Too.'"

85 Helsinki Watch, *Destroying Ethnic Identity*, 25.

86 Kelso, "'And Roma Were Victims, Too,'" 64.

87 Kelso, "'And Roma Were Victims, Too,'" 64.

88 Burton, "Navigating Global Socialism"; Pugach, "Eleven Nigerian Students."

89 Slobodian, "Bandung in Divided Germany," 654.

90 Kret, "'We Unite with Knowledge,'" 248.

91 Levy, *Ana Pauker*.

92 Verdery, *National Ideology under Socialism*.

93 Karkov and Valiavicharska, "Rethinking East-European Socialism," 18.

94 Karkov and Valiavicharska, "Rethinking East-European Socialism," 18.

95 Buck-Morss, *Dreamworld and Catastrophe*.

96 Shih, "Is the *Post-* in Postsocialism?," 31.

97 Fanon, *Wretched of the Earth*, 5.

98 Fanon, *Wretched of the Earth*, 312.

99 Fanon, *Wretched of the Earth*, xx.

100 Scott, "Re-enchantment of Humanism," 120.

101 Wynter and McKittrick, "Unparalleled Catastrophe?"

102 Weheliye, *Habeas Viscus*, 8.

103 Atletić, "Stamp Printed in Romania."

104 Proud Roma, "Strigă Tare!"

105 Kóczé et al., *Romani Women's Movement*.

106 Johnson, "Sun Ra."

107 Anderson and Jones, *Afrofuturism 2.0*, vii.

108 Drăgan, "Roma Futurism Manifesto."

109 Drăgan, "Roma Futurism Manifesto."

110 Wynter, "Columbus," 151.

111 Drăgan, "Roma Futurism Manifesto."

112 Australian Broadcasting Corporation, "One Day."

113 Clarke, *Profiles of the Future*, 108.

114 Drăgan, "Roma Futurism Manifesto."

115 Federici, *Caliban and the Witch*.

116 Federici, *Caliban and the Witch*, 141.

117 Foucault, *History of Madness*.

118 Federici, *Caliban and the Witch*, 282.

119 Kivelson, *Desperate Magic*.

120 Campagna, *Technic and Magic*.

121 Timofeeva, "What Lenin Teaches Us about Witchcraft."

122 Roy, "Dis/Possessive Collectivism."

123 Timofeeva, "What Lenin Teaches Us about Witchcraft."

124 Lenin, "Speech at the Plenary Meeting."

125 Drăgan, "Roma Futurism Manifesto."
126 Costache, "Roma Futurism and Roma Healing."
127 Costache, "Roma Futurism and Roma Healing."
128 Coțofană, "White Man Law versus Black Magic Women," 70.
129 Novakov-Ritchey, "Palpating History," 6–7.
130 Schaeffer, *Unsettled Borders*, 2.
131 Schaeffer, *Unsettled Borders*, 8.
132 Achim, *Roma in Romanian History*; Hajnáczky, "Forced Assimilation Gypsy Policy."
133 Timofeeva, "What Lenin Teaches Us about Witchcraft."
134 Stoler, "Imperial Debris," 195.
135 Richardson and Len, "Anti-NATO Days."
136 Richardson and Len, "Anti-NATO Days."
137 Marx, "Elon Musk Should Not Be In Charge."
138 Popovici, "Residences, Restitutions and Resistance"; Vișan and Frontul Comun pentru Dreptul la Locuire, *Jurnal din Vulturilor*.
139 McElroy and Popovici, "Diary from Vulturilor."
140 Gheorghe, Mark, and Vincze, "Towards an Anti-racist Feminism," III.

CODA

1   McElroy, "Dis/Possessory Data Politics."
2   Fields, "Automated Landlord."
3   Ferreri and Sanyal, "Digital Informalisation"; McElroy and Vergerio, "Automating Gentrification"; Shaw, "Platform Real Estate."
4   Fields, "Automated Landlord."
5   Mullaney, "Your Computer Is on Fire," 6.
6   Atanasoski and Vora, *Surrogate Humanity*; Irani, "Difference and Dependence"; Padios, "Exceptionalism as a Way of Life"; Roberts, "Your AI Is Human."
7   Atanasoski and Vora, *Surrogate Humanity*, 6.
8   Jordan, "Czech Play."
9   Singh, "Cold War," 68.
10 Atanasoski and Vora, *Surrogate Humanity*, 41.
11 Bledsoe and Wright, "Anti-Blackness of Global Capital."
12 Robinson, *Black Marxism*.
13 McElroy and Vergerio, "Automating Gentrification."
14 Tsing, *Friction*, 269.
15 McElroy, So, and Weber, "Keeping an Eye on Landlord Tech."
16 Gould, "Ohlone Geographies."
17 Zamfir et al., "Housing Struggles in Romania."
18 Walcott, *On Property*, 13.
19 Foucault, *Security, Territory, Population*.
20 Gilmore, *Abolition Geography*, 474.
21 Marx and Engels, *Communist Manifesto*, 484.
22 Moten, *In the Break*, 254.
23 Liu, *Abolish Silicon Valley*, 263.

Bibliography

Achim, Viorel. *The Roma in Romanian History*. Budapest: Central European University Press, 2004.

Adams, Mark B. "'Red Star' Another Look at Aleksandr Bogdanov." *Slavic Review* 48, no. 1 (1989): 1–15.

Ahmed, Sara. *The Promise of Happiness*. Durham, NC: Duke University Press, 2010.

Alianța pentru Unirea Românilor—AUR. "Programul." Accessed April 23, 2021. https://www.partidulaur.ro/program_aur.

Amin, Samir. *The World We Wish to See: Revolutionary Objectives in the Twenty-First Century*. Translated by James Membrez. New York: Monthly Review Press, 2008.

Amoore, Louise. *Cloud Ethics: Algorithms and the Attributes of Ourselves and Others*. Durham, NC: Duke University Press, 2020.

Amrute, Sareeta, and Luis Felipe R. Murillo. "Introduction: Computing in/from the South." *Catalyst: Feminism, Theory, Technoscience* 6, no. 2 (2020): 1–23.

Anastasoaie, Marian-Viorel. "Roma/Gypsies in the History of Romania: An Old Challenge for Romanian Historiography." *Romanian Journal of Society and Politics* 3, no. 1 (2003): 262–74.

Ancel, Jean. *The History of the Holocaust in Romania*. Lincoln: University of Nebraska Press, 2011.

Anderson, Chris. "The End of Theory: The Data Deluge Makes the Scientific Method Obsolete." *Wired*. Accessed February 21, 2023. https://www.wired.com/2008/06/pb-theory/.

Anderson, Reynaldo, and Charles Jones. *Afrofuturism 2.0: The Rise of Astro-Blackness*. Lanham, MD: Lexington Books, 2015.

Andrei, Cristian. "Interviu. George Simion Despre Cine e în Spatele AUR, Legionari, Rusia și Politicieni." *Politică*, December 9, 2020. https://romania.europalibera.org/a/interviu-george-simion-despre-cine-e-%C3%AEn-spatele-aur-legionari-rusia-%C8%99i-politicieni/30990612.html.

Anonymous. "The 'Light Revolution' in Romania: When Toppling the Government Isn't Enough." *CrimethInc.*, March 9, 2017. https://crimethinc.com/2017/03/09/the-light-revolution-in-romania-when-toppling-the-government-isnt-enough.

Anti-Eviction Mapping Project. *Counterpoints: A San Francisco Bay Area Atlas of Displacement and Resistance*. Oakland, CA: PM Press, 2021.

Anti-Eviction Mapping Project. *(Dis)location/Black Exodus*. San Francisco: Anti-Eviction Mapping Project, 2019.

The Apache Foundation. "Trillions and Trillions Served." YouTube, June 10, 2020. https://www.youtube.com/watch?v=3kdn2yk6nss&ab.

Arendt, Hannah. *Eichmann in Jerusalem: A Report on the Banality of Evil*. New York: Viking, 1963.

Arendt, Hannah. *The Origins of Totalitarianism*. New York: Harcourt, 1971.

Arondekar, Anjali. "In the Absence of Reliable Ghosts: Sexuality, Historiography, South Asia." *differences* 25, no. 3 (2014): 98–122.

Asbrink, Elizabeth. "The Fascist Sympathizer Who Founded IKEA." *New York Times*, January 29, 2018. https://www.nytimes.com/2018/01/29/opinion/ingvar-kamprad-ikea-fascist.html.

Aston, T. H., and C. H. E. Philpin, eds. *The Brenner Debate: Agrarian Class Structure and Economic Development in Pre-industrial Europe*. Cambridge: Cambridge University Press, 1987.

Atanasoski, Neda. *Humanitarian Violence: The U.S. Deployment of Diversity*. Minneapolis: University of Minnesota Press, 2013.

Atanasoski, Neda, and Kalindi Vora. "A Conversation on Imperial Legacies and Post-socialist Contexts: Notes from a US-Based Feminist Collaboration." In *Postcolonial and Postsocialist Dialogues*, edited by Redi Koobak, Madina Tlostanova, and Suruchi Thapar-Björkert, 29–39. New York: Routledge, 2021.

Atanasoski, Neda, and Kalindi Vora. "Postsocialist Politics and the Ends of Revolution." *Social Identities* 24, no. 2 (2018): 139–54.

Atanasoski, Neda, and Kalindi Vora. *Surrogate Humanity: Race, Robots, and the Politics of Technological Futures*. Durham, NC: Duke University Press, 2019.

Atlas & Boots. "Ranked: 100 Best Countries for Remote Workers." *Atlas & Books* (blog). Accessed May 12, 2022. https://www.atlasandboots.com/remote-work/best-countries-for-remote-workers.

Atletić, Zvonimir. "Stamp Printed in Romania Shows International Year against Racism, circa 1971." Accessed July 26, 2023. https://www.alamy.com/stock-photo-stamp-printed-in-romania-shows-international-year-against-racism-circa-87249912.html.

AT&T Tech Channel. "Interview with Author/Futurist Arthur C. Clarke, from an AT&T-MIT Conference, 1976." YouTube, February 3, 2015. https://www.youtube.com/watch?v=DivQ_cBof4w.

Augur, Tracey. "The Dispersal of Cities: A Feasible Program." *Bulletin of the Atomic Scientists* 4, no. 10 (1948): 312–15.

Australian Broadcasting Corporation. "One Day, a Computer Will Fit on a Desk (1974) | RetroFocus." YouTube, December 10, 2013. https://www.youtube.com/watch?v=sTdWQAKzESA.

Ayres, Robert L. "Breaking the Bank." *Foreign Policy* 43, no. 1 (1981): 104–20.

Bahng, Aimee. *Migrant Futures: Decolonizing Speculation in Financial Times*. Durham, NC: Duke University Press, 2017.

Baker, Catherine. *Race and the Yugoslav Region: Postsocialist, Post-conflict, Postcolonial?* Manchester, UK: Manchester University Press, 2018.

Bakić-Hayden, Milica. "Nesting Orientalisms: The Case of Former Yugoslavia." *Slavic Review* 54, no. 4 (1995): 917–31.

Baltac, Vasile, and Horia Gligor. "Some Key Aspects in the History of Computing in Romania." In *IT STAR WS History of Computing Szeged*, slideshow presentation, September 19, 2014. https://slideplayer.com/slide/3896690/.

Ban, Cornel. *Ruling Ideas: How Global Neoliberalism Goes Local*. Oxford: Oxford University Press, 2016.

Barad, Karen. *Meeting the Universe Halfway: Quantum Physics and the Entanglement of Matter and Meaning*. Durham, NC: Duke University Press, 2007.

Barad, Karen. "Transmaterialities: Trans*/Matter/Realities and Queer Political Imaginings." *GLQ: A Journal of Lesbian and Gay Studies* 21, no. 2–3 (June 1, 2015): 387–422.

Barad, Karen. "Troubling Time/s and Ecologies of Nothingness: Re-Turning, Re-Membering, and Facing the Incalculable." *New Formations: A Journal of Culture/Theory/Politics* 92 (2018): 56–86.

Barberá, Marcel Gascón. "Global Lockdown a Boon for Romania's Adult Live Cam Providers." *Balkan Insight* (blog), April 8, 2020. https://balkaninsight.com/2020/04/08/global-lockdown-a-boon-for-romanias-adult-live-cam-providers.

Baumgardner, Frank H. *Yanks in the Redwoods*. New York: Algora Publishing, 2010.

Beltrán, Héctor. "The First Latina Hackathon: Recoding Infrastructures from México." *Catalyst: Feminism, Theory, Technoscience* 6, no. 2 (2020): 1–29.

Benjamin, Ruha. *Race after Technology: Abolitionist Tools for the New Jim Code*. Cambridge: John Wiley and Sons, 2019.

Berg, Lawrence. "Banal Naming, Neoliberalism, and Landscapes of Dispossession." *ACME: An International Journal for Critical Geographies* 10, no. 1 (2011): 13–22.

Berlant, Lauren. *Cruel Optimism*. Durham, NC: Duke University Press, 2011.

Berlin, Isaiah. *The Crooked Timber of Humanity: Chapters in the History of Ideas*. London: John Murray, 1990.

Bernt, Matthias. "Very Particular, or Rather Universal? Gentrification through the Lenses of Ghertner and Lopez-Morales." *City* 20, no. 4 (2016): 637–44.

Bertrand, Natasha. "Mysterious Hacker Who Tormented the Bushes Speaks for the First Time." *Business Insider*, November 11, 2014. https://www.businessinsider.com/mysterious-hacker-guccifer-gives-first-interview-2014-11.

Beyerle, Shaazka, and Tina Olteanu. "How Romanian People Took On Power and Corruption." *Foreign Policy*, November 17, 2016. https://foreignpolicy.com/2016/11/17/how-romanian-people-power-took-on-mining-and-corruption-rosia-montana/.

Bhandar, Brenna. *Colonial Lives of Property: Law, Land, and Racial Regimes of Ownership*. Durham, NC: Duke University Press, 2018.

Bhattacharjee, Yudhijit. "How a Remote Town in Romania Has Become Cybercrime Central." *Wired*, January 1, 2011. https://www.wired.com/2011/01/ff-hackerville-romania.

Bițu, Nicoleta, and Enikő Vincze. "Personal Encounters and Parallel Paths toward Romani Feminism." *Signs: Journal of Women in Culture and Society* 38, no. 1 (2012): 44–46.

Black, Edwin. "Eugenics and the Nazis: The California Connection." *San Francisco Chronicle*, November 9, 2003. https://www.sfgate.com/opinion/article/Eugenics-and-the-Nazis-the-California-2549771.php.

Black, Edwin. *IBM and the Holocaust: The Strategic Alliance between Nazi Germany and America's Most Powerful Corporation*. New York: Random House, 2001.

Blaga, Ion. *Romania's Population: A Demographic Economic and Socio-Political Essay*. Bucharest: Meridiane Publishing House, 1972.

Blanchfield, Patrick. "Top Guns: How the NRA Became One of the Most Powerful Institutions in America." *Bookforum* (blog), April/May 2020. https://www.bookforum.com/print/2701/how-the-nra-became-one-of-the-most-powerful-institutions-in-america-23931.

Bledsoe, Adam. "Marronage as a Past and Present Geography in the Americas." *Southeastern Geographer* 57, no. 1 (2017): 30–50.

Bledsoe, Adam, and Willie Jamaal Wright. "The Anti-Blackness of Global Capital." *Environment and Planning D: Society and Space* 37, no. 1 (February 2019): 8–26.

Blomley, Nicholas. "Law, Property, and the Geography of Violence: The Frontier, the Survey, and the Grid." *Annals of the Association of American Geographers* 93, no. 1 (2003): 121–41.

Boatcă, Manuela. "Counter-Mapping as Method: Locating and Relating the (Semi-)Peripheral Self." *Historical Social Research / Historische Sozialforschung* 46, no. 2 (2021): 244–63.

Bodea, Gheorghe I. *Vida: Artist Militant*. Cluj-Napoca: Editura Dacia, 1980.

Bojin, Daniel, Paul Radu, and Hans Strandberg. "IKEA's Forest Recall." *Organized Crime and Corruption Reporting*, March 1, 2016. https://www.occrp.org/en/investigations/4990-IKEA-s-forest-recall.

Böröcz, József. "Horror of Miscegenation, Absurd Nationalist Historicism and Clear Neonazi References: Key Features of Orbán's July 2022 Speech." *Global Social Change Blog*, August 7, 2022. http://globalsocialchange.blogspot.com/2022/08/a-little-public-service-comment-for.html.

Bowles, Nellie. "How San Francisco Became a Failed City." *Atlantic*, June 8, 2022. https://www.theatlantic.com/ideas/archive/2022/06/how-san-francisco-became-failed-city/661199.

Brahinsky, Rachel, and Alexander Tarr. *A People's Guide to the San Francisco Bay Area*. Berkeley: University of California Press, 2020.

Brainspotting. "Europe Technology Talent Map." Accessed February 2, 2022. https://insights.brainspotting.ro/european-talent-map.

Brainspotting. "IT&C Talent Map Romania 2017–2018." Accessed July 20, 2019. https://www.scribd.com/document/340683595/Brainspotting-ITC-Talent-Map-Romania-17-18.

Brainspotting. "IT Talent Map: Romania, 2019–2020." Accessed February 2, 2022. https://docsend.com/view/gqhjxkg.

Brenner, Robert. "The Origins of Capitalist Development: A Critique of Neo-Smithian Marxism." *New Left Review*, no. I/104 (1977): 25–92.

Brooks, Ethel C. "The Possibilities of Romani Feminism." *Signs: Journal of Women in Culture and Society* 38, no. 1 (September 2012): 1–11.

Brown, Kristen V. "Is the Antitech Movement Obsolete?" SFGate, February 10, 2015. https://www.sfgate.com/bayarea/article/Is-the-antitech-movement-obsolete-6067623.php.

Brown, Wendy. *Undoing the Demos: Neoliberalism's Stealth Revolution*. Cambridge, MA: MIT Press, 2015.

Buck-Morss, Susan. *Dreamworld and Catastrophe: The Passing of Mass Utopia in East and West*. Cambridge, MA: MIT Press, 2002.

Bucur, Maria. *Eugenics and Modernization in Interwar Romania*. Pittsburgh: University of Pittsburgh Press, 2010.

Bucur, Maria. *Eugenie Și Modernizare În România Interbelic?* Iași, Romania: Polirom, 2005.

Bunici, Eva. "Best Work-Friendly Coffee Shops in Cluj-Napoca." *Transylvania Hostel*, 2018. https://hostelcluj.com/best-work-friendly-coffee-shops-cluj-napoca-digital-nomads-guide.

Burnett, Peter. "State of the State Address," January 6, 1851. The Governors' Gallery. https://governors.library.ca.gov/addresses/s_01-Burnett2.html.

Burton, Eric. "Navigating Global Socialism: Tanzanian Students in and beyond East Germany." *Cold War History* 19, no. 1 (2019): 63–83.

Butler, Sarah. "IKEA Enters Gig Economy by Buying Freelance Labour Firm Taskrabbit." *Guardian* (US edition), September 28, 2017. https://www.theguardian.com/business/2017/sep/28/ikea-buys-taskrabbit-gig-economy-tradespeople.

Byrd, Jodi. *The Transit of Empire: Indigenous Critiques of Colonialism*. Minneapolis: University of Minnesota Press, 2011.

Byrd, Jodi, Chandan Reddy, Alyosha Goldstein, and Jodi Melamed. "Predatory Value: Economies of Dispossession and Disturbed Relationalities." *Social Text* 36, no. 2 (135) (2018): 1–18.

Byrne, Jeffrey James. "Beyond Continents, Colours, and the Cold War: Yugoslavia, Algeria, and the Struggle for Non-Alignment." *International History Review* 37, no. 6 (2015): 923–27.

Călinescu, Roxana. "Protestele Au Devenit Un Element Constant De Contestare: Iterviu Cu Ruxandra Gubernat și Henry Rammelt." *Dilema Veche*, June 8, 2018. https://dilemaveche.ro/sectiune/dileme-on-line/protestele-au-devenit-un-element-constant-de-624764.html.

Camp, Jordan, and Christina Heatherton, eds. *Policing the Planet: Why the Policing Crisis Led to Black Lives Matter*. New York: Verso, 2016.

Campagna, Federico. *Technic and Magic: The Reconstruction of Reality*. London: Bloomsbury, 2018.

Cârje, Ion. *Irene Sau Planeta Cea Mai Apropiată*. Bucharest: Eminescu, 1981.

Carlsson, Chris. "The General Strike of 1934." FoundSF. Accessed July 19, 2022. https://archive.org/details/SanFranc1934.

Carlsson, Chris. "Hunters Point Uprising." FoundSF. Accessed June 23, 2022. https://www.foundsf.org/index.php?title=Hunters_Point_Uprising.

Cârstocea, Raul. "First as Tragedy, Then as Farce? AUR and the Long Shadow of Fascism in Romania." *Lefteast* (magazine), January 11, 2021. https://lefteast.org/first-as-tragedy-then-as-farce-aur-and-the-long-shadow-of-fascism-in-romania/.

Căși Sociale ACUM! "Humanitarian, Ecological and Housing Crisis in the Pata Rât Area of Cluj-Napoca, Romania: Input for Report on COVID-19 and Right to Housing, Issued by the UN Special Rapporteur on the Right to Adequate Housing." Accessed December 20, 2021. https://casisocialeacum.ro/archives/5013/humanitarian-ecological-and-housing-crisis-in-the-pata-rat-area-of-cluj-napoca-romania.

Căși Sociale ACUM! "To Whom Does the Smart City Belong, If . . . ?" *Lefteast* (magazine), December 23, 2021. https://lefteast.org/to-whom-does-the-smart-city-belong-if.

Cavin, Al. "The Borders of Citizenship: The Politics of Race and Metropolitan Space in Silicon Valley." PhD diss., University of Michigan, 2012.

Césaire, Aimé. *Discourse on Colonialism*. New York: New York University Press, 2001.

Chakrabarty, Dipesh. *Provincializing Europe: Postcolonial Thought and Historical Difference—New Edition*. Princeton, NJ: Princeton University Press, 2000.

Chakravartty, Paula, and Denise F. Silva. "Accumulation, Dispossession, and Debt: The Racial Logic of Global Capitalism: An Introduction." *American Quarterly* 64, no. 3 (2012): 361–85.

Chan, Anita Say. *Networking Peripheries: Technological Futures and the Myth of Digital Universalism*. Cambridge, MA: MIT Press, 2014.

Chari, Sharad, and Katherine Verdery. "Thinking between the Posts: Postcolonialism, Postsocialism, and Ethnography after the Cold War." *Comparative Studies in Society and History* 51, no. 1 (January 2009): 6–34.

Chee, Foo Yun. "EU Regulators to Examine Lawmakers' Report on IKEA Taxes." Reuters, February 15, 2016. https://www.reuters.com/article/us-eu-IKEA-taxavoidance-idUSKCN0VO19C.

Chelcea, Ion. *Țiganii din România: Monografie etnografică*. Bucharest: Institutul Central de Statistică, 1944.

Chelcea, Liviu. "Goodbye, Post-Socialism? Stranger Things beyond the Global East." *Eurasian Geography and Economics*, July 16, 2023, 1–27. https://doi.org/10.1080/15387216.2023.2236126.

Chelcea, Liviu. "The 'Housing Question' and the State-Socialist Answer: City, Class and State Remaking in 1950s Bucharest." *International Journal of Urban and Regional Research* 36, no. 2 (2012): 281–96.

Chelcea, Liviu. "Postindustrial Ecologies: Industrial Rubble, Nature and the Limits of Representation." *Parcours anthropologiques* 10 (2015): 185–200.

Chelcea, Liviu, and Oana Druță. "Zombie Socialism and the Rise of Neoliberalism in Post-Socialist Central and Eastern Europe." *Eurasian Geography and Economics* 57, no. 4–5 (2016): 521–44.

Chelcea, Liviu, Raluca Popescu, and Darie Cristea. "Who Are the Gentrifiers and How Do They Change Central City Neighbourhoods? Privatization, Commodification, and Gentrification in Bucharest." *Geografie* 120, no. 2 (2015): 113–33.

Chen, Mel Y. *Animacies: Biopolitics, Racial Mattering, and Queer Affect*. Durham, NC: Duke University Press, 2012.

Chilvers, Ian. "Tatlin, Vladimir." In *Oxford Dictionary of Art and Artists*. New York: Oxford University Press, 2009.

Chiruta, Ionut. "The Representation of Roma in the Romanian Media during COVID-19: Performing Control through Discursive-Performative Repertoires." *Frontiers in Political Science* 3 (June 7, 2021): 1–20.

Chung, Brian. "Exceptional Visions: Chineseness, Citizenship, and the Architectures of Community in Silicon Valley." PhD diss., University of Michigan, 2011.

Cinpoeș, Radu, and Ov Cristian Norocel. "Nostalgic Nationalism, Welfare Chauvinism, and Migration Anxieties in Central and Eastern Europe." In *Nostalgia and Hope: Intersec-*

tions between *Politics of Culture, Welfare, and Migration in Europe*, edited by Ov Cristian Norocel, Anders Hellström, and Martin Bak Jørgensen, 51–65. IMISCOE Research Series. Cham, Switzerland: Springer, 2020.

Clapp, Alexander. "Romania Redivivus." *New Left Review*, no. 108 (December 2017): 5–41.

Clare, John. *Poems of the Middle Period, 1822–1837*. New York: Oxford University Press, 1996.

Clarke, Arthur C. *Profiles of the Future*. London: Orion, 2013.

Cocola-Gant, Agustín. "Tourism Gentrification." In *Handbook of Gentrification Studies*, edited by Loretta Lees and Martin Phillips, 281–93. Cheltenham, UK: Edward Elgar, 2018.

Codruț, Loredana. "O Stewardesă Ryanair A EXPLODAT la Adresa Românilor Veniți din Diaspora." *Stiri pe Surse*, March 26, 2020. https://www.stiripesurse.ro/o-stewardesa -ryanair-a-explodat-la-adresa-romanilor-veniti-din-diaspora-acum-cand-nu-mai-aveti -ce-f_1445446.html.

Cohen, Kris, and Scott C. Richmond. "New Histories of Computational Personhood: An Introduction." *JCMS: Journal of Cinema and Media Studies* 61, no. 4 (2022): 158–62.

Cojocar, Adrian. "Cum s-a Reinventat Prin Investitii De 10 Mil. Euro Unul Dintre Simbolurile Industriei Din Bucuresti, Uzina Timpuri Noi." *ZF Companii*, October 13, 2011.

Coleman, Gabriella. *Coding Freedom: The Ethics and Aesthetics of Hacking*. Princeton, NJ: Princeton University Press, 2012.

Collier, Stephen J. *Post-Soviet Social: Neoliberalism, Social Modernity, Biopolitics*. Princeton, NJ: Princeton University Press, 2011.

Colliers International. "Romania Research and Forecast Report." Bucharest: Colliers International, 2018. Accessed June 3, 2019. https://www2.colliers.com/-/media/Files /EMEA/Romania/2018-Research-Reports/Colliers-Report-Research-and-Forecast -Report-2018.ashx.

Costache, Ioanida. "Roma Futurism and Roma Healing: Historical Trauma, Possible Futures, and a New Humanism." *Revista Arta*, May 23, 2021. https://revistaarta.ro/en /roma-futurism-and-roma-healing-historical-trauma-possible-futures-and-a-new -humanism.

Costache, Ioanida. "Subjects of Racialized Modernity: Romani People and Decoloniality in Europe." *EuropeNow* (blog), 2021. https://www.europenowjournal.org/2021/04/01 /subjects-of-racialized-modernity-romani-people-and-decoloniality-in-europe.

Costache, Ioanida. "'Until We Are Able to Gas Them like the Nazis, the Roma Will Infect the Nation': Roma and the Ethnicization of COVID-19 in Romania." *DoR* (blog), April 22, 2020. https://www.dor.ro/roma-and-the-ethnicization-of-covid-19-in -romania.

Coțofană, Alexandra. "White Man Law versus Black Magic Women: Racial and Gender Entanglements of Witchcraft Policies in Romania." *Kultūra Ir Visuomenė: Socialinių Tyrimų Žurnalas* 13, no. 2 (2017): 69–95.

Cristian, Deniza. "Uber Reaches 17 Cities in Romania. The App Is Now Available in Alba Iulia." *Business Review*, May 5, 2022. https://business-review.eu/business/mobility/uber -reaches-17-cities-in-romania-the-app-is-now-available-in-alba-iulia-230561.

Cucu, Sorin Radu. "Acts of Collusion: Myth, Media, and the Populist Imagination in the 2016 United States Presidential Election." *Safundi* 21, no. 3 (2020): 266–81.

Daniel, Will. "Top Tech Analyst: A.I. 'Gold Rush' Is like Dotcom Boom." *Fortune*, June 12, 2023. https://fortune.com/2023/06/12/ai-dot-com-boom-tech-analyst-dan-ives.

Dean, Martin, Constantin Goschler, and Philipp Ther. *Robbery and Restitution: The Conflict over Jewish Property in Europe*. New York: Berghahn Books, 2007.

Deoancă, Adrian. "Class Politics and Romania's 'White Revolution.'" *Anthropology News* 58, no. 4 (July/August 2017): e394–e98.

Derrida, Jacques. *Adieu to Emmanuel Levinas*. Translated by Pascale-Anne Brault and Michael Naas. Stanford, CA: Stanford University Press, 1999.

Derrida, Jacques. *On Cosmopolitanism and Forgiveness*. New York: Routledge, 2003.

Derrida, Jacques. *Specters of Marx: The State of the Debt, the New Work of Mourning, and the New International*. New York: Routledge, 1994.

Digital Nomads Romania. "Coworking Spaces in Bucharest." *Digital Nomads Romania*, November 19, 2021. https://digitalnomadsromania.com/coworking-spaces-in -bucharest.

DNLee. "When Discussing Humanity's Next Move to Space, the Language We Use Matters." *Scientific American Blog Network* (blog), March 26, 2015. https://blogs.scien tificamerican.com/urban-scientist/when-discussing-humanity-8217-s-next-move-to -space-the-language-we-use-matters.

Do, Youjin, dir. *One Way Ticket: The Digital Nomad Documentary*. 2017. https://digitalnom addocumentary.com.

Docaș, Catalin. "Ice Felix-o Afacere Extrem de Profitabil? Predat? Intereselor Imobili-are." *Digi24*, March 17, 2015.

Drăgan, Mihaela. "Roma Futurism Manifesto." *Giuvlipen* (blog). Accessed June 21, 2021. https://giuvlipen.com/en/roma-futurism.

Dreyer, Leslie. "Google Bus Blockades for a Right to the City." In *Counterpoints: A San Francisco Bay Area Atlas of Displacement and Resistance*, edited by Anti-Eviction Mapping Project, 275–78. Oakland, CA: PM Press, 2021.

Driscoll, Kevin. *The Modem World: A Prehistory of Social Media*. New Haven, CT: Yale University Press, 2022.

Dubal, Veena B. "The Drive to Precarity: A Political History of Work, Regulation, & Labor Advocacy in San Francisco's Taxi & Uber Economies." *Berkeley Journal of Employment and Labor Law* 38, no. 1 (2017): 73–135.

Du Bois, W. E. B. *The Autobiography of W. E. B. Du Bois*. New York: International, 1968.

Du Bois, W. E. B. *Economic Co-operation among Negro Americans*. Atlanta: Atlanta University Press, 1907.

Duncan, Ian. "Wild England: George Borrow's Nomadology." *Victorian Studies* 41, no. 3 (Spring 1998): 381–403.

Dunn, Elizabeth C. *Privatizing Poland: Baby Food, Big Business, and the Remaking of Labor*. Ithaca, NY: Cornell University Press, 2004.

Dunne, Sean. *The Most Dangerous Town on the Internet*. Tempe, AZ: Symantec, 2015. https://docur.co/documentary/the-most-dangerous-town-on-the-internet.

Dussel, Enrique. *Twenty Theses on Politics*. Durham, NC: Duke University Press, 2008.

Dyer-Witheford, Nick. "Digital Labour, Species-Becoming and the Global Worker." *Ephemera: Theory and Politics in Organization* 10, no. 3 (2010): 484–503.

Dzenovska, Dace, and Larisa Kurtović. "The Future of Postsocialist Critique." Paper presented at the American Association of Anthropologists Soyuz Conference, Indiana University, Bloomington, March 3–4, 2017.

Educație Civica. "Despre Proiect." Accessed February 1, 2022. https://educatiecivica.ro /despre-proiect.

Engerman, David C. "Learning from the East: Soviet Experts and India in the Era of Competitive Coexistence." *Comparative Studies of South Asia, Africa and the Middle East* 33, no. 2 (2013): 227–38.

Ernu. Vasile. *Nascut in URSS*. Iași, Romania: Polirom, 2020.

Estes, Nick. *Our History Is the Future: Standing Rock versus the Dakota Access Pipeline, and the Long Tradition of Indigenous Resistance*. New York: Verso, 2019.

Estes, Nick. "Water Is Life: Nick Estes on Indigenous Technologies." *Logic Magazine*, December 7, 2019. https://logicmag.io/nature/water-is-life-nick-estes-on-indigenous -technologies.

Eurostat. "Annual Detailed Enterprise Statistics for Services." Luxembourg: Eurostat, 2022. https://ec.europa.eu/eurostat/databrowser/view/SBS_NA_1A_SE_R2/default /table?lang=en.

Eurostat. "Foreign Control of Enterprises by Economic Activity and a Selection of Controlling Countries." Luxembourg: Eurostat, 2022. https://data.europa.eu/data/datasets /fv97prqbn7a4rrjcuusg5g?locale=en.

Eurostat. "People at Risk of Poverty or Social Exclusion." Luxembourg: Eurostat, January 10, 2022. https://ec.europa.eu/eurostat/databrowser/view/SDG_01_10__custom_2234765 /bookmark/table?lang=en&bookmarkId=c7e882b7-68b9-4465-b05a-91fb296cfb8c.

Fanon, Frantz. *The Wretched of the Earth*. New York: Grove/Atlantic, 2007.

Federici, Silvia. *Caliban and the Witch: Women, the Body, and Primitive Accumulation*. Brooklyn, NY: Autonomedia, 2004.

Ferreira, Becky. "SpaceX's Satellite Megaconstellations Are Astrocolonialism, Indigenous Advocates Say." *Vice*, October 5, 2021. https://www.vice.com/en/article/k78mnz /spacexs-satellite-megaconstellations-are-astrocolonialism-indigenous-advocates-say.

Ferreri, Mara, and Romola Sanyal. "Digital Informalisation: Rental Housing, Platforms, and the Management of Risk." *Housing Studies* 37, no. 6 (2021): 1035–53.

Ferriss, Timothy. *The 4-Hour Work Week: Escape the 9–5, Live Anywhere and Join the New Rich*. New York: Random House, 2011.

Fields, Desiree. "Automated Landlord: Digital Technologies and Post-crisis Financial Accumulation." *Environment and Planning A: Economy and Space* 54, no. 1 (2022): 160–81.

Filip, Alexandru, Madalina Kmen, and Ovidiu Tisler. "Digital Challengers on the Next Frontier: Perspective on Romania." *McKinsey & Company*, September 19, 2022. https:// www.mckinsey.com/capabilities/mckinsey-digital/our-insights/digital-challengers-on -the-next-frontier-perspective-on-romania.

Findlay, John M. *Magic Lands: Western Cityscapes and American Culture after 1940*. Berkeley: University of California Press, 1992.

Fiscutean, Andrada. "In Romania, Vestiges of Communism Boost Women in Tech." *Vice*, April 18, 2016. https://www.vice.com/en/article/jpg5x4/in-romania-vestiges-of -communism-boost-women-in-tech.

Fiscutean, Andrada. "'Life Is Pretty Good Here for IT People': Where Techies Earn Five Times the Average Salary." ZDnet, November 26, 2014. https://www.zdnet.com/article /life-is-pretty-good-here-for-it-people-where-techies-earn-five-times-the-average-salary.

Fiscutean, Andrada. "The Mix of Poverty and Piracy That Turned Romania into Europe's Software Development Powerhouse." ZDnet, August 28, 2014. https://www.zd net.com/article/the-mix-of-poverty-and-piracy-that-turned-romania-into-europes -software-development-powerhouse.

Fiscutean, Andrada. "The Underground Story of Cobra, the 1980s' Illicit Handmade Computer." Ars Technica, November 1, 2017. https://arstechnica.com/gadgets/2017/11 /the-underground-story-of-cobra-the-1980s-illicit-handmade-computer/.

Fiscutean, Andrada. "This Video Game Depicts Life in an Ultra-Nationalist Dystopia." The Outline, August 23, 2017. https://theoutline.com/post/2158/black-the-fall-game -nationalism-communism-totalitarianism.

Florea, Ioana. "The Ups and Downs of a Symbolic City: The Architectural Heritage Protection Movement in Bucharest." In Urban Grassroots Movements in Central and Eastern Europe, edited by Kerstin Jacobsson, 55–78. London: Routledge, 2016.

Florea, Ioana, and Mihail Dumitriu. "Living on the Edge: The Ambiguities of Squatting and Urban Development in Bucharest." In Public Goods versus Economic Interests: Global Perspectives on the History of Squatting, edited by Freia Anders and Alexander Sedlmaier, 188–201. New York: Routledge, 2017.

Florea, Ioana, and Veda Popovici. 2021. "Complicities, Solidarities and Everything In Between: Art and Political Engagement in the Housing Movement in Bucharest and Cluj." In Radical Housing. Art, Struggle, Care, edited by Ana Vilenica, 133–52. Amsterdam: Institute of Network Cultures.

Florida, Richard. The Rise of the Creative Class. New York: Basic Books, 2019.

Forbes Communications Council. "Câți bani a cheltuit Roșia Montana Gold Corporation în publicitatea din presa scrisă?" Forbes, March 2, 2013. https://www.forbes.ro/cati -bani-a-cheltuit-rosia-montana-gold-corporation-in-publicitatea-din-presa-scrisa_0 _8686-10173.

Forman, Mark. "Fascism Is Possible Not in Spite of Liberal Capitalism, but Because of It." Truthout, April 15, 2017. https://truthout.org/articles/fascism-is-possible-not-in -spite-of-liberal-capitalism-but-because-of-it.

Foucault, Michel. History of Madness. Edited by Jean Khalfa. Translated by Jonathan Murphy. London: Routledge, 2006.

Foucault, Michel. Security, Territory, Population: Lectures at the Collège de France 1977–1978. Macmillan, 2009.

Fraser, Nancy. Justice Interruptus: Critical Reflections on the "Postsocialist" Condition. New York: Routledge, 1996.

Freeman, Elizabeth. Time Binds: Queer Temporalities and Queer Histories. Durham, NC: Duke University Press, 2010.

Friend, Tad. "Sam Altman's Manifest Destiny." New Yorker, October 3, 2016. https://www .newyorker.com/magazine/2016/10/10/sam-altmans-manifest-destiny.

Friling, Tuvia, Radu Ioanid, and Mihail E. Ionescu, eds. Final Report. Iași, Romania: Polirom, 2005.

Fukuyama, Francis. The End of History and the Last Man. New York: Free Press, 1992.

Gal, Susan, and Gail Kligman. *The Politics of Gender after Socialism*. Princeton, NJ: Princeton University Press, 2000.

Galvan, Jill. "Occult Networks and the Legacy of the Indian Rebellion in Bram Stoker's *Dracula*." *History of Religions* 54, no. 4 (2015): 434–58.

Gentile, Michael. "Three Metals and the 'Post-Socialist City.'" *International Journal of Urban and Regional Research* 42, no. 6 (2018): 1140–51.

Getachew, Adom. *Worldmaking after Empire: The Rise and Fall of Self Determination*. Princeton, NJ: University of Princeton Press, 2019.

Gheorghe, Carmen. "Cu Fustele-n Cap Pentru Feminismul Rom." In *Problema Românească: O Analiză a Rasismului Românesc*, edited by Oana Dorobanţu and Carmen Gheorghe, 135–48. Bucharest: Editura Hecate, 2019.

Gheorghe, Carmen, Letiţia Mark, and Enikő Vincze. "Towards an Anti-racist Feminism for Social Justice in Romania." In *The Romani Women's Movement: Struggles and Debates in Central and Eastern Europe*, edited by Angéla Kóczé, Violetta Zentai, Jelena Jovanović, and Enikő Vincze, 111–34. London: Routledge, 2018.

Ghilezan, Marius. "Genetica Protestelor Din Piata Universitii." *Evenimentul Zilei*, September 18, 2013. https://www.qmagazine.ro/genetica-protestelor-din-piata-universitatii.

Ghodsee, Kristen. *Red Hangover: Legacies of Twentieth-Century Communism*. Durham, NC: Duke University Press, 2016.

Gibson-Graham, J. K. *A Postcapitalist Politics*. Minneapolis: University of Minnesota Press, 2006.

Gildea, Robert, James Mark, and Niek Pas. "European Radicals and the 'Third World.'" *Cultural and Social History* 8, no. 4 (2011): 449–71.

Gilmore, Ruth Wilson. *Abolition Geography: Essays towards Liberation*. London: Verso, 2022.

Gilmore, Ruth Wilson. "Abolition on Stolen Land." Seminar at UCLA Luskin Institute on Inequality and Democracy, Los Angeles, CA, October 9, 2020.

Goerzen, Matt, and Gabriella Coleman. *Wearing Many Hats: The Rise of the Professional Security Hacker*. New York: Data and Society, 2022. https://datasociety.net/wp-content/uploads/2022/03/WMH_final01062022Rev.pdf.

Goldman, Emma. *Anarchism and Other Essays*. New York: Mother Earth, 1910.

Goldstein, Aloysha, and Simón Ventura Trujillo. "Fascism Now? Inquiries for an Expanded Frame." *Critical Ethnic Studies* 7 (2021). https://manifold.umn.edu/read/ceso701-introduction/section/f9ffb32b-958a-4577-b03d-a6ecdb10b153#chapter1_7.

Gould, Corrina. "Ohlone Geographies." In *Counterpoints: A San Francisco Bay Area Atlas of Displacement and Resistance*, edited by Anti-Eviction Mapping Project, 71–75. Oakland, CA: PM Press, 2021.

Grady-Willis, Winston. "Explaining the Demise of the Black Panther Party: The Role of Internal Factors." In *The Black Panther Party (Reconsidered)*, edited by Charles Earl Jones, 363–90. Baltimore: Black Classic Press, 1998.

Graeber, David, and David Wengrow. *The Dawn of Everything: A New History of Humanity*. New York: Farrar, Straus and Giroux, 2021.

Graham, Stephen, and Simon Guy. "Digital Space Meets Urban Place: Sociotechnologies of Urban Restructuring in Downtown San Francisco." *City* 6, no. 3 (2002): 369–82.

Graham, Steve, and Simon Marvin. *Splintering Urbanism: Networked Infrastructures, Technological Mobilities and the Urban Condition.* London: Routledge, 2001.

Grama, Emanuela. *Socialist Heritage: The Politics of Past and Place in Romania.* Bloomington: Indiana University Press, 2019.

Grandin, Greg. *Empire's Workshop: Latin America, the United States, and the Rise of the New Imperialism.* New York: Holt Paperbacks, 2007.

Grant, Bruce. *In the Soviet House of Culture: A Century of Perestroikas.* Princeton, NJ: Princeton University Press, 1995.

Gray-Garcia, Tiny. "Ending Eviction Moratoriums Means More People Homeless on the Streets." *48 Hills*, July 11, 2023. https://48hills.org/2023/07/ending-eviction-moratori ums-means-more-people-homeless-on-the-streets.

Greenbaum, Joan. "Questioning Tech Work." *AI Now Institute* (blog), January 31, 2020. https://ainowinstitute.org/publication/questioning-tech-work-2.

Greenhouse, Steven. "In Romania, Ceausescu Is Gone but His Crippling Economic Legacy Endures." *New York Times*, August 6, 1990. https://www.nytimes.com/1990/08 /06/world/evolution-europe-romania-ceausescu-gone-but-his-crippling-economic -legacy.html.

Grellmann, Heinrich Moritz Gottlieb. *Dissertation on the Gipsies, Being an Historical Enquiry, concerning the Manner of Life, Family Economy, Customs and Conditions of These People in Europe, and Their Origin.* Translated by Matthew Raper. London: G. Bigg, 1787.

Groys, Boris. *Art Power.* Cambridge, MA: MIT Press, 2008.

Gutfrański, Krzysztof. "The Speed of Guccifer." *Obieg*, October 28, 2019. https://obieg.pl /en/171-introduction-the-speed-of-guccifer.

Haigh, Maria. "Downloading Communism: File Sharing as Samizdat in Ukraine." *Libri* 57, no. 3 (2007): 165–78.

Hajnáczky, Tamás. "The Forced Assimilation Gypsy Policy in Socialist Hungary." *Romani Studies* 30, no. 1 (2020): 49–87.

Hajská, Markéta. "'We Had to Run Away': The Lovára's Departure from the Protectorate of Bohemia and Moravia to Slovakia in 1939." *Romani Studies* 32, no. 1 (2022): 51–83.

Haraway, Donna. "A Manifesto for Cyborgs: Science, Technology, and Socialist Feminism in the 1980s." *Australian Feminist Studies* 2, no. 4 (1987): 1–42.

Haraway, Donna. *Modest_Witness@Second_Millennium. Femaleman_Meets_Oncomouse.* New York: Routledge, 1997.

Haraway, Donna. "Situated Knowledges: The Science Question in Feminism and the Privilege of Partial Perspective." *Feminist Studies* 14, no. 3 (Autumn 1988): 575–99.

Hardt, Michael, and Antonio Negri. *Empire.* Cambridge, MA: Harvard University Press, 2000.

Harris, Cheryl. "Whiteness as Property." *Harvard Law Review* 106, no. 8 (June 1993): 1707–91.

Harris, Malcolm. *Palo Alto: A History of California, Capitalism, and the World.* New York: Little, Brown, 2023.

Hart, Gillian. "Relational Comparison Revisited: Marxist Postcolonial Geographies in Practice." *Progress in Human Geography* 42, no. 3 (June 1, 2018): 371–94.

Hartman, Chester. *City for Sale: The Transformation of San Francisco*. Berkeley: University of California Press, 2002.

Hartman, Saidiya. "The Anarchy of Colored Girls Assembled in a Riotous Manner." *South Atlantic Quarterly* 117, no. 3 (2018): 465–90.

Harvey, David. *The New Imperialism*. Oxford: Oxford University Press, 2003.

Hayes, Matthew. "'We Gained a Lot over What We Would Have Had': The Geographic Arbitrage of North American Lifestyle Migrants to Cuenca, Ecuador." *Journal of Ethnic and Migration Studies* 40, no. 12 (2014): 1953–71.

Hayes, Michael, and Thomas Acton. *Travellers, Gypsies, Roma: The Demonisation of Difference*. Unabridged ed. Newcastle, UK: Cambridge Scholars, 2007.

Hayles, N. Katherine. "Unfinished Work from Cyborg to Cognisphere." *Theory, Culture and Society* 23, no. 7–8 (December 2006): 159–66.

Hellström, Anders, Cristian Ov Norocel, and Martin Bak Jørgensen. "Nostalgia and Hope: Narrative Master Frames across Contemporary Europe." In *Nostalgia and Hope: Intersections between Politics of Culture, Welfare, and Migration in Europe*, edited by Cristian Ov Norocel, Anders Hellström, and Martin Bak Jørgensen, 1–16. Cham, Switzerland: Springer, 2020.

Helsinki Watch. *Destroying Ethnic Identity: The Persecution of the Gypsies in Romania*. New York: A Helsinki Watch Report, 1991. https://www.hrw.org/reports/ROMANIA919.PDF.

Henderson, Andrew. "Best Cities to Live as a Bootstrapping Young Entrepreneur." *Digital Nomad* (blog), December 1, 2013. https://nomadcapitalist.com/2013/12/01/top-5-best -cities-live-bootstrapping-young-entrepreneur.

Heynen, Nik. "'A Plantation Can Be a Commons': Re-Earthing Sapelo Island through Abolition Ecology." *Antipode* 53, no. 1 (2021): 95–114.

Hippler, Arthur E. *Hunter's Point: A Black Ghetto*. New York: Basic Books, 1974.

Hirsch, Francine. *Empire of Nations: Ethnographic Knowledge and the Making of the Soviet Union*. Ithaca, NY: Cornell University Press, 2005.

Hochschild, Arlie R. *The Managed Heart: Commercialization of Human Feeling*. Berkeley: University of California Press, 2012.

Hoefler, Don C. "Silicon Valley, USA." *Electronic News*, January 10, 1971.

HotNews.ro. "Rovana Plumb: Proiectul Minier De La Rosia Montana Trebuie Declarat de Interes Public Exceptional, Pentru a Putea Permite Devierea Raului Corna." *HotNews.ro*, September 24, 2013. https://www.hotnews.ro/stiri-esential-15644366-rovana -plumb-proiectul-minier-rosia-montana-trebuie-declarat-interes-public-exceptional -pentru-putea-permite-devierea-raului-comana.htm.

Hu, Tung-Hui. *A Prehistory of the Cloud*. Cambridge, MA: MIT Press, 2015.

Huang, Kristin. "US General Describes 'China Threat' in Space as Chang'e-5 Lunar Mission Heats Up Rivalry." *South China Morning Post*, November 26, 2020. https://www .scmp.com/news/china/diplomacy/article/3111454/us-general-describes-china-threat -space-change-5-lunar-mission.

Hume, Brit, dir. "Mine Your Own Business on FOX News's Brit Hume." YouTube, January 18, 2007. https://www.youtube.com/watch?v=n9eWraixy2k&ab_channel =MineYourOwnBusiness.

Humphrey, Caroline, and Katherine Verdery. *Property in Question: Value Transformation in the Global Economy*. New York: Bloomsbury, 2014.

IKEA. "About Us." Accessed September 10, 2022. https://about.ikea.com/en/about-us.

Imre, Anikó. "Illiberal White Fantasies and Netflix's *The Witcher*." *Journal of Ethnic and Migration Studies* 49, no. 6 (January 11, 2023): 1570–87. https://doi.org/10.1080/1369183X.2022.2156324.

International Trade Administration. "Romania—Country Commercial Guide." July 27, 2022. https://www.trade.gov/country-commercial-guides/romania-information-communications-technology-ict.

Ioanid, Radu. *The Holocaust in Romania: The Destruction of Jews and Gypsies under the Antonescu Regime, 1940-1944*. Chicago: Ivan R. Dee, 2008.

Ioanid, Radu. *The Ransom of the Jews: The Story of the Extraordinary Secret Bargain between Romania and Israel*. Lanham, MD: Rowman and Littlefield, 2021.

Ioraș, F., and I. V. Abrudan. "The Romanian Forestry Sector: Privatisation Facts." *International Forestry Review* 8, no. 3 (2006): 361–67.

Irani, Lilly. *Chasing Innovation: Making Entrepreneurial Citizens in Modern India*. Princeton, NJ: Princeton University Press, 2019.

Irani, Lilly. "Difference and Dependence among Digital Workers: The Case of Amazon Mechanical Turk." *South Atlantic Quarterly* 114, no. 1 (January 1, 2015): 225–34.

Jakić, Bruno. "Galaxy and the New Wave: Yugoslav Computer Culture in the 1980s." In *Hacking Europe*, edited by Gerard Alberts and Ruth Oldenziel, 107–28. London: Springer London, 2015.

James, C. L. R. "After Hitler, Our Turn." In *World Revolution 1917-1936: The Rise and Fall of the Communist International*, edited by Christian Høgsbjerg, 306–48. Durham, NC: Duke University Press, 2017.

Johnson, Myles E. "Sun Ra Altered the Destiny for a Generation of Artists." AFROPUNK, May 22, 2019. https://afropunk.com/2019/05/sun-ra-birthday-destiny.

Jordan, John. "The Czech Play That Gave Us the Word 'Robot.'" *The MIT Press Reader* (blog), July 29, 2019. https://thereader.mitpress.mit.edu/origin-word-robot-rur.

The JustSpace Alliance. "Resources." JustSpace. Accessed June 10, 2021. https://justspacealliance.org/resources.

Kahancová, Marta, Tibor T. Meszmann, and Mária Sedláková. "Precarization via Digitalization? Work Arrangements in the On-Demand Platform Economy in Hungary and Slovakia." *Frontiers in Sociology* 5, no. 3 (2020). https://www.frontiersin.org/article/10.3389/fsoc.2020.00003.

Kaplan, Amy. *The Anarchy of Empire in the Making of U.S. Culture*. Cambridge, MA: Harvard University Press, 2002.

Karkov, Nikolay R., and Zhivka Valiavicharska. "Rethinking East-European Socialism: Notes toward an Anti-capitalist Decolonial Methodology." *Interventions* 20, no. 6 (2018): 785–813.

Karuka, Manu. *Empire's Tracks: Indigenous Nations, Chinese Workers, and the Transcontinental Railroad*. Berkeley: University of California Press, 2019.

Kay, Daniel. "The Digital Nomad Deception." *this is youth* (blog), December 21, 2015. https://thisisyouth.org/2015/12/21/digital-nomads-ethical-tourism.

Keller, G. Frederick. "The Curse of California." *The Wasp* 9, no. 316 (August 19, 1882): 520–21. Image taken from http://nationalhumanitiescenter.org/pds/gilded/power/text1/octopusimages.pdf.

Kelley, Robin D. G. *Hammer and Hoe: Alabama Communists during the Great Depression.* Chapel Hill: University of North Carolina Press, 1990.

Kelley, Robin D. G. *Race Rebels: Culture, Politics, and the Black Working Class.* New York: Free Press, 1996.

Kelso, Michelle. "'And Roma Were Victims, Too': The Romani Genocide and Holocaust Education in Romania." *Intercultural Education* 24, no. 1–2 (2013): 61–78.

Kenarov, Dimeter. "Romania: Mountains of Gold." Pulitzer Center on Crisis Reporting, July 16, 2012. https://pulitzercenter.org/stories/romania-mountains-gold.

Kilgore, De Witt. *Astrofuturism: Science, Race, and Visions of Utopia in Space.* Philadelphia: University of Pennsylvania Press, 2003.

Kim, Jodi. *Ends of Empire: Asian American Critique and the Cold War.* Illustrated edition. Minneapolis: University of Minnesota Press, 2010.

Kivelson, Valerie A. *Desperate Magic: The Moral Economy of Witchcraft in Seventeenth-Century Russia.* Ithaca, NY: Cornell University Press, 2013.

Kluger, Jeffrey. "Here's the Russian Ritual That Ensures a Safe Space Flight." *Time*, February 26, 2016. http://time.com/4238910/gagarin-red-square-ritual.

Kóczé, Angéla. "Race, Migration and Neoliberalism: Distorted Notions of Romani Migration in European Public Discourses." *Social Identities* 24, no. 4 (2018): 459–73.

Kóczé, Angéla, Violetta Zentai, Jelena Jovanović, and Enikő Vincze. *The Romani Women's Movement: Struggles and Debates in Central and Eastern Europe.* London: Routledge, 2018.

Koga, Yukiko. *The Inheritance of Loss: China, Japan, and the Political Economy of Redemption after Empire.* Chicago: University of Chicago Press, 2016.

Koobak, Redi, Madina Tlostanova, and Suruchi Thapar-Björkert. "Introduction: Uneasy Affinities between the Postcolonial and the Postsocialist." In *Postcolonial and Postsocialist Dialogues,* edited by Redi Koobak, Madina Tlostanova, and Suruchi Thapar-Björkert, 1–10. London: Routledge, 2021.

Kovacs, F. "Implementing Robots in 'Classical' Factories, a Difficult Task for the East-European Industries." *6th Mediterranean Electrotechnical Conference* 2 (1991): 942–44.

Kret, Abigail Judge. "'We Unite with Knowledge': The Peoples' Friendship University and Soviet Education for the Third World." *Comparative Studies of South Asia, Africa and the Middle East* 33, no. 2 (August 2013): 239–56.

Kusiak, Joanna. "Legal Technologies of Primitive Accumulation: Judicial Robbery and Dispossession-by-Restitution in Warsaw." *International Journal of Urban and Regional Research* 43, no. 4 (2019): 649–65.

Kwet, Michael. "Digital Colonialism: US Empire and the New Imperialism in the Global South." *Race and Class* 60, no. 4 (2019): 3–26.

Lai, Clement. "The Racial Triangulation of Space: The Case of Urban Renewal in San Francisco's Fillmore District." *Annals of the Association of American Geographers* 102, no. 1 (January 2012): 151–70.

Lancione, Michele. "The Politics of Embodied Urban Precarity: Roma People and the Fight for Housing in Bucharest, Romania." *Geoforum* 101 (2019): 182–91.

Lango, Luke. "AI Is Primed to Power Another Dot-Com Tech Boom." *Yahoo Finance,* May 24, 2023. https://finance.yahoo.com/news/ai-primed-power-another-dot-172106 385.html.

Larkin, Brian. *Signal and Noise: Media, Infrastructure, and Urban Culture in Nigeria.* Durham, NC: Duke University Press, 2008.

Lazarus, Neil. "Spectres Haunting: Postcommunism and Postcolonialism." *Journal of Postcolonial Writing* 48, no. 2 (2012): 117–29.

Lemon, Alaina. *Between Two Fires: Gypsy Performance and Romani Memory from Pushkin to Post-Socialism.* Durham, NC: Duke University Press, 2000.

Lemon, Alaina. *Technologies for Intuition: Cold War Circles and Telepathic Rays.* Berkeley: University of California Press, 2018.

Lenin, Vladimir. *Imperialism, the Highest Stage of Capitalism: A Popular Outline.* New York: International Publishers, 1969.

Lenin, Vladimir. "Speech at a Plenary Meeting of the Moscow Soviet of Workers' and Peasants' Deputies." In *V. I. Lenin: Collected Works,* vol. 32, *December 1920–August 1921,* 147–59. Moscow: Progress Publishers, 1966.

Levy, Robert. *Ana Pauker: The Rise and Fall of a Jewish Communist.* Berkeley: University of California Press, 2001.

Lewis, Jovan Scott. *Scammer's Yard: The Crime of Black Repair in Jamaica.* Minneapolis: University of Minnesota Press, 2020.

Liberty Technology Park. "Liberty Technology Park Cluj—A Park for Creative Ideas." Accessed May 10, 2022. https://www.libertytechpark.com/concept/.

Light, Duncan. "'Facing the Future': Tourism and Identity-Building in Post-Socialist Romania." *Political Geography* 20, no. 8 (November 1, 2001): 1053–74.

Lindtner, Silvia M. *Prototype Nation: China and the Contested Promise of Innovation.* Princeton, NJ: Princeton University Press, 2020.

Linebaugh, Peter. *Stop, Thief! The Commons, Enclosures, and Resistance.* Oakland, CA: PM Press, 2014.

Liu, Wendy. *Abolish Silicon Valley: How to Liberate Technology from Capitalism.* London: Watkins Media, 2020.

The Local. "IKEA Founder Admits to Secret Foundation." *The Local,* January 26, 2011. https://www.thelocal.se/20110126/31650.

Lonely Planet. "The Top Region to Visit in 2016: Transylvania." YouTube, November 15, 2015. https://www.youtube.com/watch?v=IEzjvhdJLaM.

Lowe, Lisa. *Immigrant Acts: On Asian American Cultural Politics.* Durham, NC: Duke University Press, 1996.

Lowe, Lisa. "Insufficient Difference." *Ethnicities* 5, no. 3 (September 1, 2005): 409–14.

Lowe, Lisa. *The Intimacies of Four Continents.* Durham, NC: Duke University Press, 2015.

Lowe, Lisa. "Rereadings in Orientalism: Oriental Inventions and Inventions of the Orient in Montesquieu's Lettres Persanes." *Cultural Critique* 15, no. 1 (1990): 115–43.

Lucia, Amanda J. *White Utopias: The Religious Exoticism of Transformational Festivals.* Berkeley: University of California Press, 2020.

Lykke, Nina. "Rethinking Socialist and Marxist Legacies in Feminist Imaginaries of Protest from Postsocialist Perspectives." *Social Identities* 24, no. 2 (2018): 173–88.

Madley, Benjamin. *An American Genocide: The United States and the California Indian Catastrophe, 1846–1873*. New Haven, CT: Yale University Press, 2016.

Maharawal, Manissa M. "Infrastructural Activism: Google Bus Blockades, Affective Politics, and Environmental Gentrification in San Francisco." *Antipode*, June 16, 2021. https://doi.org/10.1111/anti.12744.

Maharawal, Manissa M. "Tech-Colonialism: Gentrification, Resistance, and Belonging in San Francisco's Colonial Present." *Anthropological Quarterly* 95, no. 4 (2022): 785–813.

Maharawal, Manissa M., and Erin McElroy. "The Anti-Eviction Mapping Project: Counter Mapping and Oral History towards Bay Area Housing Justice." *Annals of the American Association of Geographers* 108, no. 2 (2018): 380–89.

Mahmood, Saba. *Politics of Piety: The Islamic Revival and the Feminist Subject*. Princeton, NJ: Princeton University Press, 2011.

Mahmud, Lilith. "Fascism, a Haunting: Spectral Politics and Resistance in Twenty-First-Century Italy." In *Beyond Populism: Angry Politics and the Twilight of Neoliberalism*, edited by Jeff Maskovsky and Sophie Bjork-James, 141–66. Morgantown: West Virginia University Press, 2020.

Mahmud, Lilith. "We Have Never Been Liberal: Occidentalist Myths and the Impending Fascist Apocalypse." *Fieldsights*, October 27, 2016. https://culanth.org/fieldsights/we-have-never-been-liberal-occidentalist-myths-and-the-impending-fascist-apocalypse.

Makalani, Minkah. *In the Cause of Freedom: Radical Black Internationalism from Harlem to London, 1917–1939*. Chapel Hill: University of North Carolina Press, 2011.

Makimoto, Tsugio, and David Manners. *Digital Nomad*. New York: Wiley, 1997.

Marez, Curtis. *Farm Worker Futurism: Speculative Technologies of Resistance*. Minneapolis: University of Minnesota Press, 2016.

Marica, Irina. "Cluj-Napoca and Bucharest Ranked among Europe's Best Workation Destinations in 2023." *Romania Insider*, January 6, 2023. https://www.romania-insider.com/cluj-bucharest-europe-workation-destinations-2023.

Marincea, Adina, and Veda Popovici. "Calling Fascism by Its Name: The Rise of the Radical Right and Organizing Leftist Resistance in Romania." *Lefteast* (blog), December 23, 2022. https://lefteast.org/author/adina-marincea-and-veda-popovici/.

Mark, James, and Péter Apor. "Socialism Goes Global: Decolonization and the Making of a New Culture of Internationalism in Socialist Hungary, 1956–1989." *Journal of Modern History* 87, no. 4 (2015): 852–91.

Mark, James, and Quinn Slobodian. "Eastern Europe." In *The Oxford Handbook of the Ends of Empire*, edited by Martin Thomas and Andrew Thompson, 351–72. Oxford: Oxford University Press, 2018.

Martí, Fernando. *Futuros Fugaces: Armory Chinampas*. *Just Seeds* (blog), April 2021. https://justseeds.org/product/futuros-fugaces-armory-chinampas.

Martí, Fernando. *On Indigenous Land*. In *Counterpoints: A San Francisco Bay Area Atlas of Displacement and Resistance*, edited by Anti-Eviction Mapping Project, 68. Oakland, CA: PM Press, 2021.

Martí, Fernando. *Speculation Stole Our City*. In *Counterpoints: A San Francisco Bay Area Atlas of Displacement and Resistance*, edited by Anti-Eviction Mapping Project, 336. Oakland, CA: PM Press, 2021.

Martin, Terry. *The Affirmative Action Empire: Nations and Nationalism in the Soviet Union, 1923–1939*. Ithaca, NY: Cornell University Press, 2001.

Marx, Karl. *Capital: A Critique of Political Economy*. Vol. 1. Translated by Ben Fowkes. New York: Penguin Classics, 1992.

Marx, Karl, and Friedrich Engels. *The Communist Manifesto*. Edited by Gareth Stedman Jones. Translated by Samuel Moore. New York: Penguin Classics, 2002.

Marx, Paris. "Elon Musk Should Not Be in Charge of the Night Sky." *Time*, February 3, 2023. https://time.com/6250118/elon-musk-should-not-be-in-charge-of-the-night-sky/.

Masco, Joseph. *The Nuclear Borderlands: The Manhattan Project in Post–Cold War New Mexico*. Princeton, NJ: Princeton University Press, 2006.

Matache, Margareta. "Biased Elites, Unfit Policies: Reflections on the Lacunae of Roma Integration Strategies." *European Review* 25, no. 4 (October 2017): 588–607.

Mateescu, Oana. "In the Romanian Bubble of Outsourced Creativity." In *The Routledge Handbook of the Anthropology of Labor*, edited by Sharryn Kasmir and Lesley Gill, 243–55. Oxfordshire, UK: Routledge, 2022.

Mattern, Shannon. *The City Is Not a Computer*. Princeton, NJ: Princeton University Press, 2021.

Mattern, Shannon. *Code and Clay, Data and Dirt: Five Thousand Years of Urban Media*. Minneapolis: University of Minnesota Press, 2017.

Mattern, Shannon. "Post-It Note City." *Places Journal*, February 2020. https://doi.org/10.22269/200211.

Matzal, Andra. "'Am Trăit Patru Revoluții.' De Vârstă cu România." *Scena 9*, 2018. https://www.scena9.ro/article/pompiliu-sterian-de-varsta-cu-romania.

McElroy, Erin. "Digital Cartographies of Displacement: Data as Property and Property as Data." *ACME: An International Journal for Critical Geographies* 21, no. 4 (2022): 357–71.

McElroy, Erin. "Dis/Possessory Data Politics: From Tenant Screening to Anti-Eviction Organizing." *International Journal of Urban and Regional Research* 47, no. 1 (2023): 54–70.

McElroy, Erin. "Landlord Tech and Racial Technocapitalism in the Times of COVID-19." *Foundry*, November 2020. https://uchri.org/foundry/landlord-tech-and-racial-technocapitalism-in-the-times-of-covid-19.

McElroy, Erin. "Public Thinker: Sophie Gonick on Housing Justice and Mass Movements." *Public Books*, April 26, 2022. https://www.publicbooks.org/sophie-gonick-on-housing-justice-and-mass-movements.

McElroy, Erin, and Veda Popovici. "Diary from Vulturilor 50." *Notes from Below*, October 9, 2019. https://notesfrombelow.org/article/_diary-vulturilor-50_.

McElroy, Erin, Wonyoung So, and Nicole Weber. "Keeping an Eye on Landlord Tech." *Shelterforce*, March 25, 2021. https://shelterforce.org/2021/03/25/keeping-an-eye-on-landlord-tech.

McElroy, Erin, and Manon Vergerio. "Automating Gentrification: Landlord Technologies and Housing Justice Organizing in New York City Homes." *Environment and Planning D: Society and Space* 40, no. 4 (2022): 607–26.

McElroy, Erin, and Alex Werth. "Deracinated Dispossessions: On the Foreclosures of 'Gentrification' in Oakland, Ca." *Antipode* 51, no. 3 (2019): 878–98.

McKittrick, Katherine. *Dear Science and Other Stories*. Durham, NC: Duke University Press, 2020.

McKittrick, Katherine. *Demonic Grounds: Black Women and the Cartographies of Struggle*. Minneapolis: University of Minnesota Press, 2006.

McKittrick, Katherine, and Alexander Weheliye. "808s and Heartbreak." *Propter Nos* 2, no. 1 (2017): 13–42.

Medina, Eden. "Big Blue in the Bottomless Pit: The Early Years of IBM Chile." *IEEE Annals of the History of Computing* 30, no. 4 (2008): 26–41.

Melamed, Jodi. *Represent and Destroy: Rationalizing Violence in the New Racial Capitalism*. Minneapolis: University of Minnesota Press, 2011.

Melamed, Jodi. "The Spirit of Neoliberalism: From Racial Liberalism to Neoliberal Multiculturalism." *Social Text* 4, no. 89 (December 2006): 1–24.

Meseşan, Diana. "Romanian Roulette." *Balkan Insight*, November 17, 2016. https://bal kaninsight.com/2016/11/20/romanian-roulette-11-17-2016.

Messeri, Lisa. *Placing Outer Space: An Earthly Ethnography of Other Worlds*. Durham, NC: Duke University Press, 2016.

Miciu, Cătălina. "Fabuloşii Ani '90." *Scena* 9, October 2017. https://www.scena9.ro/article /fabulosii-ani-90.

Mirabal, Nancy Raquel. "Geographies of Displacement: Latina/os, Oral History, and the Politics of Gentrification in San Francisco's Mission District." *The Public Historian* 31, no. 2 (Spring 2009): 7–31.

Mireanu, Manuel. "Incriminarea Romilor Din Baia Mare În Comunism—Căşi Sociale Acum!" *Caramida*, March 4, 2022. https://casisocialeacum.ro/archives/6870/incrimi narea-romilor-din-baia-mare-in-comunism.

Mireanu, Manuel. "Security at the Nexus of Space and Class: Roma and Gentrification in Cluj, Romania." In *The Securitization of the Roma in Europe*, edited by Huub Baar, Ana Ivasiuc, and Regina Kreide, 115–36. Cham, Switzerland: Palgrave Macmillan, 2019.

MissionCreek Video. *Mission Playground Is Not For Sale*. 2014. https://www.youtube.com /watch?v=awPVYiDcupE.

Miszczyński, Miłosz. *The Dialectical Meaning of Offshored Work: Neoliberal Desires and Labour Arbitrage in Post-Socialist Romania*. Chicago: Haymarket Books, 2020.

Mitchell, Donald. "Iconography and Locational Conflict from the Underside: Free Speech, People's Park, and the Politics of Homelessness in Berkeley, California." *Political Geography* 11, no. 2 (1992): 152–69.

Mitchell, William. *City of Bits: Space, Place and the Infobahn*. Cambridge, MA: MIT Press, 1996.

Moga, Cristi, and Ioana David. "Cea Mai Mare Tranzacte Cu Terenuri Din Ultimii Doi Ani: IKEA a Cumparat Terenul De La Timpuri Noi Pentru a Face Turnuri De Birouri Sii Locuinte." *Ziarul Financiar*, July 14, 2010. https://www.zf.ro/companii/cea-mai-mare -tranzactie-cu-terenuri-din-ultimii-doi-ani-ikea-a-cumparat-terenul-de-la-timpuri-noi -pentru-a-face-turnuri-de-birouri-si-locuinte-6557916.

Moodie, Megan. *We Were Adivasis*. Chicago: University of Chicago Press, 2015.

Moretti, Franco. *Signs Taken for Wonders: Essays in the Sociology of Literary Forms*. New York: Verso, 1988.

Morin, Gabriel. "Romania Is Not the Land of the Poor." *Medium*, January 25, 2016. https://medium.com/@gabriel_morin/romania-is-not-the-land-of-the-poor-70ce8fc5ab95.

Morozov, Evgeny. "Critique of Techno-Feudal Reason." *New Left Review*, no. 133/134 (April 2022): 89–126.

Mosovici, Pierre. "Report on the Accession of Romania to the European Union." European Parliament. Accessed July 30, 2023. https://www.europarl.europa.eu/doceo/document/A-6-2006-0421_EN.html.

Moten, Fred. *In the Break: The Aesthetics of the Black Radical Tradition*. Minneapolis: University of Minnesota Press, 2003.

Mróz, Lech. *Roma-Gypsy Presence in the Polish-Lithuanian Commonwealth: 15th–18th Centuries*. Budapest: Central European University Press, 2016.

Mullaney, Thomas S. "Your Computer Is on Fire." In *Your Computer Is on Fire*, edited by Thomas S. Mullaney, Benjamin Peters, Mar Hicks, and Kavita Philip, 3–9. Cambridge, MA: MIT Press, 2021.

Mullaney, Thomas S., Benjamin Peters, Mar Hicks, and Kavita Philip, eds. *Your Computer Is on Fire*. Cambridge, MA: MIT Press, 2021.

Müller, Martin. "Goodbye, Postsocialism!" *Europe-Asia Studies* 71, no. 4 (2019): 533–50.

Müller, Martin. "In Search of the Global East: Thinking between North and South." *Geopolitics* 25, no. 3 (2020): 734–55.

Muñoz, José Esteban. *Cruising Utopia: The Then and There of Queer Futurity*. New York: New York University Press, 2009.

Murawski, Michał. "Actually-Existing Success: Economics, Aesthetics and the Specificity of (Still)Socialist Urbanism." *Comparative Studies in Society and History* 60, no. 4 (2018): 907–37.

Mureșan, Maria. "Romania's Integration in COMECON: The Analysis of a Failure." *The Romanian Economic Journal* 11, no. 30 (January 2008): 27–58.

Murillo, Luis Felipe R. "Hackerspace Network: Prefiguring Technopolitical Futures?" *American Anthropologist* 122, no. 2 (June 2020): 207–21.

Nader, Laura. "Up the Anthropologist: Perspectives Gained from Studying Up." In *Reinventing Anthropology*, edited by D. Hymes, 284–311. New York: Vintage, 1972.

Nahoi, Ovidiu. "De Vorbă cu Ideologul AUR: Despre 'Țigani', 'Handicapați', 'Război Ideologic' și 'Revoluția Conservatoare' Care Se Amână." *RFI România*, December 11, 2020. https://www.rfi.ro/emisiunile-rfi-ro-128454-decriptaj-de-vorba-cu-ideologul-aur-despre-tigani-handicapati-razboi.

Neagu-Negulescu, Iuliu. *Arimania Sau Țara Buneiînțelegeri: Orînda Întocmirilor Omenești, După Potriva Faptelor Firești*. Bucharest: Pagini Libere, 2018.

Necula, Ciprian. "The Cost of Roma Slavery." *Perspective Politice* 5, no. 2 (2012): 33–46.

Nehru, Jawaharlal. *The Unity of India: Collected Writings 1937-40*. London: Lindsay Drummond, 1948.

Neocleous, Mark. "The Political Economy of the Dead: Marx's Vampires." *History of Political Thought* 24, no. 4 (2003): 668–84.

Ngila, Faustine. "Sam Bankman-Fried Wanted to Buy Nauru to Wait Out the World's End." *Quartz*, July 21, 2023. https://qz.com/sam-bankman-fried-ftx-nauru-court-case-money-laundering-1850662899.

Niebuhr, Robert. "Nonalignment as Yugoslavia's Answer to Bloc Politics." *Journal of Cold War Studies* 13, no. 1 (Winter 2011): 146–79.

N-iX. "Top IT Outsourcing Destinations of Eastern Europe: Market Report." *N-iX* (blog), March 28, 2023. https://www.n-ix.com/it-outsourcing-destinations-eastern -europe-market-report.

Noble, Safiya Umoja, and Sarah T. Roberts. "Technological Elites, the Meritocracy, and Postracial Myths in Silicon Valley." In *Technological Elites, the Meritocracy, and Postracial Myths in Silicon Valley*, 113–30. Durham, NC: Duke University Press, 2019.

Noi. "'Дуб Гагарина' в Калараше Вырос Из Жёлудя, Который Побывал в Космосе." *Noi*, 2018. https://noi.md/ru/obshhestvo/dub-gagarina-v-kalarashe-vyros-iz-zhyoludya -kotoryj-pobyval-v-kosmose.

NoiseCat, Julian Brave. "'It's about Taking Back What's Ours': Native Women Reclaim Land, Plot by Plot." *Huffington Post*, March 22, 2018. https://www.huffpost.com/entry /native-women-oakland-land_n_5ab0f175e4b0e862383b503c.

Nolan, Emma. "Trevor Noah Slams Racist Ukraine War Coverage by European Reporters." *Newsweek*, March 2, 2022. https://www.newsweek.com/trevor-noah-slams-racist -ukraine-war-coverage-european-reporters-1684074.

Novakov-Ritchey, Christina. "Palpating History: Magical Healing and Revolutionary Care in Rural Serbia and Macedonia." *European Journal of Cultural Studies* 26, no. 2 (April 1, 2023): 147–66.

O'Keeffe, Brigid. "The Roma Homeland That Never Was." *OpenDemocracy*, December 16, 2016. https://www.opendemocracy.net/en/odr/roma-homeland-that-never-was/.

Oman-Reagan, Michael. "Queering Outer Space." *Medium*, September 11, 2015. https:// medium.com/space-anthropology/queering-outer-space-f6f5b5cecda0.

O'Mara, Margaret Pugh. *Cities of Knowledge: Cold War Science and the Search for the Next Silicon Valley*. Princeton, NJ: Princeton University Press, 2015.

O'Mara, Margaret Pugh. *The Code: Silicon Valley and the Remaking of America*. New York: Penguin, 2020.

O'Neill, Bruce. *The Space of Boredom: Homelessness in the Slowing Global Order*. Durham, NC: Duke University Press, 2017.

Opillard, Florian. "From San Francisco's 'Tech Boom 2.0' to Valparaíso's UNESCO World Heritage Site." In *Protest and Resistance in the Tourist City*, edited by Claire Colomb and Johannes Novy, 129–51. London: Routledge, 2016.

Oprea, Alexandra. "Romani Feminism in Reactionary Times." *Signs: Journal of Women in Culture and Society* 38, no. 1 (September 2012): 11–21.

Ouředníček, Martin. "The Relevance of 'Western' Theoretical Concepts for Investigations of the Margins of Post-Socialist Cities: The Case of Prague." *Eurasian Geography and Economics* 57, no. 4–5 (2016): 545–64.

Padios, Jan. "Exceptionalism as a Way of Life: U.S. Empire, Filipino Subjectivity, and the Global Call Center Industry." In *Ethnographies of U.S. Empire*, edited by Carole McGranahan and John F. Collins, 149–70. Durham, NC: Duke University Press, 2018.

Padmore, George. *How Britain Rules Africa*. New York: Negro Universities Press, 1969.

Parvulescu, Anca, and Manuela Boatcă. *Creolizing the Modern: Transylvania across Empires*. Ithaca, NY: Cornell University Press, 2022.

Pavlínek, Petr. "Regional Development Implications of Foreign Direct Investment in Central Europe." *European Urban and Regional Studies* 11, no. 1 (2004): 47–70.

Pavlínek, Petr, and John Pickles. *Environmental Transitions: Transformation and Ecological Defense in Central and Eastern Europe*. New York: Routledge, 2000.

Pedersen, Susan. *The Guardians: The League of Nations and the Crisis of Empire*. Oxford: Oxford University Press, 2015.

Pellow, David, and Lisa Sun-Hee Park. *The Silicon Valley of Dreams: Environmental Injustice, Immigrant Workers, and the High-Tech Global Economy*. New York: New York University Press, 2002.

Penn, Malcolm G. "Romania in the Global Microelectronics World." Paper presented at the 1995 International Semiconductor Conference, CAS '95 Proceedings, Sinaia, Romania, October 11–14, 1995.

Petrov, Victor. "Socialist Cyborgs." *Logic Magazine*, September 30, 2021. https://logicmag .io/kids/socialist-cyborgs/.

Petrovici, Norbert. "Working Status in Deprived Urban Areas and Their Greater Economic Role." In *Racialized Labour in Romania*, edited by Enikő Vincze, Norbert Petrovici, Cristina Raț, and Giovanni Picker, 1–38. New York: Palgrave Macmillan, 2019.

Petrovici, Norbert, and Codruța Mare. *Economia Clujului*. Cluj-Napoca, Romania: Centrul Interdisciplinar pentru Știința Datelor, 2020.

Petrovici, Norbert, Enikő Vincze, Cristina Raț, and Giovanni Picker. "Racialized Labour of the Dispossessed as an Endemic Feature of Capitalism." In *Racialized Labour in Romania*, edited by Enikő Vincze, Norbert Petrovici, Cristina Raț, and Giovanni Picker, 39–62. New York: Palgrave Macmillan, 2019.

Petrovszky, Konrad, and Ovidiu Țichindeleanu. *Romanian Revolution Televised: Contributions to the Cultural History of Media*. Cluj: Idea Design and Print, 2011.

Pine, Adrienne. "The Field Is upon Us: Anti-Fascist Anthropology as Ethical Imperative." Paper presented at the European Association of Social Anthropologists, Belfast, July 26–29, 2022. https://nomadit.co.uk/conference/easa2022/paper/65460.

Pleter, Octavian. "Fenomenul Hacker." *Revista OPEN Tehnologia*, August 1994.

Poenaru, Florin. "Râs, Lacrimi și Priviri Coloniale." *CriticAtac*, November 15, 2010. http:// www.criticatac.ro/ras-lacrimi-si-priviri-coloniale.

Poenaru, Florin. "What Is at Stake in the Romanian Protests?" *CriticAtac*, February 7, 2017. http://www.criticatac.ro/lefteast/romanian-protests/.

Polanyi, Karl. *The Great Transformation*. Boston: Beacon, 2001.

Popa, Bogdan. "Ethnicity as a Category of Imperial Racialization: What Do Race and Empire Studies Offer to Romanian Studies?" *Ethnicities* 21, no. 4 (November 2020): 751–68.

Popa, Bogdan. "Trans* and Legacies of Socialism: Reading Queer Postsocialism in Tangerine." *The Undecidable Unconscious: A Journal of Deconstruction and Psychoanalysis* 5 (2018): 27–53.

Popa, Bogdan, and Hakan Sandal. "Decolonial Queer Politics and LGBTI+ Activism in Romania and Turkey." *Oxford Research Encyclopedia of Politics*, June 25, 2019. https://doi .org/10.1093/acrefore/9780190228637.013.1282.

Popescu, Monica. "On the Margins of the Black Atlantic: Angola, the Eastern Bloc, and the Cold War." *Research in African Literatures* 45, no. 3 (Fall 2014): 91–109.

Popovici, Veda. "Becoming Western: The Story Legitimising Neoliberalism, Violence and Dispossession in Central and Eastern European Cities." *Lefteast* (blog), June 14, 2022. https://lefteast.org/becoming-western-the-story-legitimising-neoliberalism -violence-and-dispossession-in-central-and-eastern-european-cities/.

Popovici, Veda. "Livrarea Orașului La Picioarele Capitalului: Gentrificare Și (in)Ofensivitatea Artei În București." *Gazeta de Arta Politica*, no. 5 (March 2014).

Popovici, Veda. "Residences, Restitutions and Resistance: A Radical Housing Movement's Understanding of Post-Socialist Property Redistribution." *City* 24, no. 1–2 (2020): 1–15.

Popovici, Veda. "Solidarity in Illegality: How the Corrupt East Is Already a Queer East." In *Queering Paradigms VIII: Queer-Feminist Solidarity and the East/West Divide*, edited by K. Wiedlack, S. Shoshanova, and Ma Godovannaya, 51–76. Bern: Peter Lang, 2020.

Popovici, Veda, and Mircea Nicolae. "Istoria (Nu) Se Repetă." Bucharest: Macaz Bar Teatru Coop, October 6, 2018.

Popoviciu, Tiberiu. "Contribuții ale Institutului de Calcul din Cluj la Aplicarea Matematicii În Economie: Metode Noi și Probleme de Perspectivă ale Cercetării Științifice." *Editura Academiei R.S.R.* (1969): 305–20.

Povinelli, Elizabeth A. *Geontologies: A Requiem to Late Liberalism*. Durham, NC: Duke University Press, 2016.

Proud Roma. "Strigă Tare, Eu Sunt Rom Și Mândru!" *Proud Roma Free Europe* (blog), March 31, 2021. https://proudroma.org/romania/striga-tare-eu-sunt-rom-si-mandru.

Pugach, Sara. "Eleven Nigerian Students in Cold War East Germany: Visions of Science, Modernity, and Decolonization." *Journal of Contemporary History* 54, no. 3 (2019): 551–72.

Pusca, Anca M. *Post-Communist Aesthetics: Revolutions, Capitalism, Violence*. London: Routledge, 2016.

Rai, Amit. *Jugaad Time: Ecologies of Everyday Hacking in India*. Durham, NC: Duke University Press, 2019.

Raț, Cristina. "Și țiganul este aproapele meu?" *Criticatac*, May 24, 2011. http://www.criticatac.ro/7533/si-tiganul-este-aproapele-meu.

Razsa, Maple. *Bastards of Utopia: Living Radical Politics after Socialism*. Bloomington: Indiana University Press, 2015.

Reich, Robert. "Putin Won." Twitter, January 6, 2021, 2:18 p.m. https://twitter.com /RBReich/status/1346914052568584194.

Reinhardt, Andy. "What Matters Is How Smart You Are." *Bloomberg*, August 24, 1997. https://www.bloomberg.com/news/articles/1997-08-24/what-matters-is-how-smart -you-are.

Reuters. "Piracy Worked for Us, Romania President Tells Gates." Reuters, February 1, 2007. https://www.reuters.com/article/us-romania-microsoft-idUSL0186472620070201.

Rexhepi, Piro. *White Enclosures: Racial Capitalism and Coloniality along the Balkan Route*. Durham, NC: Duke University Press, 2022.

Richardson, Joanne, and Nadia Len. *Reconstruction: Anti-NATO Days, 2008*. Bucharest: DMedia, 2009. https://archive.org/details/Reconstruction_antiNATO_days.

Rise Project. "Documentele Confidențiale ale Afacerii Roșia Montană." Rise Project, September 1, 2017. https://www.riseproject.ro/investigations/uncategorized/docu mentele-confidentiale-ale-afacerii-rosia-montana.

Roberts, Sarah. "Your AI Is a Human." In *Your Computer Is on Fire*, edited by Thomas S. Mullaney, Benjamin Peters, Mar Hicks, and Kavita Philip, 51–70. Cambridge, MA: MIT Press, 2021.

Robinson, Cedric. *An Anthropology of Marxism*. Chapel Hill: University of North Carolina Press, 2019.

Robinson, Cedric. *Black Marxism: The Making of the Black Radical Tradition*. Chapel Hill: University of North Carolina Press, 1983.

Robinson, Cedric. "Fascism and the Intersections of Capitalism, Racialism, and Historical Consciousness." In *Cedric J. Robinson: On Racial Capitalism, Black Internationalism, and Cultures of Resistance*, edited by H. L. T. Quan, 87–109. London: Pluto, 2019.

Robinson, Cedric. "Fascism and the Response of Black Radical Theorists." In *Cedric J. Robinson: On Racial Capitalism, Black Internationalism, and Cultures of Resistance*, edited by H. L. T. Quan, 149–59. London: Pluto, 2019.

Robinson, Jennifer. "Cities in a World of Cities: The Comparative Gesture." *International Journal of Urban and Regional Research* 35, no. 1 (2011): 1–23.

Rodríguez, Dylan. *Suspended Apocalypse: White Supremacy, Genocide, and the Filipino Condition*. Minneapolis: University of Minnesota Press, 2010.

Rofel, Lisa. *Desiring China: Experiments in Neoliberalism, Sexuality, and Public Culture*. Durham, NC: Duke University Press, 2007.

Rogoz, Adrian. *Omul și Naluca*. Bucharest: Tineretului, 1965.

Roh, David S., Betsy Huang, and Greta A. Niu. *Techno-Orientalism: Imagining Asia in Speculative Fiction, History, and Media*. New Brunswick, NJ: Rutgers University Press, 2015.

Roman, Raluca Bianca. "'Neither Here, Nor There': Belonging, Ambiguity, and the Struggle for Recognition among 'In-Between' Finnish Kaale." *Romani Studies* 28, no. 2 (2018): 239–62.

Romania Insider. "Over 43% of Romania's GDP Is Generated by Foreign-Owned Companies." *Romania Insider*, April 12, 2019. http://www.romania-insider.com/foreign-owned -companies-romania-gdp.

Romania Insider. "Romania's Environment Minister Confirms Massive Illegal Logging Figures." *Romania Insider*, November 25, 2019. https://www.romania-insider.com/mini ster-confirms-illegal-logging-report.

Romania Journal. "Romanian Parliament Passes the Law for Digital Nomads." *Romania Journal*, December 22, 2021. https://www.romaniajournal.ro/politics/romanian -parliament-passes-the-law-for-digital-nomads.

Romanian-American Foundation. "Technology and Innovation." Accessed August 1, 2022. https://rafonline.org/en/what-we-do/technology-innovation/.

Rorke, Bernard. "Eyes Wide Shut: Collective Punishment of Roma in 21st-Century Europe." *OpenDemocracy*, January 24, 2020. https://www.opendemocracy.net/en/can -europe-make-it/eyes-wide-shut-collective-punishment-roma-twenty-first-century -europe/.

Rosas, Ricardo. "The Gambiarra: Considerations on a Recombinatory Technology." In *Digital Media and Democracy: Tactics in Hard Times*, edited by M. Boler, 343–54. Cambridge, MA: MIT Press, 2010.

Rosca, Matei. "IKEA Funds Went to Romanian Secret Police in Communist Era." *Guardian*, July 4, 2014. https://www.theguardian.com/world/2014/jul/04/ikea-funds-romania-secret-police-communist-era.

Rosenberg, David. *Cloning Silicon Valley: The Next Generation High-Tech Hotspots*. New York: Reuters, 2002.

Roy, Ananya. "The City in the Age of Trumpism: From Sanctuary to Abolition." *Environment and Planning D: Society and Space* 37, no. 5 (2019): 761–78.

Roy, Ananya. 2017. "Dis/Possessive Collectivism: Property and Personhood at City's End." *Geoforum* 80 (March 2017): 1–11.

Roy, Ananya. "Undoing Property: Feminist Struggle in the Time of Abolition." *Society and Space*, May 3, 2021. https://www.societyandspace.org/articles/undoing-property-feminist-struggle-in-the-time-of-abolition.

Roy, Ananya, and Gautam Bhan. "Lessons from Somewhere." *Cityscapes Magazine*, September 21, 2013. https://cityscapesmagazine.com/articles/lessons-from-somewhere.

Roy, Ananya, Stuart Schrader, and Emma Crane. "Gray Areas: The War on Poverty at Home and Abroad." In *Territories of Poverty: Rethinking North and South*, edited by Ananya Roy and Emma Shaw Crane, 289–314. Athens: University of Georgia Press, 2015.

Rucker-Chang, Sunnie. "Challenging Americanism and Europeanism: African-Americans and Roma in the American South and European Union 'South.'" *Journal of Transatlantic Studies* 16, no. 2 (April 3, 2018): 181–99.

Rule, Sheila. "Reagan Gets a Red Carpet from British." *New York Times*, June 14, 1989. https://www.nytimes.com/1989/06/14/world/reagan-gets-a-red-carpet-from-british.html.

Ruse, Andrei. "Define: Hipster." *VICE*, March 9, 2013. https://www.vice.com/ro/article/mgakb3/define-hipster.

Said, Edward. *Orientalism*. New York: Vintage, 1978.

Sammon, Alexander. "IKEA's Race for the Last of Europe's Old-Growth Forest." *New Republic*, February 16, 2022. https://newrepublic.com/article/165245/IKEA-romania-europe-old-growth-forest.

Săsărman, Gheorghe. *Cuadratura Cercului*. Bucharest: Nautilus, 1975.

Saul, Nicholas. *Gypsies and Orientalism in German Literature and Anthropology of the Long Nineteenth Century*. London: Legenda, 2007.

Savio, Mario. "Sit-in Address on the Steps of Sproul Hall." Speech at University of California at Berkeley, December 2, 1964. Audio, 7:42. https://www.americanrhetoric.com/speeches/mariosaviosproulhallsitin.htm.

Saxenian, AnnaLee. *The New Argonauts: Regional Advantage in a Global Economy*. Cambridge, MA: Harvard University Press, 2007.

Saxon, Wolfgang. "William B. Shockley, 79, Creator of Transistor and Theory on Race." *New York Times*, August 14, 1989. https://archive.nytimes.com/www.nytimes.com/learning/general/onthisday/bday/0213.html.

Schaeffer, Felicity Amaya. *Unsettled Borders: The Militarized Science of Surveillance on Sacred Indigenous Land*. Durham, NC: Duke University Press Books, 2022.

Schiffman, Jeremy. "SF Mime Troupe Takes to the Bay in 'Ripple Effect.'" *San Francisco Examiner*, July 3, 2014. https://www.sfexaminer.com/entertainment/sf-mime-troupe -takes-to-the-bay-in-ripple-effect.

Schrock, Andrew. "Silicon Valley Is Not a Place." *Public Books*, April 9, 2020. https://www .publicbooks.org/silicon-valley-is-not-a-place.

Schwartz, David. *'90*. Bucharest: Macaz Bar Teatru Coop, 2018.

Schwartz, David. *Portofele Virtuale*. Râmnicu Vâlcea, Romania: Teatrul Anton Pann, 2018.

Science Direct. "Yuri Gagarin Was a Hero." *Press Reader*, May 1, 2021. https://www.press reader.com/australia/science-illustrated/20210501/283270280639708.

Scott, David. *Omens of Adversity: Tragedy, Time. Memory, Justice*. Durham, NC: Duke University Press, 2013.

Scott, David. "The Re-enchantment of Humanism: An Interview with Sylvia Wynter." *Small Axe* 8, no. 120 (2000): 173–211.

Self, Robert. *American Babylon: Race and the Struggle for Postwar Oakland*. Princeton, NJ: Princeton University Press, 2003.

Senycia, Tristan. "Developers in Romania: Insight into Their Culture and IT Market." *YouTeam* (blog), December 22, 2022. https://youteam.io/blog/developers-in-romania -insight-into-their-culture-and-it-market.

Shafir, Michael. "Polls and Antisemitism in Post-Communist Romania." *Journal for the Study of Antisemitism* 4, no. 2 (2012): 387–422.

Shafir, Michael. "Varieties of Antisemitism in Post-Communist East Central Europe: Motivations and Political Discourse." *Jewish Studies at the Central European University 2002–2003*, no. 3 (2003): 175–210.

Shange, Savannah. *Progressive Dystopia: Abolition, Antiblackness, and Schooling in San Francisco*. Durham, NC: Duke University Press, 2019.

Shaping San Francisco. "John Ross on the 1966 Armory Riot." *Shaping San Francisco*, July 15, 2007. http://archive.org/details/Clip12ArmoryRiot.

Shaw, Joe. "Platform Real Estate: Theory and Practice of New Urban Real Estate Markets." *Urban Geography* 41, no. 8 (2020): 1037–64.

Shih, Shu-mei. "Is the *Post-* in Postsocialism the *Post-* in Posthumanism?" *Social Text* 30, no. 1 (110) (Spring 2012): 27–50.

Shinn, Charles Howard. *Mining Camps: A Study in American Frontier Government*. New York: Charles Scribner's Son, 1884.

Sikor, Thomas, Johannes Stahl, and Stefan Dorondel. "Negotiating Post-Socialist Property and State: Struggles." *Forests in Albania and Romania Development and Change* 40, no. 1 (January 2009): 171–93.

Simone, AbdouMaliq. *The Surrounds: Urban Life within and beyond Capture*. Durham, NC: Duke University Press, 2022.

Singh, Nikhil Pal. "Cold War." *Social Text* 27, no. 3 (100) (2009): 67–70.

Singh, Nikhil Pal. *Race and America's Long War*. Berkeley: University of California Press, 2017.

Sjöberg, Örjan. "'Cases unto Themselves?': Theory and Research on Ex-socialist Urban Environments." *Geografie* 119, no. 4 (January 2014): 299–319.

Slobodian, Quinn. "Bandung in Divided Germany: Managing Non-aligned Politics in East and West, 1955–63." *Journal of Imperial and Commonwealth History* 41, no. 4 (2013): 644–62.

Soare, Sorina, and Claudiu Tufiş. "Phoenix Populism. Radical Right Parties' Mobilization in Romania after 2015." *Problems of Post-Communism* 66, no. 1 (2019): 8–20.

Softech. "Software Outsourcing." Accessed May 10, 2022. https://softech.ro/software-outsourcing-romania/software-outsourcing.

Solnit, Rebecca. "Diary." *London Review of Books* 35, no. 3 (2013): 34–35.

Solon, Olivia. "Elon Musk: We Must Colonise Mars to Preserve Our Species in a Third World War." *Guardian*, March 11, 2018. https://www.theguardian.com/technology/2018/mar/11/elon-musk-colonise-mars-third-world-war.

Sonneman, Toby. "Dark Mysterious Wanderers: The Migrating Metaphor of the Gypsy." *Journal of Popular Culture* 32, no. 4 (Spring 1999): 119–39.

Soper, Kate. *Humanism and Anti-humanism*. London: HarperCollins, 1986.

Spencer, Keith. "Long before Tech Bros, Silicon Valley Had a Highly Developed Society." *Guardian*, January 8, 2019. https://www.theguardian.com/technology/2019/jan/08/silicon-valley-history-society-book-ohlone-native-americans.

Spivak, Gayatri Chakravorty. *Death of a Discipline*. New York: Columbia University Press, 2003.

Squire, Rachel, Oli Mould, and Peter Adey. "The Final Frontier? The Enclosure of a Commons of Outer Space." *Society and Space* (blog), 2021. https://www.societyandspace.org/forums/the-final-frontier-the-enclosure-of-a-commons-of-outer-space.

Stachniak, Zbigniew. "Red Clones: The Soviet Computer Hobby Movement of the 1980s." *IEEE Annals of the History of Computing* 37, no. 1 (January–March 2015): 12–23.

Stan, Lavinia. "The Roof over Our Heads: Property Restitution in Romania." *Journal of Communist Studies and Transition Politics* 22, no. 2 (2006): 180–205.

Stanley, Eric. "The Affective Commons: Gay Shame, Queer Hate, and Other Collective Feelings." *GLQ: A Journal of Lesbian and Gay Studies* 24, no. 4 (2018): 489–508.

Starosta, Anita. "Perverse Tongues, Postsocialist Translations." *Boundary* 41, no. 1 (Spring 2014): 203–27.

Stevens, Nick. "A Letter from Yuri Gagarin." *Nick Stevens Graphics* (blog), September 23, 2017. https://nick-stevens.com/2017/09/23/a-letter-from-yuri-gagarin.

Stewart, Michael. "Deprivation, the Roma and 'The Underclass.'" In *Postsocialism: Ideals, Ideologies and Practices in Eurasia*, edited by Chris Hann, 145–68. New York: Routledge, 2002.

Stoler, Ann Laura. "Imperial Debris: Reflections on Ruins and Ruination." *Cultural Anthropology* 23, no. 2 (May 2008): 191–219.

Stoler, Ann Laura, and Carole McGranahan. *Imperial Formations*. Oxford: School for Advanced Research Press, 2007.

Subrahmanyam, Sanjay. "Connected Histories: Notes towards a Reconfiguration of Early Modern Eurasia." *Modern Asian Studies* 31, no. 3 (July 1997): 735–62.

Suchland, Jennifer. "Is Postsocialism Transnational?" *Signs: Journal of Women in Culture and Society* 3, no. 4 (2011): 837–62.

Švelch, Jaroslav. *Gaming the Iron Curtain: How Teenagers and Amateurs in Communist Czechoslovakia Claimed the Medium of Computer Games*. Cambridge, MA: MIT Press, 2018.

Sze, Julie. "Boundaries and Border Wars: DES, Technology, and Environmental Justice." *American Quarterly* 58, no. 3 (September 2006): 791–814.

Tadiar, Neferti X. M. "City Everywhere." *Theory, Culture and Society* 33, no. 7–8 (December 2016): 57–83.

Tadiar, Neferti X. M. "Metropolitan Life and Uncivil Death." *PMLA* 122, no. 1 (January 2007): 316–20.

Táíwò, Olúfẹ́mi O. *Elite Capture: How the Powerful Took Over Identity Politics (and Everything Else)*. Chicago: Haymarket Books, 2022.

Takahashi, Dean. "It's Alive: IBM's Watson Supercomputer Defeats Humans in Final Jeopardy Match." *Venture Beat*, February 16, 2011. https://venturebeat.com/2011/02/16/ibms-watson-wins-final-jeopardy-match/.

TallBear, Kim. "Standing with and Speaking as Faith: A Feminist-Indigenous Approach to Inquiry." *Journal of Research Practice* 10, no. 17 (2014): 1–7.

Taylor, James. "Life as a Digital Gypsy." *James Taylor* (blog). Accessed August 9, 2019. https://www.jamestaylor.me/life-as-a-digital-gypsy.

Taylor, Mary, and Noah Brehmer. *The Commonist Horizon: Futures Beyond Capitalist Urbanization*. Philadelphia: Common Notions, 2023.

Thorne, Benjamin. "Assimilation, Invisibility, and the Eugenic Turn in the 'Gypsy Question' in Romanian Society, 1938–1942." *Romani Studies* 21, no. 2 (January 2011): 177–205.

ThreatConnect. "Does a Bear Leak in the Woods?" *ThreatConnect*, August 12, 2016. https://threatconnect.com/blog/does-a-bear-leak-in-the-woods.

Țichindeleanu, Ovidiu. "Socialist Romania and Postsocialist Transition on the Path of Non-aligned Development." *Institute of the Present*, November 15, 2017. https://institutulprezentului.ro/en/2017/11/15/socialist-romania-and-postsocialist-transition-on-the-path-of-non-aligned-development.

Tiku, Natasha. "How Elite Schools like Stanford Became Fixated on the AI Apocalypse." *Washington Post*, July 5, 2023. https://www.washingtonpost.com/technology/2023/07/05/ai-apocalypse-college-students.

Tiku, Natasha. "Oakland Rebels So Sickened by Techie Scum, They Barfed on a Yahoo Bus." *ValleyWag*, April 2, 2014. http://valleywag.gawker.com/youll-probably-believe-what-these-oakland-rebels-did-t-1557036480.

Timofeeva, Oxana. "What Lenin Teaches Us about Witchcraft." *e-flux*, no. 100 (May 2019). https://www.e-flux.com/journal/100/268602/what-lenin-teaches-us-about-witchcraft.

Tlostanova, Madina. "Between the Russian/Soviet Dependencies, Neoliberal Delusions, Dewesternizing Options, and Decolonial Drives." *Cultural Dynamics* 27, no. 2 (July 2015): 267–83.

Tlostanova, Madina. *Postcolonialism and Postsocialism in Fiction and Art: Resistance and Re-existence*. New York: Springer, 2017.

Todorova, Maria. *Imagining the Balkans*. Oxford: Oxford University Press, 1997.

Todorova, Miglena S. *Unequal under Socialism: Race, Women, and Transnationalism in Bulgaria*. Toronto: University of Toronto Press, 2021.

TopCoder. "Community Statistics." Accessed August 6, 2023. https://www.topcoder.com/community/statistics?tracks[All-pills]=0&tracks[Design]=0&tracks[Dev]=0&tracks[General]=1.

Toyama, Kentaro. "The Problem with the Plan to Give Internet Access to the Whole World." *Atlantic*, December 14, 2014. https://www.theatlantic.com/technology/archive/2014/12/the-problem-with-the-plan-to-give-internet-to-the-whole-world/383744.

Tran, Kim. Twitter post, February 23, 2021, 4:46 p.m. https://twitter.com/but_im_kim_tran/status/1364345813908922370.

Tsing, Anna Lowenhaupt. *Friction: An Ethnography of Global Connection*. Princeton, NJ: Princeton University Press, 2005.

Tudor, Alyosxa, and Piro Rexhepi. "Connecting the 'Posts' to Confront Racial Capitalism's Coloniality: A Conversation." In *Postcolonial and Postsocialist Dialogues: Intersections, Opacities, Challenges in Feminist Theorizing and Practice*, edited by Redi Koobak, Madina Tlostanova, and Suruchi Thapar-Björkert, 93–208. New York: Routledge, 2021.

Tudor, Gabriel. "Bogdan Diaconu: 'Politicienii care le plâng de milă imigranților arabi să-i ia acasă și să și-i țină!'" *Academia Cațavencu*, September 24, 2015. http://www.academiacatavencu.info/actualitate/bogdan-diaconu%2D%2D"politicienii-care-le-plang-de-mila-imigrantilor-arabisa-i-ia-acasa-si-sa-si-i-tina-"-38731.

Tudor, Iulian. "Partidul România Unită și-a lansat programul de guvernare." *Romania TV*, September 21, 2016. https://www.romaniatv.net/partidul-romania-unita-si-a-lansat-programul-de-guvernare_315512.html.

Turda, Marius. *Modernism and Eugenics*. New York: Springer, 2010.

Turda, Marius. "The Nation as Object: Race, Blood, and Biopolitics in Interwar Romania." *Slavic Review* 66, no. 3 (2007): 413–41.

Turner, Fred. "Machine Politics: The Rise of the Internet and a New Age of Authoritarianism." *Harper's Magazine*, January 2019. https://harpers.org/archive/2019/01/machine-politics-facebook-political-polarization.

Turp-Balazs, Craig. "Romania Becomes Latest CEE Country to Offer Digital Nomad Visas." *Emerging Europe*, December 22, 2021. https://emerging-europe.com/news/romania-becomes-latest-cee-country-to-offer-digital-nomad-visas.

Valentine, David. "Exit Strategy: Profit, Cosmology, and the Future of Humans in Space." *Anthropological Quarterly* 85, no. 4 (Fall 2012): 1045–67.

Van Baar, Huub. "The Emergence of a Reasonable Anti-Gypsyism in Europe." In *When Stereotype Meets Prejudice: Antiziganism in European Societies*, edited by T. Agarin, 27–44. Stuttgart: Ibidem, 2014.

Vătămanu, Mona, and Florin Tudor. *Gagarin's Tree*. Accessed August 9, 2017. https://www.monavatamanuflorintudor.ro/gagarinstree.htm.

Verdery, Katherine. "Faith, Hope, and Caritas in the Land of the Pyramids: Romania, 1990 to 1994." *Comparative Studies in Society and History* 37, no. 4 (1995): 625–69.

Verdery, Katherine. "Fuzzy Property: Rights, Power and Identity in Transylvania's Decollectivization." In *Uncertain Transition: Ethnographies of Change in the Postsocialist World*, edited by Michael Burawoy, 53–82. Lanham, MD: Rowman and Littlefield, 2000.

Verdery, Katherine. *My Life as a Spy: Investigations in a Secret Police File*. Durham, NC: Duke University Press, 2018.

Verdery, Katherine. *National Ideology under Socialism: Identity and Cultural Politics in Ceaușescu's Romania*. Berkeley: University of California Press, 1991.

Verdery, Katherine. *The Political Lives of Dead Bodies: Reburial and Postsocialist Change.* New York: Columbia University Press, 2005.

Verdery, Katherine. *What Was Socialism, and What Comes Next?* Princeton, NJ: Princeton University Press, 1996.

Vilenica, Ana. "Who Has 'The Right to Common'? Decolonizing Commoning in East Europe." In *The Commonist Horizon: Futures beyond Capitalist Urbanization,* edited by Mary Taylor and Noah Brehmer, 11–38. Philadelphia: Common Notions, 2023.

Vincze, Enikő. "The Ideology of Economic Liberalism and the Politics of Housing in Romania." *Studia Universitatis Babes-Bolyai, Europaea* 62, no. 3 (September 2017): 29–54.

Vincze, Enikő. "Rampa de gunoi: Spațiul marginalității, urbane avansate rasializate în România de azi." In *Antologia Criticatac,* edited by CriticAtac, 53–67. Bucharest: Tact, 2012.

Vincze, Enikő. "Securitizarea Locativă ca Formă de Control Și ca Formă de Protecție— Căși Sociale Acum!" *Caramida,* March 4, 2022. https://casisocialeacum.ro/archives /6856/securitizarea-locativa-ca-forma-de-control-si-ca-forma-de-protectie.

Vincze, Enikő, and George Zamfir. "Racialized Housing Unevenness in Cluj-Napoca under Capitalist Redevelopment." *City* 23, no. 4–5 (2019): 439–60.

Vișan, Nicoleta, and Frontul Comun pentru Dreptul la Locuire. *Jurnal Din Vulturilor: Povestea Unei Lupte Pentru Dreptate Locativă.* Cluj, Romania: Idea, 2019.

Vladimirskaya, Tatyana. "Так Рождаются Легенды: В Молдове Никак Не Могут Найти Дуб, Который Вырос Из Желудя, Побывавшего с Гагариным в Космосе." *Комсомольская правда,* April 17, 2018. https://www.kp.md/daily/26820/3857189.

Voyles, Traci Brynne. *Wastelanding: Legacies of Uranium Mining in Navajo Country.* Minneapolis: University of Minnesota Press, 2015.

Walcott, Rinaldo. *On Property.* Windsor, ON: Biblioasis, 2021.

Walker, Richard. *The Conquest of Bread: 150 Years of Agribusiness in California.* New York: New Press, 2004.

Walker, Richard. "Landscape and City Life: Four Ecologies of Residence in the San Francisco Bay Area." *Ecumene* 2, no. 1 (January 1995): 33–64.

Walker, Richard. *Pictures of a Gone City: Tech and the Dark Side of Prosperity in the San Francisco Bay Area.* Oakland, CA: PM Press, 2018.

Wallerstein, Immanuel. *World-Systems Analysis: An Introduction.* Durham, NC: Duke University Press, 2004.

Ward, Stuart. "The European Provenance of Decolonization." *Past and Present* 230, no. 1 (February 2016): 227–60.

Wasiak, Patryk. "Playing and Copying: Social Practices of Home Computer Users in Poland during the 1980s." In *Hacking Europe,* edited by Gerard Alberts and Ruth Oldenziel, 129–50. London: Springer London, 2014.

Wattles, Jackie. "Colonizing Mars Could Be Dangerous and Ridiculously Expensive. Elon Musk Wants to Do It Anyway." *CNN,* September 8, 2020. https://www.cnn.com /2020/09/08/tech/spacex-mars-profit-scn/index.html.

Weheliye, Alexander. *Habeas Viscus: Racializing Assemblages, Biopolitics, and Black Feminist Theory of the Human.* Durham, NC: Duke University Press, 2014.

Weiss, Linda. *America Inc.? Innovation and Enterprise in the National Security State.* Ithaca, NY: Cornell University Press, 2015.

Whittaker, Meredith, and Lucy Suchman. "The Myth of Artificial Intelligence." *The American Prospect*, December 8, 2021. https://prospect.org/api/content/7fc7f7c2-5781-11ec-987e-12f1225286c6.

Wiener, Norbert. *The Human Use of Human Beings: Cybernetics and Society*. New York: Hachette Books, 1988.

Wilder, Gary. "Hasty Reflections on the Genesis of 'Concrete Utopianism.'" *A History of the Future: Utopia 13/13* (blog), January 24, 2023. https://blogs.law.columbia.edu/utopia1313/gary-wilder-hasty-reflections-on-the-genesis-of-concrete-utopianism.

Wilder, Gary. "Review of the Book: *Omens of Adversity: Tragedy, Time, Memory, Justice*, by David Scott." *Journal of Latin American and Caribbean Anthropology* 20, no. 1 (2015): 189–200.

Willey, Angela. *Undoing Monogamy: The Politics of Science and the Possibilities of Biology*. Durham, NC: Duke University Press, 2016.

Williams, Raymond. *Marxism and Literature*. Oxford: Oxford University Press, 1977.

Wolff, Larry. *Inventing Eastern Europe: The Map of Civilization and the Mind of the Enlightenment*. Stanford, CA: Stanford University Press, 1994.

Woodcock, Shannon. "A Short History of the Queer Time of 'Post-Socialist' Romania, or Are We There Yet? Let's Ask Madonna." In *De-Centring Western Sexualities: Central and Eastern European Perspectives*, edited by Robert Kulpa and Joanna Mizielinska, 63–83. New York: Routledge, 2011.

Wright, Willie Jamaal. "The Morphology of Marronage." *Annals of the American Association of Geographers* 110, no. 4 (2020): 1134–49.

Wynter, Sylvia. "Columbus, the Ocean Blue and 'Fables That Stir the Mind': To Reinvent the Study of Letters." In *Poetics of the Americas: Race, Founding and Textuality*, edited by Bainard Cowan and Jefferson Humphries, 141–64. Baton Rouge: Louisiana State University Press, 1997.

Wynter, Sylvia. "Unsettling the Coloniality of Being/Power/Truth/Freedom: Towards the Human, after Man, Its Overrepresentation—An Argument." *The New Centennial Review* 3, no. 3 (2003): 257–337.

Wynter, Sylvia, and Katherine McKittrick. "Unparalleled Catastrophe for Our Species? Or to Give Humanness a Different Future." In *Sylvia Winter: On Being Human as Praxis*, edited by Katherine McKittrick and Sylvia Wynter, 9–89. Durham, NC: Duke University Press, 2015.

Ybarra-Frausto, Tomás. "Rasquachismo: A Chicano Sensibility." In *Chicano and Chicana Art: A Critical Anthology*, edited by Jennifer González, C. Ondine Chavoya, Chon Noriega, and Terezita Romo, 85–90. Durham, NC: Duke University Press, 2019.

Young, Ayana. "Transcript: Corrina Gould on Settler Responsibility and Reciprocity." *For the Wild*. Accessed March 16, 2022. https://forthewild.world/podcast-transcripts/corrina-gould-on-settler-responsibility-and-reciprocity-encore-277.

Yurchak, Alexei. *Everything Was Forever, until It Was No More: The Last Soviet Generation*. Princeton, NJ: Princeton University Press, 2013.

Yurchak, Alexei. "Trump, Monstration and the Limits of Liberalism." Paper presented at the annual meeting of the American Ethnological Society, Stanford University, Stanford, CA, March 2017.

Zak, Anatoly. "Vostok Lands Successfully." Russian Space Web, last updated April 12, 2021. http://www.russianspaceweb.com/vostok1_landing.html.

Zăloagă, Marian. "Professing Domestic Orientalism: Representing the Gypsy as Musikant in the Transylvanian Saxons' Writings of the Long 19th Century." *Studia Universitatis Babeş-Bolyai—Historia* 57, no. 2 (2012): 1–28.

Zamfir, George. "Countering Housing Dispossession in Cluj, the Silicon Valley of Eastern Europe." *Lefteast* (blog), June 20, 2022. https://lefteast.org/countering-housing -dispossession-in-cluj-the-silicon-valley-of-eastern-europe.

Zamfir, George. "Countering Illegibility: A Brief History of Forced Evictions in Postsocialist Romania." *Studia Universitatis Babes-Bolyai Sociologia* 67, no. 1 (May 31, 2022): 37–68.

Zamfir, George, Enikő Vincze, Veda Popovici, Ioana Florea, Michele Lancione, and Erin McElroy. "Housing Struggles in Romania and in Central Eastern Europe (CEE)." *Radical Housing Journal* 2, no. 1 (2020): 149–62.

Zamfirescu, Irina, and Liviu Chelcea. "Evictions as Infrastructural Events." *Urban Geography* 42, no. 9 (2020): 1–22.

Zara. "Best Places for Digital Nomads in Cluj." *Backpack Me* (blog), January 19, 2017. https://bkpk.me/best-places-for-digital-nomads-in-cluj.

Zavisca, Jane R. *Housing the New Russia*. Ithaca, NY: Cornell University Press, 2012.

Zetkin, Clara. *Fighting Fascism: How to Struggle and How to Win*. Edited by Mike Taber and John Riddell. Chicago: Haymarket Books, 2017.

Zincă, Irina. "Grounding Global Capitalism in Cluj-Napoca, Romania." *Studia UBB Sociologia* 56, no. 2 (2011): 139–56.

Index

Note: Page numbers in italics indicate figures.

www.ingramcontent.com/pod-product-compliance
Lightning Source LLC
Chambersburg PA
CBHW020841270326
41928CB00006B/506